MW01025645

LORENZO DOW TURNER

Lorenzo Dow Turner

FATHER OF GULLAH STUDIES

Margaret Wade-Lewis

Introductory Note by Lois Turner Williams
Foreword by Irma Aloyce Cunningham

UNIVERSITY OF SOUTH CAROLINA PRESS

Published by the University of South Carolina Press
Columbia, South Carolina 29208

www.sc.edu/uscpress

Manufactured in the United States of America

17 16 15 14 13 12 11 10 09 08 10 9 8 7 6 5 4 3 2 1

Library of Congress Cataloging-in-Publication Data

Wade-Lewis, Margaret.
Lorenzo Dow Turner : father of Gullah studies / Margaret Wade-Lewis ; introductory note by Lois Turner Williams ; foreword by Irma Aloyce Cunningham.
p. cm.
Includes bibliographical references and index.
ISBN-13: 978-1-57003-628-6 (cloth : alk. paper)
ISBN-10: 1-57003-628-4 (cloth : alk. paper)
1. Turner, Lorenzo Dow. 2. Linguists—United States—Biography. 3. Sea Islands Creole dialect—Research—History. I. Title.
PM7875.G8T839 2007
427'.97308996—dc22
[B]

2006037506

The author gratefully acknowledges the following people and institutions:

Introductory note by permission of Lois Turner Williams.

Foreword by permission of Irma Aloyce Cunningham.

Geneva Townes Turner Collection of the Manuscript Division of the Moorland-Spingarn Research Center, by permission of Howard University, Washington, D.C.

"Lorenzo Dow Turner: Pioneer African American Linguist," *Black Scholar* 21, no. 4 (Fall 1991): 10–24. Reprinted by permission of the *Black Scholar.*

Lorenzo Dow Turner Correspondences, courtesy of the Melville J. Herskovits Library, Northwestern University, Evanston, Illinois.

Lorenzo Dow Turner Correspondences in the Papers of the English Department of the University of Chicago; courtesy of the Special Collections Research Center, University of Chicago Library, Chicago, Illinois.

Lorenzo Dow Turner Files in the Harvard University Archives of the Pusey Library, courtesy of the Harvard University Archives, Cambridge, Massachusetts.

Lorenzo Dow Turner Letters in the E. Franklin Frazier Papers of the Moorland-Spingarn Research Center, by permission of Howard University, Washington, D.C.

Lorenzo Dow Turner Papers, Africana Manuscripts 23; courtesy of the Melville J. Herskovits Library of African Studies, Northwestern University, Evanston, Illinois.

Lorenzo Dow Turner Papers in the Roosevelt University Archives, by permission of Roosevelt University, Chicago, Illinois.

The Thomas Elsa Jones Collection, by permission of the Fisk University Franklin Library's Special Collections, Nashville, Tennessee.

This book was printed on Glatfelter Natures, a recycled paper with 50 percent postconsumer waste content.

In loving memory of my parents,
the Reverend John E. Williams
and
Mrs. Marjorie Clark Williams

CONTENTS

ILLUSTRATIONS

INTRODUCTORY NOTE

My dear friend of many years, Dr. Margaret Wade-Lewis, has very kindly asked me to write an introductory note for this biography of my husband, in which she so effectively tells the story of his life.

This is the story of a man for whom preparation, dedication, and perseverance were the watchwords he applied to everything he undertook. The well-known adage "anything worth doing is worth doing well" must surely have been the performance standard in his family from earliest childhood. Although I entered his life in his mid-years, I recognized his daily discipline as an ingrained habit that insured his success in many areas of his life, especially in his chosen field of research. His Gullah studies phenomenally overturned all previously held theories regarding the origin of certain linguistic speech patterns extant in areas of the United States where Gullah is spoken. While his research and travels led him beyond the Gullah Islands in the quest for African retentions in Brazil and to the original African sources in Nigeria and Sierra Leone, his Gullah studies remain his most enduring contribution.

And the rest is history.

I heartily recommend your taking a journey through the pages of this riveting biography.

LOIS TURNER WILLIAMS
(Mrs. Lorenzo Dow Turner Sr.)
Chicago

FOREWORD

All too often in academia we become so involved in the particulars of our fields that we lose sight of the bottom line of all our efforts, namely, people. As members of the world community, we can little afford to do so. In this first full-length biography of Lorenzo Dow Turner, Margaret Wade-Lewis has recognized his importance and responded with corresponding action.

Lorenzo Dow Turner: Father of Gullah Studies is thorough in its scope and illuminating in its insights. Turner has earned the honor. I and other devotees of Sea Island Creole or Gullah (the term native speakers usually prefer is Geechee) have had our careers shaped in part by our contact with Turner's research, but until now, except for data in articles by Wade-Lewis, Turner's life has remained an enigma to us and to most of the world. She has turned the spotlight on him in this comprehensive assessment of his life by discussing his ideas, broad interests, and intellectual contributions. The content and style are scholarly, yet accessible to a broad audience. An important addition to the sources on Sea Island culture, biography, southern culture, American linguistic history, and African Studies, it also serves as a testament to the capacity of the American mosaic to reflect diverse cultures and voices.

I became interested in Sea Island (SI) Creole when I was a first-year graduate student at Indiana University (1962–63). One day while browsing through the stacks, my eyes fell upon Lorenzo Dow Turner's *Africanisms in the Gullah Dialect* (1949). Since American English dialectology was my major interest in linguistics and I am African American, it is no wonder that the book captured my attention.

Hours passed as I sat on the floor in front of the shelf where the book had been housed, perusing page after page, and, with each, becoming more enthralled. Over the days and weeks, I longed to pursue my new interest; unfortunately, there were no professors available to supervise research in the dialectology of creole languages.

Several years later my opportunity to conduct research on SI Creole arrived when I became a doctoral student at the University of Michigan (1966–70). Utilizing Turner's *Africanisms,* along with a few books on West African languages, I wrote two SI Creole pilot studies—"Gullah: A Dialect of English or West African?" (1966) and "Plans for Gullah in Retrospect and in Prospect" (1967).

By 1969, when I had reached the dissertation stage, only one step remained: to go to SI Creole territory and get to work. I still shudder as I hear Professor Kenneth Hill, chair of my dissertation committee, present me with that ultimatum. Yes, I had submitted a prospectus affirming that I planned to write a grammar (morphology, syntax, and semantics) of SI Creole. Yes, I had stated that the grammar would be presented in a transformational eclectic model. And, yes, I had acknowledged that no grammar in written form existed for the language. But I had never envisioned myself going to SI territory to conduct fieldwork.

Reality set in. Where was I to acquire the data for such an undertaking? Turner, in keeping with his purpose in *Africanisms,* had generally presented phonological and lexical data. My pilot studies were entirely grammatical in nature, relying on limited grammatical examples and the illustrative texts in the appendix of *Africanisms.* I was now faced with a challenge. Not only were there no written grammars; there were also no available recorded data from which to derive a grammatical analysis.

After much reflection, I contacted Dr. Turner to inquire as to whether he could share with me any SI data that would support a grammatical analysis. He graciously responded by mail, informing me that to appreciate the data, one must elicit the classificatory materials oneself. In closing, he wished me well with my fieldwork.

My choices were clear—either abandon the project or arrange to conduct fieldwork. I opted for the latter. After securing a research grant, I moved to the Sea Islands. In the process of contacting SI informants and learning to negotiate the SI physical environment, I gained immense respect for Turner's accomplishment. Just as Turner had discovered in the 1930s, I found that building a friendship network is a serious undertaking. Yet, it is logical that a self-reliant but misunderstood people would guard against curiosity-seekers. As I lived among the Islanders and developed relationships, I found them gracious and hospitable. They welcomed me into their homes, allowing me to observe natural Creole-to-Creole speech. The results of my fieldwork are my 1970 dissertation, "A Syntactic Analysis of Sea Island Creole ('Gullah')," and the revised version of it published in 1992 as *A Syntactic Analysis of Sea Island Creole.*

It is on Turner's shoulders that all of us stand. The story of Turner's family background; his resolute personality; his triumphant career as a professor of English, linguistics, and African studies in three universities; his family life; and the shifting sociopolitical context in which he made his contribution are a momentous legacy. The story of his research in Brazil at age fifty, his African fieldwork at age sixty, and his teaching and research on Sierra Leone Krio for the Peace Corps from ages seventy-two to seventy-five add to his stature as a cultural pioneer and icon.

Most of all, Turner's success in producing the first scientific account of SI Creole, thereby transforming attitudes in academia and in the larger society and making creoles the legitimate province of analysis, is a one-in-a-million accomplishment. *Lorenzo Dow Turner: Father of Gullah Studies* answers the question of how a soft-spoken university professor could single-handedly bring about such change and, in the process, advance our quest to tease out the layered intricacies of the languages we know as creoles.

It is the larger story of the recognition of African Americans as intellectuals and university professionals. Furthermore, it is the story of a man dedicated to both family and social responsibility. Turner serves as a model to us all in his fulfillment of these multiple challenges. That his legacy continues to grow confirms the value of his decades of dedicated research. This groundbreaking biography is an inspiring analysis that raises Turner's legacy to still another level. The circle has become complete. For a half century, we have studied Turner's material. Now, for the first time, we can merge the material with the man.

IRMA ALOYCE CUNNINGHAM

PREFACE

The seed for a biography on Lorenzo Dow Turner was planted almost two decades ago when, in an etymology class with John Costello at New York University, I sought to investigate the influence of African languages upon American English. That search ultimately led me to Turner's work. An analogous search, to discover my ancestors in the world of American linguistics, also led to Turner.

Over the years, as I prepared Turner articles, I did not conceive of myself as working toward a biography. It is an overdue but timely occurrence that one should appear some fifty years after *Africanisms in the Gullah Dialect* (1949) in the wake of substantial scholarly activity stimulated by sustained interest in Turner and Gullah studies.

Because this biography is the first, a full treatment is warranted. Turner was remarkable for his times, the product of a high-achieving, free black North Carolina family that dates its origins to 1799. The century of freedom the Rooks/Turner clan experienced before Turner's birth not only afforded him privileges unavailable to those born enslaved but also contributed to his appreciation of the principle that to whom much is given much also is required.

His father, Rooks Turner, received a bachelor's degree from Howard University in 1877. Shortly thereafter, he founded an educational institution that years later became the first site of Elizabeth City State University. In the 1880s Rooks Turner ran twice for statewide political office, and in 1901 he earned a master's degree. Turner's brothers undertook professional degrees—one in law and the other in medicine. Although his mother, Elizabeth, was unable to obtain an education equivalent to that of her husband and sons, she was nonetheless an inspiration and mainstay to her family. Turner's family background was the vortex that placed him on the track to achieve the extraordinary. Because no previous research has explored his genealogy, I have included a brief chapter on his family background (chap. 1), one on each of his parents (chaps. 2–3), and a preliminary family tree (appendix), based on census and archival data.

Indeed, Turner's protracted quest to recover the history and linguistic background of Gullah was consistent with both family expectations and family models of achievement. When he became the first to conduct systematic study of Gullah and then sacrificed much in the quest to document its African derivations, the first African American to document the African influence in the oral arts of Brazil, and the first to prepare books featuring phonetic transcription in Sierra Leone Krio, he was not only advancing intellectual inquiry but, simultaneously, claiming his place in the family galaxy.

Turner was steadfast in his mission, not allowing the vagaries of racism and segregation, a dearth of funds, his family, friends, social or civic obligations, or teaching and administrative responsibilities in small colleges to deter him from his research priorities. While each of these pressures circumscribed the terrain in which his ideas could come to fruition, a perusal of the Turner Collection at Northwestern University underscores the rest of the intellectual drama. Turner labored unceasingly to expand a theoretical and practical canon in linguistics and on the black diasporic cultural experience. Through analysis of and advocacy for Gullah studies, he became the preeminent African American linguist in the United States.

Turner was a quintessential academic who embraced the idea that there is no dichotomy between scholarly inquiry and community service. His social consciousness paralleled that of many of his contemporaries, among them, Ralph Bunche, Alain Locke, E. Franklin Frazier, Zora Neale Hurston, Charles Johnson, and Metz Lochard, the "New Negroes" described by Alain Locke in his 1925 anthology of the same name. A major influence shaping Turner's gestalt was his alliance with Carter G. Woodson and the Association for the Study of Negro Life and History (ASNLH). Another was the development of the American linguistic movement. Among Turner's associates was the staff of the Linguistic Atlas project: Hans Kurath, Miles Hanley, Bernard Bloch, and Guy Lowman. As he immersed himself in linguistic pursuits, he interacted with numerous others, among them, Edward Sapir, Leonard Bloomfield, Raven McDavid, and Mitford Mathews. His most influential colleague in American anthropology was Melville Herskovits. Like Herskovits, Turner was a relativist, believing in the value of each culture and respecting the folk of the people as the source of authentic culture and art forms.

Turner's life can be viewed in four stages: (1) his birth in Elizabeth City, North Carolina, in 1890 through the earning of his master's degree in English from Harvard University in 1917; (2) his tenure as instructor and head of the English department at Howard University from 1917 to 1928, including his work on his doctorate in English from the University of Chicago in 1926 and the founding and editing of the *Washington Sun* in 1928–29; (3) his tenure as professor and head of the Department of English at Fisk University from 1929 to 1946 and as chair of African Studies from 1944 to 1946; and (4) his tenure at Roosevelt College in Chicago as professor of English and lecturer in the Inter-Departmental Program in African Studies from 1946 to 1970, including his year as a Fulbright scholar in Africa (1951) and his service as director of the language component of the Peace Corps project (1962–66).

Standing astride the nineteenth and twentieth centuries, between the Harlem Renaissance of his youth and the civil rights and Black Power movements, coupled with the rebirth of the nations of a new Africa in his maturity, Turner was a seasoned traveler. He entered American linguistics shortly after the founding of the Linguistic Society of America (LSA) in 1924 and proceeded to give shape to two of its specialties—dialect geography and pidgin/creole linguistics.

At the same time Turner was a pragmatist who did not ignore literary studies. In 1931 he and two colleagues published one of the earliest comprehensive anthologies of African American literature for secondary schools and colleges.

By 1949, with the publication of *Africanisms in the Gullah Dialect,* Turner's brilliant achievement made him the "Father of Gullah Studies." He was able to accomplish for Gullah what Alex Haley accomplished for genealogy, Melville Herskovits for anthropology, Zora Neale Hurston for folklore and women's rights to self-definition, Carter G. Woodson for African American history, Hans Kurath for dialect geography, and W. E. B. Du Bois for social activism. Each believed in the remotely possible, and each sustained the effort to accomplish it over a protracted period of time. Turner was the first to bring a linguistic background to the analysis of Gullah, the first to conduct systematic interviews among its native speakers, the first to commit aspects of its grammar to paper, the first to establish conclusively that vestiges of Niger-Congo languages had survived in North America, the first to establish that black speech was a legitimate subject for scholarly investigation, and the first to offer linguistic courses at a Historically Black College or University (HBCU).

Turner conceived of *Africanisms in the Gullah Dialect* as the inauguration of a large-scale study of creoles derived from African languages. Although "creole" was a fuzzy concept until the 1960s, and Turner referred to Gullah as "a creolized form of English," he pioneered in the study of United States creoles. His master plan was to conduct fieldwork in Africa, then collect data among Romance and Germanic Creole speakers in the Guianas and on a number of Caribbean islands—in particular, Jamaica, Trinidad, Barbados, and Haiti—in order to prepare analyses comparable to *Africanisms*. He shared his vision with his Fisk University students; one of them, the Romance linguist Raleigh Morgan, undertook data collection on Louisiana Creole.

In 1943, when Fisk University became the first American University to develop an African Studies Program, Turner had become an articulate spokesperson for pan-African and interdisciplinary studies. In the decades between 1950 and 1970, his vision as a pan-Africanist scholar with an interdisciplinary pedagogy continually intensified. After *Africanisms in the Gullah Dialect,* he adopted the methodologies of social and cultural anthropology to advance his research on Brazil. He solidified his reputation as an Africanist when he lectured and conducted fieldwork in Nigeria and Sierra Leone (1951). With the advent of the Peace Corps, Turner embraced service as language coordinator and a teacher of volunteers to Sierra Leone from 1962 to 1966. The publication of two Krio texts (1963, 1965) represents another phase of the expanding fulfillment of his pan-Creole research agenda.

With increasing interest in Africa as colonialism crumbled, Turner was hired to serve as a lexicographer to prepare entries from African languages for the *Webster's New World Dictionary*. He served as a consultant for McGraw-Hill's Science Research Associates. Turner authored the article on Gullah for *Encyclopaedia Britannica* (1964) and lectured widely on syncretized forms of African culture in the Western Hemisphere. His major focus was Gullah speakers, their music, folklore, and culture; African culture in Brazil (especially Yoruban); and continental African culture and politics, both traditional and transitional. His books, articles, and book reviews recommend him as a theorist and scholar of the highest order.

Since he lived before the telephone and e-mail sharply curtailed the art of letter-writing, Turner's correspondence is rich in intellectual vitality. It provides glimpses into his relationships with contemporaries in literature, linguistics, and African diasporic culture, in and out of academia; delineates relationships with family members and friends; outlines his research agenda as it unfolded at various stages of his career; and details his day-to-day activities during his research sojourns. Because few of his letters have ever appeared in print, although they represent Turner so directly, I have been generous in the use of quotes from them and from those letters he received in response to them.

As a personality, Turner was intellectually curious and adventurous, tenacious, not seeking safety in the discipline of English, in which he received his doctorate. He reinvented himself as a linguist at a time when he was well established in his career as an English professor and when most African Americans were confined to more traditional disciplines in the academy.

Turner was energetic, typically spending twenty hours per day in work and related activities and four in sleep. He was strong-willed and not easily deterred from his priorities. He was a committed leader, finding himself selected for administrative responsibilities in each of the universities on whose faculties he served. He was a brilliant scholar and a magnet, drawing students, colleagues, and community members to him as he shared his theoretical and practical insights.

Turner's career did not develop in a linear fashion, rather in ever widening concentric circles, marked by pivotal junctures. Five of them gave shape to his intellectual and scholarly endeavors. The most important resulted from the events of the summer of 1929, when he taught at South Carolina State College and began his interaction with speakers of Gullah. The experience led him to twice attend the Linguistic Institute, while pursuing grants to investigate Gullah. The second significant juncture was his fieldwork in Gullah territory in 1932 and 1933. The third was his year-long study of African languages at the University of London in 1936–37, followed by fieldwork in Brazil in 1940–41, which allowed Turner to crack the code to document the African linguistic retentions in Gullah and the Yoruba dialect of northern Brazil and to substantiate his major hypothesis. The fourth juncture was the founding of African Studies in 1943, which created a context for Turner to explore African languages and culture in the university classroom. The fifth was his Fulbright year in Africa in 1951, when he experienced numerous African cultural and linguistic patterns he had been able to analyze previously only through secondary sources. The first four junctures were the tributaries leading to the experiential ocean that was Africa. The latter experience was the culmination of a lifelong plan to immerse himself in traditional Africa, one of the major sources of Western Hemisphere diasporic cultures. As a result, Turner was able to ascend to a new level as a specialist in African culture, one he fulfilled both within and outside the classroom until his final retirement in 1970.

It is tempting to confine Turner to his Gullah legacy, but he was far more and contributed much more. Although he earned the title of "father of Gullah studies," a biography focused only on an interpretation of his life in the context of his Gullah research would be overly narrow and misleading. Consequently, this study endeavors to present him in nuanced complexity, with Gullah studies as the centerpiece of his career but not the totality of his life.

By the end of Turner's life, he had published five books and a number of articles and book reviews, and he had prepared an impressive array of additional manuscripts, many translated from Brazilian Yoruba and Niger-Congo languages of

Africa into English. He utilized a number of them in the courses he taught. Turner's three articles on Africans in Brazil and two on the Yoruba of Nigeria were companions to the books of folklore and dictionaries that remain in manuscript form.

There is enduring interest in Turner's research, as well as growing public recognition of his contribution. During his lifetime he contributed much to the process of bringing pidgin/creole studies into the center of linguistics. Although he was not an advocate for Black English, his Gullah studies plausibly led to the conclusion that other language varieties in the Western Hemisphere derived from African languages are the legitimate province of linguistic analysis.

In the intervening half century since the publication of *Africanisms in the Gullah Dialect,* at least thirty dissertations on aspects of Gullah have appeared. Pidgin and creole linguistics and Black English / Ebonics have become constantly evolving specialties in American linguistics. Furthermore, Turner's unwavering advocacy of the study of culture in the African diaspora marks him as one of the fathers of African Studies. So broad has been his influence that it continues to grow rather than to diminish as the documents of his intellectual children and grandchildren continue to enrich the pages of books and journals and as classroom discussions continue to examine his ideas.

Africanisms in the Gullah Dialect was the first in a series of studies that established an entirely new era in linguistics. The rise of non-Western nations from colonialism to independence created the context for focusing conversations on the concerns and insights of the formerly colonized. Within a few years, two master's level linguists signaled the dramatic increase in scholarly attention to creole languages. Beryl Bailey examined a number of related Caribbean creoles in 1953. In 1958 Richard Allsopp initiated the analysis of Guyanese Creole.

At the height of the civil rights movement, J. L. Dillard, the author of *Black English: Its History and Usage in the United States* (1972), became the first to write a full-length study indicating that Black English is the descendant of a Plantation Creole. That same year William Labov published *Language in the Inner City,* which examined black urban speech, while encouraging his students at the University of Pennsylvania to undertake fieldwork projects leading to dissertations on urban speech of the young. The Labov approach was a departure from the past tradition of analyzing the speech of older, rural African Americans.

Ralph W. Fasold and Roger W. Shuy's *Teaching Standard English in the Inner City* (1970) and Geneva Smitherman's studies of Black English and education, among them, *Talkin and Testifyin: The Language of Black America* (1977), led to new interpretations of the competencies of black youth as well as methods of maximizing their educational and linguistic performance. William Stewart and others at the Center for Applied Linguistics, in Washington, D.C., initiated innovative research to enrich pedagogy and encourage the teaching of Standard English to speakers of Black English through a "bridge" or "English as a second language" approach (1970s). A half century of research too voluminous to explore in this document is the outgrowth of Turner's research.

Over the years, pidgin and creole linguistics and Black English studies have become the most rapidly advancing specialties in linguistics, with semi-annual and annual conferences, the *Carrier Pidgin* newsletter, and the *Journal of Pidgin and Creole Languages*. Each decade, examination of language in education policy rekindles the "Ebonics in the schools debate," most recently in Oakland, California, in 1996.

Gullah Studies continues to expand, starting with the early post-Turner grammar by Cunningham (1970), which was revised in 1992, and including an analysis of uniquely male/female linguistic styles in Patricia Causey Nichols's work (1976); a study of African retentions in folk culture by Mary Twining (1977); the spoken word and cultural reinterpretation by Patricia Jones-Jackson (1978); the study of tense, mood, and aspect by Katherine Wyly Mille (1990); and recent comparative analyses by Tometro Hopkins (1992) and Tracy L. Weldon (1998).

Public recognition of Turner's contribution extends beyond the doors of academia. In 1969, during Turner's final years, he was inducted into the Chicago Hall of Fame. On May 17, 1974, an elementary school in Chicago was named the Lorenzo Dow Turner Elementary School. After its closing, another elementary school, the Turner-Drew Language Academy, was established in 1999 and named jointly for Turner and Charles Drew, the inventor of the process of banking blood. Since Turner's death on February 10, 1972, a growing number of academic conferences have centered on his research. Video documentaries, numerous newspaper articles, and thousands of Web sites refer to his work. Annual Gullah festivals invoke his memory, not only on the Sea Islands, but also in states such as Oklahoma and Texas, where pockets of Georgia/Alabama/Carolina/Florida expatriates have resettled. The Penn Center on St. Helena Island serves as a clearinghouse for information on Gullah culture. The most vocal advocate for the preservation of Gullah land, culture, and traditions is Marquetta Goodwine (Queen Quet), founder and director of the Gullah/Geechee Sea Island Coalition.

On December 31, 1932, Turner offered the first presentation on his Gullah research to the members of the American Dialect Society. Coming full circle, seventy years later at its 2002 conference, the American Dialect Society offered a Lorenzo Dow Turner T-shirt to its members.[1] A biography is the logical next step.

ACKNOWLEDGMENTS

This biography is indebted to many. John Costello of New York University stimulated my love for etymology and encouraged my search for semantic items from African languages in English. The late William Stewart of the City University of New York Graduate Center assisted me in locating Turner's widow, Lois Turner Williams, and encouraged the direction of my research. Arthur Spears of City College of New York has given a great deal of sage advice over the years. John V. Singler of New York University supervised my first inquiry into Turner's contribution. Regna Darnell of the University of Western Ontario has provided both advice and inspiration. Alexander Moore of the University of South Carolina Press believed in the project at its inception and urged me along.

I owe a special debt to Lois Turner Williams, a fabulous archivist in her own right, who loved enough to discard nothing. She has given to me generously of her time, repeatedly opening her home, entrusting to me her photographs, slides, tapes, letters, and memories. Her faith that I would see this project to completion has been central to my inspiration. Similarly, Gloria Stewart, Turner Williams's sister, has been gracious during my visits, providing clarifying details. Eugene Townes, the only nephew of Geneva Townes Turner, entered my life at the opportune juncture to share documents from Geneva Townes Turner's early years in Washington, D.C., many of which were otherwise inaccessible to me.

Those who have granted interviews have played an important role in this interpretation in that they have added flesh and blood to my understanding of Turner. They are listed in the bibliography. To all those not specifically mentioned herein who have assisted in any manner, I extend my heartfelt thanks.

Several of my colleagues and friends have given generously of their time to provide careful readings of chapters or the entire manuscript, enriching it with their insights at various stages of its development: Patricia Causey Nichols, Michael Montgomery, Arthur Spears, Ian Hancock, Irma Aloyce Cunningham, Tracy Weldon, Regna Darnell, Albert J. Williams-Myers, Beverly Lavergneau, Lori Horsman, and Linda Webster. Karen Beidel and Bill Adams at the University of South Carolina Press expertly guided the manuscript through the editorial stages. Any missteps are mine.

Central to the core of this analysis are archival data. It has been my good fortune to have encountered some of the most dedicated archivists anywhere: Theresa Ferguson of the Family Research Society of Northeastern North Carolina in Elizabeth City; Edith Seiling, Gatesville, North Carolina; Clifford Muse, Howard University Archives, Washington, D.C.; Michael M. Roudette, the Schomburg Center for Research in Black Culture, New York; the staff of the Northeastern Branch of the National Archives, New York City; and Ernest J. Emrich, Library of Congress in Washington, D.C.

The repositories central to Turner's contribution are housed at Northwestern, Fisk, Howard, Roosevelt, and Indiana Universities. The most recent collection is housed at the Anacostia Museum of the Smithsonian Institution in Washington, D.C. The most extensive collection is maintained at Northwestern University, Evanston, Illinois. During my various archival sojourns, its director, David Easterbrook, and the Africana staff were consistently supportive. Likewise indefatigable has been Beth Howse, archivist, Fisk University, Nashville, Tennessee; Joellen ElBashir, curator, Moorland-Spingarn Research Center, Howard University, Washington, D.C.; Michael Gabriel, archivist, Roosevelt University Library, Chicago, Illinois; and Marilyn Graf, archivist, the Archives of Traditional Music, Indiana University, Bloomington.

The breakthrough on data related to Turner's family background, especially on Rooks Turner, was facilitated by Irene Hampton, genealogical researcher for local history and genealogy, the Pasquotank-Camden Library, Elizabeth City, North Carolina; the late Leonard Ballou, archivist, G. R. Little Library, Elizabeth City State University; and Patricia Abelard Anderson, librarian, Montgomery County Historical Society, Rockville, Maryland.

I wish to acknowledge those who helped me navigate the collections housing sources related to Turner's early life, education, development as a linguist, and linguistic history: Michelle Gachette, reference assistant, Harvard University Archives, Pusey Library; Mark Alznauer, reference assistant, Special Collections Research Center, the University of Chicago Library; Margaret Reynolds, executive director of the Linguistic Society of America; Jay Satterfield, head of Reader Services, Special Collections Research Center, University of Chicago Library; Valerie Mittenberg, reference librarian; Russ Howitt, Inter-Library Loan; and Athena Nazario, Instruction and Electronic Resources librarian of the Sojourner Truth Library, State University of New York, New Paltz. Henty Bulley, alumni officer of the School of Oriental and African Studies of the University of London, assisted in the location of records documenting Turner's year in London.

This study is richer for the assistance of Andrew Apter of the University of Chicago for his interpretation of a number of Turner's fieldwork slides; Leonard Moody of Chicago for transferring Turner's 8 millimeter Nigeria / Sierra Leone fieldwork reel to VHS format and who, with his wife Gloria has served as a member of my support network; Vivian Clark-Adams of Tulsa, Oklahoma, for generous support and assistance; Linda Franzella, Christopher Jones, Miguel de Jesus, and Joseph Shayne of the Department of Black Studies, SUNY New Paltz for clerical support; Emily Trapp, operations manager, and Douglas Short, evening supervisor, both of SUNY New Paltz Instructional Resources, for media assistance.

My nuclear family has been my regular sounding board. Turner has resided with us for many years as the subject of library trips and dinner conversations. My husband, David A. Lewis, has provided equally ardent support and critiques. Our children have likewise left their imprint—Chaka and Esi Marjorie with their technological expertise, the latter with her urgings to "be done already"; Solomon David with his bountiful optimism; and Shamell with her patience.

I am appreciative of my siblings, my brothers John, Richard, James, and Steven Williams, and my sisters Lillian Lancaster, Carolyn Bell, Mary Williams-Smith, and Marjorie Ray, who have encouraged this project with their attendance at lectures or their unwearied listening to my research sagas. I extend regards to my co-workers at Ebenezer Baptist Church, Poughkeepsie, who seldom judged while I excused myself from evening services, annual picnics, and visits to guest congregations, and to Cynthia Dozier, who regularly inquired about my progress.

This research had been made possible through State University of New York at New Paltz Research and Creative Projects Grants, United University Professions Grants, travel grants from the SUNY New Paltz Office of the Dean of Liberal Arts and Sciences, and a National Endowment for the Humanities Travels to Collections Grant, all of which I appreciatively acknowledge.

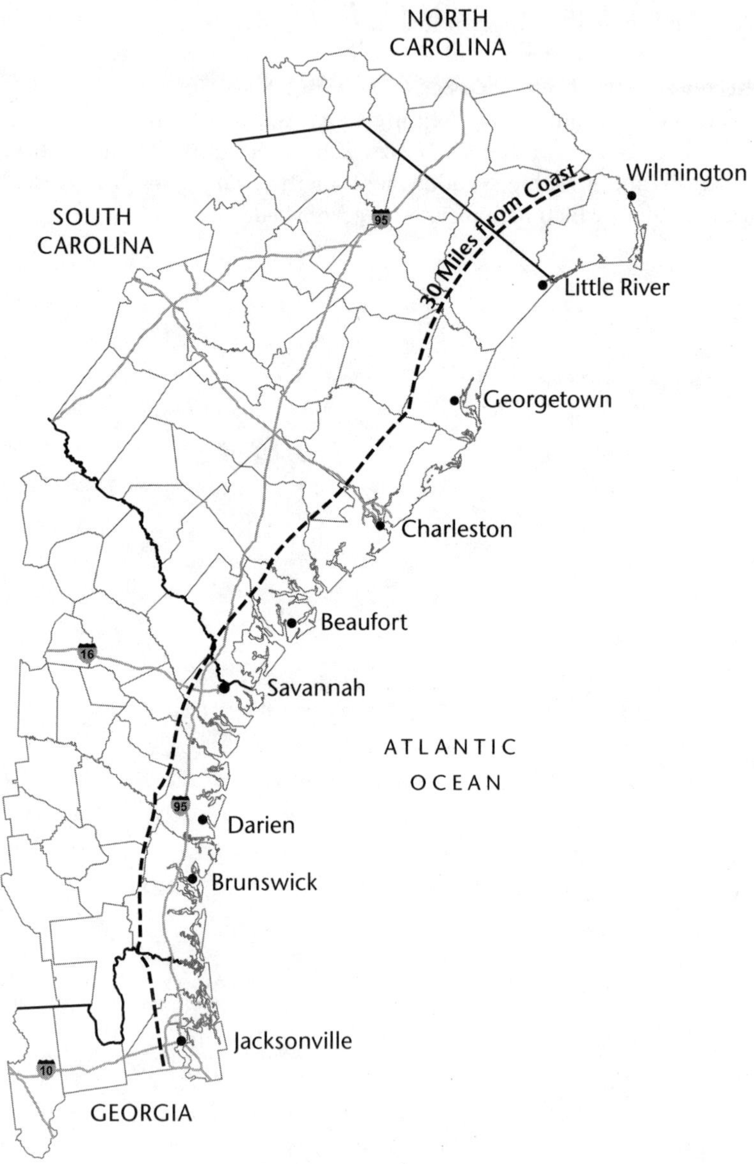

The Gullah-speaking region. U.S. National Park Service, *Low Country Gullah Culture Special Resource Study and Environmental Impact Statement* (Atlanta: NDS Southeast Region, 2004)

LORENZO DOW TURNER

1

Sally Rooks, Jacob Brady, and the Origins of the Rooks/Turner Clan 1799 AND AFTER

As the fundamental labor system of the South changed from white servitude to black slavery, the separation of Europeans and Africans became crucial to whites in order to sustain the institution of racial slavery. Once the law stipulated that a child's status as slave or free followed its mother, liaisons between white women and black men would render the equation of African ancestry and slavery ineffective, because such unions would produce free children of partial African ancestry; hence the enactment of laws that discouraged white women from choosing black partners.

—Martha Hodes, *White Women, Black Men*

IN 1799 THE ROOKS/TURNER CLAN began in Gates County, near Elizabeth City, North Carolina. By the time of the birth of Lorenzo Dow Turner in 1890, the family was in its fourth generation. The family traces its origins to a Scotch-Irish woman named Sally Rooks and to Jacob Brady, "a black man of exceeding height and large stature."[1] The best available data indicate that Sally was the daughter of Joseph Rooks, the owner of a well-known plantation that still stands, though unoccupied, on Rooks Road just off Highway 13.[2] Unlike Sally Rooks, Jacob Brady was not free. (He was probably owned by Joseph Rooks.) Laws enacted in 1715 forbade free blacks to marry whites; enslaved Africans were generally forbidden to marry anyone.[3]

One can only speculate that Sally Rooks's parent or parents at least tacitly approved of this relationship since Jacob and Sally produced four daughters within twelve years. The couple likely lived as a family. Because the free black population in North Carolina was rural and agricultural during the early generations, it was more protected "from the public attack which the rurality afforded" than those who lived in the large cities such as Charleston, South Carolina, and Baltimore, Maryland.[4] This protection compensated for the isolation. The four "Rooks sisters" thrived, becoming well-bred young women and producing descendants who have enriched the American society with their skills and talents to the present day.[5]

Nothing further is currently known about Sally Rooks and Jacob Brady. It is, however, relevant that interracial relations were less of an issue in the early centuries of the American society than after the Civil War, particularly when both the man and woman were immigrants or otherwise members of out-groups. In North Carolina there were already a number of free African Americans classified as "mulatto" whose last name was Rooks by the time Sally Rooks and Jacob Brady produced Polly in 1799. The 1860 Census for Perquimans County lists a Mills

Rooks, mulatto male, age sixty-five.[6] An Elisha Rooks, a mulatto who became the patriarch of a family of carpenters, was born in Gates County in 1790, nine years before Polly Rooks.[7]

Freedom for persons of African ancestry was the result of a number of factors. Among them were manumission, immigration, military service in the American Revolution, and being an offspring of a white or Native American or an offspring of a relationship between a white woman and a black man outside of marriage.[8] The four Rooks sisters fit into the latter category.

The first of the Rooks sisters was Polly, born in 1799. She lived for eighty-two years and died in 1881. The birth dates of the next three are approximate. Polly's siblings were Judith, born in 1802, Sally, born in 1804, and Margaret (called Peggy) born in 1812.[9] As each reached adulthood, she was able to meet and marry a free man of color.

Polly married David Rooks, a carpenter and cooper (1795–1850). Together Polly and David produced six children: Joseph, Mary, Joanna, Nancy, James, and John.[10] The children of David and Polly Rooks were the Rooks second cousins of Lorenzo Dow Turner.

The second sister, Judith, married Micajah Reid (spelled Reed in the record) on February 28, 1826.[11] Life was challenging for them: only three of their six children, Asbury, William, and Mary, survived to adulthood. They were the Reid second cousins of Lorenzo Dow Turner. Sally Rooks, the third-born sister, married Jethro (Jet) Martin in the 1820s.[12] Their children were the Martin second cousins of Lorenzo Dow Turner.

The youngest of the four sisters, Margaret (Peggy) Rooks, married Daniel Turner on April 17, 1828.[13] Daniel was a landowner, a Baptist minister, and a literate man.[14] He and Peggy moved from Gates County in search of better employment opportunities; they appear on the 1860 Census for Pasquotank County as the parents of Rooks Turner and eleven other children. Peggy and Daniel Turner were the paternal grandparents of Lorenzo Dow Turner.

By 1832 Polly, Judith, Sally, and Peggy, married to skilled artisans or landowners of color, had become members of the early black middle class. It was a heritage in which they took pride and for which they accepted both the prestige and the responsibility. Their life circumstances were far more fortunate than those of many others, enslaved or free.

At the time of the 1860 Pasquotank County Census, Lorenzo Dow Turner's grandfather, Daniel, was fifty-six years old and a farmer. The Pasquotank Country Register of Deeds Office records list him as the owner of at least sixty-nine acres of land. Furthermore, he and Peggy were both able to read and write as land deeds bear their signatures, rather than an "X."[15]

In 1860 Margaret (Peggy) was forty-eight years old. Peggy is listed with no occupation, as was often the case with entries for women who were full-time homemakers. Daniel is listed as black and she as mulatto. According to Turner, who in the 1950s—being aware of the importance of family history—listed his father's siblings, his father, Rooks, was child number nine.[16] (See the appendix for Turner's family tree.)

After the Civil War ended in 1865, one of the most hopeful signs of progress was the development of a tax-supported system of modern public education. While whites were enormously opposed to integrated schools, the majority at the North Carolina Constitutional Convention did vote for tax-supported public education for African Americans for four months of each year.[17] It is not astounding then that Rooks Turner was so exhilarated by the opportunity to receive an education that he completed the equivalent of twelve years of education in just four years.

2

Rooks Turner 1844–1926

> Those who profess to favor freedom and yet depreciate agitation are men who want crops without plowing up the ground. They want rain without thunder and lightning. They want the ocean without the roar of its many waters. . . . The struggle may be a moral one; or it may be a physical one; or it may be both moral and physical; but it must be a struggle. Power concedes nothing without a demand. It never did, and it never will.
>
> —Frederick Douglass, "The Significance of Emancipation in the West Indies: An Oration, August 2, 1857"

THE KEY TO UNDERSTANDING Lorenzo Dow Turner's tenacious personality can be found in an understanding of his parents. The Turners were an "up-headed people," ambitious, hardworking, and optimistic. Rooks, Daniel and Peggy Turner's ninth child, a member of the third generation of the Rooks clan, was born on October 24, 1844, in Elizabeth City, Pasquotank County, North Carolina.[1] He was Lorenzo Dow Turner's father. As he grew, he manifested decisiveness, impatience, a pronounced sense of civic responsibility, and the ability to influence others. Daniel and Peggy took pride in maintaining "the sixty-nine acres more or less" that Daniel owned, inherited, or purchased near Elizabeth City.[2] He sometimes became the joint owner of additional land with relatives.

> The men raised wool, flax and cotton. The women spun, dyed, wove and sewed the clothes. The men raised the large crops. The women and children cared for vegetable, herb and flower gardens.
>
> The children not only chopped in the fields and gardens, but they also took their turns at the looms. The boys did basket weaving and rug making, then sold them for pocket money in case the money could be spared. The girls pickled, preserved and learned the duties of keeping house.
>
> The men and boys went seine-fishing in the Chowan River and brought home barrels of fish to be salted for winter breakfasts. They also raised rice in the marshes of the Chowan River, which in some instances bordered the back or sides of their property.[3]

Shortly after the Civil War, the Freedman's Bureau established a school "for colored people" in Elizabeth City. The year was 1866, and the school was a first. The teachers were committed men and women of European ancestry from the North; among them were George A. Newcome, Fannie A. Newcome, and Emily S. Paduzie.[4]

In his twenties, Rooks entered school in the first grade. It does not appear that any of his siblings joined him. By 1866 many of them were already fully committed to other enterprises, having married and produced large and growing families.

Rooks applied himself with a passion as he attended the local grammar school, where Thomas W. Cardozo was the principal. The school was located on what was then Shannon Street and is currently 708 Herrington Road. Within four years, Rooks had received sufficient education to move to other challenges. Since Thomas Cardozo was committed to championing educational opportunities for the recently freed African Americans, he encouraged Rooks to enter the Preparatory Department of Howard University, in Washington, D.C., a school also founded after the Civil War. In 1870 Rooks left Elizabeth City for Washington, D.C., to join forty-eight other students in pursuit of the dream of education.[5] Among the forty-eight were the brothers John Lane and Wiley Lane, also from Cardozo's grammar school in Elizabeth City. They, too, had caught the eye of Thomas Cardozo, who had commended all three to his brother, Francis L. Cardozo (1837–1903), the Latin professor at Howard University. Wiley Lane would eventually follow in Francis L. Cardozo's footsteps, becoming Howard's first professor of Greek.[6]

Since Rooks had acquired more education than the majority of his peers by 1873, he returned each summer to North Carolina to teach others and thereby earn money to continue his own education. It was also his good fortune to come to the attention of Senator George W. Hoar of Massachusetts, one of the philanthropists from the North who "came to the rescue of hundreds of worthy and ambitious colored people during those trying days of the Reconstruction period."[7] Hoar arranged for additional funding. Rooks's interest in politics was already becoming apparent. On September 2, 1873, just before he returned to Howard University for the fall semester, he served as an election inspector, an assignment for which the county commissioners paid him four dollars.[8]

With two sources of funds, from the normal school and from Hoar, and with the supplementary assistance his family could provide, Rooks graduated triumphantly with his bachelor's degree in 1877, twelve years after emancipation and seven years after he had entered college. He then returned to Pasquotank County to serve in the education of African Americans.

Academically prepared and politically aware, Rooks embraced the awesome mission of serving as a leader and role model. He was the counterpart of Booker T. Washington, Carter G. Woodson, Ida B. Wells-Barnett, and Mary Bethune. One generation older than W. E. B. Du Bois, Rooks took seriously the imperative to educate as many others as possible. He was not a separatist but definitely a "race man" dedicated to the greater good of persons of African ancestry.

Between 1875 and 1896, Rooks was involved in at least twenty-two land transactions, six for purchases and sixteen for liens and sales. On September 17, 1879, he completed his third land transaction. It was his most significant purchase, as a two-story house and outbuildings on the property made it the appropriate site on which to establish a school. The sellers were William Shannon and his wife, Margaret. The property, costing $250, was a parcel of land "containing three acres more or less."[9] The house on the property became the school. The present address of the property is 200 Roanoke Avenue.

Rooks named the school for himself. The Rooks Turner Normal School was private and operated in summers to train teachers and during several additional months each year, as funds allowed. Rooks pursued various employment opportunities to offset the expenses of his school. Summers provided additional funds as North Carolina subsidized separate summer institutes and subscription schools for blacks and whites. These were designed to assist teachers in improving their teaching methods.[10]

Rooks regularly hosted summer teaching institutes in his building, and he taught and organized schools in other townships. Whenever possible, he taught during the fall session in a public school. The local public school for "colored" people opened the week of November 28, 1888, just after Thanksgiving and the close of the harvest season. The interest in education within the black population was so acute that two buildings were in operation, one constructed not long before 1888. According to the November 28, 1888, issue of the *North Carolinian,* "Rooks Turner and Mrs. J. R. Brown took charge of one in the new building and N. R. Newby and Mrs. Wright" took charge of the educational activities in the old one.[11]

By 1889 Rooks had distinguished himself through his dedicated work. The December 11, 1889, issue of the *North Carolinian* reported that he was appointed "principal of a Negro school. He was assisted by George A. Mabane, formerly of Windsor, North Carolina, and once a senator in the North Carolina Assembly."[12] It likely was in operation only a few months of the year as by October 6, 1890, a few months after the birth of Lorenzo Dow Turner, Rooks was administering "the colored 'Farmers and Normal Agricultural Institute.'"[13]

During December 1895, "Prof. Rooks Turner opened a school at Nixonton," one of the townships in Pasquotank County.[14] The following July found him teaching "at the tiny Pasquotank locale of Okisko."[15]

Harold Harvey Murrill dedicated a page in his master's thesis to Rooks's contribution to North Carolina history, asserting that he "was well remembered for conducting 'normal' schools (not state supported) and summer 'Teacher's Institutes' (which sometimes had some county support)." Although by today's standards, "the schools and institutes had short sessions," they were "much appreciated" by those who were privileged to take advantage of formal education. "In one sense [Rooks] Turner's educational efforts filled the gap between Thomas W. Cardozo's first known school for Blacks in Elizabeth City (1866) and establishment of what is now Elizabeth City State University—with the private, then public, graded schools complementing and later supplanting such efforts below the collegiate (or 'normal') level." Murrill concluded that "if this premise [that Rooks Turner's institutes were a bridge between Cardozo's first school and Elizabeth City State University] is accepted, obviously Rooks Turner's efforts gain additional historical significance."[16]

Because Rooks had begun with disadvantages in life that impeded his rise to prominence, he knew he had no moments to squander. Therefore, by 1880 he had met and married Elizabeth Sessoms Freeman, a nineteen-year-old woman of African, European, and Native American ancestry.[17] She had acquired as much education as the public schools afforded, the equivalent of six grades. In 1880 Rooks Turner was thirty-six. It was the first and only marriage for both.[18]

During the next ten years, Rooks and Elizabeth Turner prospered, although they endured some interpersonal tensions and economic reversals. Being a traditional man, Rooks was committed to the idea that no matter what her educational preparation, a wife should serve as a homemaker and not entrust the children to the care of others while she worked outside the home. Rooks was also determined to protect Elizabeth from domestic service, where physical and sexual exploitation of black women was rampant. Given that, he believed that he was placing Elizabeth in an advantaged position.[19] Whether she was content or chafed at these restrictions, Elizabeth apparently complied. Between 1881 and 1890, the couple produced four sons—Shelby (ca. 1881), Rooks Jr. (August 1883), Arthur (June 1885), and Lorenzo Dow (August 21, 1890).[20] According to family oral history, the four boys were intelligent, beautiful children.[21]

By 1883 it was clear to Rooks that a more encompassing effort than one individual could mount was required to organize and sustain a network of schools for the African American population. Envisioning the political arena as the ideal forum, he entered the race, along with two other candidates, on the Republican Party ticket for the seat of North Carolina state representative from Pasquotank County. The party of Abraham Lincoln was the only one open to members of the black population. One of Rooks's opponents was Hugh Cale, another educated, biracial, African American, born in North Carolina in 1840, four years before Rooks.[22] Cale had already gained credibility, popularity, and experience as a state representative from Pasquotank County in the Republican Party by the time Rooks Turner entered politics.

Nevertheless Rooks did not hesitate to challenge Cale. In the 1884 election, as a newcomer to electoral politics, he garnered 10 percent of the votes. Cale won reelection.[23] Six years later, on November 18, 1890, the *North Carolinian* reported that Rooks challenged Cale again. Five other opponents joined him. Cale was the victor, winning a fourth term.[24] Had Rooks won the election, he surely would have introduced an educational bill, as Cale soon did.

Concurrent with Rooks's educational, economic, and political commitments were his other civic involvements. He joined the Masons, the True Reformers, and the Grand United Order of Odd Fellows.[25]

Rooks's civic involvements were consistent with the political trends of the times. Three major themes characterized the black experience after 1877—"organization, uplift and increasing diversity." If African Americans were to thrive and overcome the barriers imposed by centuries of enslavement and second-class citizenship, it behooved them to consolidate their efforts. Thus, "Black community life came together in the churches, lodges, and fraternal organizations, all of which functioned as promoters of individual character and group progress." The Masons and other civic organizations "promoted solidarity, thrift, mutual aid and Christian morality right beside the Baptist State Convention."[26]

Some members of the Turner clan migrated from North Carolina during the decade of the 1880s but not the Rooks Turner branch. Acquiring funds to operate a school for African Americans was a momentous responsibility. Rooks was both bold and courageous to devote himself to it. He regularly negotiated loans using his land as collateral. Often the notes matured when he had no funds to repay them. Unfortunately, by 1886, that process resulted in a bleeding that was rapidly becoming a hemorrhage. The sale of a portion of his property that he undoubtedly found most devastating involved the three acres that housed his school. Yet it must have provided him some consolation that he was able to arrange to place the property in the hands of his friends, the trustees of the Roanoke Missionary Baptist Association, an organization in which he held membership. On July 19, 1886, Rooks agreed to sell his school and one acre of the land on which it stood. In turn, the trustees agreed to purchase two notes, which he was hard-pressed to continue paying. He retained the remaining two acres of the parcel.[27]

The Rooks Turner Normal School continued to function; however the Roanoke Missionary Baptist Association eventually established another school on the site, the Roanoke Collegiate Institute.[28] The association purchased a second acre of the original three-acre parcel from Rooks and Elizabeth Turner for $950 on July 28, 1892.[29] There the association erected the building in which it operated its Collegiate Institute for many years, until the building burned in 1935. Shortly thereafter, in 1937, the organization constructed a new building.[30]

By the 1890s a number of other citizens were concerned with making higher education opportunities available to African Americans. In January 1891 Cale introduced House Bill 383 to create the Elizabeth City Colored Normal School, a coeducational African American institution. The majority of legislators agreed with Cale; the North Carolina General Assembly ratified the bill on March 3, 1891.[31] In 1892 the state of North Carolina rented the former Rooks Turner building to house the new state-run school. It opened its doors on January 4, 1892, with a budget of $900, two faculty members, and twenty-three students from a number of surrounding counties. It was the first college in Pasquotank County dedicated to the education of African Americans.[32]

While Rooks did not operate his normal school beyond 1892, he must be acknowledged as the founder of the initial school on the grounds where the university, originally known as Elizabeth City Colored Normal School and known today as Elizabeth City State University (ECSU), first opened its doors. Now ECSU occupies another site, having moved to "its present and permanent location" on Shannon Road, renamed Herrington Road, on September 11, 1912.[33]

Rooks continued to obtain loans on his various properties. Over the years as his debts mounted, he persisted in his attempts to satisfy his creditors. On December 21, 1892, he relinquished an 80-by-200-foot lot to E. W. Dozier, to whom he owed two hundred dollars, in a note that was to be completely paid by April 12, 1893. It was a portion of the one acre Rooks Turner had retained on the original three-acre plot on the site of the Rooks Turner Normal School.[34]

In the world of Reconstruction North Carolina, it was the best of times and the worst of times for newly freed and freeborn African Americans. Because there was a smaller and less prosperous white elite in North Carolina than in neighboring Virginia and South Carolina, a "fast-growing, but ferociously struggling, middling group of all hues" looked forward to maintaining a two-party government and participating fully. They "contested power—economic, social, and political—more openly and more heatedly than many other southerners."[35] In Gates County and other portions of eastern North Carolina, there was often a black majority.

This equation applied especially in plantation areas that produced cotton and tobacco.

At election time in the 1880s and 1890s, "North Carolina's geographical, economic, and historic diversity resulted in close gubernatorial and national elections and a legislature bristling with Republican representatives. . . . Shared power among political parties meant that legal segregation came late to the state—not until 1899 did the state legislature demand that railroads provide Jim Crow cars. . . . Disfranchisement trailed the 1890 Mississippi law by a decade."[36] The warning signs of impending difficulties for African Americans increased, frequently taking the form of altercations between individual blacks and whites. Such was the case in the confrontation that resulted in derailment of Rooks's plans to continue to serve as a leader in the arena of higher education in North Carolina.

In 1896 Rooks's dream of building an expanded normal school for African Americans in his home county was abruptly relinquished to others. He did not foresee the impending catastrophe. Understanding the relationship between land ownership and empowerment, he would not have relinquished his stake in North Carolina and his real estate investments willingly. At the same time, being a forceful leader, stern and nationalistic, he did not intend to tolerate nonsense from anyone of any race or color.

The saga of how Rooks came to depart from North Carolina, relinquishing the properties that represented his plan to facilitate educational and economic empowerment, left an indelible mark on Lorenzo Dow Turner. Eighteen ninety-six was an election year. It was also the year that the United States Supreme Court turned back the clock on African American enfranchisement and progress by upholding *Plessy v. Ferguson,* declaring that "separate but equal," or legalized segregation, was the law of the land.[37]

Lorenzo Dow Turner was six years old. He had experienced enough of his strong father to sense that a black man should have a mission. Rooks, having taught summer school in Okisko in 1896, prepared to continue in the fall of the year. One day he was involved in an altercation with a white man who taunted him insultingly. Rooks was reputed to have a fiery temper, with no tolerance for insufferable discrimination. Because of the dispute, he allegedly struck the man "with the flat of an ax," knocking him to the ground. Rooks could no longer remain in North Carolina for his own safety and that of his family. Realizing that he was compelled to leave immediately, he and Elizabeth hastily packed his bags. Rooks departed "between suns," never to return.[38] One of Lorenzo Dow Turner's earliest memories was of watching his father, the decisive man with the stern face and well-trimmed beard, gather his belongings and reluctantly walk out of his family's life.

After his departure, Elizabeth was a woman alone with three growing boys, surviving on a subsistence income. Consequently she was unable to manage the rapidly maturing notes for loans Rooks had incurred. Nor was she able to pay the taxes on the remaining Turner acreage. The Turners' relative prosperity came to a jarring halt. Elizabeth was reduced to performing the domestic labor from which Rooks had attempted to protect her. Although C. Guirkin, the local banker from whom Rooks had taken several loans, died by 1899, a relative, M. L. Guirkin, was the administratrix of his estate. A note matured in 1899, resulting in an unmanageable debt. On July 22, 1899, Guirkin arranged to have the acre auctioned at the Elizabeth City Courthouse. The land was the last of the original three-acre parcel that Rooks had purchased from the Shannons in 1879 and on which his school had been established. It sat beside the property he had sold to his friends in the name of the Roanoke Missionary Baptist Association. The association continued to own the remaining lots. The sale of Rooks's final acre was the end of his noble plans for African Americans in North Carolina. In 1899 he was three years removed from Elizabeth City. His signature does not appear on the deed forfeiting the land.[39]

Nevertheless, being committed and resilient, Rooks continued to dedicate himself to community uplift. He traveled 250 miles, probably by train, to Montgomery County, Maryland, just outside of Washington, D.C. Train tracks and a station had been built in Rockville immediately after the Civil War. Montgomery County's modest population had developed agriculture and an industrial sector with factory jobs. There was a large enough African American population for the county to establish segregated public schools. There Rooks dedicated himself to teaching in the "public graded schools."[40]

Immediately he began to pursue education beyond the bachelor's degree. In 1901 he received a master's degree from Howard University, his undergraduate alma mater. He was one of the first men to receive a master's from Howard and one of a few African American men to have attained one at all.[41]

By 1902 Rooks's fortunes were again rising; he had worked his way up, becoming vice principal of Wheaton School. He moved in 1906 to the Colesville School. The year 1917 found him in the Norbeck School, and by 1920 he was at Quince Orchard School. Each school was named for a township or voting district.[42]

During his two decades in Montgomery County, little is known of how regularly he contacted his family. By 1900 he resided in the household of a black family headed by a Charles J. Vinson.[43] His occupation was "teaching school." One of two boarders, Rooks listed three children as dependents but not by name. He mentioned no wife.[44]

Circumstantial details suggest that the Turners were reunited in 1901, when Elizabeth, Rooks Jr., Arthur, and Lorenzo Dow moved to Rockville. However, the family did not always reside in the same household, possibly because of funds and space considerations. Rooks and Elizabeth experienced a final parting of the ways during Lorenzo Dow Turner's years at Howard University, around 1912.[45] During Rooks's separation from his wife and sons, he filled his life with positive activities, lecturing on issues in education and joining civic, fraternal, cultural, and religious organizations.

Wherever he traveled, his personality and preparation marked him as a leader. In 1905 the *Washington Post* ran a brief article, "Negro Teachers Conclude Session," which listed Rooks as one of the workshop speakers for the annual institute organized by teachers and administrators of the black schools.[46]

The challenges to black education were monumental. With many schools open only two to four months per year, many young blacks, boys in particular, attended only sporadically. Often the schools operated in local churches. Sometimes buildings were mysteriously destroyed by fire. Schools were few and far between.[47]

Not bowing to discouragement, Rooks continued to serve as an activist and leader. On September 9, 1913, nearly age sixty-nine, he led a delegation to a meeting of the school board to request that a school for African American children be established in Potomac. The board informed Rooks and the other delegates that it would turn the matter over to the superintendent of schools, E. B. Woods, "for further study and investigation." In 1920 there was still no black school in Potomac.[48]

Being intensely aware of the importance of the written word, Rooks authored a number of articles on education and philosophical issues.[49] He sometimes delivered them to a printer to prepare as pamphlets for distribution. In one, "The Proper Use of Time," he exhorted his readers that upward mobility was directly related to the wise use of available hours, days, and weeks in which to accomplish their goals.[50]

Permanently unwelcome in Elizabeth City, even after his retirement from the public schools in 1922, Rooks had little reason to return to his birthplace. His parents—Daniel and Peggy—and his uncles and aunts had passed away. Many of his cousins, like him, had sought formal education in other cities. Some had moved to Hampton, Virginia, to attend Hampton Institute, the alma mater of Booker T. Washington. Others moved to Atlanta to attend Atlanta University. Still others relocated to Winton, in northeastern North Carolina, on the Virginia border, to attend Winton Academy,[51] a boarding school for African Americans founded by Dr. Calvin S. Brown in 1886.[52]

At the time of Rooks's retirement, his children were adults in their thirties. He appears in the United States Census for 1920 as seventy-five years old, in Darnestown Township of Montgomery County, Maryland, without other family members.[53]

Since immediate family ties were no longer a factor, he departed from Rockville, resettling in Washington, D.C., in 1922, with his only surviving sister, Sarah Turner Bowe. She was eighty-two when Rooks retired. He moved into her household as a seventy-seven-year-old senior citizen. By then he had developed diabetes, with resulting physical complications.[54]

It seemed that despite Rooks's talents, motivation, and hard work, the sword of Damocles hung ever over his head. In his early adulthood, he was headed for prominence. He spent most of his life ahead of his times, and for that, he had paid a great price. He had committed his all, watering the tree of freedom with his dedicated labor and social activism. On the one hand, his flaring temper sometimes complicated the circumstances of his life; on the other hand, at every turn there had been cruel labyrinths of fate, and then, finally, another catastrophic situation overtook Rooks Turner on July 22, 1926. He was eighty-one years old. As for Lorenzo Dow Turner, the situation was an unanticipated episode that tested his mettle during an important passage in his life.

3

Elizabeth R. Sessoms Freeman Turner 1861–1931

Therefore, my beloved brethren, be ye stedfast, unmoveable, always abounding in the work of the Lord, forasmuch as ye know that your labour is not in vain in the Lord.

—I Corinthians 15:58, KJV

Train up a child in the way he should go: and when he is old, he will not depart from it.

—Proverbs 22:6, KJV

UNLIKE ROOKS TURNER, Elizabeth, the mother of Lorenzo Dow Turner, was born enslaved. Her mother, Mathilda, a mulatto, was born in the early 1800s. Elizabeth would have been described in the literature of her times as a quadroon, presumably having descended from a grandmother of African ancestry and a white grandfather and father. Along the way, one or more ancestors were Native American. Judging by her photographs, her African, Native American, and European genes combined in an advantageous arrangement. A study in contrasts, her hair was dark and heavy, her skin was olive, and her eyes were blue.[1]

Mathilda and Elizabeth lived on a plantation in South Mills.[2] At the time Elizabeth was born on March 12, 1861, the Civil War was about to begin. Her biological father was a white man whose last name was Sessoms. There is no evidence that she had siblings. On the back of one of her photographs is the death date of her mother, Mathilda—a Monday at 7:00 A.M. in 1865—when Elizabeth was four years old. Recorded data do not indicate who raised her. Before she was old enough to remember, her African American stepfather, Anthony Freeman, enlisted in the Union army to fight on the side of the North.[3]

By the time Elizabeth was school aged, the end of the Civil War and freedom had arrived, creating for her the opportunity to enter a local graded school. Elizabeth received "such education as the schools of North Carolina afforded," or approximately six years.[4] She was likely a good student as items in the trunk Lorenzo Dow Turner retained after she died show her to have had a meticulous style. Her handwriting was executed deliberately, with capital letters in calligraphy.[5]

As Elizabeth reached adulthood, she found favor with Rooks Turner, one of the most eligible bachelors in town. After their marriage in 1880, children arrived quickly. Consequently, when Rooks declared that Elizabeth should remain at home, she complied. The couple produced four boys in ten years—Shelby, Rooks Jr., Arthur, and Lorenzo Dow. Despite their best care and efforts, their first child, Shelby, did not thrive, dying at age two.[6]

When the fourth child was born on August 21, 1890, Rooks and Elizabeth named him Lorenzo Dow, after a traveling Methodist minister of the same name who was well known in North Carolina and across the South.[7] With their high expectations for Lorenzo Dow's life, they programmed him for greatness.

In the meantime Elizabeth, not being allowed to attend Sunday school, morning service, Wednesday night prayer meeting, choir rehearsal, or the quarterly church meetings, found bearing the vicissitudes of life more onerous. Rooks was jealous and protective. Wishing to guard his young wife from potential contact with the minister and other churchmen, he consigned Elizabeth to the home. During the week there was little time for activities other than the necessary. Her religious meditations were a private matter sandwiched between the chores required to run the household and support the activities of her energetic and demanding husband and growing boys.[8]

Elizabeth created diaries for herself by sewing loose-leaf paper together. In one of them, she maintained records of her church attendance, which was irregular while she and Rooks shared the same household. She owned two Bibles, one of which she repaired when it began to deteriorate by restitching the black covers with black thread.[9]

Howard Rabinowitz notes, "The church occupied the central position in the black community. Not simply a religious institution, it had recreational, economic, and political functions as well. Only in church affairs could blacks exercise a significant degree of independent control. . . . [The pastors were active] in most areas of community life, serving as intermediaries between blacks and whites."[10]

In the protracted period after Rooks's abrupt departure in 1896, Elizabeth, Rooks Jr., Arthur, and Lorenzo became a part of the working class. Elizabeth was often tense and worried. She was thirty-five years old. Rooks Jr. was thirteen; Arthur, eleven; Lorenzo Dow, six. She took advantage of the freedom Rooks's departure afforded to attend the Cornerstone Baptist Church on Martin Street in Elizabeth City, a church in which she and Rooks were titleholders.[11] It assisted in her survival.

Elizabeth generated income for herself and sons by taking in sewing and washing for members of the white community. The boys assisted by locating available jobs after school and in summers. They ran errands, picked apples, dug sweet potatoes, and picked cotton and berries in season. Life was challenging. There was water to be drawn and heated, wood to be chopped, a garden to be maintained, vegetables to be picked, washed, and prepared at least twice a day. Despite the challenges, somehow, each of the sons continued his education.

In 1901, when Lorenzo Dow was eleven, Elizabeth and the boys moved to Rockville, Maryland, to join Rooks. Within a few years, they had acquired a house and attempted to reconcile. Around 1912 the schism widened irreparably.[12] "There was some estrangement there" that was never successfully resolved.[13]

One by one, the sons set out on their own. Lorenzo Dow entered high school at Howard University Academy in 1906. In 1910 he entered Howard University to complete a bachelor's degree in English. Rooks Jr., the father's namesake, completed his undergraduate degree and enrolled in the Howard University Medical School. Arthur also completed Howard University in 1912. He then pursued and completed a Howard law degree.[14] All three sons had completed Howard by 1914.

In 1910, when Lorenzo Dow enrolled as an undergraduate, Elizabeth was for the most part on her own.

Her sons were out of her house but resting heavy on her heart. As Elizabeth overcame one obstacle, another arose. Just as she could breathe more easily that her sons were all on the road to educational independence, the unspeakable occurred. In 1911 Rooks Jr. contracted tuberculosis. Fortunately, because of his connections at Howard University Medical School, he was able to gain admission to the State Sanatorium of Pennsylvania at Mont Alto. High on the mountain where the air was crisp and pristine, it appeared that Rooks Jr.'s journey to recovery was quite probable.

On the inside cover of one of her Bibles, Elizabeth wrote out Matthew 8:15–16, the verses from the story in which Jesus arrived in Capernaum and healed many, including his disciple Peter's mother. The passage must have encouraged Elizabeth during Rooks Jr.'s battle with tuberculosis.[15]

Shortly after arriving at Mont Alto, Rooks mailed a postcard to his mother to provide personalized visual imagery of his surroundings and perhaps to quiet her fears for his mortality. She cherished every piece of correspondence, saving them in her trunk. The card featured the six buildings of the sanatorium. Rooks Jr. described each one:

#1 The camp in which there are about seven hundred patients. All of whom are in fairly good shape.
#2 Nurses [*sic*] home.
#3 The tents.
#4 Sun Parlor. I took a sun bath in this house this morning.
#5 Third hospital ward for men.
#6 Second hospital ward for men. My cot is in the upper end of this ward. There are fourteen patients, including two people of color.[16]

On September 30, 1911, he mailed his mother another card with an encouraging message: "Dear Mother, I am getting along fairly well. Weather is fine. Love, Rooks." The card featured an image of purple and white blooming flowers. On the top left was a statement of its source: "Made in Germany." Beside the postage mark indicating the stamp price of "one cent" was the word "DISINFECTED." Rooks Jr. wrote in ink with a fine-tipped pen in the elegant script of an educated man. The uppercase letters were rendered in calligraphy.[17]

By Christmas 1911 Rooks Jr. was still holding his own. He mailed to his mother a photograph from a brochure or magazine featuring approximately fifty men and women. It was labeled "Group of Hospital Patients." One of two African Americans, he appeared in row four. The opposite side of the sheet showed ten, mostly robust, Euro-American uniformed nurses with Santa, who was seated on the steps of the building.[18]

With Rooks Jr. struggling for his own physical survival, Elizabeth could depend on only herself and Lorenzo Dow. Like thousands of others, in the pre-antibiotic world, Rooks Jr. did not win the battle against the most dreaded infection of the early twentieth century. Like his father, he had made an impressive beginning. At twenty-nine, married with one child, he was well on the way to becoming a physician.[19] The highly recommended state sanatorium in Mont Alto, Pennsylvania, had changed the lives of many, but not Rooks Jr.'s.

All efforts at a cure failed, and he died in 1912, leaving behind a widow and a young child, Sedgwick.[20] His death left Elizabeth sorrowful, nervous, and anxious. Empathizing with her pain, whenever Lorenzo Dow or Arthur contacted her, they ended their missive with an admonition: "Don't worry" or "Be cheerful." After becoming a physician, Rooks Jr. would have been able to provide some financial assistance to relieve the drudgery of Elizabeth's daily life. The dream and the hope vanished in the pristine air of the Pennsylvania mountains.[21]

Despite the loss of Rooks Jr., Elizabeth was encouraged by the promise Lorenzo Dow showed and by his unwavering devotion to her. The two were close in spirit. While the majority of his energy during the Howard years was devoted to his studies or to waiting tables and working at other jobs to make ends meet, Lorenzo Dow regularly assisted his mother financially. The loss of his brother Rooks Jr. also caused him to be acutely aware of his responsibility in maintaining the family name by producing heirs.[22]

While Lorenzo Dow was consistently in contact with their mother, Arthur, in contrast, relocated frequently, and reached out to her only intermittently. His life was unsettled. Although he had completed his law degree in 1912,[23] he did not practice law; rather he worked in insurance, which, in part, may have accounted for some of his travel. After a decade in Washington, D.C., Arthur relocated to Detroit, Michigan.[24] Over time his restlessness and transitory lifestyle cost him several wives—Nellye, Zephra, and Effie, in that order. Arthur and his wives produced no children.[25]

Elizabeth continued to treasure cards and letters from her sons, tucking them away in her trunk. In 1924 Arthur traveled to Winnipeg, Manitoba, Canada. On June 8, he mailed her a postcard of Main Street in Winnipeg, writing, "Dear Mom, I will be back in the states tomorrow and will write you a letter. The country out here is very beautiful. I trust all are well there. Be cheerful and don't worry. Arthur."[26]

In 1929 Arthur contacted Elizabeth twice from Spokane, Washington. On the first postcard, which displayed a side view of the Monroe Street Bridge, he promised to be in touch again soon: "Dear Mother, I shall write you a letter in a few days. Hope you are well and happy. Be cheerful. Arthur."[27] On the second card, Arthur acknowledged that he should communicate with his mother with greater regularity and in more substantial detail. Although at the time he resided in St. Paul, Minnesota, he was traveling in Spokane. The card, with an expansive view of the Great Northern Railroad depot in Spokane, read, "Dear Mother, If I ever stop moving about long enough to write a letter, I will let you hear from me. Got into this town at 9:00 P.M. tonight and will leave tomorrow at 8:00 A.M. I hope to be back into St. Paul Sunday. Arthur."[28]

By 1920 Turner and his wife had become his mother's keepers. At some point during the next ten years, Elizabeth's health began to decline. No available records speak of her activities during that decade. According to her obituary, Lorenzo Dow and Arthur were her only immediate living relatives. Her obituary did not mention Rooks.

Elizabeth Freeman Turner breathed her last breath at 8:30 A.M. on Monday morning, November 23, 1931, just before Thanksgiving. She was seventy years old.[29] When the end arrived, Turner, like any other child dedicated to a parent, was far from prepared.

4

Childhood 1890–1910

> I have told you all these things, little one, because you are my son . . . and because I have nothing to hide from you. There is a certain form of behavior to observe, and certain ways of acting in order that the guiding spirit of our race may approach you.
>
> —Camera Laye, *The Dark Child*

LORENZO DOW TURNER WAS BORN on August 21, 1890, just before the harvest season.[1] He grew rapidly and learned with ease. He was charismatic.

From the earliest years of his life, he knew that he was named for one of his mother's religious heroes, Lorenzo Dow, a traveling Methodist minister. He knew that Lorenzo Dow had been fervently committed to his work, a charismatic, riveting speaker and a man who traveled far and wide to advance his mission. Until the day Turner died at 8:30 A.M. on February 10, 1972, he kept on his shelves *The Dealings of God, Man and the Devil, as Exemplified in the Life, Experience and Travels of Lorenzo Dow* (1858). He, too, embraced commitment, developed oratorical expertise, and traveled far and wide to advance his mission.[2]

By the fourth generation of the Rooks/Turner clan, many had become formally educated professionals. Others were productive working-class citizens. Turner was to become a member of the first group. In the meantime, as he developed, his parents could not know the extent to which their youngest son would exemplify the best characteristics of both the Rooks clan and their hero Lorenzo Dow—strong intellect, great energy and concentration, willingness to work without ceasing, great public speaking ability, commitment to a cause, courage, "certain ways of acting," and the fortitude to sustain and exercise the commitment throughout a lifetime. He had learned to observe those certain forms of behavior that bespoke success.

Details of Turner's childhood are sketchy. By the time his father departed from Elizabeth City in 1896, he was in elementary school, in the first or second grade. The family endured poverty. Like many neighbors, the Turners worked hard and conserved whenever and whatever they could. Often at bedtime Elizabeth would place three sweet potatoes on the coals to bake for the following day. They would serve as her sons' lunch at school—sometimes as their breakfast, too.[3]

By 1901, when Turner was eleven, segregation unlike any previously witnessed in North Carolina had been instituted. As it spread across the South, it fell particularly harshly on geographic areas that had formally practiced milder forms of repression. A major symbol of events to come was the separation of blacks and whites on the train cars after *Plessy v. Ferguson.* Alarmed by this increasingly institutionalized segregation, Rooks encouraged Elizabeth and the boys to join him in the more urban Rockville, Maryland.[4]

In Rockville, Turner's personality took shape. He did not shrink from strong commitments. Dedicated to his mother and to assisting her in making a living, Turner did not mind odd jobs. In his spare time, he played baseball. He was left-handed and developed into an expert pitcher. True to his parental teaching, he was mannerly, but at the same time charming and witty. Adults and children enjoyed being in his presence. His one surviving grade school picture shows him to be tall, slender, and serious.

Turner's early years were spent in the proverbial "little red school house," where grades one through eight commingled, teaching and learning from each other. All his days he would remember many of the lessons of his formative years, including a difficult one pertaining to the efficacy of keeping his mouth closed. While concentrating, he often allowed his mouth to hang open. One day, as the teacher spoke, Turner was jolted by a thud and felt an odd sensation. An older boy, noting his gaping mouth, had hurled an apple core into it.[5]

Performing well in elementary school and relishing the educational enterprise, Turner found no difficulty with any subject. By the time he reached high school in 1906, he was separated from his beloved mother, as the Howard University Academy at Howard University was residential. Turner was already sixteen years of age. He had spent several years out of school working to save for college and to assist his mother. Valuing long-range goals, he maintained a modest savings account at the Montgomery County National Bank in Rockville, Maryland.[6]

In high school, Turner's course of study was fifteen units covering the traditional "classical" course work of the late nineteenth century:

English	-3 Units	History	-1 Unit
Algebra	-1 Unit	Physics	-1 Unit
Geometry	-1 1/2 Units	Physiography	-1/2 Unit
Greek	-1 1/2 Units	Shop Work	-1 Unit
Latin	-3 1/2 Units	Other Subjects	-1 Unit[7]

Despite the lack of financial resources that characterized a single-parent family headed by a mother, Turner expected to attend Howard University. He worked during high school to supplement the household budget and to save funds for college, which in part explains why he was unable to enter college until the age of twenty. After his parents were permanently estranged, he became the male breadwinner for the family. Along life's way, he lost two years to the job market but gained two in maturity.

Turner's first full-time job was with the railroad as a Pullman porter. One report notes, "He 'deadheaded' Pullman cars in 37 states. Then he found a better way to make a living. In those pre–Jackie Robinson days, all[-black] baseball teams were very much in vogue. [He] used his batting prowess to advantage for eight years that saw him all the way through graduate school."[8] Turner played for the Commonwealth Giants, a baseball team comprised of the young black men who worked aboard the *Commonwealth, a* steamboat of the Fall River (Massachusetts) Steamboat Line. The team was sponsored by the steamboat company.

In the summers he traveled to New York, making his home base the residence of one of his New York relatives. Every other day, he headed down to the base of Fulton Street to embark on the S.S. *Commonwealth.* There his job was to serve as a waiter in the grand salon on the top deck until he arrived in Massachusetts: "The ship lazily bumped against its Fall River berth at 5:30 A.M. When the passengers were disembarked and the breakfast dishes cleared away, the waiters trooped down the gangway to the baseball park, destination of the day. All through the neighboring New England towns they played. At the end of each summer, Lorenzo's share of the team purse was ready to be divided between his mother and his tuition for the coming college year."[9]

When Turner applied to Howard University, given his strong high school academic background, he was accorded "Unconditioned" admittance for September 1910.[10] He embarked on an educational journey that would transform him into a second-generation college student at a time when the majority of African Americans considered themselves fortunate if they were able to see the inside of a rustic schoolhouse for four months per year for six years of their lives.

5

Howard University 1910–1914

"Alma Mater"
Reared against the eastern sky
Proudly there on hilltop high,
Far above the lake so blue
Stands old Howard firm and true.
There she stands for truth and right,
Sending forth her rays of light,
Clad in robes of majesty;
O Howard, we sing of thee.

—Words: Joseph Hunter Brooks;
music: Frederick DeWitt Malone,
both of class of 1916

WHEN TURNER BEGAN HIS ACADEMIC STUDIES, he selected English as a major. Many African American parents of his generation encouraged their children to major in English because the specialty was in consistent demand; their children likely would never become jobless. Perhaps Turner's mother and high school teachers encouraged him toward the English major. On his "Questionnaire," Turner listed his mother as the person who had influenced him the most.[1] It is also possible that, having a predisposition toward languages, he selected his major independent of parental input.

Turner came of age during an important period in U.S. history. The European ideal of Western "classical" education as a prerequisite to leadership was challenged during the Age of Enlightenment. Francis Bacon maintained that knowledge should be harnessed for utilitarian purposes. In the early decades of the republic, Thomas Paine, Benjamin Franklin, and others endorsed utilitarian education, while Thomas Jefferson, John Adams, and James Madison endorsed Western "classical" education as a prerequisite to informed participation in society. During the half-century between the end of the Civil War and the beginning of World War I, the debate intensified as the United States created a system of compulsory education. Blacks, having been excluded previously by virtue of their enslavement and of socially constructed notions of inferiority, were at last able to attend schools in limited numbers. The debate continued to be orchestrated by white male elites even while blacks, women, and Jews became "eligible" for inclusion in education institutions.[2]

The issue of whether African Americans would best be served by a technical education or one from the liberal arts and Western classical tradition was never resolved.[3] Guided by Washington's "Atlanta Compromise" oration at the Atlanta

Exposition (1895) or by Du Bois's subsequent response "Of Mr. Booker T. Washington and Others," the philosophical lines were drawn. Educated blacks were forced to follow one of two dichotomous paths. Liberal education was viewed as the opposite of industrial education or manual training, with Du Bois as the presumed spokesperson for the former and Washington the spokesperson for the latter.[4] The positions were so solidified in the press and in intellectual debates that contemporary conversations continue to utilize the dichotomy to discuss strategies for black empowerment.[5]

By the time Turner arrived at Howard University, it was already one of the leading schools in the group of black colleges that were founded immediately after the Civil War and that became known as the "Historically Black Colleges and Universities" (HBCUs). At Howard, Turner received a challenging liberal arts education from some of the finest intellects America has produced. Among those on the faculty between 1910 and 1914 were Alain Locke, one of the leading philosophers of the Harlem Renaissance and the first African American to receive a Rhodes Scholarship to England (1907); Benjamin Brawley, author and master teacher of English; Montgomery Gregory, the noted dramatist; Charles H. Houston, whom Thurgood Marshall designated the "First Mr. Civil Rights Lawyer"; Charles Wesley, historian and administrator; Kelly Miller, professor of mathematics; George Morton Lightfoot, professor of Latin; and Ernest Everett Just, biologist and author.[6]

Turner's courses for his bachelor's degree in English were, for the most part, offered in two-semester sequences.[7] They illustrate why he was immensely effective as a university professional, researcher, writer, public lecturer, and linguist. His language background was excellent, as he had completed 3 1/2 years of Latin and 1 1/2 year of Greek in high school. He added to this background six semesters of German (German I, II, and Scientific and Historical German) and two semesters of French. He was well versed as a debater, completing two semesters with an average of 90 percent the first semester and 96 percent the second. Two courses in law and one in logic contributed to the structure of his thought processes. Courses in mathematics, science, history, and philosophy added to his discipline and his perception of the world, and a concentration in English provided him with a background in both the British and Latin traditions in poetry and prose. Added to these were four semesters of composition and public speaking.[8] While none focused on the black experience, Turner gained theoretical constructs and pedagogy that would stand him in good stead for the work he would complete thirty years later.

Turner possessed a flair for organizing and writing papers. One of the assignments during his junior year for his American History class resulted in a twenty-one-page paper, "The Struggle for Democracy." Written January 27, 1913, before the opening shots of World War I, Turner's paper cited eight of the most reliable sources of the era, among them Alexis de Tocqueville's *Democracy in America* and Albert Stickney's *Organized Democracy.* His handwritten treatise was carefully outlined and developed, beginning in section 1 with an introduction, a definition of democracy, and a statement of the purpose. The second section elaborated on early struggles for democracy in North America before the American Revolution. Section 3 discussed democracy after the American Revolution, and section 4 outlined both the assets and liabilities of democracy. In section 5, the conclusion, Turner presented a quote from President Butler of Columbia University, who, in his *True and False Democracy,* declared that if democracy is to triumph, it must be carefully directed with both "intelligence and character."

Turner's paper demonstrated the careful research, thoroughness, and striving for perfection that characterized his efforts during his entire career. His political perspective had not yet been touched by experience or the fullness of time, as his discussion contained no mention of the plight of African Americans under American democracy.[9]

During his senior year one of Turner's research papers was titled "The Political Science Views of Woodrow Wilson." Submitted on April 14, 1914, and also well conceived, organized, and developed, it demonstrated that, as an undergraduate, Turner was conversant with current issues, either as a result of topics selected by his professors or by his own inclination.[10]

Turner's social life was no less rich than his academic experiences. According to the 1914 *NIKH,* the first year of the publication of the Howard University yearbook and Turner's graduation year, he was a popular student. In 1910 he was class critic. In 1912 he was assistant football manager. He was class critic again in 1913, as well as critic for the Kappa Sigma Debating Club. In 1913 he joined the all-male Howard University Debate Team, which won the championship against the team at Wilberforce University in Ohio. His classmates elected him senior-class president and a member of the advisory council; he was also manager of the baseball team. Turner's peers viewed him as a student activist, for they voted him the student "Who Has Done the Most for Howard."[11] Well known and respected on campus, Turner was a magnetic personality and a well-rounded athlete. His skills in baseball were so developed that he easily could have been a Jackie Robinson "if the time had been right." He was a generation and a half too early.[12]

Turner joined the Beta Chapter, which was the second chapter of Alpha Phi Alpha, the oldest black men's fraternity, which had been founded at Cornell University in 1906. Beta was established at Howard University in 1907. After initiation, Turner moved to the Alpha Phi Alpha fraternity house, a three-story red brick building on U Street. An official fraternity photograph shows twenty self-assured, stalwart young men dressed in black suits.[13]

The fraternity house was well maintained and furnished with a kitchen, tennis courts, and a piano in the parlor.[14] Having a piano was neither a luxury nor parlor ornamentation but rather a practical necessity. In the first half of the twentieth century, many educators became accomplished pianists. It was a requirement in most states for educators in elementary schools since classes were self-contained, with one teacher offering all subjects, including music.

As an adult, Turner stood six feet tall. He was slender, seldom weighing more than 187 pounds in his prime.[15] As a young adult, he sported a side-swept haircut, showing his wavy black hair to advantage. He was well versed in social graces and an excellent dancer, who demonstrated his skills at fraternity and sorority parties. On such occasions, he enjoyed the company of many women and men friends. Otherwise, because of his study and work schedule, there was little time for socializing. Like his father, he did not attend church or read the Bible. Having experienced the dramatically negative perception engendered by his father's strident style, Turner cultivated a more soft-spoken and tactful presence.[16]

Although Turner enjoyed being well dressed, he was careful not to spend lavishly on his wardrobe. He approved of his own good looks, though, and enjoyed posing for professional photographs, which he sent with frequency to significant others. His favorite photographer was Arthur P. Bedou, a Creole from New Orleans, Louisiana, renowned for his excellent photographs of human subjects. Bedou, the official photographer for Xavier University, maintained a lucrative business by touring other HBCUs, with Turner as one of his frequent subjects. Turner also visited Addison Scurlock (1883–1964), an excellent African American photographer, who owned a studio on U Street in Washington, D.C., which he operated with his wife and sons, Robert and George, until 1964. Scurlock was Howard's official photographer.[17] Turner purchased as many photographs as he could afford in endless poses and varieties—postcards, small oval prints, wallet-sized, 3 1/2-by-5 1/2-inch prints, 8 1/2-by-10 1/2-inch portraits, in black and white and in sepia tones.[18]

Turner's good looks turned heads. His classmates were sufficiently impressed to vote him "Most Handsome" senior. At the same time, they voted him one of four "Most Henpecked." His romantic interest was Geneva Calcier Townes, a polished, dimpled beauty. A Washingtonian born in Warren, Virginia, on August 13, 1893, Geneva was also an English major and, like Turner, possessed strong leadership skills. Her parents were both teachers: Edlow Anderson Townes, born on July 26, 1865, in Finchley, Virginia, near Danville, in Mecklenburg County; and Letitia Polina Coleman Townes, born November 25, 1867, in Albemarle County, Virginia.[19]

Turner and Geneva Townes, having both entered Howard as English majors in 1910, were inseparable. Though Geneva's first love was music, her parents, like Turner's, were of the generation that steered their offspring to degrees in core areas such as English. Geneva complied but pursued piano and voice at every opportunity.[20]

Geneva's leadership ability was evident from the beginning of her academic career. During her freshman year, she served as class secretary; as a sophomore, class treasurer; and in 1914, during her senior year, as vice president of the Classical Club and the class historian. According to her transcript, she studied Greek, Latin, and French, excelling in them all.[21]

Geneva, like Turner, completed a rigorous traditional Western education. Her classmates viewed her as assiduous, ethical, and focused; they voted her "Most Do Right" and the third "Greatest Grind," a reference to her studiousness. There is no evidence that she participated in sports, preferring instead to concentrate on voice and piano.[22]

Over the years, Turner and Geneva became two sides of one coin. Each semester they were enrolled in at least one course together. As graduation approached, their relationship progressed from friendship to their engagement. In the "Personals" pages of the yearbook, a tongue-in-cheek ode to Turner appeared. It made use of puns: "ideal," "idol," "idyll," and "idle." While the content and tone of the ode suggest that another classmate likely submitted it, it establishes that Turner and

Geneva were viewed as having a serious relationship headed for marriage. It also implied that Geneva's mother, Letitia, was less impressed with Turner than was her daughter.

> "An Ode to Lorenzo Turner"
> 'He is my ideal and I'm his idol,' said Geneva.
> 'And your love affair?' asked Grace.
> 'Is an idyll,' replied Geneva.
> 'And your fiancé?' asked Grace.
> 'He's idle according to mama,' said Geneva.[23]

The "Grace" mentioned in the poem was most likely Grace Coleman, a mutual friend and the senior class secretary. On the "Class Vote" page, Grace was selected unanimously as the "Most Brilliant."[24]

When June 3, 1914, arrived, Turner, Geneva, Grace Coleman, Eva Dykes, and more than fifty others graduated, entering the growing ranks of the black educated elite. Like Turner, Geneva earned cum laude distinction. Both indicated their plans in the 1914 yearbook: Geneva—"Will teach"; Turner—"Will do post-graduate work in English."[25]

At graduation, Turner and Geneva were two of thirty-two students to receive the bachelor of arts degree. Eighteen others received bachelor of science degrees, and six received commercial department certificates and diplomas.[26] Turner was twenty-three years old, confident, and prepared for the next step.[27] The next step was Harvard University, over four hundred miles away in Cambridge, Massachusetts.

After graduation, having not immediately located a teaching position, Geneva enrolled in Myrtilla Minor Normal School in Washington, D.C., an institution of higher education for black women, to gain further preparation for a teaching career.[28] Completing Minor as class valedictorian in spring 1916, she began teaching at Garfield Elementary School in the fall of that year.[29] Turner's further study was delayed another year while he embarked on the arduous undertaking of accumulating the funds to attend Harvard University.

6

Chicago 1914–1915

HOG Butcher for the World. . . . / City of the Big Shoulders

—Carl Sandburg, "Chicago"

LEAVING HIS MOTHER BEHIND in Montgomery County, Maryland, and Geneva in Washington, D.C., Turner traveled to Chicago with the plan of amassing sufficient funds to pursue his studies toward a master's degree. He had no fear of the unknown because Elizabeth and his life experiences had taught him resourcefulness. Turner selected Chicago for a number of reasons. It was the home of some of Turner's Overton relatives.[1] More important, since Chicago was a large city, he knew that opportunities for full-time employment abounded.

Turner had worked in the city before. During the summer of 1913, between his junior and senior years at Howard, Turner had made Chicago his summer home. Serving as a waiter in the elegant tenth-floor dining room of the former Auditorium Hotel, he had become familiar with the University of Chicago, possibly making some contacts who found him impressive and later making it feasible for him to pursue his doctorate there. The dining room was framed by broad windows that faced Lake Michigan and Grant Park. His clients were the affluent.

A half-century later, Turner recalled meeting prominent persons during his stint as a waiter. From his perspective, the most memorable was President William Howard Taft, the fattest man to have served as president of the United States, to whom Turner recalled bringing an "enormous dinner." By the time he returned to Chicago as a professor in 1946, the hotel had become the library at Roosevelt University, a place where he and his students spent many hours in research.[2]

When Turner arrived in the "city of the big shoulders" in 1914, he secured a space to reside, at 3838 Forest Avenue, and began his search for a position. Turner expected to work hard. He knew that Chicago was a rough city, and he was prepared to rise to whatever challenges faced him there. Landing a job as a porter on a long-distance passenger train on the Union Pacific line, Turner donned his uniform with pride. In the fall of 1914, on an evening trip shortly after he was hired, he was assigned to awaken an elderly couple from their sleeping-car berth and to assist them in dismounting at the appropriate stop. As the train neared a stop, Turner awakened the couple, gathered their bags, and assisted them with their coats. He exited the train, placing a step stool on the ground for them. He then assisted them in dismounting, offering his goodbye. A few moments later, as the train continued on its course, one of the experienced porters called him, "Hey, Turner, it's time to wake the old couple." Turner answered with surprise, "I let them off at the last stop." "Oh, Turner, Turner, Turner," his friend exclaimed. "That was not a station stop. That was a stop for the train to take on water!"[3]

Turner sensed his job was in danger. Predictably, when he returned to base in Chicago, his employer summoned him to the office, presenting him with a list of infractions. To his chagrin, he was dismissed immediately. The timing could not have been worse. Every month's salary was essential if he were to earn the tuition necessary to attend Harvard University.

In the subsequent days Turner "pounded the pavement" in search of employment. Often his meal for the day was "one cup of coffee and a sweet roll," as his budget would allow nothing more. Over the period of a few days, "he had walked the city of Chicago from end to end. By the close of the day, his feet were tender, his hands miserably swollen."[4] Eventually, he located a position as a clerk in the office of a Dr. R. L. Douglass at 3601 South State Street.[5] By February, Turner was optimistic that he could amass enough funds for the fall semester.

Consequently, on February 6, 1915, he applied for admission to Harvard University, in a letter to the secretary to the School of Arts and Sciences. Realizing that Harvard University admitted few persons of African ancestry, he took a modest and understated approach. "I am enclosing herewith a complete official record of my studies in college, and an application for admission to your Graduate School of Arts and Sciences, Department of English. Under separate cover I am mailing also a marked college catalogue. . . . Hoping that you will give me whatever consideration you may see fit."[6]

Turner must have waited for the news with excitement and apprehension. His wait was brief; consideration of his folder took place immediately. Of the several Howard University professors who were Harvard graduates, one or more must have encouraged Turner to consider Harvard and contacted Harvard to recommend him. The university anticipated his application, as on February 8, 1915, Mr. George W. Robinson, secretary for the Graduate School of Arts and Sciences, mailed Turner's admissions letter. "Your application for admission to the Graduate School of Arts and Sciences has been given consideration," it read. "I am happy to inform you that in view of your previous studies, you will be admitted to the School, and that you will be permitted to come up for the degree of Master of Arts upon the completion with distinction of two full years of advanced and approved work in English or English and related subjects."[7]

Turner was admitted, but with the caveat that his two years' course work be completed "with distinction." He was confident that it would. His admission was a triumph for him, his family, and African Americans as a group. He was prepared to represent them all.

7

Harvard University 1915–1917

He who enters a university walks on hallowed ground.

—James B. Conant, president of Harvard University, 1933–53

The history of blacks at Harvard mirrors, for better or for worse, the history of blacks in the United States. Harvard, too, has been indelibly scarred by slavery, exclusion, segregation, and other forms of racial oppression. At the same time, the nation's oldest university has also supported and allowed itself to be influenced by the various reform movements that have dramatically changed the nature of race relations across the nation. The story of blacks at Harvard is thus inspiring but painful, instructive but ambiguous—a paradoxical episode in the most vexing controversy of American life: "the race question."

—Randall Kennedy, "Introduction: Blacks and the Race Question at Harvard"

TURNER HAD WALKED ON "HALLOWED GROUND" at Howard University and emerged triumphant. He was the fourth man in his family to do so—first had been his father, Rooks (1877), then his brother Rooks Jr., followed by his brother Arthur (1912). In 1914 Turner was twenty-four years old and a member of the "talented tenth." Less than twenty years earlier, in 1895, William Edward Burghardt Du Bois, who made famous the phrase "the talented tenth," had become the first known African American to receive a Ph.D. from Harvard. It was a triumph for the race. Harvard would admit only an exceptional African American man—one with the potential to become a scholar and leader. Du Bois had been followed by Alain Locke in 1907, Benjamin Brawley with a master's in 1908, and Montgomery Gregory in 1910, all of whom subsequently became professors at Howard University. Carter G. Woodson, who received a doctorate in history, graduated in 1912. He was another exceptional man, serving as dean at Howard in 1919–20 while Turner was on its faculty. Now Turner had been recommended for Harvard; his turn had come to attend the most prestigious university in the country. World War I was raging, but not all men were needed for the fray to advance democracy abroad. Turner was among those anointed to continue his education to advance democracy at home.

Undoubtedly, he was aware that his being at Harvard was a symbol of slow but perceptible change. For Harvard's first 229 years, African Americans were absent from its halls, except as enslaved persons and servants. The tradition was interrupted for one session in 1850 when three African American men were admitted to the Harvard Medical School—Martin R. Delaney, Isaac H. Snowden, and Daniel Laing Jr. Almost immediately, though, they were ejected when some white students objected to their presence. Dean Oliver Wendell Holmes, the father of Justice Holmes, justified the expulsion by asserting that "the intermingling of the white and black races in their lecture rooms is distasteful to a large portion of the class and injurious to the interests of the school."[1]

By 1869 the first African Americans, George L. Ruffin and Richard Tanner Freeman, had graduated from Harvard Law School and Dental School, respectively. The trickle continued. "Probably most important," Randall Kennedy notes, ". . . is the fact that compared to the open, vicious animus with which most of white American society dealt with black Americans in the century following the Civil War, Harvard's treatment of its black students, though deficient by today's standards, constituted a welcome, and deeply appreciated contrast."[2]

Having neither family wealth nor other resources, Turner knew he had no choice but to amass funds before continuing with his graduate work. He must have recalled the stories his mother had recounted of the early days in her marriage, when Rooks and she had purchased land with plans of economic security for their sons and the establishment of a network of normal schools for African Americans. Their dreams had not been reality for Turner. He had consistently had to pursue his own. And so he would again.

In the fall of 1915, Turner moved into a room at 61 Gorham Street in Cambridge to begin his studies.[3] Occasionally, he traveled to New Bedford, Massachusetts, sixty miles south of Boston, to the home of one of his aunts, Mary Turner Reid, and her husband. He spent his weekends and breaks working as a waiter on the Fall River Line on the steamboat *Commonwealth* as it traveled up and down the Charles River delivering and retrieving tourists to and from various destinations. The trip consumed almost two hours one way. There was also service to New York City; New London, Connecticut; and Boston. On summer evenings and on weekends, he continued to play baseball for the Commonwealth Giants, a team featuring the young black men who worked for the Fall River Steamship Lines. His left arm was still in fine form. The team maintained a good winning record.

Often Turner wrote to his mother in Rockville, Maryland, sending her modest sums of money. Working part-time in hotels and restaurants to finance his education proved to be possible, even after classes began.[4] During the academic year, "there were tables to wait wherever he went. At Harvard, his table working assignment was in famed Memorial Hall, then a dining room."[5]

Harvard was not just any educational institution. Founded October 28, 1636, it was only twenty years short of its three-hundredth anniversary when Turner walked the "hallowed grounds" of Harvard Yard. By then it had graduated several American presidents (John Adams, John Quincy Adams, Rutherford B. Hayes, and Theodore Roosevelt), a few Supreme Court justices, cabinet officers, congressional leaders, literary figures, and notable men in many fields, including the sciences, arts, religion, philosophy, and medicine. Among them were Ralph Waldo Emerson, Oliver Wendell Holmes, Henry David Thoreau, Henry James, Benjamin Pierce, and William James.[6]

Turner approached his education at Harvard with the same discipline that he approached life in general. He maintained meticulous class notes in brown rectangular notebooks, approximately 5 1/2-by-8 1/2 inches, that opened at the top. Writing on both sides of the paper, he was conscious of the need to conserve. An examination of his notes leads one to assume that as he listened to a lecture, he took notes that would be of maximum assistance to him as he prepared to stand before his own classes as a professor. The name Amee Brothers Booksellers, Stationers and Engravers, in Harvard Square, was stamped on the cover of the notebooks, as may have been required of all students.[7] Turner's master's curriculum focused on English, German, and comparative literature, areas in which his undergraduate background was strong and his interest pronounced.

During Turner's Harvard years, a number of other men attended, who, like him, would subsequently become prominent, among them E. E. Cummings (1916), Eugene O'Neill (1915), and John Dos Passos (1916).[8] Given the racial climate of the time, it is unlikely that he socialized with them.

Among Turner's favorite professors were Bliss Perry, F. N. Robinson, and William A. Neilson; the latter subsequently became the president of Smith College.[9] They were among the leading professors in the American academy, and Turner completed the majority of his courses under their supervision.

Turner's Harvard University transcript indicates that he completed his course work and required examinations in four semesters, or two academic years. In each course he earned a grade of "B," some minus, some plus. History is silent on the issue of whether the grades were a reflection of his performance or a reflection of his professors' attitudes toward their black student. One is inclined to conclude the latter, based on his stellar performance in undergraduate school. There appears to have been no requirement for a master's thesis.[10]

When Turner received a copy of the *Harvard Handbook* for 1915–16, he apparently consulted it often. Pages 63 through 135 were designated "Daily Memoranda" and were to serve as a calendar/planner. For Turner they became an address book. He did not need to record his mother's and Geneva's addresses, but his one surviving brother, Arthur, is listed as the first entry. Arthur was residing in Detroit, Michigan, at 234 Melbourne Avenue. Their father, Rooks, was residing at Route #3, Gaithersburg, Maryland, in Montgomery County, not far from Washington, D.C. The third entry was the address of Dodd Mead and Company, Inc., at 4th Avenue and 30th Street in New York.[11] Turner had already begun his networking with publishing companies, a process that would result in a contract with Harcourt Brace sixteen years later when he became coauthor of *Readings from Negro Authors: For Schools and Colleges* (1931).

One of the women with whom Turner maintained contact was Jessie Hailstack, a mutual friend of his and Geneva's and later a collaborator with Geneva on a children's book. She had moved to 121 Bull Street in Charleston, South Carolina. Another was Geneva's sister Justine, who had left Washington, D.C., settling at 725 Bart Street, Portsmouth, Virginia, to pursue a teaching career.[12]

At Harvard, Turner was prepared to engage general topics related to the black experience. On May 14, 1916, he submitted a sixty-seven-page paper to Professor

C. N. Greenough, who taught English 67, or English Composition. Entitled "A Plan for the Teaching of English Composition in the M Street High School, Washington, D.C.," it consisted of a set of lesson plans for a twelfth-year English course for the most prestigious African American high school in Washington, D.C. Turner divided the weeks of the course into topics based on forms of discourse—exposition, argumentation, description, and narration. He detailed assignments for various genres, including the study of biography, poetry, short stories, literary criticism, and letter writing. As usual, he was meticulous in the development of the project in both substance and style. Although his topic involved the writing experience for African American students, the prescribed literary selections were all from the Euro-American continuum, among them traditional selections from Bret Harte, Edgar Allan Poe, Guy de Maupassant, Nathaniel Hawthorne, O. Henry, Sarah Orne Jewett, Jane Austen, William Wordsworth, and Rudyard Kipling.[13] After graduating from Harvard and with the advent of the Harlem Renaissance, Turner would embrace cultural nationalism, developing innovative approaches to incorporating the black experience in both his teaching and research.[14]

Outside of class, Turner did not lead a monochromatic life. The importance of enjoying life and engaging in activities uplifting for African Americans was part of an indelible legacy to Turner from his father. Consequently, wherever he found himself, civic activities found him. Immediately after his arrival at Harvard, Turner embarked on a continuation of the activities that characterized his years at Howard. Coming together with six other men of Alpha Phi Alpha, all of whom had joined chapters as undergraduates, Turner became a charter member of Sigma, the Boston Metropolitan Chapter. Sigma was the seventeenth chapter in the United States, founded on November 28, 1915. The men were all recent graduates of other universities and pioneers in their own right—brilliant men, among the first African Americans to pursue advanced degrees at various universities in the Boston area: Boston College, Tufts, the Massachusetts Institute of Technology, Suffolk Law School, Northeastern University, and Harvard University. Four of the seven, Turner, Earl Harrison Crampton, James Daniel McClampton, and Alford Hilton Tavernier, were graduates of Howard and members of the Beta Chapter of Alpha Phi Alpha. The remaining three were Matthew Walker Clair, a graduate of Syracuse University and the Iota Chapter, founded in 1910; Dr. Franklin Augustus Myers, a graduate of Lincoln University in Pennsylvania and the Nu Chapter, founded in 1912; and Aiken Augustus Pope, a graduate of Yale University and the Zeta Chapter, founded in 1909.[15]

Founded on December 4, 1906, at Cornell University, Alpha Phi Alpha was the first intercollegiate Greek letter fraternity in the United States established for and by men of African descent. Black students in large American universities at the time were outnumbered, marginalized, and barred from "the many opportunities for mutual helpfulness which come to groups of students through personal acquaintance and close association."[16] Fraternities and sororities provided networking opportunities during the college years and in the job market afterward.

Recognizing the necessity of networking to achieve both personal success and upward mobility for the black population, the fraternity has participated in the struggle for civil rights and human dignity for a century. Among the men who have followed Turner and his cofounders into Alpha Phi Alpha were W. E. B. Du Bois, Paul Robeson, Adam Clayton Powell, Thurgood Marshall, Andrew Young, William Gray, and Maynard Jackson. Dr. Martin Luther King Jr. was also a member of Sigma Chapter, inducted while he attended Boston University in pursuit of his doctorate in philosophy in the early 1950s. Among Alpha Phi Alpha's enterprises have been investments in life insurance companies, one of them Atlanta Life, operated by Sigma alumnus Norris Herndon of the Harvard class of 1921.[17] All of Turner's life, many of his associates, like him, were the innovators, leaders, and crusaders.

As his courses for the master's degree were concluding, Turner began to seek a full-time position. Howard University awaited his return. Entering Howard had been a dream come true for Turner, just as it had been for his father. Now he was returning. This time, though, he would enter the university's gates as a professor. At a time when almost no man or woman of African ancestry could expect a faculty appointment at a Euro-American university, there was an enterprising and creative cluster of HBCUs, such as Howard, that provided teaching and administrative opportunities for educated African Americans. Among the others were Fisk University, Morehouse College, Atlanta University, and Hampton Institute.[18] Turner was fortunate to have maintained connections at one of them. He returned to Howard in fall 1917.[19]

Turner's graduation from Harvard was not only an educational milestone; it also promised an eventual conclusion to Elizabeth's uneasy years of self-support, although her protracted wait would encompass another three years. During this time, she shared the residence of Richard and Victorine Dove Williams of Rockville.[20]

In 1917 there were 2,132 African Americans in college of a total African American population of 11,891,000.[21] Turner had achieved a master's degree less than sixty years after Emancipation, at a point when the majority of African American men continued to be trapped either in peonage in the South or in menial labor in the cities, most having limited or no literacy skills and no disposable income to change their plights. He was twenty-seven years old.[22]

8

Professor Lorenzo Dow Turner 1917–1926

Students who are poor spellers, who write or speak ungrammatically, or who habitually use incorrect or slovenly English, will be reported to the dean. When a student has thus been reported three times for defective English, his name is given to the Department of English, which shall require of him such special work as it may deem necessary; and the successful performance of this work will be prerequisite to graduation.

—*A Plan for the Study of Freshman English,* Howard University

THE END OF WORLD WAR I with the optimism and prosperity it spread in American society brought little assurance to black communities, which continued to suffer disproportionately from poverty and discrimination. On the other hand, the HBCUs were centers of talent, the promise that a new generation of African Americans could remake the social position of the group through hard work and high achievement. According to Alain Locke, "the younger generation is vibrant with a new psychology. . . . The new spirit is awake to the masses, and under the very eyes of the professional observers is transforming what has been a perennial problem into the progressive phases of contemporary Negro life."[1] This new spirit with its transformational potential defined the Harlem Renaissance and "the New Negro."

The optimism and energy resulting from it were justified. In post–World War I America, more African Americans were being hired on the faculties of the HBCUs. The number of African American students entering college increased sixfold between 1917 and 1927, with their cohort being the first generation to study medicine, law, and business in any numbers. The opportunities to study the plastic arts, performing arts, and literature also expanded at Howard, Hampton, Fisk, Atlanta, and other HBCUs.[2]

During Turner's tenure at Howard, from 1917 to 1928, he served for the majority of the years as professor and head of the Department of English (1920–28). Although he began as instructor (1917–20), he rose rapidly because of opportunity, ability, commitment, and willingness to work hard.[3] Requests for his expertise came from both inside and outside the university. In March 1923, Turner agreed to serve as a judge for the T. G. Nutter Short Story Contest, sponsored by the West Virginia Collegiate Institute, a college at which Woodson had served as an administrator.[4] At Howard, Turner served as the keynote speaker for the Fourth Annual Honors Day for the Kappa Mu Honor Society on December 15, 1926.[5]

During his fifth year, in 1922, he constructed *A Plan for the Study of Freshman English,* providing a longer revision in 1923. The epigraph above appeared first in the Howard student manual and then in *A Plan for the Study of Freshman English.* It foreshadows the quest for perfection for which Turner came to be known in his research.

A Plan not only outlined the policies and processes utilized by the Department of English but also included symbols that the professors used in correcting papers. It provided six pages of bibliography. The bibliography was designed both to list required reading and to highlight a variety of dictionaries, anthologies, atlases, and encyclopedias that students were expected to read and/or consult.

A Plan was one symbol of the importance of composition studies at Howard and the other HBCUs. If African Americans were to succeed in competition with their Euro-American counterparts, their speech and writing needed to incorporate the best of the rhetorical tradition rooted in continental African oratory and continued in slave narratives and speeches, sermons in the black churches, and rhetoric in the men's and women's activist organizations. The line of thought and rhetorical strategies of the early intellectual activists—such as Frederick Douglass, the orator and newspaper editor; David Walker, the writer; and Ida B. Wells Barnett, the newspaper editor—emphasized a rhetoric of social justice and self-empowerment that translated well into composition exercises in Turner's time and that has continued to be relevant today.[6]

As an elite institution, Howard attracted to its faculty some of the best minds in American higher education. Turner was one of them. By 1917, when Turner returned, the Howard catalog had already voiced the need for "a concerted effort for teachers in all branches to cultivate in the students the habit of using good English in their recitations and various exercises, whether oral or written."[7]

Consistent with that goal, Turner prepared challenging examinations requiring analysis, synthesis, and significant writing. Typical of them was a March 19, 1926, examination for their English 1C class. It comprised four essays to be completed in two hours:

I. After making a carefully planned sentence outline for an Expository theme with the following title: 'Some Benefits to Be Derived from a Course in English Composition,' develop your Outline, observing all the principles of composition that you have studied (Forty minutes).

II. Write a business letter to a person, firm, or institution, making application for some position which you feel qualified to fill. State your qualifications and give the names of persons who can speak concerning them (Twenty minutes).

III. Explain and give examples of, whenever possible, the following words or groups of words: (1) the uses of 'shall' and 'will' in statements involving simple futurity, in direct questions, and in indirect discourse; (2) dangling participles and dangling gerunds; (3) good use; (4) coherence and emphasis in the whole composition; (5) impropriety; (6) weak and strong verbs; (7) restrictive relative clauses; (8) non-committed conditions in past time and conditions contrary to fact in present time; (9) five rules for the use of the comma; (10) two for the semicolon and two for the colon (Forty minutes).

IV. After describing, as a whole, 'What Can Literature Do for Me,' discuss somewhat in detail the chapter that impressed you the most. Illustrate whenever possible (Twenty minutes).

(Devote ten to fifteen minutes to a careful reading of your paper in order to correct all possible errors).[8]

The contemporary thrust toward "writing across the curriculum" is pedagogically comparable to the approach being practiced at Howard eighty years ago by Turner in the Department of English, Locke in the Department of Philosophy, Kelly Miller in the Department of Sociology, and others in various social sciences departments. Simultaneously, they encouraged their students to examine the black experience with a critical eye.

> [At] Howard University, from the late teens through the beginning of the Depression, faculty, and student writing across the curriculum entered into a unique paradox where prevailing ideas and the social forces that reinforce them simultaneously had to be reproduced and contested. Specifically, writing in philosophy, English and other humanities disciplines, while it sought to reproduce certain prevailing standards, also lent new perspectives and definitions to culture by engaging in a process of questioning how the disciplines defined themselves and how through disciplinary discourse the dominant society defined African Americans.
>
> The writing assignments given by faculty at Howard University in the 1920s . . . were at once conservative, subversive and creative. Thus, teachers desired of their students writing that in form and content replicated what they presumed was being produced by students at white institutions. However, a discourse that was intrinsically hostile or blind to black experience also had to be subverted or rewritten by African American student writers. . . . At the same time, this writing created a new discourse of nation and culture, one that included both the individual and group experience and knowledge of African Americans.[9]

While the Howard catalogs and Turner's *A Plan* emphasized the development of standardized literacy skills, many courses in the curriculum transformed the canon by infusing materials on the black experience. In 1919, on the eve of the Harlem Renaissance, Carter G. Woodson taught the first black history course offered at Howard, History 33, The Negro in American History. Leo Hansberry, professor of history and uncle of playwright Lorraine Hansberry, infused African history into courses and, in 1925, organized an impressive symposium featuring student presentations on African history.[10]

By 1920 Gregory and Locke had developed the Department of Dramatic Arts and Public Speaking, along with its performance arm, the Howard Players. The nexus of the department was the course work in playwriting and theatrical production, with a major goal being "to develop the dramatic literature for the Negro theater."[11] In 1921 the new department became part of Turner's Department of English. It was one of the very first drama programs available for credit in any university in America. By 1923 the Howard Players not only were staging dramas by notable playwrights but were also staging student plays emanating from Gregory's drama courses. Furthermore, the program encouraged the growth of both male and female students. Among the writers who cited Gregory's courses as a major influence in their artistic development were Mae Miller (the daughter of Kelly Miller), Zora Neale Hurston, Eulalie Spence, Shirley Graham (Du Bois), and Georgia Douglas Johnson. Some of the works of the aforementioned writers were also included in Gregory and Locke's *Plays of Negro Life.* It is clear that during the Turner years, Howard was not only central to the development of a distinctive African American drama and theatrical style but was also pivotal in supporting the inclusion of women as central to the tradition.[12]

A number of student organizations focusing on the literary arts thrived. In 1916, the year preceding Turner's return to Howard, Locke and Gregory founded the Stylus Club to provide an extracurricular outlet for creative writers. The club limited its membership to twenty, each being selected through a writing competition. In 1919 Metz Lochard created Le Cercle Français to encourage the speaking and reading of French. Born in Haiti, Lochard was himself a native speaker and an ideal sponsor for the project.[13]

Incrementally, Turner was developing as a cultural nationalist. Woodson, Turner's friend and mentor, was already a fully developed nationalist. He founded Negro History Week in 1926 (Black History Month since 1976), edited the *Negro History Bulletin* and the *Journal of Negro History,* and founded the Associated Publishers company and the Association for the Study of Negro Life and History (ASNLH). During Turner's third year on the Howard faculty, he joined Woodson and Miller in teaching continuing education courses for public school teachers in Washington, D.C. The courses met at Minor Normal School. J. Stanley Durkee, president of Howard, opposed the offering of the courses, in part because Woodson had not first consulted him. Turner taught English, French, and German. Woodson and Miller taught sociology, history, economics, and mathematics.[14] Although Durkee threatened to cancel the courses, Turner's involvement did not appear to harm their relationship, as is evident from Durkee's letter on Turner's behalf nine years later.[15]

Turner's involvement demonstrates that he had already begun to view himself as having a larger social responsibility than was embodied in his academic position. He had not yet launched his writing career, but by 1928 he and his Fisk University colleague, Eva Dykes, had already begun to collaborate with Otelia Cromwell, a teacher at the M Street High School, to prepare an anthology of black literature all three could use in their courses.

The Howard years, with the city of Washington, D.C., as a cultural backdrop, provided the context that shaped Turner's gestalt for life. Woodson was a major guiding influence for many, including John Wesley, Langston Hughes, A. A. Taylor, Hurston, Locke, and Turner. Turner networked with Woodson, continuing his involvement with the Association for the Study of Negro Life and History and its the new leader, William Brewer, after Woodson's death in 1950. Over the years Turner variously served on the editorial board of the *Journal of Negro History,* served as book review editor, often presented at the conferences of the association, and published several articles and a number of book reviews in the *Journal of Negro*

History. While the association subsidized only one of his books, it played a major role in shaping his vision. Woodson's influence on Turner is inestimable.[16]

Woodson, whose dedication to the rescue, reconstruction, and preservation of black history was relentless and lifelong, contributed more than any other historian to the process of shifting the focus of black social history from interpretations of blacks as victims to paradigms that viewed them as major actors on the stage of history.[17] Particularly during the 1920s, before the Great Depression, Woodson hired a number of young scholars to conduct research, process government documents, and write books and articles. His vehicles were the funds from foundations, the *Journal of Negro History,* and the Associated Publishers. Hence, when Turner proposed to collect data in Gullah territory, or to collect African-derived creole data in the United States and the Caribbean, or to collect African music, folklore, and proverbs, he knew he was on solid ground because "the father of black history" was advocating such projects. Woodson enlisted scholars, both African American and Euro-American, to advance primary research in as many of them as possible. Of those Woodson nurtured and encouraged to study Gullah culture, Turner stood alone in his preparation to analyze Gullah linguistically.

Woodson himself also published continuously, serving as a model scholar. When he received a grant from the Social Science Research Council in 1927, he subsidized a number of his colleagues, among them Guy B. Johnson, Howard Odum, Thomas Woofter, Franz Boas, E. Franklin Frazier, Herskovits, and Locke, to collect research and prepare publications. Johnson, Odum, and Woofter undertook a number of projects on St. Helena Island, South Carolina, on the culture, employment, and religion of the black population.[18] In 1932 St. Helena was to become one of Turner's home bases when he collected linguistic data.

Based on a perusal of Turner's grade books, policies and examinations, and comments from former students, he was organized, firm, exacting—but not unkind—dedicated, hardworking, and effective. Dorothy Porter, who became a respected librarian and director of the Moorland-Spingarn Research Center, wrote to Turner, at the point of his retirement, that "as a former student, I will always remember your thoroughness in imparting knowledge to us."[19]

According to *ENOPRON,* the Howard University yearbook for 1920–21, there were forty-nine faculty members, including President J. Stanley Durkee and Registrar Fred D. Wilkerson. Only three of them, Turner, Ernest M. Pollard, and Leonard Z. Johnson, were in English, ensuring that the English department's workload was quite heavy. Another six taught languages: Elizabeth C. Cook (Spanish); Edward P. Davis (German and Greek); George M. Lightfoot (Latin); Metz T. P. Lochard (French); James H. N. Waring (German); and Edward C. Williams (Italian). Some of these six also may have taught some English courses.

Turner's eleven years were filled with challenges and opportunities. In the nation, it was both an exhilarating time and a frightening time. Two years after Turner returned to Washington, D.C., from Harvard, interracial strife flooded the streets. There was no road map through the turbulence. James Weldon Johnson, distinguished teacher, writer, and social analyst, referred to the summer of 1919 as the "Red Summer" because blood flowed freely in the streets. Twenty-five riots across the United States alarmed the nation, endangering and destroying both human lives and property. One of the worst took place in Washington, D.C. It lasted for three days and easily could have lasted longer if African Americans had not fought back.

Having served their country well in World War I, black citizens had developed a new mood and a new attitude. Since they had fought and died to make the world "safe for democracy" in Europe, they were determined to make it safe for themselves and their families and to gain a modicum of democracy at home.[20] At the time of the Washington, D.C., riots, Turner was in Chicago pursuing summer courses. In that setting, he would experience the tensions of the riots firsthand.

On the heels of the Red Summer, the Harlem Renaissance arrived in 1920. The atmosphere created in the country by this renaissance, and the perspectives of some of his colleagues and friends intersecting with other philosophies, such as cultural relativism fostered by Franz Boas and Marcus Garvey's nationalism, would come to influence the development of Turner's thinking about the African past, African contributions to America, and world civilization for the remainder of his life. The Harlem Renaissance ushered in a period of cultural nationalism.

Although the renaissance was centered in Harlem, it was more broadly a philosophy and an attitude. Its influence was national and, indeed, international. Langston Hughes sojourned from Missouri to New York to immerse himself in it. Dorothy West arrived from Boston to attend Columbia University. Arna Bontemps abandoned California for Harlem. Marcus Garvey migrated from Jamaica to participate.

For the socially conscious intellects of Turner's generation, a half-century removed from enslavement, the opportunity to exert a positive effect on the status of the entire group was an imperative to do so.

> [F]or Afro-Americans in the 1920s individual achievement connoted more than personal comfort and ease. The future of the race seemed to depend on men and women making it in America. Doctors, lawyers, judges, teachers, poets, writers, and actors were essential, in their achievement, because they showed that it could be done, and they leveled barriers for others. . . . Indeed, if anyone doubted that the black man's time had come, he needed only look at the awakening of Mother Africa as evidenced in the recent European discoveries and appreciation of African culture and civilization.[21]

Segments of the Euro-American population began to work more closely with the African American population and also began to show increased interest in African American subject matter. Euro-Americans participated in the Niagara Conference, the founding of the National Association for the Advancement of Colored People and the Urban League. Euro-American authors attempted fresh interpretations of African American life through drama. In folklore and anthropology, others studied African American culture, collecting materials and writing influential analyses.[22]

It is significant that a number of African Americans who were active in the Harlem Renaissance in the 1920s—among them, Ralph Bunche, Aaron Douglas, and Locke—taught at Howard University while Turner was on the faculty. Du Bois was editing the *Crisis* from New York; when Woodson left Howard, he established the office of the ASNLH in Washington, D.C. Before Turner could immerse himself in cultural nationalism, he knew he needed further education. Therefore, he began long-range plans to attend the University of Chicago.

9

The University of Chicago 1919–1926

Crescat Scientia: Vita Excolatur (Let knowledge grow from more to more, and so be human life enriched)

–Motto of the University of Chicago

TURNER'S GENERATION WAS THE FIRST COHORT of African American scholars for whom pursuing a doctorate was a possibility. Being a high achiever and surrounded by friends for whom mediocrity was not a consideration, Turner began to formulate plans to pursue a doctorate in English shortly after he joined the faculty of Howard in fall 1917. Given his family background and his own personal ambition, he knew a terminal degree was his next step. The opportunity to study at the University of Chicago, where his friend and mentor, Woodson, had matriculated a generation earlier, presented itself, and Woodson likely influenced and encouraged Turner to pursue his studies there. Woodson had cultivated a network while he pursued a master's degree in history, which he completed in 1908. Later one of the Euro-American members of the executive council of Woodson's Association for the Study of Negro Life and History was William E. Dodd, a faculty member in the Department of History at the University of Chicago.[1] He became another of Turner's mentors.[2] Dodd, like Turner, was a North Carolinian.

The University of Chicago was born in 1890, the same year as Turner. Founded by the America Baptist Education Society, funded by millions of dollars in donations over a few years from John D. Rockefeller, it opened its doors in Hyde Park on land donated by the department store owner Marshall Fields. Represented by the symbol of the phoenix, it rose on the ashes in the memories of those who survived the great Chicago fire of 1871.[3]

"Intellectually," Anthony Grafton notes, ". . . the university set itself apart from the beginning." Its first president was Ohio-born William Rainey Harper, who "set out to build a great center of research on the German model."[4] Unfortunately, Harper, having thrown himself into fund-raising, recruiting professors, "teaching intensively, [and] taking courses in other fields," literally "worked himself to death," passing away in January 1906, just before Turner entered Howard Academy.[5]

By 1919, when Turner arrived, the university was already a vital intellectual center with a broader societal outlook than many of its counterparts. Only a handful of Euro-American universities welcomed students of African ancestry. Chicago was one of them. Even though its founding organization was Baptist, it manifested an eclectic range of characteristics: it was nondenominational, admitted a few women, and held classes spring, summer, fall, and winter, including on Saturdays, providing for graduations several times per year.[6]

In 1919, because of segregation, most persons of African ancestry who attended college were admitted to the HBCUs in the South. Turner and others entering doctoral programs were notable exceptions. Each year a limited number of African Americans were selected to experience the opportunities available at the most prestigious Euro-American universities. They, like many of their peers in the HBCUs, were extraordinary humans—brilliant, articulate, hardworking, innovative, and undaunted by adversity.[7]

By the time Turner enrolled at Chicago, it was, like him, twenty-nine years old and on the path toward prominence.[8] The university expected to shape leaders in every field of endeavor. During Turner's years, several other students who became luminaries in their fields also attended. Among them were Henry Steele Commager (Ph.B. 1925; Ph.D. 1928), the historian; and Eliot Ness (1925), the high-profile police department director and inspiration for *The Untouchables*. Within years after Turner's graduation, Studs Turkel (Ph.B. 1932; J.D. 1934), the social commentator, radio host, and Pulitzer Prize–winning writer of *The Good War;* and Benjamin O. Davis (1933), the first African American general in the U.S. Air Force, also claimed Chicago as their alma mater.

Like Harvard, the University of Chicago accorded African American students differential treatment. Barred from living on campus during his periods of study, Turner resided in several households over the years. In 1919 he resided at 6432 Champlain Avenue with Essie Crews and Mellie Crews, in a supportive African American household. Turner and the Crews became friends for life.[9] Since Turner spent only his summers there, he maintained no permanent Chicago address. Rather, he lived where there was availability. During the summer of 1922, he located housing at 424 East 46th Street, Apartment #1. During the 1924–25 academic year, he lived at 5320 Maryland Avenue.[10]

Although Turner faced segregated conditions and other inconvenient social dilemmas, the structure of the curriculum met his academic needs as it allowed him to maintain full-time employment at Howard during the academic year and engage in full-time study in Chicago during the summers. Consequently, after classes concluded at Howard in late May 1919, Turner headed for Chicago. It was an eventful summer.

Hundreds of miles from Washington, D.C., Turner was threatened by the Chicago riot of the Red Summer. Enrolled in three courses, he spent many after-class hours as a waiter at the Windermere Hotel West on East 56th Street near the University of Chicago. Accounts of the riot indicate that one sweltering day in July 1919, mobs of whites roamed the black neighborhoods, terrorizing the population. Some blacks retaliated. An unknown ally rushed through the Windermere, pausing to advise Turner and the other African American workers to flee to safety. They were fortunate to escape from the premises undetected.[11]

Many others in the city were not as fortunate. By the end of the riot, the black community had sustained substantial loss of life, with twenty-three dead. Fifteen whites had died as well. The Chicago Commission on Race Relations, established to investigate the violence, included several persons Turner came to know well, either in Chicago or in Nashville after he joined the faculty of Fisk University in

Tennessee. Among the twelve commissioners were Charles Johnson, a 1917 Ph.D. graduate from the University of Chicago, an early black sociologist, and the first African American president of Fisk; Robert Park, the Euro-American sociologist, from the University of Chicago; and Julius Rosenwald, the owner of Sears-Roebuck and the philanthropist responsible for the Rosenwald Fund that would later bankroll some of Turner's research.[12]

Each available summer, Turner returned to Chicago seeking education and employment. Banquets were frequent occurrences. He worked not only at the Windermere West but also at the Tip Top Inn in the Pullman Building and in the Auditorium Building.[13] He was able to complete at least three courses during June–August of 1919, 1920, and 1922. The summers of 1921 and 1923 were the most likely periods when he remained in Washington, D.C.

Even though Turner worked as many hours as he was allocated at the Windermere Hotel and elsewhere, his finances were limited as a result of the salaries assigned to hotel employees. It was, therefore, a welcome vote of confidence and a boost to his budget that he was awarded the Smiley Scholarship for his full-time academic year of 1924–25.[14]

The scholarship was a symbol of the value African Americans have historically placed on education as it resulted from an endowment established by Charles H. Smiley. A working-class African American entrepreneur who amassed a small fortune operating a catering business on Chicago's South Side, Smiley willed more than one-fourth of his fortune to the University of Chicago. At the time of his death in 1911, his estate was valued at $11,000, of which $3,000 was set aside as an endowment for the Charles H. Smiley Scholarship. Initially, the endowment yielded approximately $150 a year. Smiley had stipulated that the funds be awarded to "poor but promising students, preferably of the colored race."[15] Turner was an ideal recipient on both counts.

Between 1919 and 1922, he completed the following courses:

Summer 1919
Shakespeare
American Literature in XIX Century
American Literature Since 1800

Summer 1920
Literature of Italy and England
English Literature of XVIII Century
Development of the English Novel

Summer 1922
Elementary Italian (Visitor)
English Literature 1832–1882
English Literary History
Early American Literature[16]

Just as Turner's academic career was of paramount importance to him, his desire to establish his own family also became a major imperative. By the summer of 1919, he and Geneva prepared to become husband and wife. Both were employed full time, Turner having completed two years as an instructor at Howard and Geneva Townes having completed three years as a teacher at the Garfield Elementary School.

The Townes family had known Turner for a number of years while he dated Geneva. For them to marry was a natural progression. It is likely that Turner's mother, Elizabeth, felt the same. On September 16, 1919, he mailed a hastily written letter to her in Rockville, Maryland. His return address was Geneva's family home at 1612 Fifteenth Street North West in Washington, D.C., which may have been his regular residence when he was in Washington, D.C. The twenty-seven rooms on three floors and a basement provided options for the Townes to gain rental income.

Turner informed his mother of his impending marriage, assuring her that he and Geneva would soon invite her to reside with them. Composing the letter in a style comprehensible to someone with rudimentary literacy skills, and not being inclined to show outward emotions, he stated matter-of-factly, "Dear Mother, We are going to be married tonight and are going right to New York. We shall remain there three or four days. I will be there Saturday. I can now arrange for you to come here sooner. I will let you know all our plans when I see you. I will also write you from New York. . . . Geneva says she will take care of me and be good to me. She sends her best love. . . . We are having a private marriage. We wish you could be here to see us married. . . . We will write you in New York. Your devoted son, Lorenzo."[17]

Turner's assurance to Elizabeth of Geneva's commitment to him contained no parallel statement of either love or commitment to Geneva. It is likely that Turner, being a man of his times, did not view such an expression as essential. After all, he was headed for the altar. He and Geneva married on September 16, 1919.[18] Rev. Isaac N. Rose, who resided on the same block as the Townes at 1616 Fifteenth Street North West, performed the ceremony.[19]

The Turners were a well-matched couple, both educated, born of educated parents, cosmopolitan, with interests in literature, education, and the arts. Turner was a commanding physical presence; Geneva was equally appealing. Side by side, he stood half a head taller than she when she wore heels. She was approximately five-feet-four; he was six feet tall. They were a perfect James Van Der Zee photograph.[20]

Having known each other for almost a decade, they must have been elated that the time had arrived when they could complete their plan to spend their lives together. Their excitement was matched by the promise of the time. America had been victorious in World War I, elevating its status from former rebellious colony to international world power. A network of HBCUs was expanding, creating unfolding opportunities for black intellectuals. Black cultural organizations in large cities were thriving. Teacher salaries were quite modest, but the Turners earned two of them. Furthermore, Geneva's parents invited them to share expenses; they settled as a couple into the Townes's family home. The Washington, D.C., Census of 1920 listed Edlow Anderson Townes as family head, Letitia Townes as his wife,

Turner as Edlow Townes's son-in-law, and Geneva Townes Turner as Edlow Townes's daughter.[21]

In the early 1920s, shortly after the Turners' marriage, the couple decided to purchase their own house at 1621 S Street. They then invited Elizabeth to reside with them. For the first time, Turner was able to provide a buffer against his mother's financial insecurity, ending her years of grueling household labor. She and Geneva were compatible, and the Turner household became Elizabeth's home for the remainder of her life. Turner and Geneva had it all—all except children.

When summer arrived in 1920, Turner returned to Chicago to complete three additional courses. That summer is most likely the occasion when Geneva audited courses with him. Elizabeth had not yet joined their household, and Geneva's sister Justine was living and teaching in Virginia, having married a physician, Dr. Frank Maloney from Maryland. Their parents were still fairly vigorous and independent.[22]

After several summers operating in the same part-time cycle, Turner became determined to complete his course work more expeditiously. He may also have been expected to complete a residential requirement. During the 1924–25 academic year, he received a full-time leave from Howard to complete his final courses. Three of the nine courses in which he enrolled were audits for his intellectual enrichment:

Autumn Quarter 1924
English Literature 1600–1744 (Visitor)
American Drama
The Renaissance and Reformation in England

Winter Quarter 1925
English Literature 1744–1790 (Visitor)
Old English Poetry
American Colonial Literature

Spring Quarter 1925
Old English—Beowulf
The Structure and Growth of Language
The Transcendentalists (Visitor)[23]

The course on the structure and growth of language may have sparked the interest in linguistics that Turner manifested six years later.

Between 1919 and 1925, Geneva immersed herself in her teaching, transferring to the Fairbrother Grade School; supported Turner's career; and organized the family social life. She sponsored writing contests for the children at her school and sponsored the literary club. She wrote the school song. She was an active member of the Nineteenth Street Baptist Church, where she and her family had been in attendance since her childhood. She spent time with her close-knit family, especially Justine.

Simultaneously, Geneva continued to pursue training in music, enrolling in private piano and harmony lessons with Mrs. Estelle Pinkney Webster and in courses at the Howard University Conservatory of Music with Roy W. Tibbs. Had she been able to afford to do so, she would have studied music full time. Consistently seeking challenges and self-improvement, she studied French under the tutelage of William Hunt, the retired consul to France. Except for the one summer when she audited courses with Turner, she remained in Washington, D.C., to manage the family affairs.[24]

By the end of spring 1925, Turner had completed his courses, the majority with Percy H. Boynton, John M. Manly, William E. Dodd, T. P. Cross, and James Napier Wilt. He had sat for the required French and German examinations, successfully passing both by November 13, 1924. They did not serve as an obstacle for him, given the strength of his college-level language background. Only one hurdle remained—the writing of his dissertation. In the winter quarter of 1924, his course on American colonial literature may have contained some content that spurred his interest in his dissertation topic.

During the following academic year, 1925–26, back on staff at Howard, Turner prepared his dissertation. His topic, an examination of antislavery sentiment in American writing, was ahead of its time for an English department in an American university as most doctoral candidates focused on the traditional topics related to the work of authors such as Chaucer, Milton, and Shakespeare. It was consistent, however, with the work of Woodson and his allies at the ASNLH. It was also symbolic of a slowly gathering trend focused on explorations of African American life encouraged by the post–World War I atmosphere and the Harlem Renaissance.[25]

Turner's working relationship with his dissertation adviser, Percy H. Boynton, was positive. Boynton was "entranced" with the topic, encouraging Turner to select it for his dissertation project. As he collected data, seeking rare documents, he became intrigued with data collection techniques, realizing years later that the research process had armed him with methodologies that prepared him for the research he would undertake during the remainder of his career.[26] When the dissertation was complete, Turner expressed his appreciation to Boynton for his "friendly and scholarly criticism."[27]

Faculty members in the Department of English held Turner in high regard. The chair, John Manly, in response to an inquiry from the Harmon Foundation prompted by Turner's 1927 grant application, responded: "Mr. Turner was a student here for several years . . . and gained the highest esteem from all who came in contact with him, for his high character as a man, for his excellent bearing as a gentleman, and for his accuracy and fullness of information as a scholar. His dissertation was a notable piece of writing."[28]

Three years after Turner's graduation, C. R. Baskering, the acting chair of the English department, recommended Turner in superlatives for a teaching position: "In my opinion, Dr. Turner has unusual originality and ability as a thinker. . . . During his graduate work . . . he ranked among the very best of our graduate students. In addition, he has an agreeable personality. He is a man of quiet dignity and tact, and won the respect of all his teachers."[29]

During Turner's intermittent absences from Washington, D.C., the welfare of his parents was among his preoccupations. After his retirement, Rooks had moved near the younger Turners, to 112 L Street, North West, Washington, D.C. By 1922 he was experiencing the most debilitating effects of diabetes, a condition that eventually forced the amputation of much of one of his legs. In the aftermath of this surgery, Turner assisted in acquiring a prosthesis for his father. On September 17, 1924, Turner and Geneva contracted with the Universal Artificial Limb and Supply Company, Inc., of 1619 F Street, North West, to build a limb. The cost was $125. Rooks liquidated a Metropolitan Life Insurance Policy to assist with the payment.[30]

Turner was not a man who expected life to be a mosaic of semiprecious stones, but often it must have seemed to him to be paved unexpectedly and ironically with shards of glass. Back in Chicago in the summer of 1926, a few days before his dissertation defense, just as his dissertation was being typed, Turner learned that his father had died. It was a serious blow and an enormous distraction during a period when focus and concentration were crucial. Furthermore, it was a paradoxical end to the life of a man who by ambition and training had been marked at midlife for greatness.

After Rooks's retirement, he had gained the blocks of time necessary to pursue the writing of his own autobiography, a significant page in the intellectual history of free black North Carolinians. Having not achieved the acclaim of a Booker T. Washington, an Ida B. Wells Barnett, a Mary McLeod Bethune, or even of his fellow North Carolinian and school founder Charlotte Hawkins Brown, he had, nonetheless, seized opportunity to serve as a factor in the education and political empowerment of early generations of postbellum African Americans in North Carolina and later in Maryland. It was a story worth sharing.

In his later years, tragedies compounded. As if losing a limb were not horrific enough, he also lost his life's work. His residence burned, resulting in the destruction of his unfinished autobiography. The state of his affairs caused him to become desperately despondent. All his life he had believed Frederick Douglass's assertion that "power concedes nothing without a demand,"[31] so he had struggled toward enlightenment and empowerment while demanding respect. His guiding light had been education. Despite his efforts, by midsummer 1926, Rooks was no longer convinced that power had conceded anything. It must have seemed to him that his life had been only a pebble in a pond. In the dawning hours of Thursday, July 22, during a walk along Rock Creek at 27th Street, he drowned.

The *Washington Post* printed a cover story on Friday, July 23, 1926, focused on the heat wave of that week, dedicating one paragraph to the drowning and in a double irony misspelling Rooks's name and simultaneously failing to acknowledge him as an educated professional and retired teacher. The headlines read: "85, No Higher, Forecast for Today; Heat Kills 2; 1 Drowns; 9 Prostrated (Cooler Weather to Prevail Over Weekend, Says Bureau; Shower Likely Today; 82-Year Old Cripple Dies in Rock Creek; One Mail Delivery Omitted)." The heat wave covered the entire Atlantic seaboard. "Washington was the hottest city east of the Rockies yesterday," the story began, "with the exception of Charlotte, N.C., where 104 degrees were recorded. This was a record there. Two other places established heat records, New Haven, Connecticut, with 100 degrees, and Asheville, N.C., with 96 degrees."[32]

The fifth paragraph detailed the official story and almost all that is known of the Rooks Turner drowning: "The death toll for the day was brought to three when Brooks [*sic*] Turner, eighty-two years old, colored, of 112 L Street, northwest, was drowned in Rock Creek at Twenty-seventh Street, where he had gone to seek relief. Brooks [*sic*] was a cripple and a passerby who observed a crutch projecting from the water discovered his body. Police believe that he slipped in the creek."[33]

Family members were less certain than the *Washington Post* that Rooks Turner had "slipped" into the creek and drowned accidentally, concluding instead that he had most likely drowned intentionally because of life reversals, including the loss of his autobiography. They added that authorities retrieved his hat from the shore, a sign to them that Rooks had been deliberate in his actions.

Even though Turner had spent a significant portion of his formative years apart from Rooks, his father was, nonetheless, a compelling force in his life. Turner was proud of him. Rooks had consistently served as a role model and symbol of ambition and leadership for the extended family. As testament of Turner's connection to his father are several photographs of an aging Rooks that Turner kept among his most cherished photographs. To lose his father on the eve of an event that was a symbol of the success his father held in highest esteem was psychologically debilitating.

Turner learned of the drowning from Geneva, who posted a telegram to him at his summer residence at 5320 Maryland Avenue, Chicago, on Thursday, July 22, the day of the drowning. It was brief and to the point: "Your father is dead. Come at once. Geneva Turner. 9:55 A.M."[34]

At 8:03 A.M. the following morning, when the Western Union Office opened, Turner posted a return telegram to Geneva, requesting that she assist with some immediate details. One was to contact the typist to ensure that the completed copies of his dissertation did not arrive in Chicago in his absence. Another was to locate his one surviving brother, to notify him of their father's death. His wire home read: "Mrs. Geneva C. Turner 1621 S. Street, N. W. Washington, D.C. Wire Arthur Get address from Helen Moore Will be home Saturday morning Tell Miss Jackson not to send the dissertation Lorenzo D. Turner 803 AM July 23, 1926."[35]

Geneva promptly acted on Turner's requests. By Saturday morning, July 24, Arthur, living in Detroit, had sent Turner a telegram. It is questionable whether the telegram reached Turner in time since he boarded an early train to Washington, D.C., on Saturday morning. In any eventuality, Turner and Geneva were alone to shoulder the responsibility for the arrangements for the burial. Arthur's telegram offered no explanation or apology for his limited involvement: "Can't come. Sending fifty. Write if you need more. Have father's picture taken for me before burial. Will write. Arthur."[36]

On the heels of the burial, Turner collected his completed dissertation from Miss Jackson, leaving Washington, D.C., for Chicago. His disappointment that his father would not be available to receive a telegram about the successful completion of his Ph.D. must have been palpable. A few days had made a galaxy of difference. With his dissertation defense ahead, he was compelled to complete preparations for it.

Being accustomed to rising to occasions, Turner knew that the days consumed in arranging for his father's final rest were all he could afford to spend in grief. He successfully defended his dissertation on August 18, 1926, three weeks after his father's demise. Except for 1924–25, Turner had completed his doctorate in summers while working full time as a department chair and professor during the academic year. His degree was conferred on September 3, 1926, in time for his return to Howard University for the fall semester as Dr. Lorenzo Dow Turner. It was a momentous occasion. Turner was the first person in his family line to receive a doctorate. He was thirty-six years old.[37]

A major social and literary analysis, his dissertation, "Anti-Slavery Sentiment in American Literature Prior to 1865," is original, comprehensive in scope, systematically analytical in approach, and methodical, dividing opposition to slavery into five categories. It analyzes nonfiction books, novels, poetry, journals, and newspapers that express opposition to slavery. Turner then categorized the philosophical stance evident in the opposition, namely, moral, religious, social, economic, or sentimental. He identified the five periods of opposition as (1) the period prior to the 1808 ban on the international slave trade; (2) 1808–31, a period ending with the appearance of the first issue of William Lloyd Garrison's *Liberator* and Garrison's emergence as a major abolitionist voice; (3) 1831–50, a period ending with the passage of the Fugitive Slave Act; (4) 1851–61, the years leading to the Civil War; and (5) 1861–65, the years of the Civil War.

Turner concluded that the major abolitionist voices in American literature prior to 1808 were the Puritans and the Quakers, with the Puritans advocating the religious and moral education of the enslaved Africans and the Quakers expressing concern for their liberation and citizenship rights. He referred to the second period as transitional. Although the antislavery sentiment in the early years of the period was mild, at the same time, it was expressed nationwide, in all the popular media, and in both the North and South. The expressions intensified in the final two years, when William Lloyd Garrison began to raise his voice, subsequently becoming the leading figure of the movement. During the third period, a "new abolitionism" gained momentum, leading to the Civil War. As antislavery sentiment gained ground in the North, it simultaneously practically disappeared from the literature of the South. In period four, the "second stage of the new abolitionism," antislavery sentiment reached its height. On the heels of the 1850 Fugitive Slave Act, a groundswell of antislavery production based on moral, religious, sentimental, and socioeconomic grounds resulted. Harriet Beecher Stowe's *Uncle Tom's Cabin* was the most effective reaction to slavery and to the Fugitive Slave Act of the period. A strong spirit of defiance led to the final period.

Turner then pointed out that in period five, antislavery sentiment appeared most often in poetry. Simultaneously, the antislavery novel reached the fullest point of its development. Much of the poetry was inspired by events of the Civil War and, as such, provided great encouragement to the Union soldiers. Among the major events influencing the subject matter of the period were the abolition of slavery in the District of Columbia, the assassination of Abraham Lincoln, and the passage of the Thirteenth Amendment.

"Anti-Slavery Sentiment in American Literature Prior to 1865" is original in its content, formal in organization, and thorough, making use of pertinent examples. The bibliography is comprehensive, followed by a useful index. The appendix comprises excerpts from two primary sources. The bibliography entries are categorized by type: "General Histories," "Histories of the Abolition Movement," "Histories of the Drama and the Stage," "Novels," "Plays," "Poems," "Essays," "Short Narratives and Sketches," "Periodicals," "Letters, Journals, Diaries, and Books of Travel," "Orations and Sermons," "Biographies and Autobiographies," and "Miscellaneous Writings."[38]

In 1925, in the absence of the Internet, print-on-demand publishers, on-line newspaper databases, and a computerized network of out-of-print book dealers, Turner and his peers were compelled to collect the entire body of their research data on site at numerous repositories. According to the Associated Publishers' edition of *Anti-Slavery Sentiment in American Literature Prior to 1865,* Turner perused the rare book collections of a number of libraries in the northeastern United States, in addition to those in the Chicago area.[39] Richard Ralston noted, "One of the obstacles [Turner] faced was that many anti-slavery documents had been burned in the hysterical moments around the Civil War. The most difficult of Turner's acquisitions was the text of Louisa May Alcott's short story 'M. L.' . . . Most copies were burned. Turner finally unearthed a copy . . . in the private Boston Athenaeum Library, where he developed a severe case of writer's cramp, copying it word for word from 9 A.M. to 10 P.M."[40]

In 1929, three years after Turner's graduation, Woodson's *Journal of Negro History* published Turner's dissertation as an issue of the journal. That same year, Woodson's Associated Publishers, with a subsidy from Turner and Geneva, published *Anti-Slavery Sentiment in American Literature Prior to 1865*.

In 1920 Woodson "had established the Associated Publishers to publish books on black history, because white publishing firms usually were reluctant to publish works by and about blacks unless a subsidy was provided. Remembering the subvention he paid G. P. Putnam's Sons to publish *The Education of the Negro Prior to 1861,* which sold well and made a profit, Woodson reasoned that if a black firm were established, it would not only provide black scholars with a medium to present their findings but also generate revenue to fund other Association activities."[41] Woodson then contacted fifty black scholars, requesting that each contribute five hundred dollars toward the establishment of Associated Publishers. Although he did not receive the level of support he had anticipated, Associated Publishers "produced many books by black scholars that white firms would not publish" between 1920 and 1930. At the same time, the publications did not increase the cash flow of the association. Consequently, by the late 1920s, when foundations decreased their contributions to the association, Woodson reluctantly adopted the practice of requesting that writers subsidize their own publications."[42]

On February 23, 1930, Woodson contacted Turner to notify him that he had produced 500 copies of *Anti-Slavery Sentiment.* He mailed 15 copies to Turner that day, informing him of an additional 235 at his disposal. The remaining 250-plus volumes were the property of the association to be offered for sale. A February 25,

1930, invoice from Woodson indicated that Turner was to pay $343.24 as his share. Turner responded enthusiastically when the slender volumes, on fine quality paper and bound in sturdy burgundy faux-leather, arrived. Woodson's March 3, 1930, letter to Turner expressed his delight that Turner was pleased with the book. Woodson affirmed that the cost was to be shared equally by the Turners and the association. Turner subsequently requested an additional 40 copies. Woodson agreed to send them to him in Nashville and to ship the remaining from Turner's 250 to Geneva at the Townes/Turner home address in Washington, D.C. In total, Woodson had 537 copies printed.[43] *Anti-Slavery Sentiment in American Literature Prior to 1865* was Turner's first published book.

Turner dedicated the book to his major supporters: "To My Wife and Mother." In the preface, he acknowledged his appreciation to his former professors Percy H. Boynton, John M. Manly, William E. Dodd, T. P. Cross, and James Napier Wilt, as well as to Woodson and Arthur A. Schomburg, the latter having made suggestions that led Turner to "several important anti-slavery productions."[44]

Although it was released in a small edition, the academic community recognized *Anti-Slavery Sentiment* as an original analysis of abolitionist philosophical positions. Although out of print for decades, it continues to be one of the standard sources libraries consult to measure the adequacy of their collections on antislavery literature. The Newberry Library of Chicago states in the description of its holdings:

> The Newberry's main strength in the field of African American Studies falls in the anti-slavery movement. With over 2000 books and pamphlets relating to anti-slavery, the Newberry has over 60 percent of the materials listed in [Dwight L.] Dumond's *A Bibliography of Antislavery in America* (1961) and 70 percent of the titles cited in [Lorenzo Dow] Turner's *Anti-Slavery Sentiment in American Literature* (1929).[45]

The African American press took note of the publication. Aubrey Bowser, the reviewer for the *New York Amsterdam News,* was immediately impressed: "The reader picks up this book expecting to be bored. At first glance it is merely a duty book, one of those things that an intelligent colored man has to read because he is expected to know something about the subject. . . . The book delightfully belies such expectations. There is something new on every page. . . . It is not generally known, for instance, that practically all the best known poets and novelists of America from 1770 to 1865 had something to say against slavery. Whittier is the chief anti-slavery poet; he was ably seconded by Longfellow, Holmes, Emerson, and Lowell."[46]

Bowser highlighted issues of racial controversy that were likely to arouse the curiosity of lay readers: "How many readers . . . know that [Louisa May Alcott] wrote 'M. L,' in which a beautiful white girl adores and marries a Negro with full knowledge of his race?" He continued, "Think of the American public of that day applauding a book that a publisher of today would shun like leprosy."[47] Appealing to the readers' sense of political awareness, Bowser noted that Turner's book also mentioned several black abolitionist writers, in particular, David Walker, William Wells Brown, James Madison Bell, and Frances Ellen Watkins Harper.

Bowser concluded with a statement focused on social responsibility, that is, "This book is far from dull for any Negro who wishes to know what a fight was waged to make him free."[48]

Alcott's "M. L.," to which Bowser referred, was published in serialized sequences in the *Boston Commonwealth* between January 24 and February 21, 1863.[49] The poignant story of an ethical young white woman and an equally ethical young biracial man who confesses to his fiancée that he is a person of African ancestry passing for white may have held special appeal for Turner, given his family history. Sally Rooks and Jacob Brady, Turner's earliest forebears in America, were in several respects the counterparts of Claudia and Paul Frere of Alcott's story. Both couples were the exception during their lifetimes, transcending public disapproval to forge a relationship across the racial divide. Alcott's character Paul bears the brand "M. L." for the name of his former plantation owner, Maurice Lecroix. Hence the title of the story.[50] It was a significant enough piece in Turner's consciousness that he selected it as one of two texts for his appendix, the other being John Trumbull's 1770 essay, "The Correspondent, No. 8."[51]

Arthur C. Cole, writing for the *Mississippi Valley Historical Review,* was restrained in his appraisal of *Anti-Slavery Sentiment.* However, he commended it for its "useful bibliography which lists the literary as well as the traditional historical sources for such a study." Simultaneously, Cole suggested that the Turner book should have been more developed, particularly in that it could have analyzed more periodicals from the Midwest, among them the *Western Citizen* and *Free West* of Chicago. From his perspective, in the absence of such materials, the strength of abolitionist sentiment in the Midwest was underestimated. Cole would have also preferred to have the volume estimate the size of the public reached by the literary appeals of each period. Such a process would have required Turner to gain sales figures from publishers; data on library circulation of published books, magazines, and newspapers; and sales figures from newspaper publishers, a process that would have been the stuff for another dissertation. If it were a possible task, the results would have been inexact at best, as some newspapers and publishers were no longer in business. Cole also noted that he often found it difficult to discern a distinction between the sentimental arguments and moral religious ones. On the other hand, he found Turner's organization in the five categories by type of argument to be a "logical" approach.[52]

At the end of the summer of 1926, Turner returned to Geneva and to Howard University for two additional years. Turner's accomplishments were stellar. With a Ph.D. in hand and a published book, he was progressing in his career. Geneva was a successful, well-loved public school teacher. The Turners were in demand on the academic/social circuit. They were middle-class Washingtonians, the owners of a well-appointed three-story, red brick row house with gleaming hardwood and tile floors. At the rear of the house, the bay windows faced a small yard where children could play safely cloistered from the dangers of the street. A one-car garage shared one side of the basement level.[53] With so much accomplished, he and Geneva turned their attention to producing children. They waited.

Geneva was thirty-three—her biological clock was ticking—and yet no children came. She was magic with children. They adored her, and she adored them. They thrived in her heart and in her classroom. At her elementary school, she sang to them and with them. She taught them to love French as she did, taught them to sing and play instruments, played piano for them, wrote plays for them and taught them to perform, and photographed them on the lawn of the school. Children were all around her in her heart, classroom, and dreams—but not in her body or her home. Arthur and his wives produced no children either. Like Geneva, Turner hungered for them, not willingly resigned to the impending reality that the Rooks-Turner line would come to an abrupt halt in a matter of decades. An unspoken anxiety from day to day, the absence of children was the source of unresolved stress in the Turner household.

10

Howard University—Turner's Final Two Years 1926–1928

Howard University has sent forth 7267 graduates to every state in the Union, to the islands of the Sea, and to Africa, Asia, Europe and South America.

—*Annual Catalogue 1927–28,* Howard University, Washington, D.C.

DURING TURNER'S YEARS ON THE FACULTY OF HOWARD, he served under three presidents—Stephen M. Newman, president from July 1, 1912, to June 30, 1918; J. Stanley Durkee, who served from July 1, 1918, to June 30, 1926; and Mordecai W. Johnson, who held the office from June 1, 1926, to June 30, 1960. Simultaneously, Turner rose from instructor of English to professor and head of the English department. Teaching and administrative service were second nature to him. Outside of class, his schedule was challenging. In 1927–28 he was chair of the Catalogue Committee, a member of the Board of Examiners, and a member of the Committee on Graduate Studies.[1]

By 1928 there were 159 members of the faculty and 21 administrators. The grounds staff, postmaster, clerks, head nurses, and secretaries added another 25 persons to the staff.[2] Howard was expanding in size, organization, and prestige. It expanded in enrollment; the positions of dean of women and dean of men were created; the central administration and faculty numbers were increased; the number of faculty members of African ancestry was increased; Congress authorized annual appropriations to the university (1928); faculty salaries improved; Howard received a "Class A" rating from the Association of Colleges and Preparatory Schools of the Middle States and Maryland; Howard University Press became operational; the *Howard Review* magazine and *Hilltop* newspaper were initiated; physical education became a department; and three years of mandatory ROTC were approved for male students.

Extracurricular activities also brought acclaim to the university. Baseball and football teams brought Howard national recognition; a number of important extracurricular organizations were founded for and/or by students, among them the Ira Aldridge Drama Club (1920) and the Historical Society (1925).

In 1926 Dr. Mordecai W. Johnson became the first African American president of Howard. He immediately began increasing the number of faculty members of African descent, following the lead of President Durkee; "he lifted Howard to greater heights than it had ever known" and was "the most dynamic of Howard's presidents . . . a builder of faculties as well as buildings."[3] One of Johnson's major contributions at the university was the forging of a cosmopolitan academic community. When asked to describe Howard, he was fond of responding in a witty fashion, "On Howard University's faculty are Negroes and whites, men and women,

Protestants, Catholics, Jews, Free-thinkers and atheists, Americans, Europeans, Latin Americans, Asians and Africans. . . . Even . . . a few Republicans."[4]

While President Johnson was building the university, Turner was building a career. Recognizing the almost total lack of comprehensive anthologies containing literature by black authors, he and two women colleagues began to edit a volume that was to become one of the earliest comprehensive literary anthologies focusing on the black experience.

Turner was part of a network of developing scholars. His 1927 grant proposal to the Harmon Foundation demonstrates that he had already consciously plotted a career trajectory that included some foundation-supported research. He was undaunted when his proposal did not meet with success.[5] He and Geneva had been married for ten years, and they were both continuing to thrive as professionals. Washington, D.C., and Howard were his homes. But then, life had other plans for him.

By all accounts, President Johnson ruled Howard with an iron fist. In his history of Howard, Rayford Logan assesses Johnson's presidency thus: "As Caesar Augustus is alleged to have said of Rome, Mordecai Wyatt Johnson could have said, with no more exaggeration, of Howard: 'I found it brick and left it marble.' . . . In office for thirty-four years, 1926–1960, a little more than one-third of the life of the University, he served longer than did any other President. A controversial figure throughout his entire administration, he knew what he wanted for Howard, and he was stubbornly determined to have his own way. As a result, his years in office were years of great progress and of a great deal of dissension."[6]

Between 1926 and 1928, Johnson called for greater emphasis on the preparation of black doctors, established a retirement plan for faculty and staff, saw the enactment of the law authorizing annual appropriations to the university, and increased appropriations for the professional schools—particularly the law, medicine, pharmacy, and dental schools.[7] At the same time, in an effort to silence legitimate criticism, Johnson divested his faculty of some of the best and most creative intellectuals in America. Alain Locke (philosophy), Metz Lochard (French), Alonzo H. Brown (mathematics), and Orlando Cecil Thornton (finance and geology) left between October 1926 and June 24, 1927; and William Henry Jones (sociology), Albert Beckham, M. Franklin Peters (English), and Lorenzo Dow Turner (English) between May 1928 and May 1929. By 1937 Arnold Donawa (dean of the dental school), Judge Fenton W. Booth, Dean Dwight O. W. Holmes (the registrar), and Professors Edward Stafford (law school), Charles V. Inlaw (law school), James Schick, and Dr. St. Elmo Brady (chemistry) had joined the exodus.

The mounting series of concerns escalated to the point at which alumni prepared a special issue of the *Howard University Alumni Magazine* entitled "The Case against Dr. Mordecai Johnson." Among their concerns were what they viewed as President Johnson's dictatorial approach; his insensitivity in the treatment of the first dean of women, Lucy Slowe, especially during her illness from the kidney disease that eventually led to her death; student unrest resulting from an "unwarranted" increase in room rent; tensions between faculty and the administration resulting in lowered morale among the students; favoritism manifested in differential salaries; insecurity over the issue of tenure; and petty and vindictive behaviors perpetuated by President Johnson.[8] It was a turbulent era. In two years at least fifteen faculty members, or approximately 10 percent of the total faculty, had been asked to depart. Johnson maintained control. He remained as Howard University president for the next thirty-two years, retiring on June 30, 1960.[9]

11

The Washington Sun—*A Venture in Entrepreneurship*
SEPTEMBER 1928–JANUARY 1929

The staff of The Sun will aim to give to the public at large a fearless, independent newspaper, carrying strong editorials, reliable news, and unique features.

—News release for the *Washington Sun,* August 1928

OFTEN ADVERSITY LEADS TO OPPORTUNITY. Between 1928 and 1929, Turner joined his surviving brother, Arthur, who returned to Washington, D.C., in the founding and editing of a newspaper, the *Washington Sun.* The press release announcing the appearance of the paper indicated that it was to be a weekly published by the Sun Publishing Company of 1918 1/2 Fourteenth Street, North West, Washington, D.C. Turner was the editor and Arthur the business manager.

According to the news release, "the first issue of *The Washington Sun,* a weekly newspaper, will appear on Thursday, September 6, 1928. . . . Whereas their purpose is national in scope, they desire especially to stimulate a wider and keener local interest in education, religion, and business, and in general to promote the civic welfare of the community. . . . Believing that you are in sympathy with these aims, they respectfully solicit your active co-operation, and hope that you will find it convenient to give them your subscription. The subscription for one year is two dollars."[1]

On July 27, 1928, Turner and Arthur began their publishing venture with a deposit of two thousand dollars, which they invested in "stock" or supplies. On September 4, they spent two dollars on advertising. The brothers maintained two meticulously detailed accounting ledgers, one for "Receipts" and another for "Receipts and Dispersals."[2]

The *Sun* format featured headline, weekly, religious, and social news, a comic strip, and advertisements. Outside the walls of Howard and academia where Turner had spent twenty-two years, more than half of the years of his life, Turner must have been both stunned and challenged. He embraced the opportunity to become reacquainted with his brother, Arthur, as he had not been since the days of their childhood. The city of Washington, D.C., and the outlying suburbs were in the scope of his lenses and on the point of his pen. He was an expert writer and thinker. He possessed savoir-faire and thus met the public well.

A number of Washingtonians looked forward to the new weekly or wished to support the Turners' venture. Immediately he and Arthur solicited a substantial list of subscribers, the first of whom was L. C. Farrar. Among the others who paid for subscriptions during the first week of operation on September 4, 1928, were some of Turner's former colleagues from the Department of English: M. Franklin Peters,

Mrs. C. E. Leak, Mrs. I. L. Stewart, M. Grant Lucas, Merrill W. Holland, Mrs. C. A. Brown (Syrna), and Mrs. M. L. Edwards.

The *Washington Sun* rolled off the press each week a finished product of which the brothers could be proud. The quality of reporting was first-rate. The paper resembled the *Afro-American* in most respects. By the second week of operation, on September 13, Turner had successfully solicited a subscription from Dr. Mordecai Johnson and Kelly Miller, the dean. By September 29 an additional colleague, the literary scholar Mercer Cook, had subscribed.[3]

The eight-page inaugural issue of September 5, 1928, became the model from which future issues were developed. The slogan of the *Sun,* consciously practiced throughout the paper, was "TO SERVE ALL THE PEOPLE ALL THE TIME." News underscoring triumphs in the progress of African Americans graced the front page, along with details of defeats and tragedies. The coverage was local, national, and international. The multifold message to the black population, like that of the other black newspapers, was: be a model American citizen, be proud of black accomplishments, be aware of the virulence of racism, work vigorously to advance both individual and group progress, and be politically active in order to foster change.

The lead story of September 5 suggested the importance of patriotism among black citizens: "65,000 Spectators Line Pennsylvania Avenue Day Parade: Colored Company Makes Brilliant Showing Wins 5th Prize—Four States Take Part—Has High Efficiency Rating Says George Watson, Fire Chief." A massive crowd lined Pennsylvania Avenue to view floats and fire engines from four states. The fire engines represented "the modern fire equipment put on display by the visiting companies." Utilizing a Hawaiian theme, the all-black company was led by the Community Center Band playing "snappy music" (early jazz). Waving proudly from the float were the fire lieutenant, J. G. B. Key, and three local women. Apparently, in segregated Washington, D.C., of the 1920s, a single company served the black community, and "throughout the ten years of its existence, it [had] shown unusual courage and good judgment in fighting city fires." Its float won fifth place. The prize was a radio. Page 8 featured a photograph of some of the uniformed firefighters standing in front of their well-kept building. Another featured Fire Lieutenant Key.[4]

One of the national stories suggested the increasing inclusion of blacks in the American drama: "G. O. P. Chieftains Plan Vigorous Campaign: To Recruit Unprecedented Registration of Negro Voters." Because the presidential election was ahead, the "colored division of the Republican National Committee" had held a conference at which it developed a strategy to "accomplish an unprecedented registration of colored citizens in every section of the country, especially in those states where colored voters hold the balance of power." The immediate goal was "to line that vote up behind the Hoover-Curtis ticket."[5]

Among the several tragedies covered in the September 5 issue was a story bearing the headline "Two More Negroes Shot by Officers . . . No Guns Found on Men or at Scene of Chase." The scenario has been repeated often in the history of black/white relations. The police reported that they had stopped two young men because the front and rear license plates on their Essex touring car did not correspond. In the process of attempting to escape the pursuing police, the driver slammed into a brick wall and then fled on foot. He was shot in the back of the head as he ran. The second man, standing on the driver's side running board, was shot in the hip.[6]

The *Sun* featured some levity. Often a comic sketch graced the back page. The inaugural issue featured the Knots family, recently arrived from Cross Roads, Pennsylvania. Described as "neighbors of yours," the well-dressed family was composed of a father, a mother, two sons, a daughter, and a grandmother. One son was "the brains of the flock," adored by his teachers "but not the kids on the block." The second son was the hungry, pudgy one. The daughter was pigtailed, slightly "fresh," and cute. The message encouraged by the comic strip was that the ideal black family is two-parent, extended, upwardly mobile, and with options—was among them, the ability to settle in various urban centers; that to be intelligent does not always bring one popularity; that life requires coping mechanisms, among them overeating (perhaps less detrimental than many others); and that women and girls must be physically attractive.[7]

One of the international stories, "Progressive Africa Now in Making Says Mr. Firestone," reported on an interview with Harvey S. Firestone Jr., vice president of Firestone, who had returned from eight weeks in Liberia, the home of 2,000,000 Africans. His message was that Firestone Plantation Company was on a mission to make Liberia "the largest American-controlled source of rubber." According to Firestone, who was interviewed at the Mayflower Hotel, the west coast of Africa had emerged from the ravages of enslavement to develop "organized trade for hundreds of miles. Schools and churches are developing. Medicine and hygiene are reducing tropical diseases. . . . Modern ideas are taking hold in the native mind. While this change goes forward, the riches of Africa are reaching the outer world in greater volume. Yet these riches have been scarcely touched."[8]

The *Sun* dedicated substantial space to church news, local commerce, politics, "Literature and Drama," history, sports from Howard University and elsewhere, obituaries, and social life. The Turners engaged their friends and associates as contributors. On occasion, the playwright Willis Richardson prepared the drama reports. "The Junior Column," prepared by Sarah M. Frazier, was dedicated to young readers, presenting articles, book reviews, and poetry. Geneva's friend Jessie H. Roy prepared the obituaries.

A number of businesses placed advertisements in the *Sun,* most selecting the least costly option. Usually Nellye Z. Turner, Arthur's wife, placed a larger quarter-page advertisement featuring her Nel-Art Beauty Salon, "Washington's Foremost Beauty Salon," at 1417 U Street North West, where "Ladies of discriminating taste" visited to maintain "a refined personal appearance." Nellye and her operators offered lemon facial packs, eyebrow arching, oil manicures, and hair care, including washing, conditioning, cutting, tinting, and especially the popular marcel. Nellye stocked "a complete line of cosmetics," providing "expert advice as to their use."[9]

Each week the subscriber list grew, with some paying one dollar for half a year and others paying two dollars for the entire year. While the list was substantial, so were the bills. Income generated by advertisements in the *Sun* was modest, and the revenue the paper generated could not support one family. Two were dependent on it. It appears that Turner was required to accomplish the bulk of the work associated with the paper. According to the accounting ledgers, he most often arranged for the supplies, a responsibility that one would assume would have belonged to Arthur, the business manager.

By the end of the Christmas season, it was clear that the sun was not shining brightly on the *Washington Sun.* A number of factors accounted for its failure. Not enough of the reading public found it "convenient" to subscribe. Many readers who were already loyal to the reigning newspaper, the *Afro-American,* likely considered one black newspaper sufficient. The *Afro-American,* which maintained offices in both Washington, D.C., and Baltimore, provided broad circulation. Furthermore, too much of the revenue was required to replenish the stock, causing the overhead to outdistance the income. The number of subscriptions, though increasing with regularity, was not adequate to pay the bills. There were too few large advertisements. By January 18, 1929, when the brothers reluctantly put the paper to bed for the last time, they were deeply in debt. To their dismay, the Turners' major venture in capitalism had lasted less than five months.[10]

In January 1929, Turner prepared to settle the accounts by assessing the remaining expenses for the newspaper. He and Arthur were at least one thousand dollars in the red, no small sum for men with little other income and nowhere to turn as the effects of the Great Depression would soon begin to blanket the minds of Americans like winter snow. In a few months, the wealthiest Americans would be leaping to their deaths over their stock market losses.

Since the paper did not sustain the family, it was fortunate that Geneva continued to be employed in the public school system and was able to provide a family income. Nellye's beauty shop likely sustained her and Arthur. During the year the newspaper sharpened Turner's business skills while providing additional professional contacts. Metz Lochard had departed for Chicago to join the staff of the *Chicago Defender.* They were to be friends for life; Lochard would cover Turner's career in the *Chicago Defender,* often contacting him to request an update on his research.

Turner's most productive years were ahead. As he had collected data for newspaper articles, his thoughts turned to teaching. In the process of searching for an academic post, he applied for a summer position at South Carolina State College, a small HBCU sixty miles northwest of Gullah territory. By the summer of 1929, there were students for Turner to meet in Orangeburg, South Carolina, who, while learning from him, would teach him lessons that would alter his perspective and simultaneously serve as the catalyst for his transforming the field of American linguistics. Turner's experience at Orangeburg would lead to the most pivotal juncture in his life and career. At the end of the summer, full-time employment at Fisk University in fall 1929 would place him in the South, where his thoughts would often turn to the Sea Islands.

12

Fisk University 1929–1932

I did not find better teachers [at Harvard than at Fisk . . . only] teachers better known.
—W. E. B. Du Bois, *The Autobiography of W. E. B. Du Bois*

THE PRESTIGE FISK UNIVERSITY ENJOYS is based on a distinguished history of innovation. Turner was well aware of its reputation as it was one of the rivals of Howard University in academics and in athletics. It opened its doors in the Federal army barracks hospital building at Fort Gillem, Tennessee, on January 9, 1866.

Fisk is one of the universities born of the efforts of the American Missionary Association (AMA), an organization founded in 1846 largely to protest the inaction of other missionary associations in abolitionist activities. It advanced nondenominational work in the South while maintaining a platform in opposition to slavery. By September 1861, when the first enslaved African Americans were freed, the AMA sent missionaries to Fortress Monroe in Virginia. By 1866 the AMA had employed over three hundred persons to teach and propagate Christianity among the newly freed men and women. The universities it sponsored continue to graduate exemplary scholars and citizens.[1]

While there were many who championed the cause of education for the freed men and women, their commitment did not ensure financial security for the HBCUs. The early struggles of Fisk and other HBCUs to gain funds for their operations are now legendary. Fisk consistently proved itself a survivor, and the Fisk Jubilee Singers played a major role in the economic stability of the university in its early years.[2] One of the first buildings, and historically the major residence for women students, was Jubilee Hall. The funds required for the erection of the building were raised by the original company of Fisk Jubilee Singers by touring Europe and singing arranged Negro spirituals.[3]

Over the past 130 years, its faculty and alumni have been among America's most distinguished intellectuals. The list includes Du Bois, Aaron Douglas, Sterling Brown, Robert Hayden, John W. Work I, II, and III, John Hope Franklin, Hazel O'Leary, Roland Hayes, Charles H. Wesley, C. Eric Lincoln, and more recently, Nikki Giovanni, Judith Jamison, Ronald Walters, and David Levering Lewis.

In 1930 Fisk became the first HBCU to earn certification from the Southern Association of Colleges and Schools. In 1933 and 1948 it became the first HBCU to be placed on the approved lists of the Association of American Universities and the American Association of University Women, respectively. In 1952 it was the first HBCU to receive a chapter of Phi Beta Kappa and to receive a chapter of Mortar Board.[4]

The history of Fisk was, however, not all peace and tranquility. During the 1924–25 academic year, student unrest bubbled over on the campus, as it did on the campuses of a number of other HBCUs. A series of convergent forces, rather than one in particular, was the cause. The early context of the HBCUs was that of educational institutions for newly freed persons and freeborn persons whose educational opportunities had been severely constricted. Many universities maintained high school departments to prepare students for college. By the 1920s, however, high school departments were being eliminated and there was a small, thriving black middle class whose college-aged children were freed enough from food, clothing, and shelter preoccupations to embrace more philosophical issues. In his history of Fisk, Joe Richardson notes, "With the growth of the black middle class and the economic betterment of a small group by the First World War, more students went to college and fewer had to work. Newspapers, moving pictures, the radio, and Northern students going to Southern schools spread new ideas. The above changes, with the concept of democracy generated by the war, the aggressiveness of returning black soldiers, the Niagara Movement, the founding of the NAACP, and the *élan vital* stimulated by the 'Black Renaissance' or the 'New Negro Movement,' combined to send a new type of student to the Black college. They were no longer timorous students who refused to fight back."[5]

Active support of alumni encouraged student revolts on a number of campuses. In the case of Fisk, Du Bois observed the campus climate with interest, commenting in articles in the *New York Amsterdam News* and the NAACP's *Crisis*. When he arrived at Fisk in June 1924, to deliver an alumni address, he denounced the policies of President Fayette McKenzie, stating that he planned "to criticize and say openly and before your face what so many of your graduates are saying secretly and behind your back." And so he did. In his address he admitted that McKenzie had been effective in raising funds, but he believed that in the process the university had "lost its soul."[6] Being fiercely dedicated to civil rights, Du Bois viewed McKenzie as overly conciliatory toward the local southerners and the education associations that allocated funds. Richardson notes that "issues of segregation were among the concerns. Fisk students had been required to sing to segregated audiences. As unrest increased, the *Fisk Herald,* the student newspaper . . . was suspended. The student government association was dissolved."[7]

The students then organized a strike. After funding for the university fell precipitously, President McKenzie resigned. The year was 1925. Some rocky days were still ahead, but the next president was more flexible in his acceptance of social change. According to Richardson, "The Good Years" were ahead.[8] In four years Turner would arrive and contribute to the making of them.

Given Fisk's history and status, it is not surprising that it would have attracted Turner and in return considered him an important acquisition. By the time he arrived in Nashville, Fisk had been in existence for sixty years. Its most recent president, newly appointed in 1926, Thomas Elsa Jones, was a Quaker born in Indiana on March 22, 1888, with a Ph.D. from Columbia University and international employment experience as director of the YMCA in Vladivostok, Siberia, and as professor of economics at Kyoto, Tokyo. Fisk was entering a period of renaissance:

"President Jones had no experience in race relations and little as an administrator in an educational institution, but he was young, vigorous, and bright. . . . Jones was soon convinced that he was 'right in the center of one of the most important developments not only in America but in the world.'"[9]

The road to Turner's appointment at Fisk began with his letter of application to President Jones, dated January 4, 1929. Turner began his quest for university employment as soon as it was clear that the *Washington Sun* was not a viable enterprise. By then his typewriter ribbon was thin, testifying that he was a committed conservationist as well as a man of limited disposable income.

The letter chronicles his career path to that juncture. The professors Turner listed as referees were a who's who of educators at their respective universities: "For testimonials concerning my work at Howard, I refer you to Dr. St. Elmo Brady, of your Department of Chemistry, and to Dean D. W. Woodard, of Howard University. Concerning my work at the University of Chicago, I refer you to Professors John M. Manly, Percy Boynton, David H. Stephens, Napier Wilt, and Tom B. Cross. Concerning my work at Harvard, I refer you to Professors Bliss Perry and F. N. Robinson, Harvard University, and to Dr. William A. Neilson, President of Smith College, Northampton, Mass., who was on the faculty of Harvard when I was there, and under whom I took several courses."[10]

On March 1, 1929, the historian Charles Wesley recommended Turner highly. Wesley added that Geneva would look forward to studying music at Fisk: "I do not hesitate in saying that I believe that he would do more than is expected of him, if you should see fit to employ him. . . . It appears also that his wife intends to accompany him, and resign her position here in the public schools. . . . So far as efficiency as an instructor is concerned, I am confident that you would make no mistake in him. Mrs. Wesley majored in English at Howard and took most of her work under his direction, and she agrees with the general opinion in this respect."[11]

Among those who submitted reference letters was former Howard University president J. Stanley Durkee, who had relocated to Brooklyn, New York, to co-pastor the Plymouth Church with Clyde W. Robbins. In his March 2, 1929, letter, Durkee stereotyped black men generally as "fair weather friends." His comments illustrate why Woodson and some other intellects condemned the paternalism of white "leaders" of African Americans and lobbied for the day when blacks would speak for themselves and lead their organizations.[12] However, Turner was a member of Durkee's approved list. Durkee recommended him in superlative terms:

> I am writing you in behalf of Lorenzo Dow Turner, formerly of Howard University. He does not know I am writing you; he did not ask me to write you; it will be a great surprise to him to know I have done so.
>
> My long experience teaches me this—you must have about you loyal Negro men if you have any hope of final success. Any of them will back you when the wind is fair, but when a squall comes it is amazing how they flee for cover. Only a few Negroes will stay on deck when they are really needed. You have one in Dr. [Elmo] Brady. God bless him! You can trust him to the death.

> Lorenzo Turner is another such man. I know him. There are exceedingly few men of whom I can speak in such terms as I can use regarding Dr. Turner. . . . I know his honesty, his loyalty, his hard work, his faithfulness to his tasks, his high scholarship and ideals.
>
> . . . He is one of the very, very few men of that University who possessed my absolute confidence. I know the man, the scholar, the gentlemen. I recommend him to you in superlative terms. . . .
>
> Strength to your arm and courage to your heart.[13]

The hiring process dragged through the winter of 1929, reaching a new level of seriousness when President Jones contacted President Johnson of Howard University. "Since talking with you I have made some rather extended investigations among the Alumni and friends of Fisk University and feel that we would not be making a mistake to invite Dr. Lorenzo Turner to become a member of our faculty. I believe I understand you to say that you would be happy if he could be well located, and that you wished it were so you could have him on the Howard Staff. . . . I have decided to give him a part with us," he wrote.[14] President Johnson replied immediately on March 8, 1929: "[We] at Howard shall be very glad to see him working with you."[15]

By April 3, 1929, President Jones was prepared to offer Turner a contract for one year, "beginning on or about September 15, 1929 and closing on or about June 15, 1930, at the salary of $2,700.00. . . . [T]he position I am asking you to fill for the coming year is that which is now occupied by Prof. Sterling Brown who has been granted a leave of absence for graduate study during the coming year. . . . [I]t is our hope that if the year seems mutually satisfactory a permanent position can be given you on our staff."[16] A few days later, on April 7, Turner responded enthusiastically: "I gladly accept your offer of a position as Professor of English Literature for the school year 1929–1930 at a salary of $2700.00, and I thank you most heartily for your great kindness."[17]

After a flurry of letters regarding housing and other logistical details, Turner sent President Jones a letter on July 20, 1929, apprising him of his summer accomplishments. After teaching summer school at South Carolina State College at Orangeburg, Turner had traveled east to utilize the Schomburg Library in New York and the libraries at Harvard and Yale as he prepared his share of the anthology *Readings from Negro Authors*.[18]

By the time Turner arrived at Fisk, he sported a more mature appearance, combing his hair back rather than to the side. Of necessity, he had become a wearer of glasses. At some point, he had purchased a Ford Deluxe Sedan.[19] He had adopted the then fashionable habit of cigarette smoking. His brand of choice was Raleigh—unfiltered. Whenever he chewed gum, it was Juicy Fruit.[20] Soon Turner purchased a life insurance policy from Ohio Casualty Insurance Company. His wallet card listed his address as the John Avery Apartments.[21]

Turner was to become a campus icon in part because of his educational background. In 1925 only two members of the Fisk faculty held doctorates.[22] In 1927 Turner was one of thirty-nine African Americans in the United States to have earned a doctorate.[23] By 1930 the Fisk faculty had hired ten of them, including Turner. Twelve other Fisk faculty members were pursuing degrees beyond the master's. Turner's hiring came as President Jones was embarking on a program to upgrade faculty salaries, one factor contributing to the increase in faculty with Ph.D.'s. Turner's salary of $2,700 was average. In general, faculty salaries at Fisk were comparable with those at other small American colleges.[24]

Fisk was moving forward. As part of its development, it phased out its high school in 1927, adding that same year graduate programs in a number of other disciplines. By Turner's arrival, Fisk had initiated master's degree programs in history, sociology, English, philosophy, and chemistry. Richardson reports, "Under the new plan, a student pursued in residence for one full year a course of study approved by the graduate studies committee. At the end of a year, a comprehensive examination was taken and an original thesis on an approved subject presented. An outside representative from a 'distinguished university,' including Harvard, the University of Chicago, and the University of Wisconsin, participated in the final written and oral examinations."[25]

Turner's acclimation was seamless. He understood the South. He knew members of the faculty. The close-knit network of Ivy League black colleges exchanged personnel. When a university professional searched for a new experience or a broader range of opportunities, it was within the network. Turner was already quite familiar with Arthur Schomburg, the bibliophile; St. Elmo Brady, one of the first five blacks to earn a Ph.D. in chemistry; and Horace Mann Bond, the educator who later became president of Lincoln University in Pennsylvania. He also knew E. Franklin Frazier, a Howard graduate of the class of 1916, who left Atlanta University, arriving at Fisk with Turner in the fall of 1929, and James Weldon Johnson, the writer who joined the faculty in 1931.[26]

Furthermore, he was an experienced teacher and administrator. Despite the assets he brought to Fisk, Turner faced the possibility that he would be compelled to locate a different appointment in one year. Geneva remained in Washington, D.C. The uncertainty regarding the permanence of the position, the illness of Turner's mother, Elizabeth, and the lack of a public school position in Nashville for her were all factors in Geneva's decision to remain in Washington, D.C. Again, as during the Harvard years (1915–17) and the University of Chicago year in residence (1924–25), Turner and Geneva were to be apart for extended periods.

After one year, a full-time position materialized. Sterling Brown, who had joined the Fisk faculty in 1928, moved on to Howard in 1929, where he remained. Nonetheless, since Elizabeth continued to suffer in declining health and Geneva was well established in her teaching position, Geneva and Elizabeth continued to reside in Washington, D.C. Turner wrote home often.

During the summer of 1929, while he was in New York collecting material for the anthology of black writings, Turner paused on July 9 to send Elizabeth a postcard with an image featuring 5th Avenue, north from 40th Street, which he mailed from Grand Central Station. It read, "I am having a great deal of success in New York finding the materials that I came for. I am leaving New York Wednesday night for Boston, where I expect to remain about two days. I shall try to be home by

Sunday. I hope you are well. Take good care of yourself. Don't worry. Shall see you soon."[27]

By 1930 Geneva had rented out the Turner house at 1621 S Street, North West, to others; she and Elizabeth had moved in with Geneva's parents.[28] The three elders were all in delicate health. Geneva's sister, Justine, who had begun her teaching career at Peabody Academy in Tory, North Carolina, in 1917, had soon relocated to Virginia to teach. In 1922 she had returned to Washington, D.C., to a teaching position at Shaw Junior High School. One year later, in 1923, she had married Dr. Frank Maloney, a physician. The relationship was short-lived. By 1930 Justine had returned home, finalizing her divorce from Dr. Maloney in 1931.[29] In their twilight years, after Edlow retired, the Townes took in two boarders to supplement the family income. Theirs was a bustling household with seven adults in residence.[30]

The separation from his family wore heavily on Turner. He must have felt much as his father Rooks had when he left Elizabeth and the children thirty-three years earlier. Still considering Washington, D.C., his home, Turner traveled at each opportunity to spend his intersessions and other breaks with Geneva and Elizabeth. The trip was 665 miles one way, a long journey in an automobile that traveled approximately forty miles per hour.

After the Christmas break of December 1929, Turner, having returned to Nashville and Fisk, paused on January 10, 1930, to write his mother a tender letter. Expressing awareness of her loneliness, her tendency to worry, and ill health, he encouraged her, informing her that he had arranged for a drugstore to deliver medication to her: "Geneva has told you that I got back safe with no accidents and am getting along beautifully in my work. Everything is going well and I like my courses very much. I am counting the days between now and March when I shall be coming back to see you. Those two months will pass before we realize it. And then it won't be long before the summer will come. . . . I am having the druggist at 16th and R Sts. bring you a package. You ought to get it in a couple of days after you receive this letter, because I am mailing a letter to him at the same time that I shall mail this letter. . . . I hope you are well and getting along well in every way. Be as cheerful as you can and I will soon be back there with you."[31]

Although Arthur had been residing in Washington, D.C., Turner found that he and Geneva were the only dependable psychological supports for his mother. It appears that he and Arthur had been at odds since their dealings at the *Washington Sun.* Arthur's lack of attention to Elizabeth compounded Turner's frustration with him. Turner's exasperation occasionally bubbled over as Arthur was inclined to be unavailable at crucial moments, as when Rooks drowned. By January 1930 he had departed for Washington State. In the meantime, his new wife, Zephra, another beautician, had not stood in the gap for Turner by visiting Elizabeth. Elizabeth was often burdened and despondent. Turner continued, "I wasn't greatly surprised at Arthur's leaving. He is no one to be depended on. Has Zephra been to see you since I left? She and Arthur are the worst people I ever saw. . . . Take good care of yourself and try not to worry. We shall come out on top soon now. Give my regards to all and write when you get the time."[32]

Although the Fisk years were filled with obligations, they were also rich in opportunities for growth. Fisk, like Booker T. Washington's Tuskegee, acquired significant financial support from a cluster of foundations, chiefly the Carnegie, Rockefeller, and Rosenwald foundations. Under President Jones's twenty-year administration, the university was a nurturing environment for scholars. The credentials of the faculty, which was two-thirds black and one-third white, grew more and more impressive. Turner found President Jones supportive of his career as he willingly provided recommendations whenever Turner applied for grants and subsequently endorsed his requests for leaves of absence. Although it was the beginning of the Great Depression, the university's growth continued, somewhat deterred but not halted, partly because of the foundation support. By 1930 its endowment was several million dollars, and "Fisk could lay claim not only to being an outstanding college for Blacks and a superior school for the South, but to being one of the better small private universities in the nation."[33]

Commingled with the triumphs were the challenges. In preparation for his third year, Turner scribbled his projected schedule for the 1931–32 academic year on a small slip of paper. It spanned the concentrations in the Department of English, that is, composition, journalism, English language, and literature:

Spring 1931

English 117 (2nd hour)	Newspaper Make-up and Headlines
English 200 (3rd hour)	Problems and Methods of English Literary History
English 102 (4th hour)	Written Composition (prescribed for freshmen)
English 123 (5th hour)	The Negro in American Literature

Fall 1931

English 101	Written and Oral Composition
English 115	Newspaper Writing and Reporting
English 135	A Survey of American Literature

Winter 1931

English 102	Written Composition (prescribed for freshmen)
English 149	American Drama
English 112	Expository and Critical Writing

Spring 1932

English 116	The Editorial and Special Feature Article
English 201	Elementary Old English
Education 113	The Teaching of English[34]

Turner was fully occupied. While serving as English department chair, he taught an average of twelve different courses per year. Although the course load was unavoidable, given the staffing of the HBCUs, it afforded few blocks of time for independent research. English 117, Newspaper Make-up and Headlines, required that Turner supervise the production of at least some issues of the college newspaper. According to the course description, the class emphasized "the mechanical side of newspaper work . . . , including copy-reading, proof-reading, the writing of headlines, and the study of make-up. The class is required to prepare issues of the college paper and to make frequent visits to newspaper and printing plants in the city." English 101 and English 102 were the prescribed freshman composition courses, requiring significant writing on the part of students and paper grading on the part of professors.[35]

A seasoned professor, with a teaching background in composition and literature and practical world experience in journalism, Turner was clearly multitalented. He was one of four English professors. His colleagues—Lillian Cashin (A.M., University of Chicago—English and Comparative Literature), Dora Anna Scribner (A.M., University of Chicago—English), and Eulacie Shamberger (A.M., Radcliffe College—English)—each had impeccable credentials, adding to the prestige of the university and its faculty. Three of the four, Turner, Cashin, and Scribner, were graduates of the University of Chicago.[36]

Just as Turner prepared *A Plan for the Study of Freshman English* for Howard, he prepared a comparable one for Fisk. Added features of the Fisk version made it a planner, with space to record the weekly schedule of writing assignments and three final pages for students to maintain a record of the titles of their themes, the dates submitted, and grades received. Another set of columns was for test dates and grades.

Though Turner and his colleagues' hands were full, their motivation was extraordinary, for they were committed to the preparation of "the talented tenth." Furthermore, in 1930, anyone with a steady university job was unlikely to complain.

Jean P. Evans, one of Turner's distant cousins who became his student in the early 1940s, transferred from Northwestern University to Fisk because Turner was there. She remembers him as a "precise and formal man, always dressed in a suit or a sweater and tie. He was challenging but fair. We had confidence in him because he knew his material and worked as hard as he expected us to work."[37]

During the summer of 1930, Turner attended the Linguistic Institute at the City University of New York, where he studied the International Phonetic Alphabet transcription method and various linguistic courses. By the time he returned to Fisk for the fall, he was already embarking on the quest that redirected his career from literature to linguistics and that would take him to the Sea Islands and Europe in pursuit of an analysis of the ways in which the Niger-Congo languages of Africa collided with English to form Gullah. The changes in American linguistics for which Turner served as a catalyst were about to begin.

Although Turner's interest in Gullah had been sparked during his years of interaction with Woodson in Washington, D.C., in the 1920s, no opportunity to analyze Gullah had been available. After the 1930 Linguistic Institute, Turner began to explore grant options to pursue research on the Sea Islands. On November 8, 1930, he wrote President Jones: "I have filled out and sent in to Mr. Henry Moe of the John Simon Guggenheim Memorial Foundation, my application for a 1931 Guggenheim Fellowship." His letter carried a request to President Jones to write a recommendation.[38]

President Jones responded immediately. On Thursday, November 13, he contacted Moe himself. Jones reminded Moe of his visit to the Guggenheim office to discuss some of the work being carried out at Fisk a year earlier. Along with his recommendation, Jones sent a Fisk catalog and a pamphlet, *Progress at Fisk University.* Since foundation support was central to the budget, President Jones was consistent in maintaining positive relations with administrators in the foundations.

President Jones approved of Turner's research agenda, which was focused on the idea of preparing "a Descriptive Grammar of the Gullah Dialect." It is worth noting that his plan to analyze Gullah predated his involvement with Hans Kurath, the Linguistic Institute, and the Linguistic Atlas of the United States Project. Woodson had already identified St. Helena Island as an African American community to be analyzed and had commissioned several social scientists to conduct research on the island.[39] Several events coincided at the appropriate moment in history, resulting in Turner's opportunity to pursue research on the Gullah language in 1932.

President Jones asserted in his recommendation that "if [Turner] can secure this Fellowship, we would be willing to release him for a year from his duties at the University." His assessment of Turner was highly laudatory: "Dr. Turner is a superior scholar and a very good teacher. He has had approximately fifteen years of experience in the college classroom and has been trained under some of the outstanding professors of English in both Harvard and the University of Chicago. His specialty is the form of the English language, such as syntax, etomology [*sic*], and the origin and development of words, phrases, and idioms. I think he is particularly well fitted to make the study which he has described to you. He is highly respected at Fisk and we anticipate continuing his services."[40]

By the end of spring 1931, President Jones had offered Turner a promotion to research professor, along with an increase in salary. In a June 6, 1931, letter, Turner wrote President Jones to update him on his summer activities and to thank him for his support: "My work at Fisk during these two years has been exceedingly pleasant and I am looking forward to next year's work with equal delight." His summer plans included teaching at Tuskegee Institute for four weeks, after which he expected to travel to New York City to spend six weeks at the Linguistic Institute. Then he would travel to Washington, D.C., and remain with Geneva and Elizabeth until classes began.[41]

Much to Turner's disappointment, he was not awarded the Guggenheim. Later that same year, he would triumph, though, when Otelia Cromwell, Eva Dykes, and he made a breakthrough with the publication of *Readings from Negro Authors: For Schools and Colleges* (1931). Published by Harcourt Brace, it was tailored to high school and college teachers, providing copious study questions and assignments. Exercises at the ends of chapters raised thought-provoking questions while requiring students to bring to bear their familiarity with both European and African American literature. It was a boon for professors with or without experience in teaching black literature and appropriate for one-semester or two-semester sequences.

The authors included in *Readings from Negro Authors* leap from the pages as a who's who of African American writers, from Phillis Wheatley to Zora Neale Hurston. Many were young innovators in 1930; Turner and his coeditors judged well as most have subsequently become well-known writers in the African American literary canon. Selections from the contemporary authors Countee Cullen, Langston Hughes, Claude McKay, Georgia Douglas Johnson, Arna Bontemps, Alice Dunbar Nelson, James Weldon Johnson, Jessie Fauset, Kelly Miller, Sterling Brown, Benjamin Brawley, Alain Locke, and Zora Neale Hurston were featured. Simultaneously, the volume did not neglect the black forefathers and foremothers, including selections from Phillis Wheatley, Paul Laurence Dunbar, Frederick Douglass, William Wells Brown, William Sanders Scarborough, W. E. B. Du Bois, Carter G. Woodson, and Booker T. Washington.

The organizational categories of poetry, stories, one-act plays, essays, and public addresses provided a good range of genres. The plays by Willis Richardson and James F. Matheus were included in their entirety. The final portion of the volume continued suggestions for study and biographical sketches of the included authors as well as a bibliography and an index of authors and titles.

Cromwell, Turner, and Dykes collaborated effectively on the volume. Turner had been able to negotiate a contract with Harcourt Brace, a major publishing company in New York. Cromwell and Dykes were two of Turner's female counterparts, with academic backgrounds and motivation as strong as his. Eva Dykes graduated cum laude from Howard with Turner and Geneva in 1914. She also majored in English, later becoming an English professor there, after first completing her dissertation in English at Radcliffe (1921), and in so doing, becoming the first African American woman (one of three the same year) to receive a doctorate.

Otelia Cromwell, a graduate of Smith College and the author of *Lucretia Mott* (Harvard University Press, 1958), taught English at the famous M Street High School in Washington, D.C., which prepared more high school graduates for "the best New England Colleges" than any other high school in the United States.[42] By 1930 she had become a professor at Miner's Teachers College, also in Washington, D.C., on the edge of the Howard University campus. Like Turner, she was a second-generation college graduate. Her father was John Wesley Cromwell, author of *The Negro in American History* (1914), also associated with the occasional papers of the American Negro Academy from 1897 to 1924.[43]

The anthologies predating *Readings from Negro Authors,* though valuable in their own right, are more limited in scope. Those appearing in the bibliography of the Cromwell, Turner, and Dykes volume and, more recently, in Richard Barksdale and Keneth Kinnamon's *Black Writers of America* (1972) are, nonetheless, useful as they assist in documenting the unfolding African American literary tradition.

Many in the academic community welcomed *Readings from Negro Authors*. Mary Louise Strong, writing a lyrically phrased review for the *Journal of Negro History,* asserted that it filled an important void: "Few textbooks have been so greatly needed as this pioneer [volume] which is praiseworthy on so many grounds. . . . To their jousts these editors bring penetrating viewpoints, scholarly minds, keen perspicacity." She then contextualized the volume, while encouraging further development of a self-conscious African American literary tradition: "Negro literature is acquiring a history. It is developing critical tendencies. It has participated in several movements. It has made available wide ranges of material."[44]

Strong then noted, as Turner and his coeditors did, that the American literary canon is incomplete in the absence of the voices of African American writers, who are as American as any other group: "The ultimate interpretation of American literature must be in terms of large issues of thought. Negro literature is the simple story of an oppressed and rising people. It is but one of the factors of that vast problem of American democracy and can be understood only in its organic relation to American literature and in the implications of American life. No one eager to understand American literature can afford to neglect this vital part."[45]

Impressed with the volume, Strong refrained from adverse comments, rather stating that any reader could lament the absence of certain selections or the inclusion of others. She concluded that the volume was first-rate: "The performance of these editors does not betray them. The laurel boughs have not withered in their keeping."[46]

The *Hilltop,* the student weekly newspaper of Howard University, greeted *Readings* as front-page news. Since Dykes was on the faculty, the headline read, "Dr. Eva Dykes Co-author of Text Book: . . . Negro Literature." Quoting directly from *Readings,* the article stated, "Negro literature demands no unique method of approach as 'no special interpretation of the rules of craftsmanship is necessary because the standards of literary form are based on universal principles.'"[47]

Readings appeared more than thirty years before the advent of the Black Arts Movement, at which time distinctive criteria were articulated for judging African-derived forms from the oral tradition reinterpreted in written form. The concept of the black aesthetic had not yet been articulated, though Hughes, Hurston, McKay, and several other writers incorporated structures and rhythms from black music, especially blues, spirituals, and jazz; from black language/dialect (African American and Afro-Caribbean); and from folklore. Later in his career, as Turner immersed himself in creoles derived from African languages—namely, Gullah, Afro-Brazilian Portuguese, Sierra Leone Krio—and in folk literature, he would recommend to teachers of black literature that they gain an understanding of the African American oral tradition in literature, including that which made use of the dialect of the folk. He came to view it as the most "authentic" black literature.[48]

If *Readings from Negro Authors* were reissued today, professors and literature devotees would find it a valuable classical compendium of significant writings from 1760 to 1930. The selections are representative of the authors included. The study questions continue to be relevant. However, the volume has been out of print for almost seventy years.

That fall Turner's world had reached a high point. His career was progressing well. He could conceptualize enough research projects for a lifetime. He was in demand as a speaker. Just past his forty-first birthday, he was young enough to go far in his profession. He had completed his second major publication, a breakthrough in several particulars. It presented in one volume the best of the growing African American literary tradition; and it had been published by a major Euro-American company without a subvention, a recognition of the importance of both the black literary tradition and the content of the particular manuscript. The year was not to end in triumph, though. Just as Turner was preparing to depart from

Nashville for the Thanksgiving holiday, he learned that Elizabeth had died on Monday, November 23. After hurriedly driving back to Washington, D.C., he spent his Thanksgiving break contacting relatives and friends while arranging for Elizabeth's final journey. Letters and telegrams poured in.

One of the first was from Arthur's second wife, Zephra. She and Arthur had moved to Detroit around 1930 and subsequently separated. When Arthur left Detroit, Zephra had remained. As far as she knew, Arthur was in Scranton, Pennsylvania. It read, "Dear Lorenzo: All my sympathy is yours. Have wired Arthur. Will wire flowers for funeral. Zephra."[49]

One of the most detailed was a Wednesday, November 25, letter from Arthur's first wife, Nellye. It is the letter of an educated woman, philosophically inclined. She took note of Turner's unwavering devotion to his mother, praising him for his sacrifices, for "a duty perfectly performed." Her admiration for Turner is clear in the letter. Referring to him as the "Pike's Peak," Nellye concluded, "You have few equals and no peers. . . . Consolation must come from within, and Lorenzo, you of all the sons have been honorable, kind, considerate, extremely loyal and devoted to the last degree to your mother. You must draw upon that perfect past now. It will sustain and comfort you. Having done all you could during the lifetime of an individual means more than all else when they are torn from us. A duty perfectly performed should make you cheerful now."[50]

Nellye did not employ the traditional philosophical stance that the pain of the loss of a loved one diminishes over time. Rather, she chose the opposite approach—that the pain increases until, at the moment of greatest stress, Turner would come to accept that through his sacrifices he had paid in full for the right to relief. Further, she invoked the idea that he had learned endurance from African American culture:

> I know that you miss her and as time goes on the missing will increase. You miss her less now than you will in years to come, but when you are prone to falter, you have that glowing satisfaction of years of sacrifice and toil to bolster you up. . . . Won't you be brave? You can; your culture will help you to understand the futility of worry and regret. It all had to be. As a loyal son, Lorenzo, you are the Pike's Peak. You have few equals and no peers. . . . Success has always been yours but it is when we are forced to undergo suffering and pain that we gather more strength. . . . I would love to be near you now. I miss Mother, too. She always meant well and she loved you more than her life. . . . I wired Arthur at 509 Adams Avenue, Scranton. . . . I have no other address. . . . When you feel better, write to me, and please know that I shall be with you through Friday and on. . . . Devotedly yours, Nellye.[51]

Turner also sent a telegram to his first cousin James Edward Reed, a cleric in New York City. Because Reed resided in midtown at 126 East Fifty-eighth Street, he may have been one of the persons with whom Turner found shelter during his research and conference trips to New York. The telegram to Reed arrived on Thursday, November 26, the day before the funeral. Reed responded the same day: "Never dreamed I was to receive the sad news this glorious Thanksgiving Day.

Well, Lorenzo! Your loss is her gain. She has gone the way we must all go sooner or later. . . . All the 'Old Timers' have 'Gone Over' and now only us 'Youngsters are left to carry on.' Extremely sorry that I cannot run over to attend the funeral of your mother tomorrow. Though absent in person, I shall be present in spirit." Reed indicated that he was unable to cancel a commitment at the Cathedral of St. John the Divine.[52]

President Jones wired Turner at 6:50 P.M. on Wednesday, November 25: "The faculty and student body of Fisk University write to express sympathy on the passing of your mother. May the only comfort that abides be with you." Turner's English department colleagues Lillian Cashin, Mable Keemer, and Dora Ann Scribner wired him as well.[53]

There are no documents to indicate that the telegrams Arthur's ex-wives Nellye and Zephra wired to him in Scranton and Detroit, respectively, reached him, or that Arthur attended the funeral. As in 1926 at the time of Rooks's death, Geneva and Turner were responsible for the arrangements and expenses. After the funeral, there was no time to dedicate to mourning. Geneva returned to her classroom and students. Turner returned to Nashville to prepare for his final examinations at Fisk but not before sending appropriate notes of acknowledgment:

> We shall always remember
> with deep gratitude your
> comforting expression of sympathy
> L. D. Turner and Family.[54]

As of November 23, 1931, Turner must have viewed himself as an orphan, without even a dependable brother to stand at his side in times of adversity. There were no children to hold his hand, nor was Geneva there to humanize his house, sharing with him the ebbs and flows of his days and weeks. Geneva was far from Nashville surrounded by her family and friends. Turner returned to Nashville with a dull ache in his lower abdomen that would plague him with increasing insistence during the years ahead.

13

The Beginnings of Gullah Research 1932–1942

> The authors . . . were not acquainted with the African languages spoken by the Negroes who were being brought to South Carolina and Georgia continually until about the beginning of the Civil War; nor were they acquainted with the speech of Negroes in other parts of the New World than the United States. It is not surprising, therefore, that they should have entertained such views of Gullah. What is surprising, however, is that they undertook the task of interpreting Gullah without feeling the need of acquiring some knowledge of the Negro's African linguistic background.
>
> —Lorenzo Dow Turner, *Africanisms in the Gullah Dialect*

AS TURNER MATURED INTO ADULTHOOD in the early twentieth century, he was a developing literary scholar with a solid background in languages and excellent connections with his peers in literary and language studies. Surely just as prescient an influence in his consciousness as cultural nationalism was his awareness of the Americanization of linguistics. Given his background, Turner was well positioned to participate in the development of a self-conscious movement to forge an American linguistic tradition distinct from anthropology and Indo-European philology. One concrete manifestation of the movement was the creation of the Linguistic Society of America (LSA) in 1924.

Three major approaches characterized American linguistics in the early centuries: the study of Native American languages, the embracing of American English as worthy of systematic analysis, and the utilization of European linguistic theories to develop distinctively American scholarship, resulting in the international field of general linguistics.[1] Turner contributed to the American English strand that explored dialects and led to the analysis of pidgins and creoles.

Turner's transformation from a professor of English composition and literature to an interdisciplinary scholar with a specialty in linguistics was accomplished over several years because of a convergence of propitious events. He could have remained a professor of English and literature quite comfortably. Guided by his own family tradition of high achievement and the Harlem Renaissance ideal of the "New Negro" as the standard bearer for the cultural group whose responsibility was to achieve as much as possible in each arena in which one was suited, his inspiring summer in Orangeburg opened his thoughts to the possibility of analyzing Gullah. Central to Turner's turn from literature to linguistics was his attendance at the Linguistic Institute, which provided intensive six-week courses in International Phonetic Alphabet transcription and the field methods essential for the study of dialect geography.

At the founding meeting of the LSA in 1924, John Lawrence Gerig, a professor of Celtic at Columbia University, called for the "spreading of knowledge of linguistics" and "the recruitment and training of linguistic scholars." Reinhold Eugene Saleski, a professor of German at Bethany College, offered the original suggestion for an institute. Edgar Howard Sturtevant of Yale University "took up the idea with energy . . . and elaborated the plan into . . . virtually the form in which it has been put into effect."[2]

According to Archibald Hill, who served as secretary-treasurer of the LSA for many years, the Linguistic Institute convened four consecutive years before the Great Depression caused it to be suspended because of financial difficulties. The first two convened at Yale University for six weeks each during the summers of 1928 and 1929. Sturtevant served as host. In 1930 and 1931 they moved to City College of New York, with Sturtevant continuing to serve as host. From their inception, they were viewed by language scholars as fulfilling a definite need—forty-five persons enrolled in 1928 to participate in thirty-nine courses offered by twenty-four faculty members. Many of the courses the first year were actually conferences of scholars, "where everyone learned from each other" in sessions anchored by a "nominal leader." The American Council of Learned Societies (ACLS) provided the $2,500 grant to support the first institute.[3]

In the summer of 1929, the second institute was historic for its role in creating a context for the development of the dialect geography/dialectology specialty. Funded by four thousand dollars from the Carnegie Corporation and an additional one thousand dollars from Yale, one of the institute conferences focused on a proposal for a linguistic atlas of the United States and Canada. Those attending the session agreed on "plans for training field workers, methods of recording, and the maintenance of an archive."[4]

By the summer of 1929, Turner had not yet become involved in the linguistic sciences. He faced a more pressing bread-and-butter imperative. In an effort to recover some of the financial loses from the newspaper venture and in an attempt to reenter academia, Turner found himself near Gullah territory. A few months after the final issue of the *Washington Sun* appeared, Turner taught summer school at South Carolina State College at Orangeburg, an HBCU sixty miles from Gullah territory. As noted earlier, this summer in Orangeburg became the most pivotal juncture in his career.

Since Turner's family had left North Carolina during his formative years, and since travel conditions along the Carolina coasts were challenging, Turner apparently had had little direct exposure to Gullah speakers. Therefore, he was surprised to experience the linguistic and cultural differences he encountered in South Carolina. His students' dialect varied in phonology, morphology, syntax, semantics, and style from other English dialects with which he was familiar; at least two women students spoke idiolects, or personal dialects, markedly different from others.[5]

Turner had had the good fortune of learning at the feet of a number of the foremost English and foreign language professors of his generation at Howard, Harvard, and the University of Chicago. His extensive language background in Greek, Latin, German, and French had sharpened his ears, enriched further by his exposure to Gothic, Middle English, and Italian. Turner inquired of the two students about their hometowns. Learning from them that they were from Johns Island, he arranged to visit them in their homes, "and he came away with the distinct impression that it was not English baby talk but some other language he was hearing. This speech was not simply a slower Southern drawl. On the contrary, it had a rapid, African rhythm."[6] Equally as important, though, Turner learned that they utilized "basket names," which he recognized as the African linguistic/philosophical practice of protecting persons from negative spiritual energy by using one name in public while maintaining a more personal one for a close relative or friend. Based on the geographical location of the college, Turner knew he was interacting with Gullah speakers.[7]

Gullah was not a new concept to Turner. By 1870 Thomas Wentworth Higginson, a pastor from New England stationed in South Carolina as an officer for the Union army during the Civil War, had commented on the unique qualities of the culture of the Sea Islands. In *Army Life in a Black Regiment* (1870), he noted African qualities in the language, music, and religion.[8] Later writers utilized the qualities in plays and stories, speculating about their origins. Before the development of clear definitions of creoles, observers spoke of the "dialect" along the coast of Georgia and South Carolina and on the Sea Islands. Its 250,000 native speakers were flung over a series of small, swampy islands off the coast and along the coastal lowland, "from Georgetown, South Carolina, to the northern boundary of Florida." According to Turner, the name of the people and their language most likely derived from the Gola cultural group in Liberia or from another cultural group from the Hamba Basin of Angola, where Africans were procured in large numbers in the nineteenth century.[9] Local residents referred to the people and their language as Geechee, no doubt because of the nearby Ogeechee River.

The survival of Gullah can be attributed to several interconnected circumstances. First, the large ratio of blacks to whites became a feature of island demographics, with twenty black families to every one white family in many areas. The overseers were often African as well, ensuring continued exposure to African language forms and less to English.[10] By 1710 Africans were already the majority. Second, newly transplanted Africans renewed exposure to African languages. They continued to arrive involuntarily directly from Africa for many generations, with "well over 40 percent" of the enslaved Africans transported to the British North America colonies between 1700 and 1775 arriving in Charleston,[11] the "Ellis Island" for enslaved Africans. Numerous others arrived from Barbados, having already participated in the creation of an English lexified African pidgin.[12] Third, many whites found the Sea Islands environmentally unsuitable given the "heat, malaria, and dampness," their general absence facilitating African cultural retentions.[13] Fourth, the relative isolation of Gullah territory—travel opportunities were limited due to the lack of bridges connecting the islands to the mainland before World War II—served to foster linguistic retention, and the nineteenth-century influx of Africans directly from Africa after 1865 renewed the traditional African linguistic and cultural patterns.[14] In *The American Language: Supplement II,* H. L. Mencken referred to Gullah as the only American dialect unintelligible to persons from other parts of the country.[15]

Over time a number of American writers had developed solid literary reputations by producing literature or collecting folklore in Gullah. Some pieces, such as Ambrose Gonzales's books *The Black Border: Gullah Stories of the Carolina Coast* (1922), *With Aesop along the Black Border* (1924), and *Two Gullah Tales: The Turkey Hunter and At the Crossroads Store* (1926) and Julia Peterkin's *Black April* (1927), were still recent when Turner arrived in Orangeburg. Among the earlier ones were Charles Colcock Jones Jr.'s *Negro Myths from the Georgia Coast* (1888) and William Gilmore Simms's *The Wigwam and the Cabin* (1845).

Even though some of these writers were bidialectal, having learned Gullah from their African American caretakers and playmates,[16] not one was a linguist.[17] They, as many of their contemporaries, wore blinders to the possibility that African languages were a central ingredient in the structure and semantics of Gullah.

As a professor of English, Turner would have been aware of the conjectures various authors offered to elucidate the differences between Gullah and other English dialects. The prevailing assumption before 1949 was that African languages had been eradicated—that Africans in America had neither retained their own languages nor influenced American English to any significant degree. The major theory traced Gullah to archaic British dialects of the seventeenth and eighteenth centuries. Some writers viewed Gullah as modified "baby talk" Africans had acquired from plantation overseers. Still others maintained that Gullah differed from British dialects because of the social backwardness, isolation, simplemindedness, and intellectual inferiority of its speakers.[18]

Reed Smith best represented those who advocated the archaic English dialect theory. In *Gullah* (1926) he outlined four pages of the features of Gullah, particularly related to phonology, morphology, and syntax, linking them to older British dialects. His analysis did not incorporate any investigation of African languages or systematic interviews of Gullah speakers.[19]

Typical of those who adopted the tenets of the racially biased theories of biological and socioeconomic determinism was Ambrose E. Gonzales, who, in the introduction to *The Black Border,* asserted, "Slovenly and careless of speech, these Gullah seized upon the peasant English used by some of the early settlers and by the white servants of the wealthier colonists, wrapped their clumsy tongues about it as well as they could, and enriched with certain expressive African words, it issued through their flat noses and thick lips as so workable a form of speech that it was gradually adopted by the other slaves and became in time the accepted Negro speech of the lower districts of South Carolina and Georgia."[20]

Several years later H. P. Johnson, describing African Americans as "an imitative part of the population," suggested that only one African lexical item had been retained in southern speech: "Apparently the Negroes have made only one contribution to the language of the English-speaking world. They have given it the word *buckra,* which means *white man.*"[21] George Philip Krapp, a Columbia University professor and an authority on the history of American English,[22] viewed Gullah as a "debased dialect of English learned by the Negroes from the whites."[23]

When Turner first began to seek grants from the Guggenheim Foundation to undertake research among Gullah speakers, though he suspected that Gullah included a greater African linguistic component than other researchers had concluded it did, he knew that his grant proposal would have a greater chance of success if it utilized the hegemonic discourse of the era. Therefore, he advocated, first, that a comparative analysis of Gullah speech from living informants with the Gullah speech in the folklore and literature of Gonzales and others be done. Second, he proposed to collect Gullah folklore—as the Grimm brothers had collected German folklore—to preserve it from extinction.[24]

After a successful year as professor of English at Fisk, Turner was invited to attend the Linguistic Institute in the summer of 1930 for the first time. Available records do not confirm who offered the invitation. However, a well-developed University of Chicago–Fisk University network shared the resources of the same major corporations, Carnegie, Rockefeller, and Rosenwald.[25] Furthermore, Fisk drew a substantial number of faculty members from the University of Chicago. Turner was undoubtedly recruited by Kurath through the Chicago-Fisk network. The two may have met while both were in residence at the University of Chicago in the mid-1920s.

The year 1930 was the third year of the institute, still under Sturtevant's direction. President Frederick B. Robinson of City College partially funded it by paying stipends to the professors who taught the courses. Two were invited from the University of Paris, Jules Marouzeau and Albert Blum, to contribute to "understanding between American and European linguists."[26]

When Turner arrived in New York, he joined more than eighty other language professors, dialectologists, and practicing linguists. The institute featured twenty-four faculty members and lecturers, among them, Franz Boas and Sturtevant. Two of the faculty members were women—Louise Pound, a professor of English at the University of Nebraska, and Helen H. Roberts, a research associate in anthropology for the Institute of Human Relations at Yale University. Twenty-one of the course participants were also women.[27] American linguistics had come into its own as an inclusive discipline. Emerging from its connection with anthropology, which had defined it largely as the discipline to record the rapidly disappearing Native American languages, it was prepared to forge its own identity.

One of its shapers was Hans Kurath, who, having arrived in America from Austria in 1907, was fascinated with the study of languages. An opportunity materialized in the early 1920s, when, as a student of German linguistics at the University of Chicago, he traveled to various regions of the United States. Being attuned to the numerous dialects he heard, Kurath was eager to undertake a systematic study of the varieties of American English, similar to a language survey undertaken in Switzerland and Italy under the direction of Jakob Jud.

By 1925 Kurath had persuaded the Modern Language Association of the value of his proposed project. As he began to organize the research process, he realized that, given the vastness of the United States, a much larger group of researchers than he had originally anticipated would be required for the data gathering. Consequently, he divided the country into nine large speech areas and began his own work in the eastern United States.[28] Simultaneously, he began to consider the possibility of recruiting other linguists to initiate work in other regions.[29] When Turner taught in Orangeburg in 1929, he may or may not have fathomed that he would become one of them and a shaper of uniquely American linguistic history.

At the conclusion of the 1930 Linguistic Institute, after Turner returned to Fisk to begin a second year, he immediately assessed his research grant options. Having applied to the John Simon Guggenheim Memorial Foundation for a grant to conduct research in Gullah territory, he wrote to his former University of Chicago professor John Manly on November 14, 1930, to request a recommendation. He noted, "I spent several weeks down there last summer," and expressed his wish to gain a fellowship "in order that I may spend the year 1931–32 on certain of these islands to complete my study." Turner enclosed the statement of his project, ending his communication with a note of appreciation to Manly: "I am certainly grateful to you for the many kindnesses you have shown me in the past."[30] A few days after Turner contacted him, Manly responded enthusiastically: "I am very glad to hear from you again. . . . [Y]ou may rest assured that I shall reply favorably to your application for a fellowship. Your project seems to me interesting and valuable . . . and I am sure you will be able to obtain aid in carrying it out from some source."[31]

Manly's encouragement was prophetic. He provided Turner with the names and addresses of additional foundations that Turner would subsequently contact on multiple occasions during his career. "If you do not succeed in obtaining a Guggenheim Fellowship, I suggest that you apply either to the American Council of Learned Societies[,] 907 Fifteenth Street, Washington, D.C. or to the Rosenwald Foundation, Arthington and Homan Avenue, Chicago."[32]

Later in the same year, on December 11, 1930, Kurath mailed a mimeographed letter to Turner and a number of other persons recommending that they participate in the data collection for the linguistic atlas project. Kurath indicated that fieldwork would begin in June of 1931. In a handwritten note to Turner's copy, he added, "The investigation will ultimately be extended Southward. I hope that you will help us then."[33]

Just as Turner had sought recommendations from Manly and President Johnson for the Guggenheim Fellowship, he had also written Kurath. Kurath responded: "I have not been asked for a letter of recommendation by the Guggenheim Foundation as yet. Shall I send one without waiting for the request?"[34]

Turner's reply was immediate. On Christmas Eve, December 24, 1930, he answered Kurath, informing him that he would forgo his plans to spend the summer in South Carolina in order to attend the 1931 Linguistic Institute. Expressing his enthusiasm for gaining further skills in collecting and analyzing dialect data, Turner articulated the position that is the key to his having redefined his career: "Since I received your letter, I have decided to attend the Linguistic Institute again and to take Professor Jud's course of lectures and probably some courses that will help in my future work on American dialects. . . .[35] I shall always be happy to take an active part in work on dialects as I am qualified to take. I like it better than any work I have ever done."[36]

In closing, Turner suggested that Kurath send the recommendation to Henry Allen Moe at the Guggenheim Foundation "without waiting for the request."[37] In retrospect, it is clear that by 1930 the descriptive linguist in Turner had been born.

Turner was remarkable in his willingness to reinvent himself well into his academic career. As an established and respected English professor and department chair, he could have continued on the same path until retirement. He had already coedited a major literary anthology from a major publishing company. Many publication opportunities no doubt lay ahead as they did for his peer and fellow Harvard graduate Sterling Brown.

Turner's discovery of linguistics and his access to linguistic education through the Linguistic Institute were the catalysts that made his transformation a rational option, but opportunity alone does not account for his willingness to begin his career anew. Four characteristics imbued him with the fortitude to pursue his linguistic interests: his solid background in the history and structure of the English language and other Indo-European languages, which provided him the tools to assess Gullah as being structurally and semantically unique; his family background and prior success at achieving the extraordinary at each stage in his life; his desire to fulfill the "talented tenth" imperative to achieve in as many arenas as his talents permitted; and his embracing of the Woodsonian vision and quest to document the history of blacks so that the world would experience them as major factors in world civilization.

Having embraced the challenge, Turner faced numerous others. He was compelled to commit to the blocks of time necessary to learn meticulous phonetic transcription and linguistic field methods; acquire a firm background in the settlement history of Gullah territory; earn the confidence of Gullah speakers so that he could gather the most authentic data; learn the phonetics and grammatical structures of dozens of African languages, some for which there were no written grammars or dictionaries; verify the connection between Gullah and other creoles in the Western Hemisphere; immerse himself in the African aesthetic in order to interpret the music, dance, and material art forms; win grants continuously to advance his field studies; struggle alone as there were no other trained Gullah specialists with whom he could compare notes; juggle a full teaching load with courses across several disciplines; manage his schedule as department head/administrator for almost all of his career and still carve out time for writing; and, last but not least, sacrifice substantial family time to pursue his new career path.

Turner's new career path was a momentous and often lonely undertaking but one he found invigorating as it provided stimulating challenges and ensured his continual intellectual development as well as his place on the cutting edge of the linguistic discipline. The sequential steps above were necessary before *Africanisms in the Gullah Dialect* could reach completion. It is no wonder that the volume was years in the making. No one has yet surpassed his achievement.

When the summer of 1931 arrived, Turner was compelled to secure funds for his six-week study period in New York by teaching summer school. Although he did not return to South Carolina State College, he did remain in the South, traveling to Alabama to teach at Tuskegee Institute. The timing of the schedule at

Tuskegee apparently made it possible for him to participate in the Linguistic Institute.[38] After the Tuskegee session, he hastened to New York to attend the fourth annual Linguistic Institute. Seventy-four others arrived from around the country. The all-male teaching staff comprised nineteen persons, among them Clive H. Carruthers, a professor of Classical philology at McGill University, and Roland Kent, a professor of comparative philology at the University of Pennsylvania. Among the seventeen women participants were Adelaide Hahn, an assistant professor of Latin and Greek at Hunter College; Alice Hill Byrne, dean and professor of Greek at Western College in Oxford, Ohio; and Rachel Sergeant Harris, a graduate student at Brown University and one of the few women field workers for the Linguistic Atlas project.[39]

The ACLS had provided a subvention of two thousand dollars, a portion of which was utilized "to bring Dr. Jakob Jud, editor of the *Italian Dialect Atlas,* and Mr. Paul Scheuermeier, his field worker, to teach a course on the problems of preparing an atlas."[40] The course, Les Problèmes de la Préparation d'un Atlas Linguistique, was Turner's first immersion in fieldwork methodology. He also gained intensive immersion in the International Phonetic Alphabet system for transcribing phonetics and analyzing linguistic data. The lessons of that six-week period solidified his initial preparation to undertake linguistic research.

Turner was at the heart of the unfolding American linguistic movement. The major excitement at the 1931 institute emanated from the launching of the Linguistic Atlas of New England (LANE) project, conceived of as the initial stage of the Linguistic Atlas of the United States and Canada (LAUSC) project. Participants also composed and tested the LANE eight-hundred-item questionnaire.[41]

According to Hill, "the session gave valuable training to the *Atlas* workers, such as Bernard Bloch, Guy S. Lowman, and Martin Joos. The fruit of this training, of course, was the final publication of the great American research works, the *Atlas of New England.*"[42] Hill neglected to mention Turner in his "History of the Linguistic Institute." Turner's participation was significant as he was the first and only African American scholar in the Linguistic Society of America and the only African American in attendance. He studied under Jud shoulder-to-shoulder with Bloch, Lowman, and Joos. Over the years, furthermore, Turner single-handedly carved out the Gullah studies specialty, a defining moment in American linguistics—a breakthrough in dialect geography and creole studies—adding to the atlas a profile on an African American population. Other fruits of the training were Turner's three articles on Gullah and, subsequently, his book *Africanisms in the Gullah Dialect* (1949), with empirical evidence that vestiges of the Niger-Congo languages had been retained in the United States. While Turner was as integral a part of the history of 1930 and 1931 institutes as any scholar in attendance, he is rendered invisible in Hill's "History of the Linguistic Institute." The result is a distorted and fragmentary historical record.

In a related approach, Harold B. Allen, in his voluminous, informative article "Regional Dialects, 1945–1974," neglected to mention Turner in his discussion of the dialect geography research conducted in the "Middle and South Atlantic States," which included South Carolina and Georgia.[43] In contrast, throughout other sections of the article, Allen described the publications of researchers who focused on particular geographic areas in their books, articles, and dissertations. To Allen's credit, later in the article he dedicated an isolated paragraph to Turner's *Africanisms in the Gullah Dialect* under the heading "West African Languages." There he referred to "[t]he distinguished work of Lorenzo Turner (1949) on Gullah."[44]

By 1931 Turner had become a linguist and viewed himself as one.[45] He formalized his relationship with the Linguistic Society of America and was its putative first African American member. Around the same time, he joined the American Dialect Society.[46] In 1932 he joined the International Phonetic Association.[47]

It has generally been assumed in the linguistic community that the opportunity to study Gullah materialized, capturing Turner's interest and fortuitously becoming one of his many projects. On the contrary, the research opportunity was the realization of one of Turner's long-held aspirations, according to a contemporary news article. The *Providence Evening Bulletin* reported, "For years it was his goal, while he was a student at Howard, later during graduate work at Harvard from which university he took his master's degree and the University of Chicago where he obtained his doctorate. Though his home has for years been in Washington, Dr. Turner was born in North Carolina. Having always known of the Gullahs, his plan for recording their speech did not become a reality until a few years ago."[48]

Early in the 1931–32 academic year, just as Manly had suggested, Turner prepared a grant proposal for the ACLS. He waited. On March 5, 1932, Donald Goodchild, secretary of fellowships and grants, sent a Western Union telegram to Turner at Fisk with astounding news: "Awarded thousand dollars Please consider confidential until notified by letter= Goodchild."[49]

Turner was ecstatic. That same day he wired Geneva at her parents' address: "I have just received a telegram informing me that I have been awarded one thousand dollars for that study. I will give you details in my next letter. Lorenzo."[50]

On March 18, 1932, Goodchild posted the promised follow-up letter to Turner, confirming that he had been awarded the grant.[51] It was Turner's first research grant, a victory, but inadequate to replace a full semester's salary. Fortunately, President Jones awarded him a grant in aid from Fisk University. Assured of the two sources of funds, he formulated his plans. He was armed with the International Phonetic Association transcription process and the eight-hundred-item Linguistic Atlas questionnaire. His recording device was a Fairchild Aerial Camera Corporation "recording machine," also provided by the American Council.[52]

Perceiving the significance of his impending research and the importance of maintaining a high profile in his career, Turner prepared a news release, forwarding it to a number of newspapers along with a current photograph. Several of those on the African American syndicate responded. The *Baltimore Afro-American,* the *New York Amsterdam News,* the *Washington Times,* and the *Nashville Journal and Guide* all covered the unfolding story of the scientific investigation of Gullah. The *Journal and Guide* article, "Professor Studies Dialect: Lorenzo D. Turner," noted, "This dialect is rapidly disappearing, and Dr. Turner's purpose is to make a permanent record of it, not in conventional spelling, but by means of phonetic symbols. Phonographic records will serve as the basis for his study."[53] The press was interested for several reasons: Turner had been awarded a grant from the ACLS for his research, no doubt one of the first African Americans to receive such an award; his study of Gullah was in and of itself a first; and he was the chair of the Department of English at prestigious Fisk University.[54]

Turner's conscious path toward the publication that became *Africanisms in the Gullah Dialect* unfolded in stages. During the first stage of fieldwork in spring 1932, he planned to record Gullah in the Linguistic Atlas format. By the second stage, in summer 1933, he surmised that he should write separate Gullah monographs on phonology, morphology, and syntax while he simultaneously yearned to discover the source of the distinctive characteristics of the language. By the third stage, when he would spend the summer at the 1934 linguistic workshop at Brown University, he was committed to seeking answers to the question of the degree to which African languages had influenced Gullah.

In Turner's proposal to the ACLS for "A Descriptive Grammar of the Gullah Dialect: Statement of the Project," he advocated the immediate analysis of Gullah in order to "make a permanent record of it" before societal changes caused it to disappear: "Even though their speech, which is unique among the dialects of the country, has undergone little or no change since the seventeenth century, such a condition cannot long obtain, for contact with the outside world, which modern means of transportation and increasing advantages make inevitable, is daily becoming more and more easy and the distinctive characteristics of these people and their speech are gradually but surely disappearing."[55]

Turner's original intent was to utilize IPA transcription to record the speech of his informants, making "[c]omparisons . . . between certain words and phrases in Gullah and those in some of the British dialects of the seventeenth and eighteenth centuries." The concrete evidence that Gullah was more than seventeenth-century "English" developed as a result of his immersion in Gullah during 1932 and thereafter.[56]

Turner settled in the Sea Islands for the first time in the early months of 1932 and remained until September.[57] It was a riveting intellectual moment. He knew that he was on the cutting edge of a new field. To dissolve the suspicions of the Gullah people, who were accustomed to ridicule for their cultural and linguistic uniqueness, Turner sought out three distinct types of community leaders in Charleston to serve as intermediaries—a minister, a teacher, and a mortician.[58] There he became the first linguist to carry out systematic interviews of Gullah speakers. His informants spoke into his bulky, cumbersome electric recorder that weighed more than thirty pounds and utilized stainless steel magnetized wire the size of strands of human hair. The 3 3/4-inch diameter by 1 1/2-inch thick standard reel held 7,200 feet of wire. Turner placed the spool of wire on the supply reel. It moved through a groove in an electromagnetized head connected to an amplifier and microphone to the take-up reel, at a speed of 15 inches per second. Each spool absorbed approximately one hour of audio. When the wire tangled or broke, Turner trimmed the ends neatly, tying them into a square knot. Given the recording speed, he lost only a small amount of data in the process.[59]

The research process was both invigorating and challenging. Residing at 517 Rutledge Avenue in Charleston, South Carolina,[60] Turner arrived by boat each morning on one of the islands. Before he had begun data collection, his local contacts had arranged for him an introduction to informants. Having indicated to the residents that he was researching the history of the islands, he was able to encourage them to explore topics about which they were enthusiastic—the earthquake and tidal wave of August 1886, their religious life, music, dance, slavery, plantation life, farming, and freedom—thereby diverting attention from their idiolects in order to capture the creole in its most natural form.[61] Sometimes Turner interviewed individuals; other times he interviewed entire groups.[62]

Because of the rustic nature of the islands, electricity was in short supply. Sometimes Turner was invited to a site where it was available: "The religious shouts and spirituals were taken in an electrically fitted small building on the islands belonging to a northern woman who [had] bought one of the beautiful colonial plantation houses and become interested in the Turners' linguistic project."[63] On other occasions, Turner ferried informants to the mainland in order to take advantage of the electricity there.[64]

The northern woman was Lydia Parrish, who along with her husband, the American painter Maxfield Parrish, resided in Vermont but spent their winters on St. Simon Island. As an avocation, Parrish collected Gullah music. Turner collected some for her.[65] She published her findings as *Slave Songs of the Georgia Sea Islands* (1942).

In addition to Parrish, Turner gained the confidence and support of Dr. Y. W. Bailey and other officials of the Penn Normal, Industrial, and Agricultural School on St. Helena Island. In the preface to *Africanisms in the Gullah Dialect,* Turner paid special tribute to Mr. and Mrs. J. P. King. On Edisto, Wadmalaw, James, and Johns Islands, South Carolina, he found that the Rev. W. M. Metz, Lillian A. Patrick, Mrs. M. Fields, and Lorene Poinsette were especially supportive.[66]

The unending toil of Turner's days, filled with the grand surprises of stories told in a lilting language, was rivaled only by the long nights spent listening to and transcribing his data. It was a labor of love. Over the weeks and months Turner recorded in his notebooks the phonetics of his informants, chosen to conform to the Linguistic Atlas criteria, which called for at least two informants from each county, one "old fashioned and unschooled" and another of "the middle class who had had the benefit of a grade-school or high-school education."[67] He interviewed twenty-one Gullah speakers, filling a notebook on each with the details of his or her idiolect. To ensure that his data reflected differences from various generations, he intentionally selected two speakers over the age of sixty and one speaker between forty and sixty years of age from each of seven areas. In Georgia, Turner focused on Harris Neck and Brewer's Neck, Sapeloe Island, and St. Simon Island. In South Carolina, he focused on Edisto, Johns, St. Helena, and Wadmalaw Islands.[68]

Turner, an expert photographer as a result of his work as a newspaper editor, took black-and-white shots of his informants. Although no photographs appear in

Africanisms in the Gullah Dialect, no doubt because of cost constraints, Turner sometimes made photocopies of the photographs for course handouts that he distributed to students along with the informants' narratives.

While no fieldwork diary for Turner's Gullah work has been located, his various grant applications describe his methodology and accomplishments. Further, in 1934, at Kurath's request, Turner prepared a description of his field methodology to serve as a guide to other dialect geographers. Turner reported that as a rule he "spent six hours a day in field recording in each community, allowing two hours for each interview." The island he visited on a particular day depended in part on the tides and the schedule of the boats. He learned that he needed to make six to eight visits "to each informant before the worksheets were completed. . . . On the whole, the informants were generous in imparting information and seemed to enjoy the interviews," especially hearing themselves on the recordings. "To insure the fullest cooperation from [his] informants, [he] found it desirable to compensate them. [He] gave them tobacco, small parcels of groceries, or occasionally money."[69]

Turner's methodology evolved as his expertise as a field worker increased. Over time he collected data through three distinct but overlapping processes. The first involved the use of the Linguistic Atlas questionnaire, which contained one- or two-word responses that Turner transcribed phonetically. They are contained in his Linguistic Atlas notebooks on microfilm at the Joseph Regenstein Library of the University of Chicago.[70] His oral field recordings do not evidence the distinct and isolated questionnaire responses. Turner may have gleaned the responses in part from the spontaneous speech he recorded in the second process.

The second process involved machine recording the spontaneous oral performances of his informants as they sang, prayed, or recounted their life experiences. The original recording are preserved in the Archives of Traditional Music at Indiana University, Bloomington. They evidence African linguistic phonology and syntax but not semantics.

The third process, and the one most central to the thesis of *Africanisms in the Gullah Dialect,* involved Turner's immersing himself in Gullah culture so that his informants viewed him as a trusted insider. No Turner notebook or diary has been located that gives a key to how he achieved the collection of the six thousand "Africanisms," four thousand of which are incorporated in his book. They do not appear in his Linguistic Atlas notebooks or in the oral field recordings. The summer of 1933 may have been the occasion when Turner began to crack the Gullah code.

On the other hand, Michael Montgomery suggests, "it is possible that he began collecting by observation from the beginning. [The] naming practices [and other terms from African languages] represented communal and private knowledge that the Gullah did not readily share with outsiders, so that Turner was able to gain their trust enough for them to open their inner world to him was really what made the difference. Unless they had recognized a kindred spirit in Turner early on, *Africanisms in the Gullah Dialect* would never have been possible, no matter how hard Turner might have worked or how often he might have visited."[71] Turner maintained the data that was to become *Africanisms in the Gullah Dialect* in his personal files. It now appears in several draft forms in the Turner Collection at Northwestern University.

Turner interviewed men and women whose names and oral presentations are now part of American linguistic history. Among them was fifty-year-old Amelia Dawley from the Harris Neck peninsula, Georgia, who sang a Mende funeral chant for him in the summer of 1933.[72] Although Dawley was unaware of its purpose and translation, she was otherwise quite familiar with the song. Turner listed it as the first Gullah text in chapter 9 of *Africanisms in the Gullah Dialect.* It would be eight years before he could achieve a satisfactory translation, in this case by Solomon L. Caulker, a Mende student and minister with whom he interacted in 1941.[73]

Turner could have only suspected that the Dawley song was "the longest text in an African language that has been preserved by a Black family in the United States" and that it would continue to reach across time and space.[74] A half-century later Mary Moran, the daughter of Amelia Dawley, still remembered it in Gullah territory, and in Sierra Leone a Mende woman sang it, and it became the subject of the documentary *The Language You Cry In,* by Joseph Opala: "Everyone come together. Let us struggle (work hard). The grave is restless. The grave is not yet finished. Sudden death cuts down trees, borrows them; the remains disappear slowly. . . . Let his heart be perfectly at peace."[75]

The full text was provided to Opala and Cynthia Schmidt in 1997 by a Sierra Leonean linguist, Tazieff Koroma, and translated by Koroma, Edward Benya, and Opala. The head woman, Baindu Jabati, of the Mende village Senhum Ngola, recalled the song because her grandmother, understanding the value of a diminishing tradition, had insisted that she learn it. According to Jabati, women, traditionally charged with Mende funeral arrangements, sang the dirge in a ceremony called *teijami* or "crossing the river." *Teijami* was one aspect of the final graveside ceremonies for both men and women. Performed on the third day after a woman's funeral and the fourth day after a man's funeral, it symbolized the process of bridging the worlds of the living and the dead. Family members spent the night and a portion of the following day at the gravesite performing the final rites. After preparing and eating rice, the participants completed the ritual by turning the empty rice receptacle upside down, leaving it on the grave as a farewell symbol.[76]

On St. Simon, Turner recorded Julia Armstrong singing a Vai-Gullah song featuring food crops—rice, okra, and the need to plan for the future in moderation, to "eat some and save some."[77] He met Eugenia Hutchinson on Edisto, recording her as she sang another Vai song, a funeral chant similar to the one from Amelia Dawley. He met the seasoned elder, Diana Brown, who recalled slavery, vividly apprising Turner in the narrative he recounted as "Hard Times on Edisto" of the time the Red Cross distributed rice but somehow bypassed her house and that of four other elders. Given her age, experience, and the deep creole (language variety far from English in both grammar and vocabulary) she spoke, Turner considered her an ideal informant. He recorded her on multiple occasions; on one of them, she prayed a Gullah version of the Lord's Prayer. During the fall of 1932, Turner initiated the process of recording the life experiences of formerly enslaved African

Americans, a practice that was later continued in a large-scale project sponsored by the Works Progress Administration from 1936 to 1938.

Diana Brown, age ninety, was one of two who recounted her experiences of 1886, during and after the earthquake, when "that tide . . . [did] carry the people right down to the creek. Some dead on the place. You go there and meet some man broken."[78] Rosina Cohen of Edisto Island also recounted her recollection of the earthquake, while Hester Milligan of Edisto Island and Hanna Jenkins of Waccamaw Island shared the experiences of their religious conversions, in "Seeking Religion."[79]

One of the men Turner recorded was Prince Smith, who described, in "Farming on Wadmalaw during Slavery," the planting process in detail. In the beginning of his narrative, he detailed the preparation of the soil for the seeds: "When time come to set out to work, you list ground. From top of the bed, you bring the grass all down to the valley till the land done fix that way. Now when time to bank the ground, you will take your hoe in your hand again and now bank that land all around. There ain't any plow. When you get through with all that, and everything straighten up, and time come to plant, then you trench up top of the bed and put the seed in and cover up."[80]

Prince Smith's second narrative, "Punishing the Slaves on Wadmalaw," illustrates that Turner had become a trusted insider as it describes a recollection one would not likely recount to an outsider. Typical of slave contexts, the punishment regimen was designed to foster fear and maintain domination by dispensing pain capriciously. Often the punishment was not for notable transgressions but rather "if you couldn't done task. . . . Then they had a raw lash . . . flat. They don't give you a cut on your clothes; you naked. They cut you some place and the blood drain down on you. . . . Sometimes they draw out the traces from the buggy . . . and give you ten or fifteen lash."[81]

For each narrative in chapter 9, "Gullah Texts," Turner provided the IPA transcription on the left page and the English orthographic version on the right page. He was careful in his English translations to preserve some creolized features from the idiolect of each informant. In the case of Prince Smith, Turner maintained zero /s/ for third person singular, e.g., "time come__"; auxiliary verbs, e.g., "done fix"; zero copula, e.g., "you __ naked"; zero articles, e.g., "You trench up __ top"; zero /əd/, e.g., "everything straighten__"; and zero /s/ for noun plural, e.g., "fifteen lash__."[82]

Turner's final Gullah texts are from Samuel Polite, an elder from St. Helena Island. Polite recounted several narratives about his occupations, first as a farmer, in "Making Manure on St. Helena Island," and then, in "The Chief of the Stevedores," as a worker at the docks. Years later, to Turner's dismay and sorrow, Polite met an unexpected death when his pipe fell on his chest while he labored on his farm, seriously burning him. It was the summer of 1944. Polite was one hundred years old. He did not survive to see the publication of *Africanisms in the Gullah Dialect.*[83]

As Turner recorded informant after informant, he became more disillusioned with the "archaic English" and "baby talk" hypotheses. "No matter how many times Turner listened to [oral materials in Gullah]," Richard Ralston states, "he could not make English out of them. Meanwhile, the more he observed of Gullah dances, the more music he absorbed, the more he became convinced he was viewing an African derived culture that he did not fully understand."[84] According to Turner himself, "Finding in Gullah so many words and constructions that could not be explained on the basis of English . . . I decided that I should study several West African languages with a view to finding, if possible, an explanation of these strange characteristics."[85]

His desire to crack the code was insatiable. Increasingly, he considered another hypothesis: that is, if Pennsylvania Dutch had survived as a German dialect in America because of the relative isolation of its speakers, would not Gullah be "African language / English" because of the isolation of its speakers? Several researchers had already documented Pennsylvania Dutch as a German dialect in the United States.[86] No similar research had been conducted on the background of Gullah speakers. Pondering the possibilities inherent in this question led Turner to continue to seek historical data on the transportation of Africans to the Western Hemisphere and to consider the question of how to gain competence in African languages.

While the general public regarded Gullah as "broken English," the staff of the Linguistic Atlas anxiously anticipated an opportunity to examine Turner's data for the new insights it would reveal about American speech varieties. The four central members, director Hans Kurath, associate director Miles Hanley, assistant editor Bernard Bloch, and principal field investigator Guy Summer Lowman Jr., realized that Turner was exploring a linguistic gold mine. Lowman traveled with Turner during the summer of 1933 to sample the data.[87] According to Turner, the experience was awkward:

> A few years ago, I invited the late Dr. Guy S. Lowman, Jr. . . . to accompany me on one of my field trips to the Sea Islands. I wanted to see whether the impression Dr. Lowman got of the Gullah words, many of which were clearly not English, was similar to my own. On one of the Sea Islands, during an interview with one of my informants, Dr. Lowman unintentionally used a tone of voice which the informant resented. Instantly the interview ended. Apologies were of no avail. The informant refused to utter a word. In all the remaining interviews during that trip I talked and Dr. Lowman remained discreetly silent. On my return to the Sea Islands several weeks later, I was confronted on every hand with this question, *mɛk unə fa brIŋ dI bʌkra?* Meaning, "Why did you bring the white man?"[88]

In regular contact with Kurath, Turner periodically submitted his worksheets, accompanied by wire recordings, to the atlas headquarters at Yale in 1932 and Brown University thereafter. Kurath provided written feedback, particularly on processes to capture less broad and more precise transcriptions.[89] Eventually Lowman recorded speech samples from Turner's major informants.[90] By September 1932 Turner had traveled to New Haven to confer with Kurath, prompting Kurath to indicate his satisfaction with Turner's achievement: "I think you have been eminently successful in collecting the materials for an intensive study of the speech of Negroes on the islands along the coast of South Carolina. All students of American

English will welcome the appearance of an accurate account of the speech of these islands. Your texts will be genuine and accurate, and I look forward with pleasure to an authoritative treatment of the language on your part."[91]

Since the wire recordings were fragile, Turner often paid seventy cents per twelve-inch double-faced recording to have them copied to rubber, aluminum, or acetate. Turner would mail the wire recordings to Kurath, who, after listening to them, would send them to a Mr. Stone to be copied and returned with their originals to Turner.[92]

Turner's colleagues at the American Dialect Society likewise maintained contact with him as his fieldwork progressed. In late 1932 *Dialect Notes* featured a report, "Progress of the Linguistic Atlas," that mentioned the status of "the collection of New England material." The report then turned to the South. "The second area to be investigated will probably include Virginia, North and South Carolina, and Northeastern Georgia. . . . Professor Lorenzo D. Turner, of Fisk University . . . was able to study intensively the Gullah dialect as spoken in the islands off the coast of South Carolina. He has made over sixty phonograph records, and completed twelve transcripts, using the Atlas work sheets. Copies of these transcripts are now in the headquarters of the Atlas."[93]

As Miles Hanley, secretary of the American Dialect Society, completed plans for the annual December meeting, he mailed a form letter from Warren House at Harvard to the society members. "Circular Letter to Persons Interested in American Dialect, Especially Gullah" notified society members and nonmembers that they were invited to Turner's presentation on Gullah. Pointing out that Turner had spent a number of months on the Sea Islands "to study intensively the speech of negroes living in the islands off the coast of South Carolina," he established the time as December 31, 1932, at 11:00 A.M., in Room 22 of the Yale University Law School. "As usual," the meeting was being "held jointly with that of the Modern Language Association of America in New Haven."[94]

For the first time, on December 31, 1932, Turner began introducing other linguists to his research. (He also presented a lecture on his data at the New York Public Library's 135th Street [Schomburg] Branch during Christmas break.[95]) Turner was bringing to the table his fieldwork as a trained linguist and as the first researcher to view Gullah as more than a casual observer. Many recognized the presentation as a breakthrough. Before this time, "there was no understanding of Gullah as a dynamic, coherent, and distinct language, one with an evolving, adapting, and patterned structure and a complex history of its own. Rather, early commentators had seen Gullah as a collection of words corrupted either from English or as a repository of archaic features preserved from contact with whites and traceable to dialects from the British Isles."[96] Turner described Gullah as a distinctive linguistic variety as he played selectively from among the recordings he had collected during six months of 1932 on Johns, Edisto, Wadmalaw, and St. Helena Islands.

In discussing his research methodology, Turner explained to the audience that his interviews utilizing the Linguistic Atlas questionnaire had resulted in not only worksheets but also more than one hundred recordings. He then elaborated on some unique aspects of tone, syntax, and morphology. In his discussion Turner noted a number of the features now documented as being prominent in African-derived creoles, among them, zero final consonants ("and" = /an/), zero copula ("Thine is the kingdom" = /dɒɪn ___ dɪ kɪŋdəm/), zero final *r* ("power" + /pɒwə/), and zero *eth* ("those" = /doz/). Turner also indicated semantic items with second-syllable stress in English that have first-syllable stress in Gullah, among them, "July," "hotel," "begin," and "machine." One of the recordings Turner played featured a Gullah version of the Lord's Prayer.[97]

In the Yale presentation, Turner noted that on some islands the Gullah was further from the Standard English continuum than on others, so that he, a native of nearby North Carolina, "was compelled to take an interpreter with him" to Edisto Island. His informants were "three native subjects on each of the four islands who had a minimum of contact off the islands." He underscored that the speech of the women selected was less influenced by "the marks of outsiders" than that of the men, suggesting the idea of a creole continuum, although he did not use the phrase. It did not enter regular usage until the 1960s.[98]

Hanley had also notified the press of the American Dialect Society lecture. A *New York Times* reporter arrived to cover the lecture. The following day, Sunday, January 1, 1933, the *Times* headline read, "Records in Gullah Heard by Linguists: Dialect of Coastal Negroes of South Carolina Is Presented at Yale Session (Unique Study Described)."[99] On Monday, January 2, 1933, the *New York Times* featured a second article titled "Topics of the Times: Gullah."[100] Turner, having discussed his one hundred recordings, the Gullah version of "The Lord's Prayer" (probably from Diana Brown), and several phonological characteristics, concluded by drawing parallels between Gullah and Oxford English. The article made no comment, however, on the possibility of African-language influence, which suggests that since Turner could not yet provide corroborating evidence, he did not raise the issue in his initial lecture. It did note that "there is an almost startling resemblance here to Oxford English, at least as we read it in this country. The Gullah speakers say 'een' heaven just as Oxford—and Boston very often says 'has bean,' where most of us say 'had bin.' And 'fuhgive' and 'delivuh' and 'powuh' exhibit the same careless, slurring liberties with 'er' and 'or' sound that is the privilege of the British upper classes."[101]

Additional newspapers took note of the lecture, especially those on the African American syndicate. On Saturday, January 14, 1933, the *Washington Sentinel* ran an article, "Gullah: South Carolina Dialect Studied by Linguists." After detailing the context of Turner's presentation, it pointed out the uniqueness of Turner's research by noting that most of those whom he had interviewed had minimal exposure to life beyond their home islands and that, "their parents for several generations had been natives of the islands."[102] The *Pittsburgh Courier,* the same Saturday, featured "Records of Strange Gullah Dialect Made for Scientists." A sidebar listed a number of Gullah semantic items and their English translations.[103]

On April 13, 1933, Turner received notification that the ACLS had awarded him three hundred dollars to continue his Gullah research.[104] Therefore, during the summer of 1933, he returned to the Sea Islands for data collection on the Georgia side. Geneva accompanied him as a collaborator. They received their mail in care of, and no doubt resided with, a Dr. Jackson at 1506 Albany Street, in Brunswick, Georgia.[105]

During the following summer, from June 16 to September 8, 1934, both Turners attended a linguistic workshop at Brown University in Rhode Island. Kurath had joined the faculty at Brown in 1931 as a member of the German department. Although Kurath was the organizer and many of the principals were the same, the workshop at Brown was not sponsored by the Linguistic Society of America.

The *Providence Evening Bulletin* ran an article on August 13, 1934, prompted by the Turners' attendance at the 1934 workshop. During the winter of 1932, Geneva, still an elementary school teacher by day, had "spent her evenings studying phonetics in order to be ready to become her husband's associate and scribe" in the summer of 1933. At the 1934 workshop, together they reported on the progress of the research, often smiling "in recollection of the occasions when they heard the stories in the south."[106] The article also noted that "Mrs. Turner worked intensively with her husband on the Georgia islands recording on paper what he was taking by machine,"[107] a reference to her transcribing data onto the eight-hundred-item Linguistic Atlas questionnaire.

A second article, "Linguists from All Parts of Country Meet at Brown University," from the *Providence Journal,* was illustrated with a photograph of those in attendance. The roster—Bert Emsley of Ohio State; Claude Wise of Louisiana State University; Herbert Penzl, Hans Kurath, Bernard Bloch, and Mrs. Norman Kilpatrick of Brown; Elizabeth F. Gardner and Margaret Chase of Mt. Holyoke; Marguerite Chapallaz of University College of London; Samuel J. McCoy of William and Mary College; Mrs. Bernard Bloch of Wellesley; Jane E. Daddow of Vassar; Archibald A. Hill of the University of Virginia; and Eston E. Ericson of the University of North Carolina as well as the Turners—stands as testimony that Turner was well connected with his contemporaries in the world of language studies and linguistics.[108] *Dialect Notes* of the same year listed Turner as a member of the summer staff for the Linguistic Atlas project.[109]

By the winter of 1934, Turner was prepared to pursue the African retentions hypothesis in earnest. On December 3, 1934, he contacted Leland at the ACLS, saying, "My work on the descriptive grammar of the Gullah dialect is progressing well." Turner broached the subject that would define the core of his life work, establishing a connection between Africans in Gullah territory and those in the British West Indian islands of Jamaica and Barbados. "I have become curious to know more about the speech of the latter group [West Indians], as well as something of the possible African influence on the speech of both groups. To be able to make the proper kind of investigation of this subject, I shall need some acquaintance with the speech of the Negroes in those sections of Africa from which the West-Indian and the Sea-Island Negroes of America came."[110]

His conversations with Lowman had led Turner to consider studying African languages at the School of Oriental (and later African) Studies at the University of London. Lowman, having earned a doctorate from the University of London in 1931,[111] had apprised Turner of the course offerings on the phonetics of African languages. Turner wrote Leland, "I have talked with Dr. Guy S. Lowman, of the

Linguistic Atlas staff, concerning the matter, and he informs me that the preparation I need can be obtained at the School of Oriental . . . Studies at the University of London."[112]

The major purpose of Turner's letter to Leland was to initiate a dialogue about the possibility of a grant to pursue studies of, first, the phonetics of African languages (nine months), then Jamaican Creole (three months), to be followed by Barbadian Creole (three months). At that point he expected that he would be prepared to construct a comparative analysis of Gullah, Jamaican, and Barbadian, with an eye toward documenting the African language influence in all three. Turner requested application forms, indicating his desire to study in London in fall 1935.[113]

His plans did not progress as rapidly as he had proposed. The ACLS did not award him funds to spend that fall in London, although he would go there in 1936–37, and he pursued alternative options as his burning commitment to cracking the Gullah code propelled him forward. He was unable to silence the call to locate answers to the mystery that Gullah represented.

According to the statement of work for a later grant proposal, Turner spent approximately fourteen months all together in Gullah territory gathering linguistic data and making between "250 to 300 double-faced phonograph records of folktales, proverbs, songs, prayers, sermons, and other narratives."[114] Although Turner interviewed a number of additional speakers over the years, the original twenty-one were his major informants. When he returned to the Sea Islands in the summer of 1933, his purpose had been to expand his study with data from the Georgia islands. From March 13 to March 23, 1938, he arranged for other professors and graduate students to cover his classes while he spent ten days collecting data in the Sea Islands.[115] The week in March 1938 was Turner's first opportunity to listen to his Gullah informants with the new ears and insights he had cultivated at the University of London. He returned again in the summer of 1939, and he engaged in data collection on the Sea Islands for the last time in 1942.[116]

Over a period of years between 1932 and 1949, Turner presented several conference papers on Gullah.[117] He was thorough in his approach to evaluating the sources of the loan words and in attempting to establish correspondences between Gullah and other Western Hemisphere creoles in areas with significantly large African populations. The quest found him seeking opportunities either to study linguistics or to conduct fieldwork in the identified geographic regions.[118]

Between Turner's initial presentation on the final day of 1932 and the publication of *Africanisms in the Gullah Dialect* in 1949, he published three articles on Gullah. The first, "Linguistic Research and African Survivals," appeared in 1941 in the *ACLS Bulletin,* after Turner presented a version of it in 1940 at the ACLS Conference on Negro Studies. His major thesis was that Gullah researchers were confronted with several handicaps. The first was the adamant stance of "American students of language" that the African element in Gullah was negligible. He mentioned Ambrose Gonzales, H. L. Mencken, Reed Smith, and Guy Johnson, in particular. Noting that Gonzales had overlooked many Africanisms by describing them as "corruptions" of American English lexical items, Turner pointed out several examples. Among them was /loni/, which Gonzales believed was a corruption of *alone.* Turner's research indicated that it was plausibly the retention of the Mende root /loni/ ("standing, is standing"); /taloni/ ("he is standing"); and /i loni/ ("he is not standing"). He found it troubling that in Mencken's 1937 edition of *The American Language,* Mencken asserted that African Americans had inherited no "given names from their African ancestors." According to Turner, Mencken made this claim even though, "so far as I know, [he] never made any inquiries of the Gullahs concerning their given names."[119] After quoting statements from each of the four previously mentioned commentators in which they repudiated the African retentions hypothesis, Turner asserted, "It should be noted in fairness to the writers whose views on Gullah have just been quoted, that the Gullah Negro when talking to strangers is likely to use speech that for the most part is English in vocabulary, being different in this respect from his speech when he talks to his associates and to members of his family."[120]

Turner then clarified an issue that several contemporary researchers have pondered, that is, why his early field transcriptions manifested few IPA transcriptions of phonemes, tones, and semantic items from Niger-Congo languages. "My first phonograph recordings of the speech of the Gullah Negroes contain fewer African words by far than those made when I was no longer a stranger to them. One has to live among them to know their speech well."[121] Turner surmised that the questioning of the presence of African-language retentions was a handicap unique to the American context, as, "I should think that in Brazil, for example, it would be taken for granted that there are such survivals."[122]

A second handicap facing both linguists and ethnologists was the dearth of "adequate historical documents" to track the importation and geographic resettlement of Africans to the Western Hemisphere. He noted that the problem was more severe in Brazil than in the United States as the Brazilian government had ordered many documents pertaining to slavery to be destroyed circa 1888; Elizabeth Donnan's *Documents Illustrative of the History of the Slave Trade to America* (1930–35) had proven "most helpful" in verifying the numbers of Africans from certain territories on the African continent who were resettled in their eventual homes in the United States.[123]

If the dearth of documents on the numbers and ethnic backgrounds of Africans removed from various geographic areas in Africa presented a research dilemma, a third and equally confounding handicap resulted from the dearth of reliable historical and anthropological studies of the African ethnic groups under consideration. Turner spoke favorably of the work of Melville Herskovits on Dahomey (now Benin), W. D. Hambly on the Ovimbundu, Henri Labouret on the Mandingoes, and William Bascom and Joseph Greenberg on the Yoruba and Hausa. He called for research on the Wolof, Bambara, Mende, Vai, Twi, Gã, Fanti, Temne, Susa, Kongo, Mandinka, Ibo, Efik, and Fula. Turner underscored the need for studies undertaken by Africans themselves and by Americans, in addition to those undertaken by Europeans.[124]

A fourth handicap was the dearth of grammars and dictionaries of African languages. In English-speaking geographic areas of Africa, with a few notable exceptions, "missionaries who have had little or no training in linguistics" had compiled most of the work. With the exception of the work of Delafosse and Labouret in French-speaking territories, the same reality pertained. Consequently, Turner called for descriptive linguistic analyses featuring phonology, morphology, syntax, and semantics, including "the marking of lexical tones and well-developed texts."[125]

After studying African languages and, subsequently, subjecting his data to scrutiny informed by his recent insights, Turner was able to determine that "a great many Mende and Vai were sold on Harris Neck, Georgia, and on other plantations nearby, because most of the many African words I have collected there are from these languages." He asserted further, "Likewise, there must have been a great many Kongos sold on St. Simons Island, Georgia," since, "in many families on this island, the names of all the children are Kongo words. This is true also of the names of birds, animals, and plants."[126]

In his conclusion Turner listed a number of the linguistic and anthropological studies he had found helpful. He then called for studies similar to his to be undertaken in other African American communities where African cultural and linguistic retentions were likely to be abundant, among them sections of Louisiana, southern Alabama, Mississippi, and the eastern edges of Florida, North Carolina, and Virginia. The proposal that was considered the most radical by his contemporaries was the suggestion that certain white communities "where contact between the races has been close" be studied for "African linguistic survivals."[127]

Some of Turner's recommendations have been pursued in part, with a number of researchers conducting comparative research related to black and white dialects, more in the North than in the South. Between 1936 and 1938 field workers collected narratives and music from formerly enslaved African Americans for the Federal Writers' Project.[128] The first systematic investigations of black/white speech relations developed from the editing of the field records of the *Linguistic Atlas of the Middle and South Atlantic States* (*LAMSAS*). Kurath concluded, "The speech of uneducated . . . [blacks] exhibits the same regional and local variation as that of the simple white folk."[129] A few years later Raven I. McDavid and Virginia McDavid utilized *Linguistic Atlas* methodology to compare black/white southern speech, in the first article documenting twenty or more African terms (such as goober, gumbo, and okra), several grammatical elements, and phonological forms adopted by whites. McDavid expanded his observations in a number of other articles, among them his 1972 article coauthored with Lawrence M. Davis.[130]

The black informants made up 20 percent of the one thousand interviews recorded in Georgia, Florida, Alabama, Tennessee, Arkansas, Mississippi, Louisiana, and eastern Texas during fieldwork for the *Linguistic Atlas of the Gulf States* (*LAGS*), completed in 1983. Almost 15 percent of the informants for the *Dictionary of American Regional English* (*DARE*) were black.[131] In the 1970s Walt Wolfram and Wolfram and Donna Christian analyzed white southern and Appalachian speech for parallels to black speech. In the 1980s Ralph W. Fasold et al. debated the divergence issue.[132]

In "Notes on the Sound and Vocabulary of Gullah," Turner described the Gullah-speaking region, his research methodology, and the African background of the

Gullah people. He then listed by name his twenty-one major Gullah informants across six islands and one mainland area, elaborating on the phonetics of Gullah, particularly the vowels and consonants. He described the tonal nature of eight West African languages, that is, the high, mid, and low tones that influenced Gullah most substantially, as well as the glides from one tone to another. His focus was on the eight languages for which he was able to locate verification of the tone markings in articles and dictionaries, namely, Twi, Fante, Ewe, Ibo, Efik, Ibibio, Vai, and Yoruba. He identified eleven vowels, three diphthongs, and eighteen consonants in Gullah. For the first time linguists were provided data illustrating the systematic nature of the Gullah phonetic system: palatal plosives; the zero consonant clusters; zero final /r/; zero /r/ before consonants; /l/ in medial position where other dialects of American English utilize /r/; a number of African-language consonant combinations in initial position, such as /kp/, /gb/, /mp/, /nd/, /nt/, and /ɽ/; and the velar nasal in initial position.[133]

In the next section of the article, Turner discussed retained African/Gullah proper names, making a distinction between Niger-Congo semantic items utilized in actual conversation and those semantic items, phrases, and sentences utilized only in songs. He presented a list of semantic items with their IPA forms in African languages side-by-side with the English pronunciations and glosses.

For the first time in print, Turner indicated the breadth of his work. By 1942 he had collected five to six thousand lexical items, with "approximately four-fifths of these . . . now used only as personal names." Some of these were the "basket names," exclusive, personal names used only by family and friends. To illustrate the African naming practices among the Gullah, Turner categorized the names by circumstances: time of birth; physical condition or appearance of child; temperament, character, and mental capacity; religion, magic, and charms; greetings, commands, and explanations; and place of birth. Among the Gullah, [sam bi] is a male name whose origins Turner documented to Kongo "worshiper." A "vigorous, active" child might be named [ka' mal e] from the Bambara. Turner detailed terms utilized in conversation, among them ['bi di'bi di], "a small bird" in Kongo; [gʌm bɔ], "okra" with variants in Tshiluba and Umbundu; [ŋ gu ba], "peanut" with variants in Kimbundu, Umbundu, and Kongo; and one of the most widely dispersed African roots, [tot], "to carry," with variants in KiKongo, Kongo, Kimbundu, Umbundu, and Mende. Each of these semantic items and a number of others, particularly pertaining to verbs of action and the names of animals, plants, and food, were well known throughout the South. However, Turner apparently did not wish to make claims larger than he was prepared to substantiate. Therefore, in his research he focused only on Gullah, leaving additional claims to others.[134]

"Notes on the Sounds and Vocabulary of Gullah" is written with the same meticulous detail and scholarly attention as *Africanisms in the Gullah Dialect,* which was to follow in eight years. The editor's note preceding the article pointed out that the "Notes" section was extracted from "the wealth of [Turner's] forthcoming book," which will "probably be published by the Linguistic Society of America."[135]

Turner's third Gullah article was "Problems Confronting the Investigator of Gullah."[136] Appearing one year before *Africanisms in the Gullah Dialect,* it outlined four prerequisites for conducting Gullah research. They were adequate knowledge of conditions surrounding the importation of Africans to the Western Hemisphere; acquaintance with the speech of Western Hemisphere Africans who have had no contact with seventeenth- and eighteenth-century English in areas such as Brazil and Haiti in order to compare their speech characteristics with those in Gullah; familiarity with African culture and with languages—including the phonology, morphology, syntax, semantics, and tones—in the areas from which Western Hemisphere Africans were taken; and sufficient acquaintance with Gullah informants so that they "will feel no necessity for using a form of speech which they commonly reserve for strangers."[137]

To illustrate the African-language influence in Gullah, Turner offered semantic items that others had labeled as nonsense words. He then indicated their phonetic forms and etymology in African languages. In the process, he explained the absence of the voiced *th* sound, [ð] *eth,* the use of aspect, the use of the "verbal adjective," and the approach to word formation. The article provided an excellent glimpse of Turner's research methodology and samples of his data on the Gullah Creole.[138] He subsequently incorporated major concepts and portions of the three articles in the introductory chapters of *Africanisms in the Gullah Dialect.*

Making use of his own intuitions, heightened by the linguistic background acquired from the two Linguistic Institutes, the linguistic workshop at Brown University, and the instruction from Ida Ward and others at the School of Oriental Studies, Turner was determined to construct an indisputable case for retained Africanisms. In the process, he utilized methods that were not fully articulated until years after the publication of his major work. His criteria for determining if semantic items were genetically related prefigured those Joseph Greenberg articulated in *Essays in Linguistics* (1957). According to Greenberg, if terms from different languages are related, their similarities will be the result of more than chance. There must be recurrent phonetic resemblances, semantic plausibility, breadth of distribution (in languages of the same family or subgroup), length of the form, participation in parallel irregular forms, and occurrence of sound correspondences found in other etymologies which are strong on the same grounds. That is, the sequence of phonemes must be similar; the lexical items must be similar or related in meaning or could have plausibly resulted from an original meaning; they must appear in several genetically related languages; they must contain a number of phonemes or consist of more than one syllable; and the related languages must contain other lexical items that are parallel in phonological structure.[139] Underlying Turner's Gullah research is use of the major elements of these criteria, as is evident in chapter 3, "West African Words in Gullah," the core of *Africanisms in the Gullah Dialect.*[140]

Turner had played a major role in defining creole studies at the ground floor, at a juncture before creoles had gained centrality in linguistic research and when "the few sources that existed were inaccessible to most scholars."[141] Turner referred to Gullah as "creolized English,"[142] focusing on the work of Americans who reproduced Gullah fictionally or commented directly on it, that of Africanists who produced dictionaries and grammars of African languages, and that of African retention theorists from the Caribbean and Latin America.[143]

Turner's study of Gullah and the paths to which it led him transformed him into a linguist and creolist and into an early cultural nationalist. Among the influences in the transformation was the development of the Harlem Renaissance. Turner was a "New Negro," to use Alain Locke's 1925 phrase from the book of the same name. Born at the cusp of the new century, Turner was socially conscious and adventurous. His cultural nationalism, no doubt sparked by his father but kindled by Woodson and his colleagues in the Association for the Study of Negro Life and History, was reinforced and complemented by the cultural retentions model of the Harlem Renaissance era. That model incorporated national and international movements, including European romanticism, Marcus Garvey's nationalism, and the Boasian concept of pluralism/particularism. It was the theoretical opposite of the assimilation model.

During Turner's years at the University of Chicago, the Chicago school of sociology was in vogue. Its major proponent, the sociologist Robert Park, utilized an assimilation model of race relations, proposing that whenever non-European people interact for a significant period with Europeans, adaptation follows a sequential pattern. That is, competition leads to conflict; conflict leads to accommodation; and accommodation ultimately leads to assimilation. From Park's perspective, virtually nothing African had been retained among blacks in the diaspora.[144] Park influenced a generation of sociologists and other social scientists, among them E. Franklin Frazier and Charles S. Johnson.[145]

Turner did not adopt the tenets of the Chicago school. It is worth noting that his exposure to it was significant, first during his years as a graduate student in Chicago between 1919 to 1926 and then at Fisk, where he was in contact with Park and E. Franklin Frazier, author *of The Negro Family in the United States* (1939). Frazier served on the faculty at Fisk from 1929 to 1934.[146]

Turner's protracted study and analysis of Gullah, his study of Louisiana Creole, Brazilian Portuguese, and Sierra Leone Krio, the major foci of his career and energy, would not have figured prominently in his life had he been an adherent of Park's views. When Turner and Frazier both conducted research in Brazil in 1940–41, Frazier did not accept or analyze the retention and syncretism of African culture in Brazil, except in religion, while Turner did. The most logical explanation for Frazier's position lies in his strong adherence to the tenets of the Chicago school of sociology.

By the summer of 1935 Turner was in search of another creole in the United States derived from an African language. Each June, President Jones mailed Fisk faculty members a letter requesting that they respond to five questions related to summer plans. Turner's July 4, 1935, return letter indicated that he was teaching summer school at Alcorn A&M College in Mississippi, "and spending my weekends making phonographic recordings of Creole in Louisiana. From July 9 to 20 I shall give all my time to this work, making New Orleans and Lafayette, Louisiana my headquarters; then I shall proceed north by way of Nashville."[147]

Turner remained in Louisiana at least until July 22, during which time he collected ten recordings, some speech, and some music. He recorded Jessie Covington and Paul Juon singing a Liszt and Chopin duet; other music in Louisiana

Creole, sometimes by unidentified persons; and Creole conversations with George Doyle (a former New Orleans police officer), Roman Bourges and Emma Broussard, Alvina Charlot, Josef Damas, and Louis (Le Tête) Napolean, among others.[148]

Over the next few years, Turner would embark on a number of journeys that would forge him into a pan-African creolist and cultural historian.[149] The first would lead him not to Africa but to Europe and to the University of London.

Lorenzo Dow Turner at his desk, 1949. By permission of Lois Turner Williams, Chicago

Rooks Turner (Lorenzo Turner's father) in later years. By permission of Lois Turner Williams, Chicago

(left) Elizabeth Freeman Turner (Lorenzo Turner's mother). Photograph by Addison Scurlock; used by permission of Lois Turner Williams, Chicago

(below) Lorenzo Dow Turner as a child, ca. 1898. By permission of Lois Turner Williams, Chicago

Rooks Turner Jr. on veranda, ca. 1910. By permission of Lois Turner Williams, Chicago

Arthur Turner in academic attire on receiving his law degree from Howard University, 1912. By permission of Lois Turner Williams, Chicago

Lorenzo Dow Turner (*1st row, 2nd from right*) on the Howard University baseball team, 1912. By permission of Lois Turner Williams, Chicago

Lorenzo Dow Turner (*2nd row, 3rd from left*) and the Beta Chapter of Alpha Phi Alpha, 1912. By permission of Lois Turner Williams, Chicago

(above) Lorenzo Dow Turner (*center*) and the Howard University Debate Team, 1913. By permission of Lois Turner Williams, Chicago

(left) Lorenzo Dow Turner, 1914. Photograph by Addison Scurlock; used by permission of Lois Turner Williams, Chicago

Lorenzo Dow Turner, 1929. Photograph by Arthur P. Bedou; used by permission of Lois Turner Williams, Chicago

Geneva Calcier Townes Turner, ca. 1929. By permission of the Moorland-Spingarn Research Center, Howard University, Washington, D.C.

(above) Lorenzo Dow Turner (*3rd row, 3rd from left*) and Fisk University faculty, 1929. By permission of Fisk University Franklin Library Special Collections, Fisk University, Nashville

(left) Gullah informant on porch, 1932. By permission of Lois Turner Williams, Chicago

Lois Morton and Lorenzo Dow Turner on their wedding day, September 1, 1938 (*left to right:* Claudia Jenkins, Lois Morton Turner, Lorenzo Dow Turner, Robert Hemingway). By permission of Lois Turner Williams, Chicago

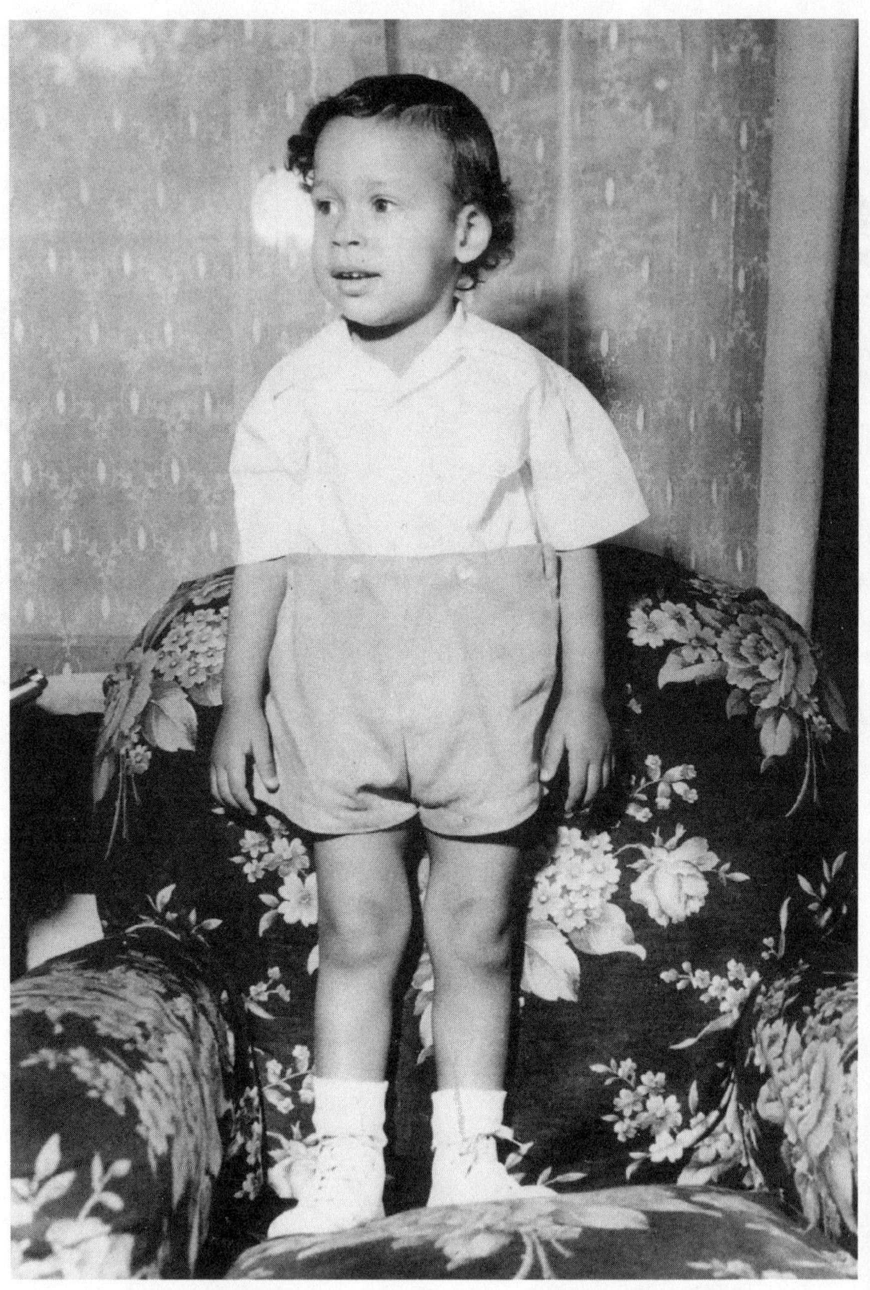

Lorenzo Dow Turner Jr. (age 2), 1945. By permission of Lois Turner Williams, Chicago

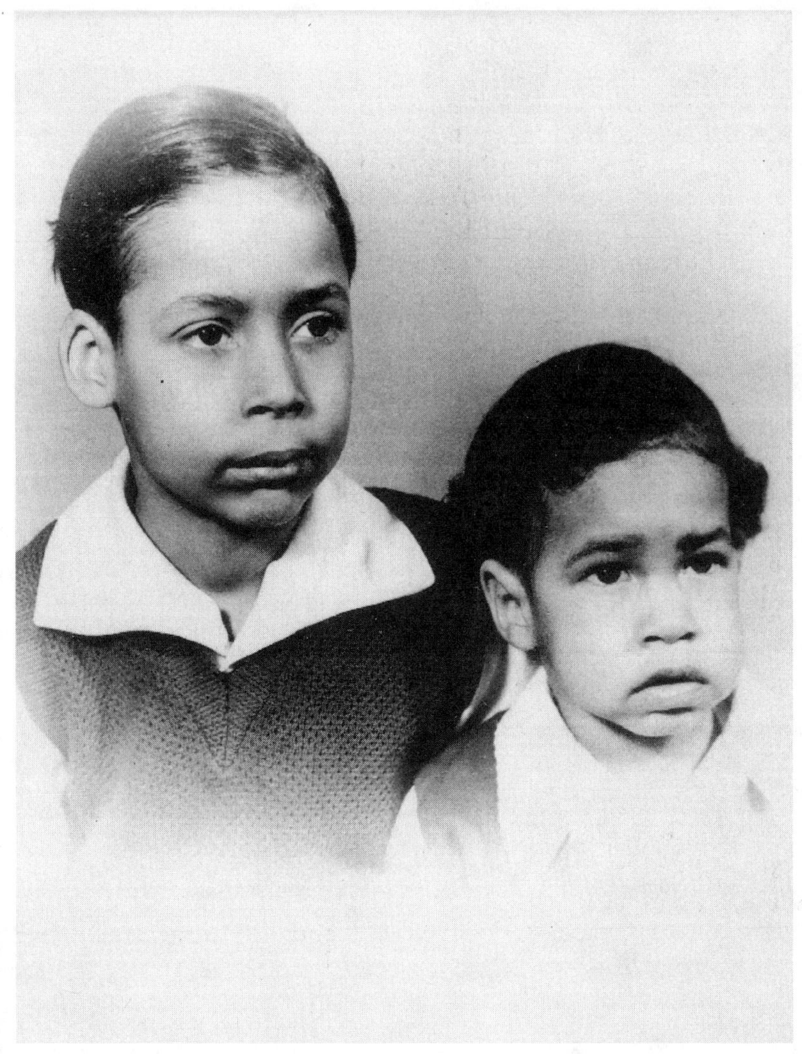

Lorenzo Dow Turner Jr. and Rani Meredith Turner, ca. 1951. By permission of Lois Turner Williams, Chicago

Theodora Maria Cardoza Alcântara (African name: Adʒaji), Brazil, 1940. By permission of Lois Turner Williams, Chicago

The present and former heads of a Dahomean cult ("born in Brazil of Dahomean parents. Both speak Fõn fluently") in Bahia, Brazil, 1940. By permission of Lois Turner Williams, Chicago

Donald Pierson, E. Franklin Frazier, Marie Frazier, and Lorenzo Dow Turner in Brazil, 1940. By permission of Lois Turner Williams, Chicago

Group at Fisk University. *(Front row):* Ako Adjei, Fatima Massaquoi, Charles S. Johnson (sociology); *(second row):* Lorenzo Dow Turner, Mark Hanna Watkins (anthropology), Jacob Motsi, Edwin Smith, ca. 1943. By permission of Fisk University Franklin Library Special Collections, Fisk University, Nashville

Yoruba prince in Nigeria, 1951. By permission of Lois Turner Williams, Chicago

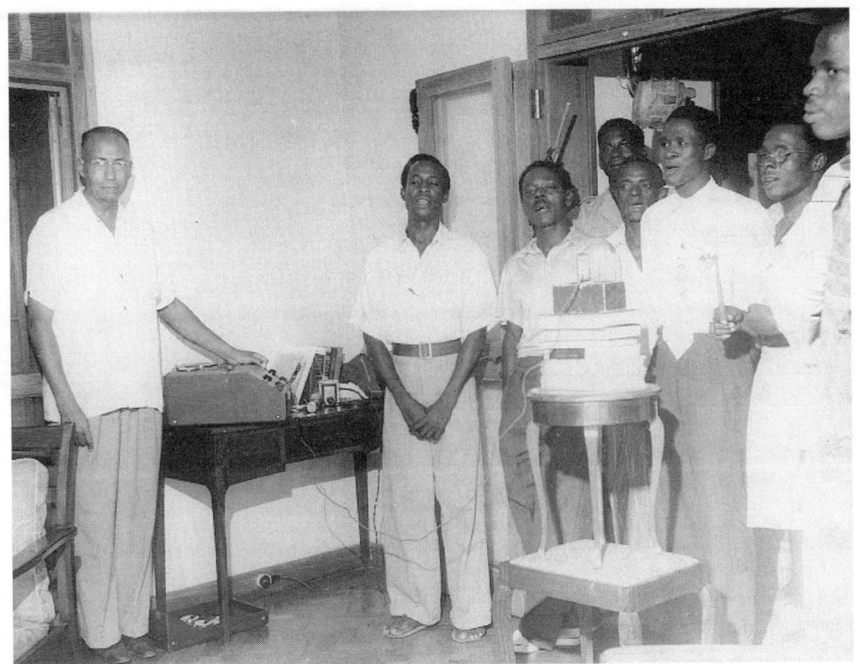

Lorenzo Dow Turner recording men singing in Nigeria, 1951. By permission of Lois Turner Williams, Chicago

Lorenzo Dow Turner's most prized African sculptures. By permission of Lois Turner Williams, Chicago

Lorenzo Dow Turner with talking drum, Chicago, 1952. Photograph by Norman Sklarewitz for the *Pittsburgh Courier,* used by permission of Roosevelt University, Chicago

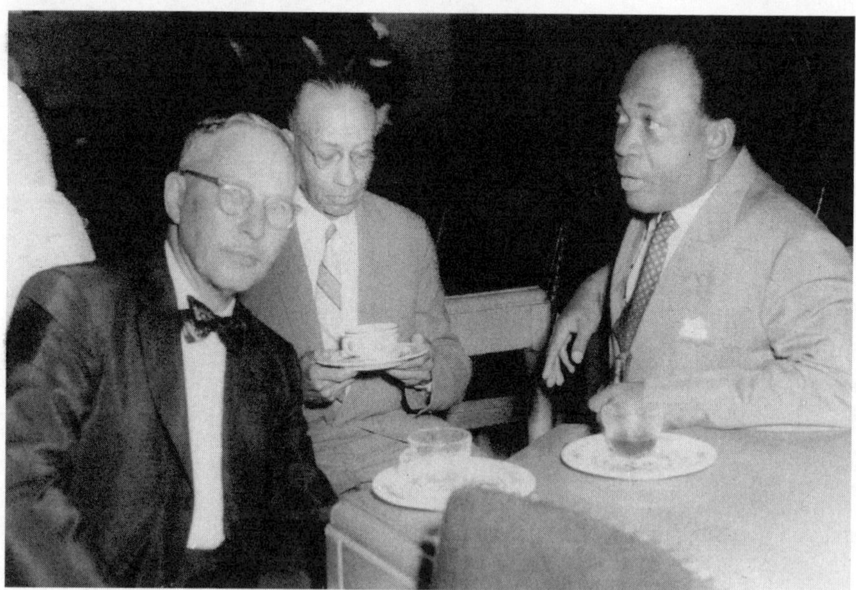

Left to right: Melville Herskovits, Lorenzo Dow Turner, and Kwame Nkrumah (president of Ghana) at Roosevelt University, October 15, 1958. By permission of Lois Turner Williams, Chicago

14

The University of London 1936–1937

> For almost 160 years London's university institutions have played a leading and innovative role in the development of higher education. From the pioneering days of the 1820s, when the first colleges were established to challenge the supremacy of Oxford and Cambridge, London has been in the forefront of educational advance.
>
> —Publicity Office, University of London

ALTHOUGH THE UNIVERSITY OF LONDON dates from the 1820s, the School of Oriental Studies was not founded until 1917. It continued to bear the name School of Oriental Studies until 1938, a year after Turner had completed his work, after which it was renamed the School of Oriental and African Studies.[1] Prior to 1930 "the world-center for the study of Africa had been the University of Berlin. But with Hitler's rise to power, many faculty members moved to the University of London."[2]

By 1917 formalized colonialism in Africa was almost two decades old and deeply entrenched. Europeans who planned careers in government service or missionary work in African countries needed some grounding in African languages to navigate the cultural terrain; the school served their needs. Other students were bankers, members of the military, or employees in business houses. Some were "occasional students" who attended when time permitted. Over time the school received grants in three-year cycles from the Rockefeller Foundation, "towards the development of research into African linguistics and phonetics. . . . The funds [were to] be devoted exclusively to linguistic research, to be conducted both in London and in Africa."[3] A number of individuals, corporations, and businesses provided yearly grants. The list for the year ending in July 1936 covers almost an entire page.[4] It underscores the extent to which European nations depended on the School of Oriental Studies to prepare personnel for government and corporate service in the colonies.

Turner, realizing that it was necessary to study African languages in order to construct an accurate analysis of his Gullah data, began to seek grant support. After the 1934 workshop at Brown University, he began to make inquiries of foundations. In the meantime, seeking to draw cross-linguistic comparisons, he decided to explore the African element in Louisiana Creole. His need for summer employment may have been his original motivation to consider Alcorn. On the other hand, his active pursuit of a Louisiana Creole research site may have fortuitously coincided with his having received a teaching appointment in a Mississippi university near the Louisiana border.[5] In any case, Turner agreed to teach in the seventy-second summer session at the Alcorn A&M College in Lorman, Mississippi, also an HBCU, from June 5 to July 9, 1935.[6]

When the session concluded, Turner traveled to nearby Louisiana, spending the remainder of his summer near New Orleans, locating and interviewing informants and recording data in Louisiana Creole.[7] His methodology replicated the Linguistic Atlas structure that he utilized for his Gullah fieldwork. Since French was among the languages he had studied at Howard during the 1911–12 academic year, he was able to summon enough French to analyze the French element in Louisiana Creole. His analysis of the African element would have to wait until his year in London. By the end of summer 1935, Turner had assembled a large corpus of Gullah Creole data and a smaller one of Louisiana Creole, the raw material he planned to subject to his African-language retentions hypothesis as he pursued and absorbed African-language phonetics and morpho-syntactic structure in London.

In the fall of 1935, Turner contacted Moe of the Guggenheim Foundation regarding his research funding proposal, indicating that he wanted to study African languages at the University of London in order to identify the non-Indo-European element in Gullah. On March 14, Moe mailed him a letter of regret. On March 30, 1936, Turner received a list of 1936 recipients, along with their topics and affiliations.[8]

At a time when blacks were tokens afloat in the sea of foundation grant awards, foundations often considered one award to an African American to be sufficient. In 1936 the one was not Turner. It was the second occasion the Guggenheim had failed to support his research. Some evaluators may have considered the idea that someone could study African languages in London, and then return to the United States and document African linguistic retentions in an African American creole far-fetched. Since creole was not yet a well-defined linguistic construct, most Americans viewed any form of African American speech as simply an incorrect, uneducated version of English. This stereotypical view was reinforced by popular literature and the nascent movie industry that depicted black dialectal patterns as indicators of inferiority and ignorance.

The single black recipient of a Guggenheim for 1936 was a deserving choice. Turner's former Howard University student and the first black woman anthropologist, Zora Neale Hurston, was awarded a grant for "the gathering of material for books on authentic Negro Folk-life, in particular a study of magic practices among Negroes in the West Indies."[9]

Evaluators were undoubtedly able to visualize the possibility that Hurston's efforts to record traditional black folklore would lead to a successful publication. They were familiar with the preservation of the Negro spirituals and viewed them as a model for Hurston's research. But the connection between Gullah in the United States and grammatical retentions from languages in Africa must have seemed a larger leap to those accustomed to the hypothesis that African Americans had been divested of all traces of African culture during their enslavement from 1619 through 1865 and beyond. Evaluators did not have to make that leap in Hurston's case, as they likely viewed African American and Afro-Caribbean folklore as having evolved in the Western Hemisphere with little or no African cultural infusion.

Another advantage in Hurston's favor was that her research had already gained validity with the publication of *Mules and Men* (1935), a collection of African American folklore gleaned from her fieldwork in Polk County, Florida, where she had crystallized cultural forms from the folk in the turpentine camps, the phosphate mines, and the juke joints. The book also reflected research she conducted in New Orleans on the philosophy and practice of voodoo. In 1936 Turner's Gullah research had not yet begun to appear in print.[10]

If being marginalized by foundations because of racial prejudice was not enough, Turner and like-minded scholars also faced a more insidious type of rejection, which severely hampered the research efforts of those who wished to document aspects of the black historic and cultural past:

> The racial exclusivity of the major foundations ensured that the controversial black proposals would not be funded and that the most conservative black social scientists would be rewarded with research money; black nationalists, Marxists, and ardent integrationists had little chance of receiving grants. Not surprisingly, black applicants were judged by different standards than those used for their white counterparts. Creativity and originality were not valued when assessing the merits of black research proposals. Rather, black applicants were judged on the facts they presented, their previous research and writing experience, and their politics.
>
> Research projects that promoted interracial cooperation and racial accommodation received backing. . . . Money was provided for studies on subjects such as methods to enhance business opportunities for blacks, black migration, urban conditions, and crime and the black community.[11]

Although Turner's plans had already hit the rocky shoals of the foundation seas, he was not dissuaded from his mission. The same day he received the "no thank you" letter from the Guggenheim, he composed a letter to Leland, the permanent secretary of the ACLS, informing him that his Guggenheim application had been "voted on unfavorably." Noting his commitment to his project, Turner stated that he was determined to take a year's leave from Fisk at half salary to pursue his research in London. He welcomed suggestions from Leland concerning alternative sources of financial assistance.[12]

Demonstrating his faith in his project, Turner began to make plans. That he had achieved the major accomplishments of university degrees on a shoestring contributed to his resolve that he could endure a similar experience in London. Since it was his sabbatical year, he was eligible for full salary for one semester or half salary for the academic year. At the same time, he was a married man with an employed wife. He could summon family resources if no other funding was forthcoming. In view of that assurance, Turner donned his marching gear. In an April 6, 1936, letter, he contacted Daniel Jones at the University of London. Jones was also secretary of the International Phonetic Association. Turner enclosed sixteen shillings for a "subscription for ordinary membership" in the association for 1935 and 1936, also requesting bulletins "describing courses in English Phonetics, General Phonetics, and the Phonetics of African languages." Providing a statement indicating the context for his interest, Turner continued, "For the past three years I have been studying Gullah . . . and have almost completed a descriptive grammar of this dialect." He then outlined his methodological strategy: "Next year at the University of London, in addition to pursuing certain courses in phonetics, I should like to study the phonetic structure of certain West African languages with a view to determine, if possible, the nature and content of African survivals in Gullah."[13]

Around that same time in 1936, Turner received a hastily written note from Lowman, still the Linguistic Atlas project principal field investigator. The note was scrawled on the stationery of the Shamrock Inn in Washington, D.C., near the Capitol Building and the Library of Congress. Lowman was in Washington on business, having conferred with Leland. According to Lowman's note, he had raised Turner's case with Leland, who had responded favorably to the idea of Turner's studying African languages at the School of Oriental Studies. Lowman, having had the opportunity to study phonetics with Daniel Jones while he completed courses toward his 1931 Ph.D.[14] could vouch for the value of the opportunity.

Lowman was encouraging. "Dr. Leland would like you to write a letter to the American Council of Learned Societies (907–15th Street, Washington, D.C.) stating your desire to study a year in the Department of Phonetics of University College, and in the School of Oriental Studies . . . , also of the University of London. I presume that you want to go there this coming fall. As soon as he receives the letter he will undoubtedly do for you what he can in his official capacity. He seems very favorably inclined. . . . I advise you to go to London. You will have a month's vacation at Christmas, and again at Easter when you can visit Paris."[15]

In June 1936 Lowman contacted Turner again. Turner had remained at Fisk, with plans to return to Washington, D.C., after July 15. Concerned that Turner's plans might not come to fruition, Lowman offered him personal funds for the London trip. In the same letter he informed Turner that he had mislaid his suitcase in his travels. Among the contents were his thesis and one of Turner's monographs. In a return letter to Lowman of June 21, 1936, Turner thanked him for his "letter and for the assistance you offered." Indicating that he did not wish to receive a gift, he left open the possibility that he might borrow funds if other options were exhausted. "If I find after reaching England that I need temporary financial assistance, I shall feel free to call upon you." Expressing concern over Lowman's lost thesis, Turner assured him that "it does not matter a great deal about my monograph which was lost, because I have another copy."[16] Since they had worked in Gullah territory together before, Turner wished to confer with Lowman before his London departure.

> Will it be possible for me to see you after that time? If you can spare the time, I can arrange to take you to South Carolina to interview again one of my informants. At any rate, I shall want to talk with you both about my Gullah study and my proposed work in London. I plan to leave for London in September.[17]

While Turner's first preference was to conduct fieldwork in West Africa, that option was unavailable to him.[18] Furthermore, although the field was rich in oral primary data, few specialists were available to provide instruction or to commit African languages to written form. On the other hand, the University of London had already trained students in the languages and cultures of Africa. There were a few professors in London with firsthand experience in African languages who were able to provide instruction, some of them with the aid of graduate students from

African countries. A limited number of audio tapes and written grammars were also available.[19]

In 1936 the following professors were on staff in the Department of Languages and Cultures of Africa:

Ethel O. Aston. Lecturer in Swahili.
Rev. G. P. Bargery. Part-time Senior Lecturer in Hausa.
Ida C. Ward, D.Lit. Nigerian dialects. (*With African Assistants*). Senior Lecturer in Phonetics and Linguistics.
N. Tucker, M.A. (Capetown), Ph.D. Comparative Bantu and Sudan Languages. Senior Lecturer in African Phonetics and Linguistics.
Bernice Honikman, M.A. (Capetown). Southern Bantu Dialects (*With African Assistants*). Assistant Lecturer in Phonetics.
Professor Lloyd James. Temporary Head of the Department.

Three faculty members taught phonetics in the Department of Phonetics and Linguistics, not necessarily related to African languages. One of them, J. R. Firth, was to be one of Turner's contacts.

Lloyd James, M.A. (Cantab.). Professor of Phonetics in the University of London. Head of Department.
R. T. Butlin, B.A. Senior Lecturer in Phonetics.
J. R. Firth, M.A. Part-time Lecturer in Linguistics[20]

On August 11, 1936, Turner mailed a letter from 1612 Fifteenth Street, North West, in Washington, D.C., which became the Turner home after Geneva's parents died, to G. W. Rossetti, the secretary of the School of Oriental Studies, requesting an application of admission. Therein he stated his intention to pursue "courses in the Department of Phonetics and Linguistics both at the School of Oriental Studies and at University College. . . . I shall probably not be able to decide upon the specific courses I need until I arrive in London and consult with certain professors . . . but I am especially interested in the Phonetics of West African languages."[21] Turner then made clear the urgency of his request: "While applying for my passport visa at the British Consulate in Baltimore, I was advised that before leaving the United States I should be able to furnish immigration officials with a letter indicating that I have been admitted to the University of London. For that reason, I would like to be admitted to the School of Oriental Studies as soon as possible, paying in advance the appropriate fees. When you send me the form of application for admission, will you indicate what fees I should need?"[22]

As he prepared paperwork for his trip, Turner continued to seek funding. According to his Fisk University annual faculty report of 1937, he was successful only in gaining the ACLS grant of $750 to maintain his recorder and a grant-in-aid from the Fisk University Humanities Institute. In Turner's "Profile of a Scholar," there is indication not of a 1936–37 American Council grant but rather of a 1937 award, which represents support for his summer research in Paris.[23] As Turner continued to formulate his plans, he began to contact colleagues who could offer other suggestions and strategies.

Leland contacted him on August 21, 1936, as a follow-up to their earlier correspondence. Turner was operating with a used recorder owned by the ACLS. Leland advised him to ship it to Lincoln Thompson, the president of Sound Specialties Company in Waterbury, Connecticut, "with instructions to overhaul it and put it in good order, and then hold it subject to directions from these offices." Turner was then to write Thompson, informing him to expect the recorder and requesting that he mail the bill to the offices of the ACLS.[24]

In Leland's letter, he made additional suggestions, among them that Turner write to Melville Herskovits, "giving him some idea as of your plans, and soliciting his suggestions, particularly with respect to a possible visit to West Africa after your work in London." Next, he recommended that Turner register with the American University Union at 1 Gordon Square. Leland indicated that he was preparing a letter of introduction for Turner to its director, Willard Connely, and noted that "the University Union is maintained to be of service to American students and professors who are traveling in the British Isles. It will be especially useful to you with regard to such practical matters as admission to the British Museum."[25]

Leland's complimentary and supportive letter of introduction for Turner, also dated August 21, 1936, was enclosed ("you are free to use [it] as you have occasion"), along with individual notes to Daniel Jones and Lloyd James. The letter stated in part, "This Council knows Professor Turner to be a competent and distinguished scholar in his field of work, and bespeaks of him the helpful attention of those to whom he may present this letter."[26]

By 1936 Kurath had worked with Turner for four years. On August 29, 1936, Kurath contacted Firth in London to alert him to Turner's impending arrival and to enlist his support. His letter on Linguistic Atlas letterhead from Brown University stated in part, "May I present Professor Lorenzo D. Turner . . . to you? Professor Turner has been working for several years on a study of the speech of negroes on the sea islands along the coast of South Carolina and Georgia."[27] Kurath emphasized Turner's quest to identify the non-English aspects of Gullah: "[He] has come to realize that certain features of pronunciation and of morphology are not parallel in any dialect speech of the white population in this country. He now wishes to familiarize himself with the structure of a number of African languages to see whether certain peculiarities of Gullah are to be attributed to the influence of the languages spoken by the negroes before they learned English. The task of establishing the existence of such carry-overs is doubtless a very difficult one, but it must be undertaken sooner or later. Dr. Turner will greatly appreciate any assistance that you may be able to give him in his stay in London."[28]

The application that Turner had requested arrived expeditiously from London. After returning it immediately, along with transcripts from Harvard and the University of Chicago, Turner soon received a letter, dated September 8, 1936, from the secretary of the School of Oriental Studies thanking him for his application and the three guineas for his registration fee. Turner was accepted. He was scheduled to study Phonetics and West African Languages. Classes were to begin on Thursday, October 8, before the date he expected to depart from the United States, but he was assured that he would be interviewed when he arrived, at which time he could pay his remaining fees.

Turner received another letter posted the following day, September 9, 1936. It was an acknowledgment from H. E. Foster, the registrar of University College, stating "The members of the Phonetics staff will be available for interview on the Tuesday, Wednesday, Thursday and Friday preceding the opening of the session on October 5th, and will be glad to see you on the morning of any one of those days."[29]

Turner's plans were gaining momentum with each written transaction. That same day, he acted on Leland's recommendation to contact Herskovits for suggestions on the African languages that likely influenced Gullah significantly. His detailed letter on September 9 invited suggestions while commending Herskovits on his previous research. The correspondence is important in that it serves as a report on the status of Turner's research in 1936. "Before the work is ready for publication, however, I feel that I should know something about the languages spoken in those sections of West Africa from which the Gullah Negroes were brought as slaves, especially since certain features of the pronunciation, morphology, intonation and vocabulary of Gullah are not paralleled in any dialect spoken by the white population in this country. I intend, as soon as it is convenient, to visit other parts of the New World—for example, certain parts of South America, Jamaica, Haiti and other West Indian islands—with a view to studying the speech of Negroes there."[30]

Having set the stage, Turner then described his research plan and his rationale for considering certain West African languages as the source of differences between the Gullah Creole and English:

> Next month (October 7) I shall sail for London, where I shall spend a year at the School of Oriental Studies of the University of London studying the phonetic structure of certain West African languages, particularly many of those spoken in sections from which Negroes were brought to South Carolina and Georgia. The fourth volume of Professor Elizabeth Donnan's *Documents Illustrative of the History of the African Slave Trade to America* gives Angola and Congo as the source of the largest number of slaves (approximately 25,000) concerning whose arrival in South Carolina between 1733 and 1807 there is definite record; Sierra Leone and Liberia (Grain Coast) furnished the second largest number (between 14,000 and 15,000); Ashanti, Togo, Dahomey, and Nigeria (Gold Coast and Slave Coast) were third, with nearly 11,000; and Senegambia was fourth, with about 10,470. Whereas nearly all the slaves from Congo came to South Carolina near the end of the period, I find that those from Angola are pretty well distributed throughout the period from 1733 to 1807, more than 23,000 arriving between 1733 and 1738. Other sections furnished comparatively few slaves. It is obvious that many of the slaves were subsequently sent to other places and many in other places were brought to South Carolina, but these figures will be valuable to me as a guide in my selection of the appropriate West African languages for study.
>
> I shall certainly appreciate any suggestions you may care to give me.[31]

A week later Herskovits responded in a cordial letter, recommending languages to serve as the focus of Turner's study: "Your letter of the 9th came while I was on my way home after a summer in the East, and I hasten to answer it. I am glad you are going on with your work on Negro speech, and I am sure you will find the leads to African correspondences quite numerous."[32] He suggested to Turner that though some cultural groups were procured for the Western Hemisphere in large numbers, from his perspective, they were not necessarily the groups that exerted the greatest cultural and linguistic influence. "I would suggest that you specialize in the linguistic characteristics of the region from Western Nigeria, Dahomey, and the Gold Coast; more particularly Yoruban (Nago), Fõn (Ewe) and Twi. I realize that there are other regions of West Africa from which greater numbers of slaves were derived. At the same time, I am coming more and more to have the feeling that it was the peoples from this area and the linguistic stocks I have mentioned who set the patterns for . . . the Gulla [*sic*] Islands and the British West Indies."[33]

Herskovits knew that Turner wished to solidify his theoretical expertise of African languages with practical work in the field. For that purpose, he alluded to a potential informant in Ghana:

> "Are you planning to work in the field? Should you go to West Africa and work in the Gold Coast, I would be more than glad to give you a letter to the informant whom I used when I was among the Ashanti in 1931. The young man would, I believe, be ideal for your purposes: he is the son of a Chief, teaches in one of the Wesleyan Mission schools, has good command of English and is of the highest intelligence. However, I assume that such plans are a matter for the future. Mrs. Herskovits and I are shortly bringing out a volume with the Columbia University Press entitled 'Suriname Folklore.' In this book, in addition to a collection of tales in text and translation and Dutch Guiana Negro songs, we have included a discussion of certain aspects of the linguistic problem."[34]

Herskovits offered to lend Turner copies of his notes.

On September 30, 1936, immediately after receiving the Herskovitses "Linguistic Notes," Turner contacted Herskovits with a brief letter of thanks, at the same time expressing an interest in fieldwork in Africa: "In making my selection of the West African languages for study I shall take your suggestions. I find your 'Notes' very interesting and illuminating. I think the correspondences you reveal are highly significant. I am returning the 'Notes' under separate cover and shall want to purchase a copy of *Suriname Folklore* as soon as it comes off the press. My plan is to spend several months on the West Coast of Africa after completing a year's study at the School of Oriental Studies in London, if finances permit. I shall keep you informed of my progress."[35]

Although each week an increasing number of Turner's plans reached fruition, he must have been exhilarated when he received the small, lime-green schedule of classes, *School of Oriental Studies Time Tables for the 21st Session, 1936–37,* for there on page 27 he found "Dr. Ward—Courses will be arranged as required. Ewe, Fante, Gã, Mende, Twi, Yoruba."[36]

By September 6, Turner had submitted his registration fee for a course on phonetics and West African languages that cost three pounds and three shillings. The course was to meet for the entire academic year 1936–37 for four hours each week. A month later, by October 6, shortly before his departure for London, Turner paid for his course on West African languages. The cost was fifteen pounds, four shillings, and six pence. Being eager to maximize his experience, Turner paid one pound as membership dues to join the International Institute of African Languages and Cultures on October 21. By October 23, he had paid one pound to gain privileges to use the School of Oriental Studies Library in Clarence House on Matthew Parker Street.[37]

Determined to pursue his project, Turner forged ahead, traveling by ship to London in early October 1936 and renting a room at 32 Arcadian Gardens, Bowes Park, London, to engage in his research in earnest. Though his room did not provide the amenities, such as central heat, to which he was accustomed, he embraced his austere existence with the anticipation that a greater goal was within his reach. In class he found Ward the key to his quest for the analytical tools to phonetics and structure of West African languages. She was an experienced teacher of African languages. By the time he met her, she had already published articles and books on the Bantu languages, possible sources of the African language influence in Gullah. Having lived and conducted research in West Africa, she and R. F. G. Adams, an inspector of education in Nigeria, had lobbied to have the orthographic system of the International Institute of African Languages and Culture (IIALC) as the standard orthography for African languages. That system, created in 1927 and presented in a pamphlet titled *Practical Orthography of African Languages,* contained eight vowels and twenty-eight consonants, with */gw/*, */kw/*, and */nw/* having been added to represent some of the Ibo phonemes. After its adoption, it was popularly referred to as the "Adams-Ward Orthography."[38]

Turner's timing was opportune since two years after his study leave, in 1939, Ward returned to eastern Nigeria, leading a research expedition to examine some Ibo dialects for possible use for literary purposes. She hoped to encourage the development of a standard Ibo, utilizing "central" Ibo, which covered the Owerri and Umuahia areas, with special inclination toward Ohuhu dialect. Over time writers, publishers, missionaries, and Cambridge University accepted Ward's "standard Ibo."[39]

During 1936–37, under Ward's tutelage, Turner was able to begin to crack the Gullah code. As he concentrated on the phonology, morphology, syntax, and semantics of Niger-Congo languages, formerly unexplained features of Gullah began to make sense. He learned as much as was possible in the year of Ewe, Efik, Gã, Twi, and Yoruba in order to examine his Gullah data in view of this newly gained expertise.[40]

Six weeks after Turner arrived in London, on November 15, 1936, he paused to contact President Jones of Fisk to apprise him of the status of his research. The letter serves as a record of Turner's research accomplishments in London. After detailing the adjustments required, Turner detailed the triumphs. He was disappointed that there were "far fewer conveniences than in America. Library facilities are more limited than I expected, the libraries close quite early, and the almost universal absence of central heating makes effective research far more difficult than in America."[41]

He indicated that his work with Ward was progressing well and that, in addition to her own background as one who had resided in West Africa, it was helpful that she utilized informants who were native speakers. Turner was already finding greater confirmation for his major hypothesis about Gullah than he had expected. He wrote, "Apparently most of the Negroes (according to statistics) who were brought to South Carolina and Georgia during the period of slavery came from sections of the West coast where these languages and a few others were spoken. The resemblances between these languages and Gullah are much more striking than I had supposed. Many of the constructions are identical, *and* there are close correspondences in intonation and inflections."[42]

As Turner immersed himself in the analysis of African languages, his awareness of the distinction between dialects and creoles was developing. He mentioned to President Jones the failure of earlier researchers to note the grammatical patterns of Gullah beyond the vocabulary. "These scholars, being unacquainted with the characteristics of West African languages, have been observing only the Negro's vocabulary, which is essentially English. They have overlooked other characteristics which are far more significant."[43]

Mentioning others in London besides Ward with whom he interacted regularly in the academic enterprise, Turner affirmed his satisfaction with the opportunities available to him:

> I am also doing some advanced work in phonetics under Professor Armstrong of University College. I am finding all my work quite interesting. The Africans with whom I work are graduates either of Oxford or London University and make excellent informants. The professors are nice to work with and seem very much interested in my project. Through Sir William Craigie, who frequently comes to London from Oxford, I have met several prominent scholars in the field of English literature and language, have attended meetings of the British Philological Society and the Royal Society of Literature, and have heard several very interesting and inspiring lectures.[44]

On December 18, 1936, Jones responded to Turner's letter, expressing enthusiasm over his quest to analyze African survivals and simultaneously suggesting the value of Turner's research to Fisk: "I have your letter of November 15, and I have enjoyed its contents very much. You seem to be utilizing your time to good advantage. Your project is most interesting and should throw valuable light upon this much-mooted question of African survivals in America. I am glad that you are having the opportunity which should be of benefit both to you and to Fisk."[45]

By the end of winter, Turner had forged connections with the African community in London. On March 18, 1937, he received a handwritten letter from W. Ofari Atta of West Hampstead inviting him to Mort Lake to "join a party of Gold Coast students who are going to see the collections of Gold Coast and Nigerian art assembled by Mr. Corkin and Captain Armitage."[46] At that point in Turner's academic year, he opted to conserve his weekends to focus on his studies. Another opportunity arose, however, to view the exhibition in the summer of 1937.

Over the months, Turner eagerly scrutinized the African language materials available to him as he consulted with Ward. The more he learned of West African languages, the more he realized that making the sacrifice to spend a year in London had been a judicious decision. Turner was energized by his findings related to the connections between African languages and Gullah, and his study had increased his eagerness to embrace African cultures and traditions in the context of the continent. Following the leads offered him, he began to make plans for his trip to Paris in August, noting that "French scholars have done excellent work on West African languages, and I wish to avail myself of some of the facilities offered in Paris."[47]

In early summer Turner traveled to Paris to interview and record a number of Africans from French-speaking territories. Through good fortune, he impressed Professor Henri Labouret, director of the International Institute of African Languages and Cultures, who arranged to have Turner assigned a tent/office on the fairgrounds of the Exposition Internationale (an international exposition of arts and crafts) in Paris. Not only did Labouret make valuable suggestions to Turner, he also directed visiting Africans to him. Many of them were officials representing countries where French was the colonial language. When they arrived at his door, Turner played Gullah recordings, hopeful that they would find some materials recognizable, and "Turner found link after link [between Gullah and some of the African] languages."[48] He also discussed with the African visitors details of the structures of Ewe-Fõn, Bambara, and Wolof. His funding source was the ACLS.[49] Turner's African informants in Paris confirmed the insights he had reached in London in his studies with Ward. By the end of summer 1937, Turner had found the key. He held in his hands the evidence he needed to codify many unique aspects of Gullah.

Before the summer ended, Labouret, who was also familiar with Arabic, suggested that Turner study it in an attempt to ascertain the extent to which Islamic Africans who had been transported to the Gullah islands had left their footprints on Gullah Creole.[50] Turner recognized the suggestion as being worthy of future consideration.

As unique as Turner's experiences were, he was not the first African American to discover the linguistic resources and make his way to the African-language scholars at the University of London. Three years before, in 1933, Paul Robeson, on a European tour, was drawn to delve into the African past. His growth in consciousness was in part the result of controversies that swirled around his role in the movie *The Emperor Jones,* which stereotyped people of African ancestry in ways that many viewed as deeply damaging to the psyches of persons of African and Euro-American ancestry. Often members of the press questioned Robeson on issues related to race. His biographer Martin Duberman notes, "Newly vocal on themes that had quietly engaged him intellectually for years, his excitement grew, and he began an energetic effort both to broaden his own insights through formal study and to incorporate the emerging new perspectives into his concert work and his future plans. Robeson had always enjoyed the study of language; now it became a passion. He enrolled in the School of Oriental Studies . . . to do comparative work in African linguistics, with the eventual goal . . . of taking a Ph.D. in philology."[51]

Although Robeson did not realize his plan to earn a doctorate in philology, his registration card for the School of Oriental Studies confirms that he enrolled in a phonetics course during the first term and KiSwahili during the second term of 1933–34.[52] According to Robeson, he also pursued the study of West African languages. Since none appear on his registration card, he most likely pursued them as an auditor as time permitted. In them, he found "a homecoming":

> I went to the London School of Oriental Languages, and quite haphazardly, began by studying the East Coast languages, Swahili and the Bantu group which forms a sort of Lingua Franca of the East Coast of Africa. I found in these languages a pure negro foundation dating from an ancient culture, but intermingled with many Arabic and Hamitic impurities. From them I passed on to the West Coast Negro languages and immediately found a kinship and rhythm and intonation with Negro English which I had heard spoken around me as a child. It was to me like a homecoming. . . . It is my first concern to dispel [the] regrettable and abysmal ignorance of its own heritage in the negro race itself.[53]

By October 1936, when Turner arrived, Robeson's performance schedule had demanded his attention, and he had moved on to continue his artistic pursuits. Robeson left a large footprint though. Three-quarters of a century later, the School of Oriental and African Studies memorialized him. On April 16–18, 1998, a three-day conference was held in celebration of his life and contribution. Furthermore, in fall 1998, a new residence hall, christened the Paul Robeson House, opened in his honor.[54]

It is likely that Robeson and Turner were the first African Americans to study at the University of London. They were, however, not the first Americans. Founded in 1917, the school kept records that are preserved in its annual *Reports of the Governing Body and Statement of Accounts*. They do not indicate country of origin for students in the early years, but the report for 1918 does reveal that four students were enrolled in Swahili. Two persons, a Captain O. A. R. Berkeley and a Miss M. H. Werner, received First Year Certificates. Enrollment in the language courses mushroomed almost immediately. By 1920 "the number of students who studied African languages, exclusive of Arabic, was forty-nine, the subjects being Chi-Nyanja, Hausa, Luganda, Sesuto, Swahili, Yao, Yoruba and Zulu."[55]

By 1931 students are listed by country of origin for the first time. Seven from the United States were in attendance. By the time Turner arrived in 1936, the number had reached a historic high of eleven. Just as Fisk University and the University of Chicago were enriched by Rockefeller money, so was the School of Oriental Studies. In 1932 the Rockefeller Foundation donated three thousand pounds and planned to do so for a three-year cycle. In 1936 the foundation began the donation cycle again, with three thousand pounds pledged for each of the next three years, a fact that in part might explain the increase in attendance of students from America. The purpose was to contribute "towards the development of research into African linguistics and phonetics."[56]

After a year of study, Turner was prepared to blend business with pleasure. Geneva was to spend the summer with him. At the end of her academic year, Geneva arranged for a cruise on the third-class plan of the S.S. *Aquitania,* the "World's Wonder Ship." It embarked from pier 90, situated off 25 Broadway at 6385 Fifth Avenue in New York, on June 30, 1937. The George Bell Elementary School (her most recent teaching appointment) celebrated the occasion by preparing farewell notes, one from the French club and others from the principal and teachers. Margaret Bow, a Turner cousin, sent a bon-voyage note. Justine and her growing four-year-old son, Eugene, who still resided in New York, arrived at the pier to wish Geneva bon voyage in person.[57] She did not travel alone. According to her photographs and notes, her sailing companions were her friends Catherine and Mimi.

Shortly after Geneva's arrival, the Turners constructed a travel schedule that provided exposure to many of the major cultural events and tourist sites in England and France. On Sunday afternoon, July 11, at last the opportunity arrived for them to view the art collection at Leyden House. The Turners traveled to Mort Lake as part of a large group of invited guests. The display was as dazzling as they could have imagined, one of the most impressive assemblages of African art in Europe. This introduction to museum-quality African art probably became Turner's standard for the African sculpture he collected fifteen years later when he traveled and lived in Nigeria and Sierra Leone. Furthermore, Turner was an African American celebrity. According to Geneva, "Lorenzo and I were invited here to the home of Mr. and Mrs. Corkin to tea and to view the collection. Lorenzo was invited to lecture and to play his records to the guests (about 80). They were wealthy people with a charming daughter of eighteen years and a son just out of college. A most interesting afternoon."[58]

The program for the afternoon stated that Maurice Corkin had been a political officer in Benin. He was an associate of Sir Cecil Armitage, who has been on a quest for the Golden Stool of the Ashanti. Even though Armitage had not succeeded in capturing the stool, the two men had procured six thousand pieces of art from Dahomey (now Benin) and the Gold Coast (now Ghana). According to the description of the display, there were silk hangings, which were flags of the Gold Coast, wrist knives, bracelets, Ashanti gold weights representing various occupations, basket work, ivory trumpets, drums, guns, spears, carved wooden figures, a large xylophone, staffs, quivers, Ashanti stools, bronze masks, lamps, numerous drums, swords, and much more.[59]

Turner and Geneva could not have selected a more stimulating summer for their Europe odyssey. Geneva chronicled it with care, retaining every brochure, program, ticket stub, map, and train schedule. After her return to Washington, D.C., she lovingly assembled an attractive scrapbook, affixing each item creatively and writing the commentary in silver ink. At some point in July, the Turners attended one or more activities associated with the coronation of Their Majesties King George VI and Queen Elizabeth. They kept the "Souvenir Programme" and purchased a postcard of the coronation chair. Turner commissioned an artist to paint Geneva's portrait.

Geneva was able to share with Turner the experience of the 1937 Exposition Internationale. Between his interviews, they attended the Folies Bergères starring Josephine Baker, purchasing a copy of the program that displayed a sensuous color drawing of "La Baker" au naturale—without her banana skirt. They selected a cinema for a double feature—*Marinella* and *Maria Chapdelaine,* the latter featuring Madeleine Renaud and Jean Gabin. They purchased a copy of *L'Image*. They visited Libraries Flanmarien. They ate gourmet cookies and saved the tin to store their undeveloped film.

They traveled to Stratford-upon-Avon on August 9 to visit the home of Shakespeare and then attended the Shakespeare Festival. On August 15, they boarded a train to Oxford. Ann, a new Scottish friend whom Geneva met in her European travels, accompanied them. With her guidance, they made their way to Scotland to visit Oban, Edinburgh, the highlands, and a castle. On August 18, they visited Canterbury. They sojourned to Cambridge on August 26 to visit Trinity College.[60]

The summer of 1937 was a glorious time that recaptured the exhilaration of the Turners' romance from their Howard University days. They had been married eighteen years, but only during the first ten years (1919–29) had their employment situations allowed them to reside in the same household regularly. It had been years since they had been able to spend such pleasurable blocks of time together.[61] Now that all four of their parents had been laid to rest, Geneva was free to make plans with Turner, giving the couple much to consider. However, providence would have it otherwise. Memorable and idyllic though their summer had been, they were wise to record their shared moments for all time. All else would be falling action. The summer was their crescendo. There would not be another.

15

Lois Gwendolyn Morton 1918–1938

My childhood was ideal—much like Anne's of Green Gables.
I was sheltered and happy.

—Interview with Lois Turner Williams,
Chicago, Ill., September 15, 2002

TURNER WAS INVIGORATED by his research. As he studied African languages with Ward in London and interviewed native speakers of African languages, he became more and more certain of his thesis—Gullah's distinctiveness lay largely in the features it retained from Niger-Congo languages. His hunger to conduct fieldwork in Africa among native speakers in order to achieve immersion in the intricacies and nuances of their languages and cultures was profound. Unfortunately, the time had not arrived when educated North Americans of African ancestry were welcome in the colonized African countries.

Furthermore, the Depression was still grinding on. Finding himself without funding, Turner returned to the United States. Leaving Geneva again in Washington, D.C., he sojourned to Fisk. He knew he would have to harness his hunger, placing his energies in teaching and data collection in America.

Turner's frequent trips to visit his family in Washington, to attend conferences, and to travel to research sites made it necessary for him to own his own car. On September 8, 1937, having returned from London, he paused briefly in Washington, D.C. There Turner traded in his older Ford Deluxe Sedan at the Steuart Motor Company and purchased a new blue 1937 Ford Deluxe Sedan. He was allowed one hundred dollars as a trade-in for the older Ford, paid forty-nine dollars down, and financed seventeen payments of forty dollars each through the Universal Credit Company. He later sold the 1937 Ford before he departed for his research year in Brazil. In 1942, after his return from Brazil, he purchased a 1941 black Ford Sedan, also from Steuart Motor Company. It was the final vehicle he would own in the United States.[1]

It was September 1937. Turner did not arrive in Nashville a day too soon. The opening convocation was a major event at Fisk in which faculty members were expected to participate. Being dutiful, Turner attended.

At the end of the convocation, Lillian Cashin, one of Turner's colleagues in the Department of English, approached him. Accompanying her was a poised, demure, forty-something woman. Cashin introduced the woman to Turner. She was Myrtle White Morton, a 1916 graduate of Fisk, who informed Turner that she was a home economics teacher in Louisville, Kentucky. Her husband, Clifford Morton, likewise a Fisk graduate of 1916, was a high school principal. Her purpose in returning to Fisk was to accompany her daughter, Lois Gwendolyn Morton, as she entered the university in pursuit of a master's degree in English. In May 1937 Lois had completed her bachelor's degree in English from the Municipal College for Negroes (later renamed the University of Louisville), in Kentucky. Having introduced her daughter to Turner, Myrtle Morton added, "Dr. Turner, please take good care of my little girl."[2] It was a request that would permanently impact all their lives.

Lois was a head-turning beauty—willowy, well proportioned, standing all of 5 feet 3 ¾ inches high. A daughter of the diaspora, with tinges of the African, and larger doses of the Native American and European branches, her youthful face spoke of innocence while her spirit spoke of ancient times. Outwardly she appeared young and vulnerable, but her essence housed a solid, tempered core. Born in Crawfordsville, Arkansas, on February 4, 1918, the eldest of three children to solidly middle-class, educated parents, she had traveled and lived with them in a number of towns, including Gastonia, North Carolina, when she was seven. There both parents were employed at Lincoln Ridge Academy, a high school for African Americans funded by the American Missionary Association. Living at the boarding school with her family, Lois had met a cross section of aspiring young people, including Ernest Kalibala, a native of Uganda and the first African she recalled meeting. As a young adult, Kalibala completed his doctorate in sociology at Harvard and returned to Uganda to found the Aggrey Memorial School.[3]

When Lois was eleven-and-a-half, her parents relocated to Ocala, Florida, to teach at Fessenden Academy. A year later the Mortons gathered up the children again, this time moving to Bloomington, Indiana, so that both Clifford and Myrtle could gain further education at Indiana University—Clifford, a master's degree in education, which he began full-time and later completed during summers between 1932 and 1935; and Myrtle, the second two years leading to her bachelor's degree in home economics, which she completed in 1932.

Lois entered Bloomington High School at age twelve. The year was 1930. For the first time in her life, she experienced integration, being one of twenty-seven black students in a school of two thousand. She excelled academically, but she assigned her social life a mixed review. When the Mortons returned south, to Louisville, Kentucky, where her father became a principal in 1933, Lois's mother was compelled to commute to another town for employment because of the nepotism rule. As a result, by age fourteen, Lois was responsible for a number of day-to-day household tasks. She also assisted her father with the care of her younger siblings, Andrew (born August 21, 1921) and Gloria (born July 5, 1923), becoming responsible for her own and Gloria's clothing and hair. The lesson to Lois and her siblings was that families must be hardworking, cooperative, role sharing, and flexible in order to support each other's growth and the survival of the family unit. It was a lesson Lois would subsequently put into practice in her own adult family life. Her experiences, adapting to new towns and school systems, hastened her advancement toward maturity and self-reliance.[4]

In 1937 at Fisk, Turner hired Lois as a student-worker in the English department office. "I graded papers, conducted some research, and assisted with clerical work. As compensation, I was paid $20.00–$30.00 per month from funds available to the university through a government grant," she recalled.[5] Turner saw Lois at some point every day, either in class, in the office, or both. "I enrolled in his courses in phonetics, Chaucer, Old English, and history of the English language." She and Frank Yerby were two of the graduate students in English in 1937.[6] They were both of the highest caliber—prepared, articulate, confident, assertive, and ambitious. Both were artists by temperament and practice—Yerby a writer, and Lois a painter.

Turner must have sensed that each would make him proud in the future, but he viewed Lois as the prize. She humanized his office with her lilting Kentucky accent, winning smile, and willingness to tackle any task. Lois's father had persuaded her to love the arts but study English as a buffer against unemployment. As she tackled her graduate courses and undertook her thesis research, she was all business, but she knew that she was in love. "For me it had been love at first sight. Nevertheless, I approached my work in a professional manner," she remembered, and despite the formality they both maintained, "a strong attraction between us was building as a result of frequent consultations about the progress of my thesis research."[7]

On one occasion, just before Easter 1938, Lois left Turner a note written lengthwise on the unlined side of a three-by-five-inch card, requesting a meeting with him to discuss some revisions. It read, "Dr. Turner: Should you come by your office, here, and have the time, I wish you would see me about 4:45 or 5:00 to discuss my thesis. I have done some more since I saw you last. If, however, you can't see me and should chance to read this, please tell me on this card, so I won't be waiting. Thanks and Happy Easter. Lois M."[8]

Within a few months, Turner was unable to imagine life without Lois. There was one complication. Turner's wife of eighteen years was devoted and steadfast. Together Turner and Geneva had weathered the years of sunshine and storms—growth in their careers, friends, social life, trips and research, the sharing of common goals, made bitter by the death of his brother, Rooks Jr., the illnesses and demise of all four of their parents, complicated career choices, the friction of separation, and the hunger for children who did not come.

When Rooks Sr. had drowned on July 22, 1926, his heart had been broken from life's reversals. When Elizabeth had died on November 23, 1931, she was sad and anxious, tired and worn from struggling to survive. Geneva's father, Edlow, had grown increasingly frail until his death on August 28, 1935. Then Letitia had followed suddenly and unexpectedly on December 30, 1937. At some point in the spring of 1938, Justine had returned to Washington, D.C., from New York, where she had completed a master's degree in education from Columbia University. She was ill at the time. Her young son, Eugene, by then a slight but charming cherub of four, born October 9, 1933, was the only child in the Towneses immediate family. His care fell to Geneva during her sister's convalescence.[9] Geneva loved him as her own and looked forward to participating with Justine, a single parent, in his long-term care and rearing. She had developed into the responsible nurturer.

From Geneva's perspective, she had not only endeavored to be an exemplary wife; she had also been a model daughter and daughter-in-law. She had not joined Turner in Nashville, and though her absence had caused stress in their relationship, they both understood why. She had joined him during summers whenever possible. Her desire to be with him was secondary to her belief that a prerequisite for a stable family life was a consistent home base. Furthermore, being a dutiful daughter/wife, she had been constrained to assist in the care of both his mother and her parents.[10]

Although Geneva was an adherent of the Bible, she had not literally "cleaved to her husband" because his path was impractical to follow for one who wished to maintain a stable family life. And at that time a woman who took a leave from her position was not guaranteed the option of returning. The realities of her life were often in paradoxical contrast to the desires of her heart. She did not view Turner as being particularly pragmatic, but she loved him and understood that he needed freedom and her support to conduct research. She took pride in sharing in his accomplishments.[11]

Family responsibility had consistently impeded Geneva's attempts to leave Washington, D.C. Just as Turner had been his family's mainstay, she had been hers. After standing by his mother and her parents in life, she had purchased the family plot in Lincoln Memorial Cemetery and arranged to lay their bodies to rest after death. Furthermore, no teaching position had ever materialized for her in Nashville. The Turners were one of thousands of black married couples separated by the job market. After having set down roots in Washington, D.C., it was questionable whether she would ever view relocating to Nashville as a reasonable alternative. Yet, the Turners' European working vacation provided a sample of future possibilities. When Geneva considered the context of her life and the rationale for her decisions, it seemed an irony too cruel for words for Turner to leave her just as she was free to plan life with him.[12]

Turner ached with the pain of his dilemma; but images of Lois had woven themselves through his mind and heart. Although she was reserved, he sensed the romantic feelings were mutual. Occasionally over the 1937–38 academic year, he had gathered students to attend a play in Nashville. Lois and Yerby were regulars. Turner could see that Frank Yerby was also attracted to Lois. From Turner's perspective, Lois did not manifest more than collegial interest in Yerby. She was well bred and gently raised. Turner viewed Lois as an ideal mate—educated, attractive, mature beyond her chronological age, socially appropriate—and young enough to produce children.[13]

By April 1938 Turner had spoken to Geneva about a divorce. He traveled to Washington, D.C., in early April for the Easter break. On April 10, Lois sent a telegram to him there, indicating that she was running out of books for her thesis research. A voracious reader, she had completed her scrutiny of the thirty-six novels available to her. "NOVELS EXHAUSTED, 36. IF NOT SUFFICIENT BRING MORE," Lois said, ending her missive, "WORRIED. LOIS MORTON."[14] The libraries in the Washington, D.C., area provided a larger selection of resources than those in Nashville.

During late spring or early summer 1938, Geneva appeared in person in Nashville to confer over the divorce papers. She and Turner had agreed to state that the grounds were desertion on his part. Geneva was devastated but dignified. In a sense the relationship had run its course; it was a marriage of attrition. Once there had been almost total overlap in their worlds. By 1938 there was a fissure between them—widened by the years of separation, the absence of children to serve as glue, and other factors—that seemed unbridgeable. Geneva decided not to obstruct Turner's efforts to end their relationship.[15]

The stage was set for Turner to approach Lois about his freedom to pursue a relationship with her. And he did. "Soon," she says, "our courtship was discreetly underway [*sic*]. We walked, talked, ate, held hands and sometimes hugged and kissed. On one occasion, at a Fisk University faculty/student social, we danced together."[16] For Lois it was an awkward but exhilarating time. Consequently, when Turner raised the issue of marriage in May 1938, she was reduced to tears of confusion. How would she tell her parents? What would she say to her classmates and friends? How could she proceed so swiftly from graduate student to wife of the chair of the English department?

One weekend in early May when Lois's mother, Myrtle, came to visit her daughter at Fisk, Turner raised with Myrtle the issue of marrying Lois. Myrtle was stunned but expressed little opposition. In a whirlwind, the three visited jewelry stores, locating the appropriate rings for the engagement and wedding.[17]

After Myrtle returned to Louisville, Kentucky, and conferred with Lois's father, Clifford, both began to express increasing disquietude. Turner had spoken to Myrtle but not Clifford. Appropriate social etiquette dictated that Turner should have asked Clifford for Lois's hand in marriage. For Clifford, flags went up. What did it mean? What else was there? The age difference? Lois was twenty; Turner was forty-eight (forty-three according to Turner) and several years older than Lois's mother. What about Lois's career? She was their first child and an artistic prodigy. Her parents reasoned that with appropriate education in art, her potential might lead her to become an Edmonia Lewis or a Meta Warwick Fuller. Should she not wait until she was older and more established in her career to marry? She was just beginning to develop as an independent intellect. Would an older man stifle her aspirations and confine her to housekeeping and childbearing? Would the social life of Fisk and the surrounding Nashville community be supportive of a young bride with a groom who was considered one of the prizes of Fisk? What would their friends and associates say about their lovely daughter marrying an older man? A divorced man? Divorce was a word one whispered in 1938. Since the days of "no fault" divorce had not arrived, someone would have to bear the blame. Was he a philanderer? How did a married man allow himself to fall in love with his young student? Would he be faithful and respectful? How could Clifford and Myrtle know?

Lois reports that "amid the tumult, I continued research for my thesis. I prepared a ninety-five page analysis on illustrations in black novels, a topic that combined my literary interests with my artistic ones. In 'Illustrations in Recent Novels of Negro Life' [1938], I examined the illustrations in five-hundred books along three indices—the history of illustrations in books; the choice of media and appropriateness for the particular text; and the effectiveness of the illustrations 'apart from the media.'"[18]

As Lois prepared for her thesis defense, in keeping with the Fisk tradition, Turner invited Miles Hanley, a specialist in James Joyce from the University of Wisconsin, to serve as the external evaluator. Like Turner, Hanley was a literary scholar / linguist. He continued to teach in both disciplines, English and linguistics, focusing on New England dialects in the latter. He was one of Turner's colleagues from the Linguistic Institute, the Modern Language Association, and the Linguistic Atlas Project. His evaluation was especially appropriate on the occasion of Lois's defense, "lest there be a whisper of favoritism" on Turner's part. After scrutiny, Turner and Hanley considered Lois's thesis both original and relevant, assigning it an honor grade, and Lois graduated in triumph.[19]

She was one of a growing number of students seeking master's degrees at Fisk. In December 1938, one semester after her graduation, Dean A. A. Taylor released a report announcing that since the first master's of science degree had been awarded to Frederick Augustine Browne in chemistry in 1928, 570 students from eighty-seven different colleges, thirty-four states, and two foreign countries had attended master's programs at Fisk. "Not one student who received a degree had failed to receive approval of the outside examiner. Usually the visiting observers were pleasantly surprised" at the level of expertise of Fisk graduate candidates.[20]

In May 1938, having completed her master's degree, Lois returned to her parents' home in Louisville. Since they were well-connected educators, her graduation was covered in the press. On July 9, 1938, the *Pittsburgh Courier* printed a photograph of Lois in her graduation attire, with the caption, "Miss Lois Gwendolyn Morton, twenty-year-old daughter of professor and Mrs. Clifford M. H. Morton, who received her master of arts degree in English from Fisk University. . . . She is an honor graduate of Louisville Municipal College."[21]

Lois's new status was mesmerizing to her: "From my perspective, the engagement was the real news. I had consistently excelled in educational endeavors but never before been an engaged woman. Most of the courting took place that summer." Exhilaration and ambivalence combined in equal parts in her emotional fiber, but her parents did not share her excitement. From their perspective, Lois had been an exemplary daughter; never before had she been the source of their continuing discomfort. As a teen, she had won a scholarship to an art school in the Midwest. Her parents, convinced that she should not leave home until she was older, refused to allow her to accept the scholarship. "I was profoundly disappointed," she remembers. "I had relinquished the dream of art school. By 1938, I was a young adult. I did not wish to compound my losses by giving up love."[22]

When the spring semester ended, Turner drove from Nashville, Tennessee, to Louisville, Kentucky, to visit Lois each weekend. The trip was 175 miles each way. In good weather, it required at least five hours travel time. Turner checked into a local hotel, retrieving Lois from her parents' home on Saturday mornings and returning her on Saturday evenings. They strolled and sat in the local park, spending quality time together. Between trips, Turner wooed Lois with weekly letters. Lois eagerly awaited them, responding to each. In the meantime, Clifford and Myrtle remained distant, viewing Lois as being in total rebellion. They referred to him as "Dr. Turner." He queried her about her position vis-à-vis him, inquiring as to whether she had "a mind of her own" strong enough to resist the quiet pressure from her parents. "I was in love," she remembers, "suspended dangerously between my new love and my loving family. That summer, because of the inner turmoil, I wept often" on his shoulder.[23]

Lois analyzed the summer as follows: "I felt myself being propelled along by forces I could not totally control nor truly wished to halt. I had completed two degrees beyond high school. I was a woman physically and emotionally. Prepared for the challenges of adult life, I reasoned that life was a series of unknowns with litmus tests to be passed and not failed. If danger lay ahead, my twenty years of living had prepared me for it. My year at Fisk had been all that I had hoped for, with freedom, independence, and opportunities for growth, both intellectual and social. Within one year, I had earned a master's degree and located my own fiancé."[24]

The Mortons, Lois, and Turner planned the wedding for Thursday, September 1, 1938, at 3:00 P.M. Clifford insisted that it be held in their home rather than in a church. It was an intimate and elegant affair with family and a small cluster of friends. Lois's first cousin on her father's family side, Claudia Jenkins, served as the bridesmaid. The best man was Robert Hemingway, a musician at Fisk, who had become one of Turner's lifelong friends. Myrtle expertly designed and sewed all the dresses. Her own was black. While black and white weddings are fashionable in the twenty-first century, in 1938 a black dress was the attire for a funeral. Turner and Hemingway wore white suits, rendering the black especially evident. Lois and the guests did not miss the symbolism. The guests were quiet and restrained. Clifford and Myrtle's smiles were strained. Periodically, Lois shed tears. She was a whirling vortex of emotions. Turner was tense. Lois recalls that "one moment of relief arrived with the entry of Mother's older half-sister, my Aunt Edna, who was tall, full-figured, and elegant. As she rushed to hug me, she lifted me bodily from the floor."[25]

The *Louisville Defender* ran a two-column article in its society pages covering the wedding in its September 1938 issue. "Miss Morton in Pretty Marriage to Fisk Instructor" described the occasion in detail. The minister was Rev. T. S. Ledbetter. After the reception, at which Turner and Lois were presented "many useful and beautiful gifts, the newly weds changed to traveling clothes and made their hurried departure for Nashville, Tennessee." Their honeymoon was "in the east." While the article mentioned that Clifford gave Lois away, it made little mention of Myrtle's involvement on the day of the wedding and no mention of her attire. The accompanying photograph featured the immediate bridal party without Lois's parents.[26]

The night after the wedding, Lois's father spoke quietly to her, sending her on her honeymoon with a traditional mantra: "Lois, I could not bring myself to forbid you to marry Dr. Turner. But if you have made your bed hard, you must lie in it."[27]

"Daddy was a stern and disciplined man. I was certain that he meant every word. I was just as convinced that Mother felt constrained to concur. Over the years, my parents maintained a formal but cordial relationship with Dow, referring to him as 'Dr. Turner' for the remainder of his life—and theirs," according to Lois.[28] At the same time, Lois's father, being a local administrator and the president of the Fisk University alumni organization in Louisville for many years, arranged to have Turner speak at Louisville Municipal College on several occasions. He respected Turner as a scholar; he also wished to assist Lois and her family financially.[29]

From Lois's perspective, "My wedding day was the beginning of a grand adventure, similar to a ride on a massive roller coaster. I was proud to be Mrs. Lorenzo Dow Turner. Dow was proud to have me as his wife. Some stretches on the trip were exhilarating; others were dismal. I did not complain to my parents, regardless of the height of the peaks, the speed of the trip, or the suddenness or depth of the drops on the journey."[30] The roller coaster did not always deposit her at the end of the day in the bed of her dreams, and over the ensuing thirty-five years, Lois found many occasions to contemplate what life might have held for her had she chosen to lie in a different bed.

16

Yale University FALL 1938

> The university is essentially a living thing. Like other organizations it must grow by casting off that which is no longer of value and taking on that which is. . . . Meantime, it will always be true that where the great investigators and scholars are gathered, thither will come the intellectual elite from all the world.
>
> —From the inaugural address of James Rowland Angell, President of Yale University, 1921

LOIS RECALLS THAT "AS NEWLYWEDS we lived in Dow's apartment for a short time. In January 1939, we rented a house on South Street. After Dow's research year in Brazil, we rented another house at 900 14th Avenue South, near the Fisk University campus. We lived there until 1944 when we purchased our own home 1015 Villa Place."[1]

Looking forward to the years ahead, the newlyweds' plan was for Turner to pursue teaching and research and for Lois to pursue the study of visual arts. They would travel and study together. An opportunity too momentous to reject soon presented itself when Turner was selected to spend the fall semester of 1938 at Yale University to study with Edward Sapir on a grant from the ACLS. Turner's colleague Mark Hanna Watkins spent the same semester studying with Sapir at Yale. Watkins, one of the first black American anthropologists, had been one of Sapir's star students at the University of Chicago. Sapir supervised his dissertation, after introducing him to his informant, Hastings Kamazu Banda, a native speaker of Chichewa, who later became a physician and who was the president of Malawi from 1964 until 1994.[2] Like Turner, Watkins was strongly involved in linguistics. Sapir generally dissuaded students from majoring in linguistics, however, because of the dearth of employment opportunities in the discipline, suggesting, rather, that they opt for anthropology.[3]

Sapir was the only formally trained linguist among the many Boas students at Columbia University in the early twentieth century. Language became the lens through which Sapir interpreted culture. Over time his concern for the "pragmatic classification of culture" was transformed into "a sensitive awareness of the meaning of culture in the human experience." Sapir became a something of a leader in the humanistic school of anthropology. Because of his fieldwork in the western states and, later, Canada, he "became aware . . . that cultural diversity was a human phenomenon—something to be cherished and protected. . . . Complexity was no valid measure of the good life. Simple cultures might be organized with far more sensitivity for human personality than the depersonalized life of the industrial culture of the West."[4] Among those also associated with the humanistic tradition are Ruth Benedict, Robert Redfield, and Watkins.

Joining the faculty of the University of Chicago in 1925, Sapir arrived just after Turner had completed his course work in English. If the two did not meet in Chicago, they met a few years later. In 1931 Sapir was attracted to Yale by a joint appointment in the departments of anthropology and linguistics. Yale had received an infusion of Rockefeller funds, making fellowships and other types of supported research possible.[5] Among the other linguists who availed themselves of the opportunity to study with Sapir at Yale were Stanley Newman, Fang-Kuei Li, and the young married couple Mary Haas and Morris Swadesh.[6]

Sapir was the central figure in the development of the "First Yale School" of linguistics in the 1930s. The "Second Yale School" under the influence of Leonard Bloomfield followed in the 1940s.[7] In theoretical perspective, Sapir's vision was broader than that of many of his peers in that he embraced the concept of the "functional equivalence of languages"; that is, the idea that though their elements may differ in style and variety, no language is superior to another.[8] His approach, therefore, held special appeal for innovative linguists such as Turner, with his interest in African-influenced creoles, and Watkins, with his concern for Bantu languages. It must have been encouraging to work directly with a linguist steeped in fieldwork on non–Indo-European languages who embraced the theory of "functional equivalence" at a time when many others still referred to non-Western and AmerIndian languages as "primitive."[9]

Constantly on the outlook to continue his study of linguistics, Turner recognized the Yale opportunity as valuable. At some point Turner had acquired a copy of the journal, written in Arabic, of an overseer, prompting him to consider investigating the possibility of Arabic retentions in Gullah. Simultaneously, given the historic contact between African Americans and Native Americans in the South, Turner could not be assured that he had turned over every stone until he had also investigated the possibility of Native American influences.[10] Sapir was familiar with both Arabic and Native American languages.

Going to Yale promised to meet Lois's needs, too, as she could pursue advanced studies in art in the Yale School of Fine Arts. Therefore Turner and Lois gathered many possessions into their blue 1937 Ford and headed for New Haven. From Nashville, the trip was just over one thousand miles. Once they arrived, the newlyweds moved to 482 Sheldon Avenue in nearby Hamden, Connecticut.[11]

The *Nashville Defender* marked the Turners' departure with a brief article on September 23, 1938. "Mr. and Mrs. Lorenza [*sic*] D. Turner Studying at Yale" reported,

> Dr. Lorenzo D. Turner, head of English at Fisk University, left the city Sunday accompanied by Mrs. Turner, in route to Yale University, New Haven, Conn., where he will spend one semester participating in a seminar on Comparative Problems in Primitive Languages. This seminar will be conducted by Professor Edward Sapir of the Departments of Anthropology and Linguistics. Dr. Turner goes to Yale on a grant from the American Council of Learned Societies. While in New Haven he will continue his work on a volume dealing with African survivals in the speech of Negroes in the coastal region of South Carolina and Georgia. Mrs. Turner will pursue courses in the Yale School of Fine Arts.[12]

In Turner's copy of the *Graduate School Bulletin of Yale University for the Academic Year 1938–1939,* his handwritten notes indicate that he planned to take Advanced Phonetics and Phonemics, Research in Linguistics, and Comparative Problems in Primitive Languages. Although the *Bulletin* indicates that none of the three was scheduled for the fall of 1938, Turner may have arranged to pursue the content of the courses through independent study. All three were courses that Sapir usually taught.[13]

Lois immediately contacted the School of Fine Arts and acquired its list of course offerings. Her handwritten notes indicate that she planned to enroll in three courses—one with Lewis Edwin York, an associate professor of drawing and painting; one with Theodore Diedricksen, an assistant professor of drawing; and one with Richard Adams Rathbone, an assistant professor of drawing and painting.[14] She subsequently selected four. Pictorial Art, Painting, and Pictorial Composition were all offered by Rathbone; Drawing was taught by Diedricksen.[15]

Lois was gratified for the opportunity to expand her horizons. The art school she was forced to forfeit as a teen was no longer an issue. She found the prominent artist Richard Rathbone to be an especially challenging teacher, and she welcomed each new adventure: "Rathbone's practice of displaying our work in order from superior to poor was humiliating—until the day my painting ranked best in the class."[16] During the evenings, the Turners conferred over meals, discussing Turner's linguistic projects and Lois's most recent paintings, relishing each other's company while formulating their short- and long-term goals. The Yale semester was a stimulating beginning for a marriage between two intellects.[17]

On December 17, at the end of the fall semester and just before returning to Fisk, Turner contacted President Jones. His letter served as an update of his academic activities for fall 1938: "I am spending most of my time working on my book and attending two seminars in Linguistics conducted by Professor Sapir. . . . I am also studying Arabic." Elaborating on the relevance of Arabic to his research, Turner stated, "Some of the slaves who were brought to Georgia were Mohammedans who had a knowledge of Arabic, and one of them wrote a diary in his native African language, using Arabic script and several Arabic sentences. One of the Arabists here is assisting me in translating the Arabic portions of the diary. Afterwards I will begin work on the West African parts."[18]

Turner had used his semester well. Besides his formal classwork, he had met Rev. Henry C. McDowell, a former missionary in Ngalangi, Angola. Upon his return to the United States, McDowell had become the pastor of the Dixwell Avenue Congregational Church in New Haven. Turner's contact with him proved productive, as McDowell made available to Turner materials he had brought back from Angola "relating to the Umbundu language."[19]

The one major setback during the semester had been the illness of Sapir from heart disease. Having experienced one heart attack during the summer of 1937, he then suffered a second in fall 1938 and was "ordered to bed by his physician."[20] Sapir subsequently succumbed to heart troubles on February 4, 1939. He was fifty-five years old.[21]

By then Turner had returned to Nashville, but Sapir's death at midcareer was a serious blow to the small but thriving linguistic community. During the latter portion of Turner's residency, Yale arranged for Sapir's classes to be conducted by "a Dr. Emeneau, who had recently returned to Yale from India, where for the past three years he has been working on certain Dravidian Languages."[22]

Continuing to make presentations on his expanding Gullah data, Turner reported to President Jones: "On December 12 I read a paper before the Linguistic Club of Yale University on West African survivals in the vocabulary of Gullah. . . . I am also to read a paper at the annual meeting of the Modern Language Association of America which convenes at Columbia University during the last three days of December."[23]

In the closing days of 1938, Turner attended the conference of the Modern Language Association. The uniqueness and seminal nature of his research was now and again noted in the national press. *Newsweek* magazine briefly covered the presentation in its education section on January 9, 1939. "At the 55th convention of MLA, Turner, English Department Head at Fisk in Nashville[,] traced 400 colloquialisms back to African dialects," it reported. Among the semantic items cited were "jumbo," "goober," "tote," and "buckra."[24]

Turner informed President Jones that he would return to Nashville "a day or two before Christmas for conferences with some of our graduate students in connection with their theses for the M.A. Degree." He then expected to return to Yale to complete the semester, returning to Nashville "about January 26" in time for the second semester.[25]

After the Turners returned to Fisk in the spring of 1939, the honeymoon was over; the marriage began in earnest. Lois reached her twenty-first birthday on February 4, 1939. Turner erroneously believed he had discovered the perfect baby doll and expected to play the role of a dominant father. Lois's angelic baby face and lilting dialect belied the solid, mature core and strength of character underneath. "What I lacked in experience in male/female relations," she remembers, "I more than compensated for in confidence, tough-mindedness and experience in the dynamics of living in a strong interdependent two-parent family. I was a woman of my times, who expected to be supportive, making sacrifices in the interest of my husband's career, but I, nonetheless, expected dialogue around family issues, reciprocity, and contact with the professional academic community as a faculty woman, not just as a faculty wife. My expectations were often unmet. In some regards, so were Dow's, especially on those occasions when he viewed me as manifesting youthful behaviors for which he entertained little tolerance."[26]

Early September 1939 provided another experience that matched the stimulation of the Yale semester in the Turners' developing relationship. When Turner returned to the field on St. Simon's Island, Lois and her mother accompanied him. He was proud to introduce his new wife and her mother to his Gullah informants. Not only that, he was delighted with the companionship. While Turner interviewed informants, recording new materials for his corpus, Lois examined the surroundings for artistic subjects. She selected four girls of graduated ages, creating tender, sensitively rendered charcoal portraits of their heads and shoulders.[27]

At some point after his return from London in September 1937, Turner had shipped his typewriter to a company to have a number of the traditional keys replaced with International Phonetic Alphabet symbols, specifically to make possible the processing of his Africanisms manuscript. Not having had the advantage of a course in typing, he utilized his own "hunt and peck method" to prepare his manuscripts.[28]

After his return from Yale, Turner remained at Fisk for three semesters before departing for Bahia, Brazil, in 1940 in search of Africanisms in Brazilian Yoruba and Afro-Brazilian culture. Lois was eager to spend the year abroad with him. Turner was anxious to have her accompany him. Unfortunately, funds were inadequate to support them both. At the same time, Turner was uncomfortable with leaving Lois alone in Nashville for a variety of reasons, among them, the cost of sustaining two households and the many young men who found Lois attractive. Nor was he reconciled to the idea that she should accept a teaching position in a local college or a public school. Eventually he determined that they should close their apartment in Nashville and place their belongings in storage, and that Lois should return for the year to her parents' home in Louisville. His decision was nonnegotiable.

As Turner sold his 1937 Ford to raise additional funds for his journey, Lois wept tears of disappointment. His triumph was her tragedy. Her respect and adoration for her parents could not outweigh her pain and her certainty that the time had come for her to reside in her own home with her own husband. She recounts, "Only my love for Dow made bearable the humiliation of returning to Louisville alone, to withstand the questioning stares of small town folk who had read two years earlier that I had won a prize in marriage, a handsome professor and English department chair at Fisk University. One year was far too long to languish as a sheltered, youthful bride."[29]

17

Brazil and Back 1940–1941

From my study of the importation of slaves from Africa in Brazil, and from the knowledge I have at present of Negro speech in Brazil, I find that with few exceptions the West African languages which have influenced the sea-island speech of South Carolina and Georgia appear likewise to have influenced the speech in certain parts of Brazil, particularly Bahia and Pernambuco.

—Lorenzo Dow Turner, "Statement of Work," February 17, 1940

TURNER'S QUEST TO LINK AFRICAN PEOPLE in the Western Hemisphere to their African past was lifelong. He approached the process through lectures, courses, research, publications, and the maintenance of relationships with persons of African ancestry in the United States, Africa, and Brazil, as well as with persons of European ancestry with related interests.

By 1939, two years after Turner's year in London, his perspective on the centrality of the African experience to the lives of persons of African ancestry internationally was being conceptualized in cultural anthropological ethnographies. With the onset of World War II, there was increasing interest in Brazil as a haven for intellectuals escaping the turbulence of the European continent. Simultaneously, a small social network of scholars in the United States and the Caribbean were examining the African presence in their various countries, attempting to understand it in broadly similar terms, that is, in terms of their status as "other" in their societies; the race variable; and the appreciation of African origins and retentions in language, culture, and family life.

The large Afro-Brazilian presence in northeastern Brazil became the focus of a number of researchers. Turner was one of them. While he was in London during the 1936–37 academic year, Henri Labouret had encouraged him to consider Brazil as another source of African diasporic culture. From available historical documents, Turner had learned that, "in marked contrast to the U.S. slaveholders' practice of breaking up [African] families and discouraging all semblances of Africanisms, just the opposite had been true in Brazil. [Africans] arriving near Bahia had been allowed to set up cult houses, serving as the same sort of center of worship that they had known in Africa."[1]

The reestablishment of traditional religious centers had facilitated the retention of African languages, art objects, music and musical instruments, ceremonies, and ceremonial objects in Brazil. Much after Turner's major research appeared, other research verified the retention of African plastic art techniques in the Western Hemisphere, most substantially in the southern United States in Georgia and the Carolinas, the same areas where African linguistic retentions were most pronounced.[2]

By early 1939 Turner had begun to seek grants for his Brazilian fieldwork. His proposal to the Rosenwald Fund met with success, as George M. Reynolds, the director of fellowships, informed Turner on April 12, 1939, that he had been awarded $3,100 "to assist you in carrying forward your study of phonetics and linguistics in accordance with the plan of work which you submitted to our Committee."[3]

In late May 1939 Turner contacted Melville Herskovits at Northwestern University to suggest that they meet to discuss Turner's future research. As Herskovits was the most prestigious anthropologist in the United States, and an Africanist as well, foundations were inclined to seek his opinions before granting research funds. Therefore, it behooved promising scholars to ensure that Herskovits was familiar with their research agenda. Turner offered to visit him. His plan at that juncture was still to prepare several separate monographs on Gullah, each focusing on the major elements of languages—the phonology, morphology, syntax, and semantics. Envisioning an additional one on intonation, he expected to compare aspects of Gullah to the relevant tone languages in Africa.[4] He wrote Herskovits:

> I shall be in Chicago early in June and should like very much to talk with you. If June 10 or 11 is convenient to you, I will come on either of those days. . . . You will be interested to know that I have collected in coastal Georgia and South Carolina approximately 3000 West African words. The sections furnishing the greatest number of words are Sierra Leone, Gambia and Senegal, Angola, Togoland, and the Gold Coast. At least forty percent . . . are used as proper names among the Gullahs.[5]

For Herskovits, June was not a workable month. He responded to Turner on October 17, requesting two papers, the one on Gullah, which Turner had read at the conference of the Modern Language Association in December 1938, and Turner's unpublished Africanisms manuscript. It was the most important letter of Turner's career and, indeed, of his entire life, as his response resulted in quotes from his unpublished Africanisms manuscript appearing in Herskovits's *The Myth of the Negro Past* (1941), the most influential book of the most influential anthropologist of the generation. It further legitimized Turner's developing research while ironically it did not result in a Carnegie Foundation research grant. His withholding the manuscript would not have changed the philosophy of the granting organization. The Carnegie Foundation, which funded Herskovits's fieldwork for *The Myth of the Negro Past,* was adamant in its stance that people of African ancestry receive only limited funds for research on the black experience. Turner was not among the elected, possibly because his research focused on language rather than politics, economics, or another social science. E. Franklin Frazier received Carnegie funds for his research in both Brazil and Haiti. The publication of *Africanisms in the Gullah Dialect,* though the book was essentially complete, was delayed eight years more.[6]

A week later, on October 24, Turner responded in the affirmative to Herskovits's request, indicating the status of his manuscript and suggesting another date for them to meet:

> Since I last heard from you, I have been working pretty steadily on the Gullah vocabulary with respect to African survivals. I expect to have the manuscript completed in about four to five weeks and shall be glad to have you examine it before I have it published. Will that be early enough for your purpose? If not, I can send you examples of the African words in Gullah from each of the groups into which I have divided them. In selecting names for their children, the Gullahs have used African words which describe conditions surrounding the birth of the children, such as the place of birth, the time of birth, the temperament of the child, its physical appearance, the state of its health, the condition of the weather, or other surroundings, etc. My list of proper names, accordingly will fall into about twelve or fifteen of these categories, with the names in each group arranged alphabetically. The list of words that are not proper names will be alphabetical throughout.[7]

Turner then summarized the results of his data collection on the Sea Islands, indicating that the final list would contain more than four thousand words.

Turner revised his plans, suggesting a meeting with Herskovits in Chicago around Thanksgiving. He added, "I should like also to talk with you concerning my plans for further study of African survivals in the speech of New World Negroes. If you are going to be in Chicago during the last week in November, I can arrange to come there at that time."[8]

The meeting marked the beginning of a mutually beneficial, though unequal, relationship that lasted until Herskovits's death on February 25, 1963, three years before Turner's formal retirement. By 1940 Herskovits was familiar enough with Turner and his work to recommend him to funding agencies. Early in the year, Turner submitted a funding proposal to Leland, who was by then the president of the ACLS, for funds to supplement the $3,100 from the Rosenwald Fund. Leland contacted Herskovits for comment on March 6, 1940:

> You are familiar with Lorenzo D. Turner's plans for Brazil, and you doubtless know that he has secured a grant for $3100 from the Rosenwald Fund. He needs, however, a thousand dollars more for a good recording machine (a Lincoln Thompson at $700, including the gasoline generator), and three or four hundred dollars more for discs and for the expenses of informants.
>
> I am encouraging him to apply to our Committee on Grants in Aid of Research for a grant of $400 ($300.00 for discs and $100 for expenses of informants), but it seems to me that the machine should be purchased by Fisk University and be its property; accordingly I am asking him to discuss this with the administration of the University.
>
> Meanwhile, it would help me to have your own opinion of his work, and especially of his proposed investigation in Brazil. I enclose the memorandum which he furnished us.[9]

Leland requested that Herskovits respond to the issue of whether or not Turner knew Portuguese: "There is one question raised by our Advisory Board, namely, that as to his equipment in Portuguese. Do you know anything about that? And in your opinion how important is it for him to have a good knowledge of Portuguese?

I know that he worked in Paris with French Negroes without much more than a rudimentary knowledge of French. It seems a sort of paradox that a man can work in linguistics without knowing languages, but in primitive linguistics scholars do that all the time."[10] Leland was clearly aware of the tradition among European linguists of studying non-Western languages and, indeed, writing grammars of them, with no background whatsoever. He seemed, however, to be unaware of the breadth of Turner's background in Latin and Romance languages.

Leland attached a copy of Turner's proposal for study in Brazil. Therein Turner had indicated that, after the Brazilian research, he expected to conduct research in "British and Dutch Guiana, the West Indies and elsewhere in the New World."[11] Herskovits was utilizing a similar approach in his anthropological research, as was E. Franklin Frazier in his sociological research.

Six days later, on March 12, 1940, Herskovits responded to Leland: "Turner came to Evanston to talk to me three or four months ago, and I advised him to apply for a special grant to cover the recording machine and records, since it was perfectly apparent to me as I went over his budget that it would be impossible for him to go to Brazil and do the work he contemplates and buy recording apparatus and records on a grant of that size." Herskovits had recommended to Turner the type of recorder he himself had used in Trinidad, for which he had been able to utilize Carnegie Corporation Funds. "With this in view, I sent him the literature I had and also the cost figures I assembled on the basis of my own expedition to Trinidad last summer. You may remember that the Carnegie people gave me a budget for that trip that permitted me to acquire one of those machines."[12]

Herskovits advocated that Turner be allocated foundation funds for a reliable recorder if Fisk University was unable to provide them. His rationale was that the quality of the field tapes should be "of practically professional caliber," an acknowledgment of the value of Turner's research. "I think it would be excellent to have Fisk acquire the machine, but if they do not, I hope the door will not be closed to the chance of either the Council or Stevens of the GEB [General Education Board] getting one for him. The improvements that have been made in recording machines in the last few years are considerable. Working under conditions of great handicap, I was able to bring back records that people in the broadcasting studies who have heard them tell me are of practically professional caliber. Acetate is quiet—that is, without scratching—and makes possible linguistic recordings that are far and away superior to anything that can be achieved on aluminum."[13]

On the issue of the soundness of Turner's research plan and methodology, Herskovits was unequivocal in his general support, while taking the liberty to circumscribe the focus of the research. He said, "I think Turner will do a good job in Brazil. For one thing I suspect he will work into Portuguese, but since his problem is essentially that of phonetics and grammar, I do not believe that a knowledge of the language is nearly as important as it would be if, for instance, he were to study social relationships. Frankly, I do not take very seriously the non-linguistic aspects of his project—for example, this matter about molding children's personalities has probably just been thrown in as a bright idea."[14]

On the issue of competence in the language, Herskovits pointed out that the Brazilian researcher Gilberto Freyre had informed him that English speakers would readily be available to be of assistance, in particular, some native Brazilian scholars who were also pursuing African influence in Brazilian culture: "I am told by Gilberto Freyre that there are many people in the intellectual group who know English, and I am sure that with letters to Freyre and Ramos and others, there will be students who will jump at the chance of being allowed to help Turner and thus provide him with interpreters who can gather his material quite satisfactorily for him until he himself masters Portuguese. I understand, however, that he is studying the language and that he has been studying it for some months, so that he should land in Brazil with a pretty adequate knowledge of it."[15]

Herskovits then recommended that Turner be allocated a recorder as soon as possible so that he could become thoroughly familiar with "its idiosyncrasies and those of the generator before he leaves." Herskovits further recommended that Turner "send it [the recorder] or bring it here for a thorough check-over by Mr. Phillips, an expert who has been of inestimable help to me and who will certainly catch anything that might need adjustment in the machine, as well as be able to give Turner many important tips on its use in the field such as only an expert with Phillips' training can give."[16]

In closing, Herskovits added, "I believe that Professor Turner is highly qualified to carry out the project for which he has applied. His work in the Sea Islands has turned out very significant materials, and the preparation for his research, which he obtained while in London working with West Africans, will stand him in good stead; he will be, I believe, the first trained linguist with such a background to study Brazilian Negro dialects."[17]

In his review of the proposal, Herskovits recommended that Turner be allocated "one or two hundred dollars more," which was two or three hundred dollars less than both he and Leland knew would be necessary. Simultaneously, he discounted the relevance of Turner's plan to analyze children's speech while concluding that the overall relevance of collecting a corpus of Afro-Brazilian data outweighed any perceived flaws in the research methodology. He wrote, "There are two points that might be made concerning this project. For one thing, I do not believe that Mr. Turner has asked for as much money as he should have, and I would like to see the committee appropriate one or two hundred dollars more than has been requested since I feel that an added efficiency in working over this project could be obtained if an extra amount of this order were made available to Professor Turner. I have the feeling that it would be well if the research were concentrated on the recording and analyses of texts and in recording songs by adults."[18]

By mid-year 1940 Turner had firmly developed his fieldwork plans. His base of operation was to be northern Brazil, particularly around Bahia, among the Brazilian Yoruba population, and he would employ a process similar to the one he utilized in Gullah territory. By then a seasoned field worker, Turner's intent in Brazil was to make a holistic examination of African retentions in the oral arts—linguistics, music, dance, folklore, and religious rituals.

In late June, after depositing Lois with her parents in Louisville, Turner traveled to New York by train, leaving soon after for Brazil aboard the *Uruguay*. He traveled tourist class. During the days aboard the ship, he concentrated on continuing his study of Portuguese. Immediately after his arrival in Rio de Janeiro, Turner wrote to Frazier. In 1934 Frazier had resigned from Fisk, in part because of conflicts with Johnson over the most effective methods of presenting issues of race in scholarly literature.[19] He had then accepted a position at Howard, where he taught and conducted research for the remainder of his career. Turner and Frazier were friends for life. Frazier, on a Carnegie Foundation allocation related to Gunnar Myrdal's *An American Dilemma* (1944) project, was to join Turner in Brazil, where Turner's base was the Hotel Florida, at Rua Ferreira Vianna, 75–77, Rio de Janeiro.[20]

The major purpose of Turner's letters was to brief Frazier on processes essential to his preparation for the journey. They also provide insight into Turner's Brazilian research agenda. Turner planned to become fully conversant in Brazilian Portuguese by learning standard Brazilian dialects from a native speaker. He wrote, "I have been here nearly two weeks, and am beginning to get accustomed to the Brazilian way of life. The language is very difficult to speak and to understand when Brazilians speak it. I am taking five lessons a week and living at a hotel where no English is spoken. I plan to remain here until the middle or last of September. By that time I hope to have the language well enough in hand to begin my research in Bahia."[21]

Turner had selected the provinces in which the African populations were concentrated. In several weeks he expected to confer with Donald Pierson, the Euro-American sociologist who was teaching at the Escola Livre de Sociologia e Política in São Paulo. Pierson, like Turner and Frazier, was a graduate of the University of Chicago.[22] The book resulting from Pierson's 1940 fieldwork is *The Negro in Brazil: A Study of Race Contact at Bahia* (1942). Turner wrote to Frazier:

> I intend to remain in Bahia six months, in Pernambuco three, and in Maranhão three months. If time permits I may spend three weeks each in Alagoas and Sergipe. In these four states, the customs of the Negroes appear to be more primitive than anywhere else. I am told also that in certain parts of Minas Gerais many African customs have survived. I shall probably go there, too. I shall meet Pierson in São Paulo this weekend.
>
> What are your plans? If I can give any suggestions about your travel in Brazil, let me know. I came on the *Uruguay* (American Republics Line) tourist class. Everything was fine. . . . I stayed ten days at the Pax Hotel, Preia do Russell, 108, and paid $2.00 a day for room and board (private bath). There is some English spoken there. At the Florida, where I am now staying, I pay $40.00–$45.00 a month for room and board. There is no English spoken here.[23]

Frazier responded immediately, prompting Turner to mail him a second letter on July 26, 1940, expressing pleasure that he would arrive soon. Turner commented on the difficulty of acquiring competency in Brazilian Portuguese. Simultaneously, he provided Frazier with numerous details that would be helpful in his planning for the trip. Because of Frazier's inquiry, Turner volunteered to book housing for Frazier and his wife, Marie. Turner wrote:

> This language here is hell. These people speak so fast that it is still difficult for me to understand most of what they say. I can ask for anything I need, but when I ask on the streets for information, the answers are often more confusing than enlightening. My linguaphone set hasn't been as useful to me as I had hoped it would be. With the exception of two records, it is entirely European Portuguese, which is different in many ways from Brazilian Portuguese—both in vocabulary and construction. . . . You asked about a room with bath at this hotel. . . . If you wish me to, I will engage a room here for you. Is Marie coming? Guests are constantly coming and going, but the sooner you engage the room, the better.[24]

Looking forward to having a familiar friend and researcher in Bahia, Turner noted that "it appears that we shall be going to Bahia together. The fare from here to there is only about $10.00 on a Brazilian boat. There is no American boat going from Rio to Bahia. I may rent a small furnished house in Bahia where I can do my recording without disturbing anyone. If I can make any other suggestions, let me know."[25]

Frazier soon arrived. In Brazil, Turner and Frazier's contacts welcomed them as celebrities. They were the subjects of interviews for newspaper articles, invited to *candomblé* ceremonies, and introduced to middle-class and wealthy Afro-Brazilians. Turner interviewed the women who were the present and former heads of the Dahomean cult in Bahia. Both were born in Brazil of Dahomean parents. Both spoke fluent Fõn. He purchased three African drums and four rattles from one of the cult houses in Bahia. He met Theodora Maria Cardozo Alcantara, one of the middle-class women who utilized her African name /adʒa ji/ (low, low, high tone), which means "a child having a caul around the neck at birth." He interviewed Señor Maxwell Assumpcão Alakiʒ and his wife and three children, who presented him with an autographed photograph of the family in Western business attire.[26]

During the course of the year, Turner recorded approximately sixty persons, many of them religious leaders. His data consist of four major types: (1) materials from African-Brazilian cults (*candomblé*), as they sang and spoke, that illustrated Yoruba percussive techniques, Angolan and Kongo idioms, and call and response; (2) *capoeira* singing and dancing, with small groups providing call and response in African/Portuguese, rhythms from the *berimbau* (with and without *caxixi*), and the *pandeiro;* (3) popular secular music (some perhaps from the radio); and (4) language informants who conversed, counted, and spelled, usually in Portuguese. Turner recorded Manuel de Silva providing drumming on more than one occasion, as well as Nestor de Nascimento, a well-known popular musician, who sang in an Angolan language, accompanying himself on the guitar. On one occasion, he sang a farewell song. Turner attended Carnivale and recorded vocal and instrumental music.[27]

Turner took notes and recorded a number of acetate discs of both speech and music.[28] In addition to collecting materials on Brazilian–West African cultural patterns, he sometimes played Gullah recordings to his Brazilian informants. As he suspected, Afro-Brazilian Portuguese was infused with Yoruba and Ewe-Fõn, in particular. He found that when he played Gullah tapes to Africans of the religious cult communities near Bahia, his informants recognized some lexical items, tones, and music styles.[29] Turner was, therefore, able to document another profound level of verification that Gullah and Afro-Brazilian Portuguese were related and both infused with a substratum of Niger-Congo languages.[30]

Against the backdrop of Turner's research abroad, as he traveled long distances with bulky, weighty equipment, attempting to function in a new language, struggling to economize on an inadequate budget, his life in America often became secondary to him. He overlooked the reality that he and Lois were partners in a young marriage requiring nurture. Like his father, Turner tended to be controlling and not inclined to share his wife's attention while also limiting her options. So as he placed his research priorities at the center of his life, his letters to Lois often caused her to feel neglected. More important, without the option of pursuing employment outside her parents' home, with no resources to continue the study of painting, and with no independence, Lois felt she was stagnating.[31]

In a letter of September 17, 1940, she raised the issue of her career. Her desire to enter the employment arena was grounded in the reality that one could not afford to allow viable opportunities to pass. There was significant discrimination against married women, especially those of childbearing age, on the assumption that their work lives would be interrupted by family responsibilities, especially by pregnancies and care for young children. The young Mrs. Turner wrote her husband, "With everyone going to school to study or teach, I feel rather out of things. I really should have a job teaching somewhere. I need a year's experience or two in order to hold a really good job. One can't ever tell when it may become necessary. When one is married it is more difficult to get jobs, though."[32]

Two weeks past their second wedding anniversary, Lois tactfully reminded Turner to purchase a reasonably priced keepsake for her. She preferred that he make the selection rather than allowing Marie Frazier to choose it. She wrote, "Darling, I wonder if you see anything pretty there that you'd like to bring me. It could serve as my second anniversary present. If I were choosing, I should like to pick it (because you always spend too much), but since I probably won't get there, you try to be economical and bring me something not too expensive as my watch. You know 'pretty' well what I would like—of course something I could keep."[33]

Lois inquired about the Fraziers. Indicating that they had arrived in time to travel on the boat with him from Rio to Bahia, Turner informed her that the local papers had run stories on Frazier and him. The richness of research opportunities in the field and the positive reception accorded the two were assets. The liability was the interpersonal relations among the three. Already Turner's patience was fraying: "The Fraziers are getting more and more on my nerves every day—especially Mrs. Frazier. . . . She . . . hates dark people and is hardly courteous to them."[34] Turner found it paradoxical that anyone wishing to study the culture of people of African descent would harbor color prejudice against them.

On October 14, 1940, five weeks after his September 7 arrival in Bahia, Turner sent Lois a letter by airmail indicating that he had become "sick with a diarrheal condition due to something I ate." His residence was the Palace Hotel at Rua Chile, 20. Turner wrote that he had "been in my room for two or three days, but I shall be able to go out tomorrow." He explained that "such a condition is almost unavoidable here until one gets accustomed to the food and water. I called in a colored doctor, and he has given me medicine that has helped me greatly."[35]

Describing the cultural context, commenting on the color issue in passing, Turner expressed optimism about the abundance of research data for his study: "Nearly everybody is colored here. It is a very interesting place—the oldest city in South America and older than any city in North America. The African material is very rich. There are some Negroes here who were brought from Africa as slaves and who still speak their native language. There is a church here almost entirely lined with gold. It is nearly 400 years old. At the time it was built, gold was very plentiful and cheap. There are 365 churches in the city—nearly all Catholic."[36]

As the months passed, the Turners wooed each other countless times by airmail. In early January 1941, Lois began to make plans for Turner's return. Of high priority was a house. "What about a house in Nashville? I told you I couldn't get the one we had in mind," she wrote. Lois was conscientious in processing his mail: "I am still taking care of your mail. Important letters I feel I cannot get to you on time, I return along with your address to the senders."[37]

Turner's data collection progressed as planned. He focused on language and culture, and Frazier on family life and race relations.[38] Pierson, their third collaborator, also analyzed race relations.[39] After a few months, Turner and Pierson both concluded that African influence was widely evident. Their conclusions did not, however, alter Frazier's perspective; he observed African retentions in Afro-Brazilian religion only.[40] On February 4, 1941, Turner contacted Herskovits, declaring enthusiastically, "The field here is rich in African material and I am having no difficulty finding it."[41]

After four months, Frazier headed for Haiti, while Turner remained in Bahia. They had no doubt debated their differing hypotheses. Turner was convinced that the evidence of African retentions in northern Brazil was so compelling that Frazier would abandon his former hypothesis. In his February 4, 1941, letter to Herskovits, Turner expressed his belief that firsthand contact with Afro-Brazilian culture would convert Frazier to the African retentions school: "He is no longer in doubt about African survivals in New World culture. From now on he will observe the American Negro through different but wiser eyes. This trip to Brazil has indeed been a revelation to him."[42]

When Herskovits responded, he did not comment on Frazier's perspective; rather he expressed his enthusiasm over Turner's success in locating African retentions in yet another diasporic location: "Naturally, this is an extremely important job and it will be a great help to have so much material of this kind available when your data will achieve publication."[43]

As spring arrived, Turner moved to Pernambuco. By April 1941 he had settled at Avenida 7 de Setembro, 142, perhaps the small house he had wanted so as not to disturb his neighbors as he played and analyzed his field tapes. His funds were running low; his thoughts were turning to Lois and home. "Your letter came today, and I am answering it immediately. I enjoyed reading your letter immensely. . . . [All] of them are very sweet and cheering to me in this strange 16th century town. Much as I enjoy your letters, they cannot take the place of you. But the weeks are passing rapidly and I shall soon be with you," he wrote.[44] Having contemplated the importance of Lois's career as an artist and wishing to be supportive, Turner outlined a general plan detailing how they could both accomplish their goals:

> I do so much want to live forever happily with you. I am counting the days that remain before my return. We shall have to work out a plan whereby you can continue your work at Yale and also have a baby or two. That will be one of the first subjects we will discuss when I return. I am eager, as you know, for you to get more training in art. With the kind of training they give at Yale, you can become a great artist. Maybe you can get in two summers there or in New York or Chicago before 1943. Then I can be with you to help with details about the house. We could take our meals in a good restaurant and while you are in class I can be writing on a book and attending lectures in Linguistics. The facilities are excellent at Yale, as you know.[45]

Among the highlights of Turner's year in Brazil were his opportunities to immerse himself in the culture of Yoruban/Brazilian (Nagôs) communities. He had located and documented "several thousand African words, a large number of which are used by the Gullah."[46] He had purchased four Afro-Brazilian women's garments, musical instruments, artwork, and photographs.[47] Having observed African percussion style, dances, music, religious practices, and folklore, upon his return to Nashville he taught Lois a traditional Afro-Brazilian dance, which she in turn taught four women students at Fisk. They performed it in the authentic garments that Turner had purchased.[48]

A growing body of references on Afro-Brazilian culture appeared a few years before and after Turner's fieldwork.[49] A full-length dictionary on Africanisms in Brazilian Portuguese was not completed until forty years after Turner's year in Brazil, when John T. Schneider published the *Dictionary of African Borrowings in Brazilian Portuguese* (1991).[50]

Turner published three articles from his Brazilian research. It is clear from their focus that Turner's vision of culture had become holistic. For him the methodologies of cultural anthropological ethnography provided a broader context for interpreting the language and culture. The first paper to appear was "Some Contacts of Brazilian Ex-Slaves with Nigeria, West Africa," in the *Journal of Negro History* in 1942. It pointed out that in 1890, two years after the abolition of slavery in Brazil, a decree signed by Ruy Barbosa, minister of finance, mandated the burning of all documents related to African enslavement in Brazil. Hence, the traditional documents on which social scientists rely to reconstruct the history, sales, roles, and migration patterns were destroyed. Therefore the oral data from former slaves and their descendants, and the documents they had maintained, became valuable resources to persons wishing to research their African backgrounds. In the 1940s there were many such persons living in Brazil. According to Turner, "Many of them were born in Africa, still speak fluently their native language, frequently have in their possession valuable papers and pictures relating to West Africa, and correspond regularly with their relatives living there."[51]

Turner concentrated on the syncretized culture of the Yoruba-Brazilians, or Nagos, since they constitute the largest and strongest African influence. He reported that their influence was followed by that of the Dahomeans and Angolans. In addition to religious syncretism, music, dance, and linguistic retentions, the article described the nature of the contacts between Afro-Brazilians and their relatives in Nigeria: they undertook trips to Africa for visits and for extended stays; corresponded with relatives and friends; and traded in textiles, tobacco, sugar, dried beef, and cachaça, a drink made of sugar cane and water. Within the article, Turner reproduced copies of letters, passports, and certificates of birth, baptism, marriage, and burial of Africans in Brazil who maintained ties with relatives in Nigeria. He concluded by pointing out that the Yoruba in Brazil have great reverence for Africa, then encouraged researchers who study Brazil to acquaint themselves with the nature of the African influence in order to produce accurate results.[52]

The second article, "The Negro in Brazil," was written for the informed lay public.[53] Turner developed a sociohistorical analysis, comparing the experience of slavery in the United States to that in Brazil. Indicating that the Brazilian Africans were procured from roughly the same regions as those in North America, principally from the area extending from Senegal to Angola—including the countries of Senegal, Gambia, Guinea, Sierra Leone, Liberia, Ghana, Togo, Dahomey (now Benin), Nigeria, Congo, and Angola—he noted that they were resettled largely in northeastern Brazil. Putting down roots in Bahia, Maranhão, Pernambuco, Minas Gerais, Alagoas, Sergipe, and Rio de Janeiro, they found the climate similar to that in West Africa. Consequently, they were able to re-create familiar industries, including growing cotton and producing sugar.

Painting a rather idealized picture of life for Africans in Brazil, Turner underscored a number of particulars in which they were advantaged socially over Africans in the United States and elsewhere in the Caribbean. He noted that they were often manumitted, possessing, as a result, all the rights and privileges of any other citizens, and they were born free if their fathers were free Europeans. Entire nuclear families were freed if the number of family members reached ten. Under Brazilian law, Africans were to "enjoy special privileges" for 85 to 104 days per year, which included the right to work for financial remuneration. By the end of formal slavery in 1888, millions of Afro-Brazilians were already free. With this backdrop established, Turner discussed the religious practices as "the most fruitful source of African survivals" in the Western Hemisphere. He noted that "native African religious ceremonies are basically the same as they were when brought to Brazil during the period of slavery. In these communities one can still see authentic African dances . . . and artifacts and hear authentic African drum rhythms, songs, chants, prayers, and stories. From these African . . . communities both religious and secular songs and dances, as well as other elements of African culture, have spread throughout Brazil and far beyond its borders."[54]

In the second portion of the article, Turner outlined the Afro-Brazilian contributions to folklore, language (including several thousand African words that have been permanently incorporated in the vocabulary of Brazilian Portuguese), architecture, the plastic arts, sciences, the military, and politics. He pointed out that a number of Afro-Brazilians returned to Nigeria after 1888, contributing to architecture, education, and the economy in notable ways. Concluding with a quote from the Brazilian analyst Gilberto Freyre, Turner emphasized that the lengthy collision of cultures in Brazil resulted in "integration, or balance of contending elements, rather than segregation, or sharp differentiation, of any of them or violent conflicts between them."[55]

The third article, "African Survivals in the New World with Special Emphasis on the Arts,"[56] was reminiscent of "The Negro in Brazil." While the focus was Brazil, Turner's approach was cross-cultural, also presenting data on Africans in the United States and various Caribbean islands. Using as examples African retentions in language, folk literature, religion, art, and music, Turner reasserted one of his major themes, that myths related to Africans and African culture could be laid to rest if more persons would become serious students of African culture.[57]

Turner returned from Brazil with a significant corpus of folklore, particularly folktales, some history, and music, original and unpublished at that time. While some of the data are in manuscript form, much is also captured on the approximately six hundred twelve-inch discs recorded in and around Bahia. They evidence that West African languages were still spoken in northeastern Brazil by formerly enslaved Africans and their descendants, the major ones being Yoruba, Ewe, Fõn, and Kimbundu.[58] Had Turner been able to shepherd his Brazilian folklore into print, it would have been among the first such works in the United States, a seminal contribution to a synthesis of Afro-Brazilian culture.

After Turner's return to Nashville, the rigors of his position at Fisk did not afford him the time or resources to compile the full range of the cultural data he had collected. However, his articles on Brazil demonstrated that his research was solidly anchored in the African retentions hypothesis and in interdisciplinary analysis. All three articles highlighted the degree to which Africans in northern Brazil were aware of their Nigerian heritage and the ways in which that heritage was reflected in syncretized forms of music, dance, dress style, folklore, and religion, as well as in the contacts they maintained with Nigeria. These articles foreshadowed his cross-disciplinary work (with an anthropological focus) that became central to his teaching and public lectures after he joined the faculty of Roosevelt College in 1946.

Turner continued to be committed to his research agenda. According to his 1946 grant proposal to the American Philosophical Society, his intellectual contributions were still to be the compiling of grammars, dictionaries, and analyses of retained semantic items from African languages in North American creoles, as well as collections of folklore and music.[59] He still looked forward to conducting fieldwork in Africa, Jamaica, Haiti, and British and Dutch Guiana; he chose his potential fieldwork sites carefully as they would yield data on both Afro-Germanic and Afro-Romance creoles.

Before the African Studies movement in the United States was under way, Turner's conception of the importance of African diasporic studies in the curriculum was already well developed. On Sunday, May 31, 1942, the Alpha Lambda Chapter of Alpha Phi Alpha in Louisville, Kentucky, featured Turner in one of the Louisville Pan-Hellenic Council forums. Addressing the topic "Education for Citizenship," he made a case for the inclusion in the curriculum of data on African culture, African diasporic culture in America and Brazil, and the experiences of enslaved Africans in the Western Hemisphere. According to a report of his talk in the *Louisville Defender,* Turner maintained that there were "several factors in effective education for citizenship" that were "frequently and sometimes intentionally neglected in our education scheme. . . . If all races . . . were made aware of the offerings of Africans and their New World descendants, a better world would result."[60]

Turner then set about to dispute a series of commonly held myths about blacks, among them that blacks were childlike and submissive, with enslaved Africans in America representing the most degraded of all Africans; that African culture was "savage" and unable to withstand external pressures, so that in contact with another culture, Africans could not maintain their own heritage; and that blacks have no past about which they can take pride. He indicated that a test of the effectiveness of the propaganda was that the majority of African people in America had become convinced that they had no history or culture worthy of systematic study.

The reality, Turner stated, is that the records of "insurrections, suicides, infanticides, and run-aways" refute the myth of an African submission to enslavement; that many enslaved Africans were persons of "high birth" who were captured and enslaved through warfare; and that West Africans have ancient languages and cultures that compare "favorably with all others." Contrasting the attitude of African people in America with those in Brazil, Turner asserted that Afro-Brazilians were aware that the Africans had brought "the best in music, art, the dance, and folklore" to Brazil.[61]

Turner concluded his presentation by challenging African Americans to take pride in their culture, both on the African continent and in the diaspora. Further, he admonished them to "educate other races and groups in the appreciation of African culture," by teaching courses in African languages, civilizations, and art at the college level, in part because of the contributions of Africa to "modern culture."[62]

The themes developed in Turner's lecture were central to his message for the remainder of his career. Many were echoed in the introduction to *Africanisms in the Gullah Dialect,* which would appear seven years later.

While Turner returned to the United States in July 1941 still buoyed by the results of his data collection, he was immediately dashed to earth by the political realities at Fisk. Financial support for the college was in decline, in part because of World War II. Consequently, the university had embarked on a retrenchment program that was to divest it of a number of productive faculty members.[63] M. Franklin Peters had been one of Turner's friends and colleagues since their days together at Howard University (1923–28). Turner had later recommended him to Fisk, and he had joined the faculty of the English department in 1936, while

Turner was on leave in London. According to a 1936 letter from President Jones to Turner, Peters was an exemplary addition to the faculty: "There is a fine spirit on the campus and first rate class work seems to be in progress in every department. Dr. Peters gave his first public, dramatic performance about two weeks ago. Although unfortunately I was not in the city, I have heard many favorable comments as to the quality of the presentation."[64]

In Turner's absence, though, and without consultation with him, President Jones eliminated Peters from the faculty. Jones had also submitted his own resignation to the board of trustees, to be effective on January 1, 1941, in part concluding that since the most recent financial campaign had faltered, new leadership was warranted. Jones noted in a letter to Turner, "Since there were no funds to employ additional personnel, the teaching and administrative duties of the faculty had to be increased."[65] Jones's most pressing reason for wishing to resign, though, was to become director of the American Friends Service Committee's Civilian Public Service, an organization dedicated to organizing conscientious objectors against the war. Being a conscientious objector himself, Jones found the position appealing. But rather than accepting his resignation, the board of trustees granted him a leave of absence for 1941. In addition, the board granted him several months leave each year for the duration of World War II, until 1945, a situation that caused the bulk of administrative burdens to fall to Dean A. A. Taylor. Alumni were soon to complain of "unfavorable conditions" on the campus.[66]

Immediately after learning of Peters's dismissal, Turner sent the president a strongly worded four-page, double-spaced, typed letter questioning the reasons for the decision while making a case for its reversal. After confessing his great surprise "on reaching the campus" that Peters had been dismissed, Turner underscored that the Peters matter was "of very grave concern to me as head of the Department of English. . . . I suppose the action was due to the program of retrenchment, which the University has found it necessary to adopt, but Professor Peters informs me that no explanation for the dismissal was given him."[67]

Next, reminding President Jones of the workload in the Department of English resulting from the university's English requirement for students, Turner argued, "If the economic status of the University demands that the Department of English dispense with one of its four full-time teachers, it is unfortunate for Fisk University. . . . For adequate instruction in English there should be at Fisk four full-time English teachers. The dismissal of Professor Peters leaves only three. . . . At Fisk English is required of all students—eleven semester hours at a minimum."[68]

Turner emphasized the exigency of having persons trained specifically in composition to offer the English department's writing courses. In closing, he made the case that the status of the English department would be seriously compromised without Peters and that the quality of instruction the students received would suffer: "Professor Peters is the best equipped in training, experience, and temperament of all the teachers of English we have had during the twelve years I have been here. His leaving would seriously cripple our work."[69]

On numerous previous occasions, President Jones had responded to Turner in a warmly supportive manner. In 1941, though, in the face of a shrinking budget, the president had sharpened his elbows for the battle. His tone in the return missive was clinically detached: "Regarding Professor Peters' case, I regret to say that there is little that can be done about it. Necessary retrenchments . . . have affected not only Dr. Peters but other faculty members." President Jones, suggesting that he would confer with Turner at some unspecified future juncture, informed Turner that he would be out of town but expected him to meet with Dean A. A. Taylor.[70]

Peters was not reinstated. After the Peters affair, Turner no longer felt that he enjoyed the position of a favorite son. From his perspective, his unwavering loyalty to Fisk and President Jones, as well as his exemplary performance, had been rewarded with deception. He was undoubtedly angered that President Jones had not consulted him and allowed him to make a case for the preservation of his department. At the same time, he was remorseful that he had not been able to protect the position of his colleague and friend after having invited him to Fisk. For the remainder of his tenure, Turner was restive, wary of President Jones, and concerned that continued declines in funding might not bode well for his job security at a crucial time in his career and family life.

Two weeks later Turner received the grim news that Guy Lowman had been killed in an automobile accident near Auburn, New York.[71] Born in 1909, Lowman was thirty-two years of age. By the time of his death on August 3, 1941, Lowman had interviewed more than one thousand informants residing in towns and villages along the eastern seaboard of the United States and Canada, employing his keen intuition and fieldwork techniques.[72] The loss must have been painful for Turner. Lowman was not only a talented field researcher; he had also been one of the consistent supporters of the direction of Turner's Gullah research.

Continuing with his research agenda, Turner published one article and two book reviews in 1942. "Some Contacts of Brazilian Ex-Slaves with Nigeria, West Africa" and a review of Sterling Brown et al., eds., *The Negro Caravan: Writings by American Negroes* appeared in Carter G. Woodson's *Journal of Negro History.* Turner's review of Herskovits's best-known volume, *The Myth of the Negro Past,* appeared in the *Journal of Negro Education* from Howard University.

Turner continued to be in demand on campus and in the academic world of the HBCUs. On February 2, 1943, he received a letter from Robert J. Sailstad, coordinator of the Communication Center at Hampton Institute in Virginia, requesting that he spend two or three days there evaluating Hampton's English program. Sailstad offered to pay Turner's expenses and an honorarium. In a return letter shortly thereafter, Turner agreed to make the evaluation.[73]

After visiting Hampton in early March 1943, Turner mailed Sailstad his analysis, laid out over a number of pages. In the early pages, he advocated a traditional composition program, featuring courses offered by full-time faculty with expertise in composition. On page four, Turner advocated a three-hour course on black literature that would include "a study of the Negro folk literature, since this constitutes a much more distinctive contribution to American literature than the more sophisticated Negro literature." Realizing that such an approach should be grounded in discussion and analysis of African culture and contributions, Turner suggested that "in connection with this folk material some attention should be given to the American Negro's African cultural background." He offered to furnish "a list of significant books with this important background material."[74]

On the fifth page, Turner focused on the value of understanding distinctive African American language forms: "Almost every interpretation given by Negro authors of Negro dialect in the United States has to be rewritten because these writers who have attempted to explain it had no acquaintance whatever with the American Negro's African linguistic background. It is always difficult to appraise properly the literature of our contemporaries; and unless college students acquire a sane critical approach to literature, they will not be able to interpret it properly."[75] He was already far beyond most of his peers in stressing an African-centered paradigm in black literary criticism.

By summer Miles Hanley had invited Turner to the University of Wisconsin to present a series of lectures on his Gullah research and on the data he had collected in Brazil. Turner accepted. His general theme focused on African survivals in both Brazil and the United States. In an August 7, 1943, article, the *Chicago Defender* announced: "Fisk Professor Concludes Colorful Lecture Series." Turner's four presentations were "The Yorubas of Brazil in Story and Song," "African Religion and Secular Music from Brazil," "Varieties of Brazilian Portuguese," and "Africanisms in the Gullah Dialect of Coastal South Carolina and Georgia."[76]

By the early 1940s Turner's theoretical framework reached well beyond an analysis of language and literature. At its center was an interdisciplinary synthesis that demonstrated that African retentions and reformulations survived in the heart of the cultures of people of African descent in the Western Hemisphere. He concluded that if he could not physically touch the African continent, he could at least foster a holistic understanding of it within and outside the classroom.

18

Fisk University and the Founding of African Studies 1943–1946

> There is some basis for belief that in the Western Sudan especially, perhaps also in Nyasaland, and other places . . . the native people will have a larger share in the development of their country and in the shaping of their own destinies. It is not a disparagement of their inherent abilities nor their present accomplishments to say that Africans will need assistance in these tasks.
>
> —Fisk University brochure on African studies, 1943

FOR TURNER, 1943 WAS AN EXCELLENT YEAR. He participated in the founding of the African Studies Program at Fisk, the first in the nation. Often Northwestern University is cited as the first such program, but Northwestern actually initiated the first outside an HBCU, in 1948. The distinction of having the first African Studies Program to offer degrees at the bachelor's and master's levels belongs to Howard University in 1954, under the direction of Mark Hanna Watkins.

At Fisk, six scholars were associated with the program: Charles Johnson, the director and chair of the Department of Social Sciences; Robert E. Park, sociologist and professor emeritus from the University of Chicago; Edwin Smith, president and cofounder of the International Institute of African Languages and Cultures in Great Britain; Ina C. Brown, a social anthropologist; Mark Hanna Watkins, a linguistic anthropologist; and Turner. In addition, the program attracted a number of continental Africans to Fisk, among them the Vai princess/social scientist Fatima Massaquoi and Jacob Motsi, the Setswana informant for Watkins.[1]

The program offered a broad range of courses. Its catalog stated that it had a multifold mission: (1) to widen students' social and intellectual horizons while releasing their thoughts and feelings from the "limitations of a restricted national, ethnic and monocultural vista"; (2) to provide a scientific treatment of African culture and issues for university students, especially the scientific investigation of cultural, psychological, and biological data; and (3) to prepare African students for service in their home countries.[2]

Turner and his colleagues, foreseeing the end of colonialism, looked forward to the collaboration between Africans and African Americans in the process of building a stronger, freer Africa. Written by Watkins, the program description stated: "The American Negroes, related as they are genealogically and historically to the Africans, would appear to be distinctively adapted for work in this sphere. Their claim for the privilege and opportunity for the undertaking must be supported by adequate preparation. The human urge for such alliance must be buttressed with the acquaintance, forbearance, and objectivity which result from long and careful study. Action that is based on concrete data and rational attitudes will have greater efficacy than that which is motivated by romantic impulses alone, however noble may be the intentions that are bound up with the latter."[3]

The three major goals of the Peace Corps are evident in Fisk University's African Studies Program, which predated the Peace Corps by twenty years.[4]

African Studies created a positive stir, each year attracting for the university's Spring Fiesta speakers at the cutting edge of their disciplines.[5] Its purpose was to celebrate African cultures in the Western Hemisphere. Therefore, the speakers were usually proponents of the African retention hypothesis. The April 14–16, 1943, seminar on Africa was among the most memorable, featuring Suzanne Comhaire-Sylvain of the University of Haiti on the influence of African languages on Haitian Creole speech.[6]

Comhaire-Sylvain was an excellent choice as she had initiated the body of research on the retention of Africanisms in North American culture with her study *Le Créole haïtien,* in which she described the morpheme classes and noun and verb phrases of Haitian Creole. At the end of each section, she outlined "la base française" and "la base africaine." Her careful evaluation led her to conclude that Haitian Creole lexical items largely derive from French, that is, have French as their source, with Ewe-Fõn as the major source of Haitian Creole morpho-syntax.[7] Herskovits, the other featured speaker, presented "Patterns of Music in Africa and the New World," a lecture which he illustrated with recordings.[8]

On the home front, Turner anxiously anticipated fatherhood. In 1943 Lois was twenty-five and pregnant with the Turners' first child. Turner was in his fifty-fourth year. Lorenzo Dow Turner Jr. made his appearance on a warm summer night, July 1, at 12:14 A.M. Turner's joy overflowed. Before dawn he ran through the neighborhood, knocking on doors, awakening his colleagues to announce, "It's a boy!"[9]

The Turner household was transformed. Turner's pride in fatherhood was matched by Lois's pride in motherhood. She set about to sew a wardrobe for baby Lorenzo. Now and again Turner would pause from his research to drive Lois and baby to Louisville to visit his Morton grandparents and his Aunt Gloria. One such occasion was the summer of 1944, when Lorenzo Jr. celebrated his first birthday. They were part of the high society in the African American world, and as such, their activities were monitored with interest by the press.

The *Louisville Defender* covered Lois and Lorenzo Jr.'s summer visit to Louisville on its society page on July 8, 1944. Lois's younger siblings were home as well.

> The MORTON "KIDS" of West Madison were all home together again. . . . LOIS MORTON TURNER of Nashville; GLORIA, a student at Talladega College; and ANDREW, a student in army medical training at Meharry Medical College. Andrew came 'all the way from Nashville for the baby's birthday' . . . even though the baby lives in Nashville, too; and he sees him often . . . LORENZO TURNER JR., son of Lois and DR. LORENZO TURNER, of Fisk University. Lois and little Lorenzo will be here for about two weeks longer . . . visiting her mother and dad, the CLIFFORD

> MORTONS and her sister. Andrew spent just the weekend. Gloria had a recent visit from her classmate and roommate, JULIA REID of Jacksonville, Alabama. Mrs. Morton entertained for the young lady at luncheon and at cards.[10]

It was a fulfilling period for the Turners, both in their personal lives and in Turner's professional life. During the second year of their marriage, for Lois's birthday in 1940, Turner had purchased a Singer sewing machine. Being the daughter of a home economics teacher, she was well schooled in the art of homemaking. She decorated their home in an appealing manner. After the birth or Lorenzo Jr., she did not hesitate to tackle any project, whether pants, shirts, or winter items such as hats and snowsuits.[11]

One of the highlights of Lois's career occurred in the spring of 1945 when she was offered a full-time appointment as an English professor at Tennessee State University. Assigned to teach both English composition and literature courses, Lois found the position a dream come true. Tennessee State, like Fisk, was in Nashville, and the opportunity to teach there provided the career she had longed for since completing her master's degree.[12]

Turner became one of the caregivers for two-year-old Lorenzo Jr. The challenge was for Turner to integrate his son into his own routine, for at least the hours when Lois taught her classes. After Turner dropped Lois off for her classes, he performed his daily activities, returning to retrieve her when the academic day concluded. The family then shared a joyous reunion. All was well for a few weeks until the challenge of fulfilling childcare responsibilities with an already demanding schedule became burdensome from Turner's perspective. Consequently, he admonished Lois to resign her position and return to homemaking full-time. She reluctantly complied, having taught one semester. She was hoping for another opportunity at a university career when Lorenzo Jr. reached school age, but the appointment at Tennessee State was the only university position she had the opportunity to accept during her career.[13]

Turner, being a committed and talented man, was taxed in every way. His opportunities to pursue his own research were becoming more limited. By the winter of 1944, Watkins had taken a sabbatical, accepting the newly created Lichtstern Fellowship at the University of Chicago. He would follow his fellowship period with a semester of research in Mexico City at the Universidad Nacional de Anthropología e Historia.[14] His absence created a greater burden for Turner in that Turner was compelled to accept additional administrative responsibilities.

Outside of class, Turner was responsible for constructing schedules for graduate students to confer with African informants. Given the World War II economy, there were no funds for the expansion of the African Studies faculty. Charles Johnson, the original head, was also the Social Sciences Division chair and head of the Social Science Institute (later the Race Relations Department). To compound the difficulty, Park died in 1944. The six faculty members who participated in the program were reduced to four at a time when the department was still at an embryonic stage.[15]

On September 29, 1944, shortly after classes had begun, President Jones sent Turner a stern directive alluding to "the problem of African Studies," and noting, "the course which seems open to my associates and me is to request you to accept the position as Acting Head of the Department of African Studies for the year 1944–1945."[16] Turner received a similar directive for the 1945–46 academic year.

Despite his commitment to African Studies, Turner must have viewed the new position as an unwelcome burden. President Jones's letter offered a reduction in workload in that Turner was to be freed from teaching undergraduate English courses. At the same time Jones indicated that Turner was to continue to instruct and advise graduates and teach "such other courses as agreed upon by you and Dean A. A. Taylor." While no specific salary increase was mentioned, President Jones directed Turner to confer with him about "the duties of this new appointment and the budgetary arrangements involved in it." Among the new responsibilities was organizing the annual African Studies lecture series.[17]

By 1944 Turner had concluded that his work at Fisk was finished. There seemed little possibility, short of leaving the university, to carve out greater space for his own research. He began to extend feelers for positions elsewhere. Lois was also becoming restive in the Nashville community: "Prejudice was worse than in Louisville, and I did not look forward to raising a child there."[18]

Nashville was at least 25 percent black, a reality that failed to alter relations between blacks and whites. Blacks were "a functional part of the whole and yet isolated from the mainstream system of institutions."[19] By 1930 Nashville had become a thriving city of 154,000, with a range of industries and enterprises. A number of colleges and universities called the city their home. It was one of the vital transportation hubs of the South; cultural life was rich and varied. At the same time, segregation was stifling. Economic disparities between blacks and whites were glaring. There was "much lower black family income, underrepresentation in white collar occupations and years of school completed, overrepresentation in unskilled labor and illiteracy. . . . [T]he infant mortality rate for [blacks] in Nashville was nearly double that for whites. . . . [blacks] were restricted to one branch of the library, had separate wards in the general hospitals, separate parks, segregated seating in transportation and theaters, and were excluded from all retail jobs."[20]

The New Deal initiated by President Franklin D. Roosevelt in 1933 did not deal out resources rapidly enough to relieve the joblessness and poverty of the black population. By 1944 lynching had increased. The wartime economy did not reach to the bottom of the underclass to provide economic recovery from the Depression. Although Roosevelt had described the South as "the nation's number one economic problem," admitting that "one third of a nation [was] ill-housed, ill-clad, ill-nourished," he, as his predecessors, was reluctant to tackle segregation, realizing that his political base in the South could be eroded.[21]

As Turner struggled with his worklife dilemmas, the prospect of an ideal research project hovered on the horizon. On March 6, 1945, Dr. Halfdan Gregerson, vice president of the Inter-American Educational Foundation in Washington, D.C., contacted President Jones to inquire of Fisk's interest in a multidisciplinary project in Haiti involving Haitian Creole, music, and other aspects of the Haitian culture. Over the course of a few months, President Jones undertook negotiations with Gregerson.[22] Turner was to be among the scholars involved in the project.

In an April 9, 1945, letter to Daniel Wilson, Turner summarized the demands facing him. Wilson, as the secretary of the American Dialect Society, had requested a copy of Turner's paper to have it typed for *Publications of the American Dialect Society*. The paper became "Notes on the Sounds and Vocabulary of Gullah." Turner responded to Wilson, indicating that he would type it himself:

> If you will give me the date of your deadline, I shall be grateful. It so happens that this year I find that I am doing the work of three able-bodied men. For example, I am serving as chairman of two departments; am a member of eight active committees (sitting in meetings on an average of ten hours a week); carrying a teaching load of fourteen hours (including a composition course in which there are thirty-seven students, each writing two themes a week—I have no theme reader); am responsible for the selection of six lecturers (specialists) for three seminars on Africa and the Caribbean to be held on April 26, 27, and 28 during our Festival of Music and Art; am supervising the preparation of two A.M. theses; am trying to get my manuscript on *Africanisms in the Gullah Dialect* into Bernard Bloch's hands by the first week in May; am preparing four lectures to be given at one of the colleges here in Nashville early in May; and am preparing for publication a thirty-page bulletin of our Curriculum in African Studies which must be off the press by April 26. Several weeks ago I accepted an invitation from Dr. E. E. Lowinsky to give a lecture at Black Mountain College, North Carolina, early in May; but as I look over my schedule, I am almost certain that it will be humanly impossible for me to leave Nashville at that time. I can't recall the night when I got more than four hours' sleep. My wife swears she will leave me if I don't spend more time at home with her and the baby. You can see my predicament.[23]

In the same letter, Turner indicated that the content of his Africanisms manuscript was complete. The manuscript awaited a final version, as Turner had not located an appropriate typist to process it. His major work would be delayed four more years.[24]

On June 2, 1944, Turner contacted Howard H. Long, an administrator charged with hiring in Washington, D.C., to apply for a position at Miner Teacher's College, which would make it possible for him to return to Washington, D.C. He enclosed under separate cover a "few publications," adding, "I shall come to your office on June 9, unless in the meantime I am advised by you to the contrary."[25] No available correspondences indicate that Turner was invited for an interview or offered a position.

In the meantime, in Nashville Turner's plate was overflowing. His salary was $4,800 per year. As the sole breadwinner for the family, he was compelled to seek grant options for his impending sabbatical year of 1945–46. Much to his relief, his application to the Rosenwald Fund was successful. An April 25, 1945, letter to Turner confirmed that he had been awarded $2,500 "for a twelve month period to enable you to complete and publish three volumes of Afro-Brazilian folk material."

Under the signature of Mrs. William C. Haygood, the acting director of fellowships, the letter requested that Turner "let us know at once whether or not you can accept the fellowship."[26]

In summer 1945, Turner joined the summer teaching faculty at Atlanta University.[27] He departed from Fisk with the expectation that a fieldwork experience in Haiti would be his next major venture. Turner requested that Lois serve as his collaborator.[28]

The Haitian project promised an ideal linguistic context within which Turner could continue his exploration of North American African language derived creoles. That he would collaborate with the Haitian Department of Education in recording Haitian Creole, transcribing it, and then developing enough of a prescriptive grammar to create instructional programs in Haitian Creole for the schools in the rural areas was an ideal next step.

Turner's prospects were derailed in early August when Roger Dorsinville of the Commission Coopérative Haitiano-Américaine d'Éducation Département de l'Instruction Publique in Port-au-Prince raised the concern that aristocratic Haitians would oppose the project: "We are meeting strong opposition from French-speaking people who are against the vernacular language (creole) as a teaching means. They are aristocratic people (thinking that creole is vulgar), or against its phonetic spelling (they are tradition-minded people who think that we should rather teach creole written like etymologic French). . . . So we expect that, after careful study, you'll kindly indicate any change toward a more French like phonetic spelling of creole."[29]

After further negotiations with Johnson and the Haitian government, Turner's portion of the Haitian project was tabled indefinitely. The Haitian government was not prepared to dive into the uncharted waters of creole studies. John Work Jr., the prominent composer/arranger from a family of Fisk musicians, left for Haiti in the summer as a consultant to the music program. He returned to Fisk in mid-September. Watkins also departed to conduct fieldwork in Haiti. He did not return to Fisk but rather accepted a position as visiting professor of linguistics at the Escuela Nacional de Anthropología e Historia in Mexico City, Mexico.[30]

Turner completed the teaching of summer school at Atlanta University, but without the Haitian project, he was short of adequate funds to pursue a full-year's sabbatical. Although the Rosenwald Fund had awarded him $2,500, he was reluctant to accept it as it would not fully fund the processing of his Brazilian data and compensate for the loss of his faculty salary.[31]

Just as Turner was resolved to forgo his sabbatical and return to Fisk to the Herculean routine of balancing two departments, English and African Studies, on his shoulders—both with less than full staffing—he availed himself of the opportunity to use the library at the University of Chicago. While there, the director of the Rosenwald Fund, which was based in Chicago, suggested that he present a series of lectures at the newly established Roosevelt College. The lectures may have been arranged to allow him to utilize the Rosenwald grant. Conferring with two members of the English department, Kendall Taft, the chair, and Wayne A. R. Leys, Turner created a lecture schedule.[32]

Turner's lectures were well received. After he returned to Fisk in late fall of 1945, Leys wrote to him, "inviting him to become visiting professor of English" for the spring quarter of 1946. He accepted, returning to Chicago in February 1946.[33]

During Turner's final year at Fisk, still burdened with responsibilities in both departments, his Brazilian data was, nonetheless, on his mind. During the intersession, he prepared a proposal to the American Philosophical Society. On January 8, 1946, Turner mailed his request, which asked for $750 to prepare three volumes. The first was to be an annotated book of secular and religious songs in Yoruba with English translations; the second an annotated collection of Yoruba texts consisting of folktales and other narratives, orations, and prayers with English translations. True to his Brazilian grant proposal, the third volume was conceived of as a collection of bedtime stories told in Portuguese to the children of the religious cult houses of Bahia, Brazil, with the scenes and characters from African culture. Turner had consulted with John Work Jr., his music department colleague, who had agreed to prepare the music transcriptions for the first volume.[34] It was a momentous undertaking.

Since Turner carried on an active research agenda, the opportunity to gain access to facilities at which he could more readily conduct research was a burning desire. In a spring 1946 letter to James Napier Wilt, one of his former professors at the University of Chicago, Turner informed him that he was handicapped by the "woefully inadequate library facilities in Nashville." He looked forward to access to more adequate research facilities and the opportunity "to do many of the things I have wanted to do for a long time."[35]

Furthermore, Fisk was changing perceptibly. Turner was not alone in the inclination to consider another appointment. After twenty years of service, President Jones had concluded that the time had arrived for him to embrace opportunities beyond the doors of Fisk. Since there were more middle-class African Americans with the formal education to administer their own institutions, some faculty, students, and alumni began to articulate more volubly the need for a change in administration. President Jones was willing to oblige. Since he was a Quaker, an ideal opportunity presented itself when he was invited to become president of his alma mater, Earlham College, a Quaker institution in Indiana. By 1945 Jones was reconciled to the growing discontent among black intellectuals over the Euro-American leadership of African American institutions.[36] By late 1945 he had resigned with plans to remain at Fisk until summer 1946. With Jones's departure, Turner knew that Fisk was entering a period of uncertainty.

The ensuing contest over the presidency was hard fought. Several able men applied. Turner's choice was his ally and Alpha Phi Alpha fraternity brother Charles Wesley. The board of trustees favored his colleague Charles Johnson, the social scientist. Johnson won, becoming the first black president in the history of Fisk, effective 1947.[37]

After a grueling winter with an endless array of burdensome responsibilities, compounded by reservations about the changing of the guard at Fisk, Turner wrote President Jones on April 22, 1946, tendering his resignation: "My decision to resign has been reached as a result of the opportunity that has come to me to carry forward my work in my chosen field to greater advantage than has been possible at Fisk University." Turner did not elaborate on the details of the opportunity, simply granting that "I have enjoyed my work here during the past sixteen years."[38]

Jones was in his final month at Fisk. So was Turner. Turner was not, however, taking a leap into the totally unknown. By then he had already received an offer from the new college bearing the name of one of the most popular and revered presidents in American history.

19

Roosevelt College and the Publication of Africanisms in the Gullah Dialect 1946–1966

Roosevelt University was founded in 1945 to provide opportunity for learning and teaching in conditions of freedom and equality. The University seeks to develop individuals who will be dedicated to the essential themes of a democratic society, who possess not only the intelligence refined by an understanding of the history of man . . . but possess the courage to create in the world the conditions under which the welfare of the individual will ever remain at the center of human endeavors.

—Roosevelt University Bulletin, 1965–66

ON MARCH 26, 1946, TURNER RECEIVED an appointment letter from President Edward J. Sparling of Roosevelt College in Chicago, offering him "$3,500.00 in 12 installments," to begin on September 1, 1946.[1] He had impressed English department chair Kendall Taft and College of Arts and Sciences dean Wayne A. R. Leys and come highly recommended by James Napier Wilt.[2]

Established in 1945, named for President Franklin Delano Roosevelt, and situated in downtown Chicago, Roosevelt College (later University) was conceived of as an experiment in racial diversity and harmony. Like Fisk, Roosevelt was private. President Sparling was familiar with Turner's work since Turner had visited and lectured at the college during the previous semester, in Roosevelt's first year of operation.

Leaving Lois behind in Nashville to sell their house at 1015 Villa Place, Turner relocated to Chicago during the summer of 1946. While there, he purchased a large Victorian house at 4036 Ellis Avenue in the historic district. Familiar with Chicago from as early as 1913 when he was employed in hotels and aboard trains, he admired the neighborhood. The sturdy, red-brick house had captured Turner's imagination because of its potential. It was also reminiscent of the rowhouse he and Geneva owned. The stained glass windows gave it elegance. Built-in bookcases graced the parlor. The front yard was seventy feet from sidewalk to house. The secluded backyard was three-hundred feet deep, ideal for family and social gatherings and for the play activities of Lorenzo Jr. and future children. The five bedrooms on the upper floors were well-lit and roomy. The twelve-foot ceilings on the first floor and ten-foot ceilings on the second floor added to the spacious feel of the residence. On the second floor was an elegant ballroom with a half-bath. Turner visualized subdividing it into individual bedrooms to obtain rental income. The living room fireplace was adorned with tiles from the Minton Works of London, each depicting a scene from British history. Because Ellis Avenue is near Lake Michigan, cool breezes provided pleasant relief during the hottest days of the summer. The walls were constructed of massive bricks, increasing the possibility that the house would be comfortably cool in summer. The location was ideal.[3]

Turner signed a contract agreeing to pay the $6,000 mortgage in sixty monthly installments. When fall arrived, the family occupied the house. They subsequently subdivided the second floor, increasing the number of available bedrooms. Contrary to Turner's assumption, the house did not generate enough income through renters to pay for itself. Consequently, two years later, he contacted Irvin Jacobs and Company to refinance the mortgage, requesting that the mortgage application be amended to $7,800 in eighty-four installments.[4] Turner was in a financial mire. His new salary was $1,300 less per year than it had been in Nashville, and the cost of living was far greater in Chicago. A second son, Rani Meredith, born May 13, 1948, had just joined the family, a turn of events that, though a cause for joy, also resulted in the need for a larger cash flow.

From the outside, the house was awe inspiring, but time and experience living on the inside resulted in another view of it. It was a leviathan, requiring coal for fuel, and being "drafty and nearly impossible to heat in the coldest weather."[5] In its earlier life, the house had been truly elegant. By the time Turner purchased it, however, it bore the weight of poor maintenance at the hands of its owners, two elderly bachelor brothers. Their hygiene and housekeeping also left much to be desired. Lois set about to adapt it to the Turner family, with sometimes discouraging results.[6]

She was not fond of the house. Turner's plan was that the three of them would reside on the first floor in the parlors while renting out the five bedrooms on the second and third floors to supplement the family income. Over time, he reasoned, not only would the family derive a substantial income, but there would also be funds for maintenance. Turner continued to be committed to the idea that Lois should remain at home, with homemaking and childrearing as her primary responsibilities. He assumed that there would also be hours of solitude during the day for Lois to pursue her artwork. Given her responsibilities, including the care of two young children, the regular pursuit of art projects became a luxury that time seldom permitted. Furthermore, Rani Meredith developed asthma and a series of allergies, which caused mother and child many tedious days and sleepless nights.[7]

The Turners converted the first floor to their living quarters. Being a humanitarian by temperament, Turner sometimes invited students from Africa to live cost-free in exchange for data on their languages and cultures. Among them was Olatunde Adekoya, a Yoruba speaker from Nigeria, who lived with the Turners for two years. Over time other African students resided with them. Among the other tenants were the artist John Wilson, his wife, Julie, and their two young children.[8]

Although Roosevelt was a fresh experience, returning Turner to a cultural center with impressive library facilities, funds continued to be a source of tension. Turner opened a checking account at the First National Bank of Chicago. There was usually too much month at the end of the money. The Turners were optimistic that residing in Chicago, economic opportunities through publishing and presentations would flood to him to offset the decrease in salary.

The *Chicago Defender* greeted Turner's appointment with enthusiasm, viewing to it as "one of the most encouraging signs on the academic horizon." The editor noted that in the past several years, "a number of Negro scholars have been given temporary posts in outstanding white universities," but Turner's was a breakthrough. The *Defender* regarded Turner as the first African American in a full-time faculty position at a Euro-American university. Viewing appointments of "eminent men" as "one of the most effective means through which the canker of racial prejudice can be combated," the editor described Turner as "a very quiet, unassuming and mild-mannered man," adding that, "beneath it all glows the incandescent fire of a vigorous and searching intellect, nurtured by long years of sound scholarship. . . . [H]e will do honor not only to his race, but also the faculty and student body of Roosevelt College."[9]

At the time Turner joined the faculty of Roosevelt, he was a senior-level faculty member. He had already participated in the creation of an African Studies Program. For the remainder of his career until his formal retirement in May 1966, his assignment was as professor of English and, by 1952, as director of the Interdisciplinary Program in African Studies.

Roosevelt was liberal and integrated at its inception. Because it was both new and small, in some respects the context was similar to that in the HBCUs—the salary was low and the workload high. But Turner was enthusiastic about joining the faculty since he was encouraged to pursue his intellectual interests. Furthermore, he viewed Roosevelt as a test case for democracy. In an article President Sparling encouraged him to prepare a year after he joined the faculty, Turner asserted, "There is no doubt that the program being carried out at Roosevelt College is the most encouraging, and the most practical demonstration of democracy we have yet had in the field of higher education. For centuries, we have been quite distinguished for our speeches on democracy in education, but not for doing anything about it. We cannot at present envisage the effect of this trend upon our total life, but my guess is that its influence for good will be tremendous."[10]

Turner elaborated on the assets of Roosevelt—its organization, recruitment policies, and administrative/faculty decision-making structure. He praised it for being the first college to receive accreditation from the North Central Association after less than one year. Commenting on the issue of academic freedom, increasingly a concern on campuses at the end of World War II, Turner asserted that it "is nowhere better exemplified than at Roosevelt. . . . *There is faculty control of academic matters by vote*" (Turner's emphasis). Further, Turner pointed to the recruitment of faculty as nondiscriminatory since "thirty percent of the faculty represents the so-called minority groups, among which are nine Negroes. . . . But as the Dean of the College said recently, 'Teachers are hired at Roosevelt College for ability and training alone. We do not consider their race or religion when interviewing them *because these are unimportant matters. We are concerned only that they can deliver*'" (Turner's emphasis).[11]

The absence of a quota system for students resulted in multicultural diversity on the campus at a time before most colleges had considered it. Turner said, "They are all just students at Roosevelt College, constituting an animated crazy quilt, all pieces of which are woven of the same material, with only the colors different."[12] Roosevelt provided educational opportunity to both domestic and foreign students, including Africans, African Americans, and Jews, at a point at which many universities silently barred all these groups.

Finally, Turner expressed his sense of satisfaction that Roosevelt had developed an innovative and culturally diverse curriculum. The course offerings were several decades ahead of the times in promoting a global perspective. "One interesting feature of the curriculum," he wrote, "is a series of culture courses, two of which may be offered in lieu of a year of modern foreign language. These courses include a study of the culture of China, India, Latin America, Africa and its contribution to Western civilization."[13]

If Turner envisioned that being on the faculty of a new university would relieve him of some of the pressures of time and the dearth of financial resources that had assailed him in previous contexts, he was badly mistaken. By working incessantly, though, he was able to continue his research.

According to Gail Frazier-Clemons, a distant cousin who was a student in Chicago in the 1960s, Turner "was cordial but amazingly focused." Whenever she approached his study, which was the first door to the left after the vestibule, he invited her in, speaking with her a few moments. Then, if she did not observe her cue to depart, he would incorporate her into his research by playing one or more of his field tapes. He utilized the same strategy with all comers.[14] Both Lois and her sister Gloria, who often visited in summers, noted that Turner had "amazing powers of concentration." He was able to tune out background noises, including the play activities of Lorenzo Jr. and Rani Meredith, the television, and the telephone. Gloria's summer visits offered some relief for Turner, as she voluntarily typed several of his African manuscripts.[15]

Turner supplemented his salary with funds from speaking engagements as often as possible. He was a wanted man, an African American griot par excellence. Since he was an excellent orator, his message was usually well received; so the demands on his time were massive. In contrast, typically the honoraria accorded him were as small as twenty-five dollars.[16]

Churches were frequently his lecture venues. On Sunday, March 23, 1947, he addressed the members of the Good Shepherd's Congregational Church at 57th and Prairie Avenue on African culture in Brazil. His 4:30 P.M. lecture was sponsored by the Chicago Tougaloo College Club.[17] Several years later Turner offered an "African Safari," sponsored by the Women's Guild of the First English Evangelical Church of Chicago at 3062 Palmer Square. The lecture also featured a 12:30 P.M. luncheon with African-inspired delicacies for $1.50.[18]

By the spring of 1947, Turner had agreed to an appointment as an adult education lecturer for the Adult Education Council. For many years, he regularly offered night courses for the Chicago Central YMCA.[19] The alumni associations of the HBCUs also sought Turner's expertise. A May 31, 1947, article reported that Turner served as the keynote speaker for the Chicago chapter of the Meharry Medical College Alumni Association, at its victory banquet in celebration of having raised $195,000 toward its $200,000 goal. The event convened at the "swanky Morrison Hotel," attracting two hundred guests.[20] Turner also served as host when two HBCUs honored Langston Hughes.[21]

As Turner continued to offer courses in the traditional English curriculum, his opportunity to teach African Studies courses materialized after his return from Africa.[22] One of his mainstays was African Culture and Its Survivals in the New World, one of the Culture Studies courses.[23]

For his classes, typically Turner constructed essay examinations that were guaranteed to challenge test-takers for the duration of the class session. The questions encouraged both recall and reasoning, covering major theoretical issues.[24] One of Turner's Chaucer examinations required the following:

I. After writing from memory the first 18 lines of the "Prologue," explain the general plan of *The Canterbury Tales.* (Include references to the time, places, number of tales and of characters, function of host, etc.).

II. What are the chief merits of the "Friar's Tale" and the "Summoner's Tale" as narratives? Illustrate.

III. Write a paragraph on four of the following, including 2 and 4:
   1. Chaucer's handling of his sources in the "Knight's Tale."
   2. Principal verse forms used by Chaucer in *The Canterbury Tales.*
   3. Evidence for placing Chaucer's birth between 1340 and 1345.
   4. Preterite-present verbs and the weak declension of adjectives in Chaucer.
   5. Some literary parallels to *The Canterbury Tales* that Chaucer may have been familiar with.
   6. The Marriage Group of *The Canterbury Tales.*
   7. "The Clerk's Tale" as satire.

One of his English literature open-book examinations required students to

I. Define the following terms and demonstrate (from the text) their use: 1) blank verse, 2) heroic couplet, 3) Petrarchan sonnet, 4) feminine rhyme, 5) assonance, 6) masculine caesura, 7) anacrusis, 8) imagery, 9) farce, 10) melodrama, 11) catalectic line, 12) terza rima.

II. Write a criticism of Shelley's "To a Skylark" (p. 485), stressing form and ideas.

III. Selecting the two plays upon which you have not yet reported, discuss the social significance of one and write a character sketch of the hero in the other.

In Turner's History of the English Language examination, students were asked to demonstrate their grasp of both historical changes in English and contemporary trends in the discipline. For example, Turner expected students to express some familiarity with the focus of the professional journals:

I. Since the Middle English period, changes in grammar have been relatively few and those in vocabulary extensive. Explain this specifically and somewhat fully.

II. Indicate the changes which the following long vowels underwent between Old and Modern English periods:

   /a:, æ:, e:, i:, and u:/.

III. Comment upon <u>five</u> of the following, including 1), 2), and 6):
   1) Brief history of the pronouns <u>that</u>, <u>which</u>, <u>who</u> and <u>its</u>.
   2) Prescriptive Grammar and the Doctrine of Usage.

3) Spelling Reform.
4) The Society for Pure Engish.
5) Chief Sources of American English.
6) Linguistic Journals in the United States.
7) Scientific Interest in American English.

IV. Regional Pronunciation (cultivated) in the United States.

One of his phonetics examinations administered to senior students expected them to

I. Give roughly the location of the three linguistic areas of the United States and the distinguishing characteristics of each.

II. Illustrate the approximate tongue positions of each of the following vowels and consonants: /i, u, o, a, ʃ, t, l̩, ɫ/.

III. Transcribe in phonetic symbols one command, one request, and one question and give the intonation of each.

IV. Explain the following terms: cardinal vowels, rising and falling diphthongs, syllabic consonant, vowel, consonant.

V. Is the vowel of sins longer or shorter than that of seat? Why?[25]

Outside of class, Turner was determined to work regularly on the analysis of his Gullah materials. A year before arriving at Roosevelt, he had discussed the publication of his Africanisms manuscript with Kurath, who agreed to write "a few introductory paragraphs" for the book. At the same time, Kurath agreed to provide "some suggestions on parts of the phonology and the morphology that you may want to consider." Closing with a vote of confidence, Kurath stated, "I regard your book as an important contribution in the field of American English."[26] However, no Kurath introduction appears in any edition of *Africanisms in the Gullah Dialect.*

As Turner settled into his position at Roosevelt, he continued to play an active role in professional organizations. According to the June 1948 issue of *Progress,* he was named to the advisory committee of *American Speech* for 1948–49.[27]

In the process of re-editing the manuscript, Turner sharpened his focus on those elements of Gullah that were most likely derived from the thirty Niger-Congo languages for which he was able to establish clear ancestry. He had collected six thousand semantic items and utilized the four thousand for which he could make the strongest case on linguistic grounds.[28]

Turner finished retyping the book. Far from the South and the Sea Islands, with a completed manuscript in hand, he increased his attempts to have it published. Although his allies in the American Dialect Society had welcomed his research for more than ten years, locating a publisher who was willing to wager that the manuscript of a reference-style book on Gullah would sell was no easy task. His efforts to shepherd *Africanisms in the Gullah Dialect* into print are indicative of the complications he faced finding publication opportunities during his entire career.

On April 9, 1945, Turner contacted Daniel Wilson, still secretary of the American Dialect Society, concerning possible publication opportunities, to no avail.[29] Turner then sent a letter to J. M. Cowan, the secretary of the Linguistic Society of

America. Cowan responded on February 7, 1946, informing Turner that it would cost the society $1,719 to print the 308-page book. He added, "I should like to see it appear in our Monograph Series." There was one caveat. The LSA would require a subsidy in order to undertake the project. While Turner's sense of urgency was pronounced, Cowan's was not: "There is no urgency about the matter since the press assures me that they have such a large backlog of work that it would be some time before they could get at the composition."[30]

Turner then contacted the ACLS. Over the course of his career, Turner had found it to be the organization most responsive to his applications for research funds. Cowan was also a principal there, serving as director of the Intensive Language Program. He answered Turner on May 21, 1946, indicating that two members of the Standing Committee on Research had responded favorably but that Turner's manuscript would be placed on hold until the American Council had received new funds for publications.[31]

Next, Turner contacted Donald Young, executive director of the Social Science Research Council. Young responded on July 3, 1946, with less than encouraging news: "I am very sorry that it is not possible for this Council even to consider giving assistance to publish your Gullah manuscript. For one thing, we have no money whatever which can be used to help defray printing costs of work, which was not conducted at least in part under our auspices. We have no endowment and practically all of our money is given to us for specific purposes."[32]

Providing a potential lead, Young referred Turner to the American Philosophical Society, where a number of colleagues who knew Turner served on the Committee on American Linguistics and Archaeology, among them Leonard Bloomfield, Waldo Leland, Edgar Sturtevant, and Alfred Kroeber.[33] That option led to a dead end.

Turner then contacted the University of Chicago Press. The press expressed a willingness to consider the manuscript if some organization would provide a subsidy. Turner took heart. During the summer of 1947, he labored over suggested revisions for the final draft. When they were complete, he visited the University of Chicago Press office on 5750 Ellis Avenue to deliver the manuscript in person, only to learn that Elizabeth L. Titus of the editorial department was not available. Several weeks later, on August 15, Titus contacted Turner, expressing her regrets that she had missed his visit and informing him that "a recent bulletin from Donald Goodchild, Secretary of Fellowships and Grants of the ACLS informs us that the Council will not act upon applications for subsidies before November." She was empathetic with Turner over the delay, "knowing how hard [you] worked to complete [the] revisions."[34]

As Turner bided his time, he continued to present Gullah data in conference papers. In December 1947, he was one of eighty-six persons who gathered in Detroit for the annual meeting of the American Dialect Society. It convened at the Book-Cadillac Hotel on December 30, from 11:00 A.M. to 12:30 P.M. He was one of three presenters. Harold Wentworth of Temple University described "The American Dialect Dictionary," E. H. Crigwell of the University of Tulsa discussed "Experiments in State-Wide Dialect Collecting," and Turner presented "Problems Involved in the Collection and Treatment of Africanisms in the Gullah Dialect."

Turner's paper subsequently appeared as "Problems Confronting the Investigator of Gullah" in *Publications of the American Dialect Society* (1948).[35]

As the new year arrived, Turner continued to pursue publication opportunities. On January 13, 1948, Goodchild, secretary for fellowships and grants for the ACLS, contacted him to inquire about his progress.[36] In his response Turner indicated that the manuscript was on hold as he had been in contact with the University of Chicago Press, which, like the Linguistic Society of America, wished to receive a subsidy.[37] The ACLS voted to assist. On May 18, 1948, Turner received a "Notification of Award" letter from the ACLS, arranging to offer the University of Chicago Press $1,500 to subsidize the publication of *Africanisms in the Gullah Dialect.* The arrangement called for the press to publish it no later than May 15, 1950, reimbursing the ACLS from the proceeds within five years.[38] The benefit of the arrangement to Turner was that *Africanisms in the Gullah Dialect* would be published, issued by a prestigious university press. The dilemma was that little had changed. A subvention was still being required, just as it had been twenty years earlier with the publication of *Anti-Slavery Sentiment in American Literature Prior to 1865.* Furthermore, although Turner had worked for almost two decades to publish *Africanisms in the Gullah Dialect,* the conditions under which it was to be issued made it unlikely that he would experience any financial remuneration. It was to be born in debt.

The University of Chicago Press published *Africanisms in the Gullah Dialect* in mid-1949. The press catalog, *Books for Fall, 1949,* listed it as "due out in July, 300 pages. 6 x 9—Illustrated." The price was $7.50. A dust cover of bright green bordered in light green protected the light green binding. The title was printed in white, on a cover that bore no graphics beyond lettering, suggesting the scholarly nature of the book.[39]

The usual discussions of *Africanisms in the Gullah Dialect* and Turner's career indicate that he labored on the project for seventeen years. In reality, according to multiple correspondences from Turner to Herskovits, Wilson, and others, by the time the book was published, it had been complete, except for the final typing of the preface and last two chapters (the appendix) for almost a decade.[40] On the other hand, Turner himself suggested the protracted time frame, stating in the preface to *Africanisms in the Gullah Dialect* that "the present study is the result of an investigation that has extended over a period of fifteen years."[41] He had been a long-distance runner, never abandoning his research for projects that could have been accomplished with less intensive, original empirical research.

The Gullah revolution was coming into its own. In 1941 Herskovits had quoted from Turner's still unpublished manuscript.[42] In 1948 H. L. Mencken completed the second supplement of *The American Language.* It was reviewed in the *Charleston Post and Courier.* W. D. W., the reviewer, noted that Mencken included a section on unique features of Gullah. For the first time, Mencken had varied from his original line, adopting Turner's thesis. Quoting from Turner's work, Mencken detailed a number of African names that Turner had documented as being in use in Gullah territory. Among them were "Agali" (Wolof) *welcome;* "Alamisa" (Bambara) *born on Thursday;* "Anisa" (Vai) *very beautiful;* "Holima" (Mende) *patience;* and "Sina"

(Mende) *a female twin.* Mencken described Gullah territory as the only area of the United States where persons of African ancestry had maintained African naming practices. Going further, he quoted Turner as having asserted that, "in some families on the Sea Islands, the names of all the children are African. Many have no English names, though in most cases the African words in use were nicknames. Very few of the Gullahs of today know [the] meaning of these names; they use them because their parents and grandparents did so."[43] Also in 1948, Mitford M. Mathews had published a few terms from African languages in *Some Sources of Southernisms.*

Turner traced the etymologies of Gullah semantic items to approximately thirty sister languages of the Niger-Congo Family. The book contained arguments for phonological and syntactic influences, and provided selected Gullah texts—transcribed phonetically—and explanations of morphology, particularly the use of tense, number, and gender.

When it was complete, Turner's "list of African-derived vocabulary (pages 190–208) was much longer than that of any previous scholar, and his compilation of personal names (pages 31–189) was staggering. More important, his careful description of aspects of syntax (pages 209–22), morphology (pages 223–31), word formation (pages 232–39), pronunciation (pages 240–48), and intonation (pages 249–53) marked a turning point in thinking about Gullah. After Turner, African influence on all aspects of Gullah was inarguable."[44]

When *Africanisms in the Gullah Dialect* appeared, the academic establishment that had described Gullah as archaic British dialects, "baby talk," and "broken English" was provided ample evidence of the African influence. Turner listed alphabetically four thousand terms, many of them personal names, the other terms used in conversation, stories, songs, and prayers, with their phonetics in both Gullah and the African languages in which they have been attested.

The book was greeted with a lively range of commentary in academic publications and the news media. Both linguists and nonlinguists reviewed it. James W. Ivy of the *Crisis* called it "an original contribution to American linguistic scholarship. . . . [Turner] has done for Gullah what Renato Mendonça and Jacques Raimundo did for Afro-Brazilian; Suzanne Comhaire-Sylvain and Jules Faine for Haitian Creole; and Fernando Ortiz for Afro-Cuban. *Africanisms in the Gullah Dialect* squashed forever the assumption that Gullah is a 'pidgin' dialect."[45]

Except for the *New York Times,* the Euro-American press had not covered the beginnings of Turner's Gullah research in 1932. However, the societal changes in post–World War II America resulted in some southern newspapers turning the spotlight on *Africanisms in the Gullah Dialect* in 1949. Mel Most of the *Charleston Post and Courier* weighed in on October 16, 1949: "A lore never revealed to white men has been wrested from his people by a painstaking negro professor. His search uncovered astonishing survivals of African culture and more than 4,000 African words, names and numbers still spoken among 250,000 negroes in a corner of the United States." Most described Turner's book as "too technical for lay readers," but asserted, "Students of American English found Gullah is the missing link that introduced many Americanisms used by people who never dream they're talking African."[46]

Most embraced the validity of the research in *Africanisms in the Gullah Dialect:* "Turner's book means the end of theories that African culture left no trace here." Commenting on the naming practices, he noted that the Gullah people had been exposed to both Islam and Christianity before they were unceremoniously dislodged from their African homes: "The names show that many of the Gullahs' ancestors were Moslems. . . . For example, Fatima and Safiyata, the names of a daughter and a wife of Mohammed [*sic*]." Citing the use of "Ameena" as the closing in Gullah prayers, Most indicated "Other words show Christianity had reached them before they left Africa."[47]

Three weeks later, John Bennett, a northern writer who lived in Charleston after marrying into southern aristocracy but knew little about southern dialects, denounced Most's article and Turner's thesis. From Bennett's perspective, only one hundred Gullah terms of African origin remained; names and other lexical items that could be identified were "remnants of original African tongues. But they have no more to do with the negro-English dialect than the broken scraps of yesterday's breakfast in the garbage can have to do with today's dinner menu," because "to be an integral part of any language or dialect, the words in question must be a part of the vocabulary of that speech and in common employ as a vehicle of communication . . . in other words, a recognized part of the local vernacular."[48]

The historian Herbert Aptheker reviewed *Africanisms in the Gullah Dialect* in *Masses and Mainstream.* Noting that earlier writers had failed to give serious consideration to the African language impact on Gullah, Aptheker referred to previous explanations of Gullah's origins as "vicious claptrap adopted by the distinguished academicians of our multi-million-dollar institutions of mis-education. . . . Since the words Gullah and Geeche themselves are taken directly from the names of two different West African peoples, one would have thought that these scholars would have investigated possible African sources for the language they were discussing. . . . [I]magine going to the trouble of studying West African languages, when explanations like 'clumsy tongues' and 'baby talk' will do!"[49]

Africanisms in the Gullah Dialect was covered widely in speech and language journals. Robert Hall, writing for *American Speech,* issued a positive and supportive review. He would later amend his position, but initially he claimed, "Previous investigators of Gullah had apparently not troubled to investigate the languages of West Africa (whence came most of the slaves imported to the Americas), so convinced were they that African influence could be discounted *a priori*. . . . So far as the survival of Africanisms in Gullah is concerned, Turner's evidence is decisive, and we must now consider the older viewpoint (which considers African influence negligible) as definitely superseded. . . . In the study of American English, Turner's book is not only noteworthy, it is revolutionary."[50]

George Wilson, writing for the *Quarterly Journal of Speech,* presented an enthusiastic review, utilizing phonetic transcription to render examples from the text. He considered it an asset that Turner included "twenty-eight pages of Gullah songs, narratives, descriptions. . . . in phonetics, with accompanying literal translations in English." Calling the finding of over three thousand African names "of immense linguistic and historical significance," he pointed out that "almost no other writer has found any of them, or paid attention to them if he has found them."[51]

Wilson concluded by commenting on the validity of Turner's field methods: "Dr. Turner has set a good example for others who would collect and study dialect: accept no one else's theories, but study thoroughly the background of the speech and the speech itself firsthand; use all good methods of collecting material —questionnaires, phonograph records, spontaneous interviews; live among the speakers and gain their confidence; discuss their language with them."[52] And Wilson's final statement suggested a number of disciplines for which he considered *Africanisms in the Gullah Dialect* useful: "Besides being immensely valuable to lexicographers and phonologists, this book should prove valuable also to historians, sociologists, anthropologists, and onomatologists."[53]

Not all reviews were laudatory. Morris Swadesh in *Word* expressed a number of concerns. He commended Turner for having collected three thousand names and hundreds of other lexical items, declaring, "This is a remarkable achievement, forcefully demonstrating the essentiality of decent human rapport for effective fieldwork in linguistics or in any other social sciences." At the same time he criticized Turner for reporting ejective consonants in Gullah, comparing them to ejectives in Hausa and Zulu. From Swadesh's perspective, "It is clear that Gullah has no phonemic contrast between non-ejective and ejective," rather an occasional ejective resulting from "variation of the typical unaspirated stops." Further, Swadesh wanted Turner to have detailed the breadth of distribution of African language terminology within Gullah territory, noting how frequently across broad geographical distances certain terms were utilized. As a result, he objected to Turner's use of the concept of "survivals," suggesting that "influence" would have been a more appropriate concept. In closing, Swadesh stated, "Turner's work constitutes a valuable collection of material and serves to indicate the scientific problems that can be fruitfully studied in Gullah." He ended with an expression of hope that Turner would continue to study Gullah.[54]

Watkins, Turner's former Fisk colleague, provided the same review of *Africanisms in the Gullah Dialect* for *American Anthropologist* and the *Journal of Negro Education*.[55] His major criticism was "flaws" he observed in phonological and morphological analysis: "One cannot determine from the descriptions and the texts . . . the precise number of Gullah phonemes," since "Turner shows a tendency to discuss symbols rather than sounds." He noted "unwarranted generalizations" about grammatical features, pointing out that Turner indicated the absence of passive voice in Gullah but that it appeared in a transcribed text in Turner's appendix.[56] Further, he found Turner's discussion of the "verbal adjective" "not in accord with current principles of morphological analysis."[57] Watkins's generally favorable reviews were short of examples to illustrate his objections. He concluded that the volume "suffers some shortcomings from the point of view of linguistics, but it shows clearly that Gullah has some of its roots in Africa—which is its primary objective."[58]

Raven McDavid, known for harsh critiques, reviewed *Africanisms in the Gullah Dialect* for *Language*. Raised in South Carolina, McDavid viewed himself as a specialist on its history and culture. He began by praising Turner's preparation, research skill, and the factual nature of the book:

> Turner has had several advantages over every previous investigator of Gullah. In addition to the obvious fact that as a Negro he could approach the Gullah people on terms of intimacy denied to any white investigator . . . he has been trained in dialect geography and field methods by the staff of the Linguistic Atlas; he has studied African languages and has checked his materials with native speakers of many languages in the areas from which the Gullah Negroes were probably transported; and he has investigated also the creolized Portuguese spoken by Brazilian Negroes. On the basis of data at his disposal he has identified several thousand items in Gullah with possible African sources—a mass of evidence which should go far forward correcting the tendencies of previous investigators to dismiss the African element in Gullah as inconsequential. The presentation in the present book is soberly factual, the conclusions are conservative, even the details are rarely questionable.[59]

But then the review became more scathing. First, McDavid denigrated the value of Turner's overall contribution, claiming that the "new book is not the work which linguists have looked for. A descriptive grammar of Gullah has long been needed; it is not provided for here."[60] Second, he issued a volley that any linguist would consider a serious blow when he objected to the arrangement of the data: "The arrangement . . . suggests that its purpose is not primarily linguistic." Third, he called for a more extensive treatment of phonology since both Gullah and West African languages have fewer phonemes than Standard English, and since "the phonemic system of Gullah and the phonemic values of individual allophones show striking uniformity in all communities where the dialect is spoken, although these communities occur discontinuously along three hundred miles of coast in the region in which dialects of American English show the greatest local diversity."[61] Fourth, McDavid objected to the omission of several books and articles from the bibliography.[62] Fifth, he raised the archaic English retentions argument, questioning why certain features found widely in both southern speech and in Gullah should be ascribed to African linguistic influence.[63] Finally, McDavid suggested that Turner should have plotted the geographic distribution of each semantic item within Gullah territory, including the names, a process that would have required far more extensive interviewing and thus necessitating more fieldwork time and funds than were available to Turner.[64]

Turner and McDavid had interacted extensively for several years before 1949, during linguistic conferences. While Turner was at Roosevelt, McDavid had relocated from Cornell University in Ithaca, New York, to the nearby University of Chicago. On one occasion, they had considered a collaborative writing project. McDavid visited the Turner home at least once in October 1949. Hence, Turner had grounds to believe that McDavid respected his research and comprehended the constraints under which the Gullah research had been developed.

When *Africanisms in the Gullah Dialect* appeared, McDavid wrote Turner to inform him of his plans to review it for both *Language* and the *Charleston Evening*

Post. Turner was likely encouraged that the review for *Language,* the most prestigious journal in the field, was in empathetic hands. McDavid's initial contact with Turner suggested as much. In contrast, the developing review took quite another turn. In his initial letter to Turner, McDavid seemed impressed: "I've just finished going through the *Africanisms* for the first time (I generally have to read a book at least twice or three times when I'm doing a serious review—and I'll probably want to do more than that with yours, since I want to see a good job done for *Language;* I think I told you that Bloch officially confirmed his oral statement to me). It looks even better than it did in MS form. The texts are especially interesting to me: I spent a couple of hours reading them aloud, just to see how they went."[65]

Later in the year, on November 13, 1949, when McDavid's draft of the review was complete, he corresponded with Turner again, hinting that his review would not be entirely favorable: "As you would probably suspect, in reviewing for *Language* I'm making a little more of some of the slightly adverse criticisms I hinted at in my review for the *Charleston Evening Post* . . . chiefly developing from the fact that most linguists I think would like to see a fuller description of the structure of Gullah. But I think I am keeping these in proportion, so that there will be no question about the review being favorable."[66]

On November 28, McDavid mailed another letter to Turner, this one containing a copy of his finished draft of the review for *Language.* His "slightly adverse criticisms" comprised the majority of the review: "This is the final form—some notes unchecked, but the opinions are there as I phrased them," he wrote. McDavid must have been aware of the potential damage to Turner's reputation as a scholar, the perceived value of *Africanisms in the Gullah Dialect* to linguists, as well as its sales potential. Therefore, he added, "I don't think it will hurt the book."[67]

This researcher has located no replies from Turner to McDavid's letters. However, Turner's reaction to the review is expressed in a letter he sent to Raleigh Morgan, his former Fisk student who was completing a doctorate in Romance linguistics at the University of Michigan in Ann Arbor. Morgan had contacted Turner to inform him of the refusal of the *Charleston Daily News* to print a short but largely favorable review of *Africanisms in the Gullah Dialect* submitted by McDavid.[68]

Turner's response to Morgan gave McDavid the benefit of the doubt: "Although McDavid's review of my book in *Language* contains several errors of fact and judgment due to his lack of acquaintance with certain features of African languages and with problems involved in my study, he did bring out many good points." Turner then reacted to the statement that the book should have been a descriptive grammar. Even though his initial plan had been to construct a grammar of Gullah, as he studied African languages over the years, he realized that the primary source data necessary for such an analysis, that is, grammars of African languages, had not yet been written. According to Turner, "In the first place, the book was not intended as a descriptive grammar of Gullah. Again, the kind of morphological and tonal treatment he expected is impossible at present because no comparable scientific treatment exists for the thirty or more African languages upon which Gullah draws. Had he consulted me before he wrote the review, I could have cleared up much of his confusion."[69]

The publication of *Africanisms in the Gullah Dialect* represented an intellectual breakthrough that captured the public imagination from coast to coast. Reviewers analyzed it in newspapers from South Carolina to California. On May 3, 1950, Elizabeth Wright of the University of Chicago Press contacted Turner to inform him that the press office had received copies of reviews from a number of journals and newspapers. There were duplicates of many, which she forwarded to him.[70]

Africanisms in the Gullah Dialect was a source of pride for many and a source of interest for others. Even though it did not generate income for Turner, he was optimistic that it could be of financial benefit in other ways. L. D. Reddick, a former Fisk student of Turner's and, by 1949, the librarian at Atlanta University, wrote Turner to inform him of the nine-thousand-dollar Anisfield-Wolf award. Established in 1934, it was dispensed each year to an author of an outstanding book.[71]

By the end of the year, on December 28, 1949, a few months before his death, Woodson contacted Ralph Linton of the anthropology department of Columbia University to recommend Turner to the Anisfield-Wolf Committee: "I understand that the Anisfield-Wolf award is offered each year to encourage the publication of books designed to improve race relations in this country. I desire therefore to speak a word for Doctor Lorenzo D. Turner's *Africanisms in the Gullah Dialect.* This book is eloquent evidence of Doctor Turner's development as an authority on English as spoken by Negroes on the Islands off the coast of Georgia and South Carolina."[72]

Woodson suggested the depth of Turner's preparation and dedication, pointing to Turner's study of African languages. Referring to him as "one of the most productive scholars specializing in the English language," Woodson viewed the award as an investment in Turner's future research: "In tracing these origins he has shown ripe scholarship in mastering the essentials of the native languages spoken in Africa as well as the influences from these sources on the languages spoken in the Western Hemisphere. He has discovered thousands of expressions that have thus crossed the Atlantic and [has] given them an original treatment. This achievement entitles him to rank as one of the most productive scholars specializing in the English language. Anything which you may do to enable him to publish other works for which he has collected most valuable data will greatly aid scholarship in the modern world."[73]

Like Woodson, Turner believed that he was an ideal candidate for the award. Therefore, two months earlier he had written to Paul Corbett, sales manager for the University of Chicago Press, to suggest that he encourage Herskovits to prepare a review of Turner's book for the *American Anthropologist* or the *Journal of American Folklore*.[74]

Although Herskovits had praised Turner's work in manuscript form, quoting from it to bolster his case for retained African culture in the Western Hemisphere in *The Myth of the Negro Past* (1941), he prepared no review of it. Given Herskovits's prestige in academia and influence with funding agencies, his review would have been the single most important one in print. Turner did not receive the Anisfield-Wolf Award. It was an exciting prospect but one of many levels of confirmation and acclaim that eluded him.

Despite controversy, *Africanisms in the Gullah Dialect* has stood the test of time. Previous researchers had commented on a limited range of features while Turner examined Gullah systematically, providing plausible explanations for its distinctiveness. In their introduction to a new edition of Turner's book, Katherine Wyly Mille and Michael B. Montgomery write, "He began simply by refusing to accept the views of previous scholars and by considering an African source whenever there was a good reason to do so. In the process he forever changed the understanding of Gullah."[75]

In 1949 Turner was fifty-nine years old, with great energy to forge ahead. The study and analysis of other creoles influenced by African languages awaited him.

By the summer of 1949, it seemed that Turner's plan to generate additional income through lectures was likely to bear fruit. In the wake of rising societal agitation for and interest in integration, G. James Fleming, the secretary of the Race Relations Committee of the American Friends Service Committee in Philadelphia, engaged Turner for a lecture tour. In addition to presenting his research, he was expected to assess the quality of race relations wherever he traveled. When, for example, Turner spent the week of May 1–7, 1949, at the State University of Iowa, he "made twenty-two presentations, including seven classroom lectures, with an average attendance at each lecture of thirty persons, gave three lectures before faculty groups, ten before student groups, one address at an off-campus worship meeting, and one public address before students, faculty and citizens of Iowa City."[76]

Turner held many one-on-one and group interviews, at which he was well received. He wrote "I had personal interviews with approximately seventy-five students and twenty-five faculty members and attended five dinners and four teas. The over-all response was excellent, and I reached an approximate total of 1100 persons."[77]

Turner's impression of Iowa City was favorable, except for his assessment of the quality of life for black and Jewish students. He reported to Fleming that the approximately 160 "Negro" students were denied accommodations in the residence halls and in the homes of local residents (with the exception of four white families and four local black families); denied most jobs on campus, including assistantships; and had access to neither barber nor beauty shops in the town. There were no blacks on the faculty and only "two or three Negro department assistants doing some sort of clerical work. One of these is connected with the Department of Romance Languages."[78]

Turner also reported "considerable anti-Semitic sentiment both on the campus and in the city," though having greater resources, "the Jews are not nearly so greatly handicapped as the Negroes." In concluding, Turner recommended that "the appointment of a well-qualified Negro as a permanent member of the faculty would be an excellent first step in the direction of improving race relations both in Iowa City and on the University campus."[79]

Wherever Turner's career path led him geographically, his commitment to the work of Woodson and the Association for the Study of Negro Life and History was continuous. For decades, he served as an assistant editor for Woodson's journals, the *Journal of Negro History* and the *Negro History Bulletin.* On April 23, 1949, Woodson, as editor in chief, contacted Turner regarding the plans of the ASNLH to publish an *Encyclopaedia Africana,* informing Turner that he had appointed him to the editorial board for the project:

> At the meeting in this office of January 8, called to secure the cooperation of outstanding scholars in completing the ENCYCLOPAEDIA AFRICANA, it was voted that the Editor-in-Chief appoint an editorial board to determine matters of policy and also to secure the cooperation of a still larger number of scholars as consultants. You were appointed a member of the board of consultants. It is understood that this service is cooperative, and no compensation will be allowed except in case of traveling expenses or other debts incurred in performing some special services required by the management. All assigned articles when accepted by the staff, however, will be paid for at the rate of two cents a word. Kindly inform us whether or not you will thus cooperate.[80]

Turner immediately began to evaluate articles for inclusion in the encyclopedia. Later in the year, on October 11, 1949, he recommended to Woodson three articles and two book reviews in rank order. The articles were Jessie P. Guzman's "Monroe W. Work and His Contributions," Sidney Kaplan's "The Miscegenation Issue in the Election of 1864," and L. D. Reddick's "The Negro Policy of the United States Army, 1775–1945."[81]

Turner enclosed eight dollars to cover a two-year subscription to the *Journal of Negro History,* simultaneously expressing his support for the new project by assuring Woodson, "I shall be glad to do whatever I can on the *Encyclopedia.*" In closing, Turner noted Woodson's support for *Africanisms in the Gullah Dialect:* "I certainly appreciate the nice things you said about my book."[82]

Woodson died one year later, leaving the encyclopedia project incomplete. A similar project was to be created by W. E. B. Du Bois when he settled in Ghana in 1961. The Ghanaian government under Kwame Nkrumah, its first president after independence, commissioned it. Du Bois's death in August 1963 halted the project.[83] However, it found new life under Kwame Anthony Appiah and Henry Louis Gates Jr. Issued in 1999, dedicated to W. E. B. Du Bois, and entitled *Encyclopedia Africana: The Encyclopedia of the African and African American Experience,* it covers a range of topics central to the history and contemporary life of African people in the United States, the Caribbean, and Africa. Topics are treated from the perspectives of politics, economics, the military, religion, the family, education, and the arts.[84]

Immediately after Woodson's death on April 3, 1950, Mary McLeod Bethune, the president of the association, appointed Rayford W. Logan, the Howard University historian, as director of the association and editor of both the *Journal of Negro History* and *Negro History Bulletin.* The board meeting was to convene in October 1950, at which time a permanent director and editor were to be chosen. On May 18, 1950, Logan wrote Turner to indicate that the organization was counting on his continued support: "I have accepted this responsibility because I feel assured of the continued assistance and cooperation of the Assistant Editors. I feel so confident of your continued devotion to the work created by Dr. Woodson that it would be gratuitous to ask you for a specific assurance of your advice and cooperation."[85]

Wishing for full attendance at the meeting, Logan invoked Woodson's memory as he urged Turner to attend: "Dr. Laurence D. Reddick has already initiated plans for the October meeting of the Association. We will want to make this first Meeting since the death of Dr. Woodson a worthy tribute to his memory, and I hope that you will begin now to make plans to attend it."[86]

On June 15, 1950, Turner responded, informing Logan that he had just returned to Chicago after an "absence from the city for several days." Giving Logan his vote of confidence, he assured him of his continued support. Turner was undoubtedly relieved that Logan had accepted the editorship, and indicated the same to Logan: "I am very happy to learn that you have accepted the responsibility of serving as Acting Director of the Association and Editor of *The Journal* and *Bulletin*. For several years I have thought of you as the most suitable person in every way to assume the heavy tasks in the event Dr. Woodson became unable to carry on. You can rest assured of my fullest cooperation. I can realize what a sacrifice you are making considering the many other heavy responsibilities you are carrying."[87]

Turner then assured Logan of his plans to attend the meeting in October. In the same letter, apparently in response to another letter from Logan about the peer review process for articles accepted for publication in the *Journal of Negro History*, Turner described the process Woodson had utilized: "As to the prize research articles and reviews, I never considered myself chairman of the Committee of Judges. Dr. Woodson usually read the eligible articles and reviews, sent them to me, and I, after reaching my decision, sent them on to Dr. Savage at Lincoln University. Savage and I sent to Woodson our votes. Woodson decided on the winners after considering the votes of the three of us. He usually sent the articles and reviews to me late in September, allowing sufficient time for Savage and me to read them before the fall meeting of the Association."[88]

After World War II ended, new interest in the intellectual exploration of non-Western cultures developed. For Turner, Africa was still the place he yearned to touch. His fieldwork in Nigeria and Sierra Leone, which lay ahead, would be high points of his career.

20

Africa at Last! 1951

> My research is now going very well. Interesting material is to be found everywhere. A few days ago one old man gave me out of his head 170 proverbs, each one illustrated with a story or sermon. I have three hours of recording (3 one-hour spools of wire) from him alone. He is in the latter 70s and is a real artist. Before I leave here I may need to order more spools of wire. There is so much fascinating material that I hate not to record it. Today a woman sang for me several lullabies and other songs in Yoruba. I will have enough material to keep Adu busy translating for a long time.
>
> —Turner to Lois Turner, Wednesday, May 2, 1951

BEGINNING IN THE EARLY 1930S, when Turner had become convinced that the Niger-Congo element in Gullah was much greater than many others had assumed, he had aspired to conduct fieldwork in Africa. His ardor has been heightened when he lived in northern Brazil in 1940 among Yoruba speakers, some of whom not only knew their relatives in Nigeria but in some instances had visited them as well. Further, he wished to gain the background to interpret his Brazilian Yoruba folklore more adequately by immersing himself in the source, Nigerian Yoruba culture, through which he would develop a more nuanced sense of African philosophy underlying the culture.[1] The obstacles to that goal were immense, in particular, lack of funding for a sustained fieldwork experience resulting from assumptions among anthropologists and other social scientists that made it difficult for black Americans to receive grants for research in Africa.

Given that context, it was not until the Fulbright program was established in 1948 that Turner's opportunity arose. As soon as the United States Department of State initiated the program, Turner began to make inquiries about support for his anticipated work.

The project he proposed would have occupied several researchers for a few years. First, he planned to examine the eight Yoruba dialects in Nigeria, "collecting Yoruba folklore, and putting into written form, with English translations, as much of the unwritten folk literature as time permits." Second, Turner intended to utilize the Linguistic Atlas methodology as he prepared a special worksheet. He would interview informants from the eight dialect groups for several months each, supplementing his phonetic transcriptions with wire recordings. The result was to be "sufficient information for making a scientific analysis of the sounds, syntax, morphology, and tones."[2]

Turner proposed to utilize the data for multiple purposes—to prepare "a descriptive grammar of the dialects . . . , an analysis of their tones . . . , a study of the vocabulary . . . , an annotated collection of the folktales . . . in Yoruba with English translations . . . , an annotated collection of miscellaneous folk material, such as proverbs . . . , orations, sermons, prayers, narratives of religious experience, life histories of informants . . . , and a collection of folk songs representing each of the provinces, with music transcriptions and with the lyrics in both Yoruba and English." When his documents were in print, Turner expected that his original primary source data would be a rich repository sought after by others, among them ethnologists, social anthropologists, and sociologists, who would utilize the material to analyze the relationships between myth, ritual, and social structure; comparative musicologists, who would analyze the music; psychologists and intercultural educators, who would study the "impact of European civilization" upon Yoruba culture; and historians specializing in Brazil, who would gain deeper insight into the social relations and migrations between Brazilian Yorubans and their Nigerian relatives.[3]

One of Turner's references for the Fulbright award was Ida Ward at the University of London. On March 18, 1949, Turner wrote to her, thanking her for visiting him and his family in Chicago and for encouraging him in his attempts to gain a fellowship. "For a long time I have been looking forward to spending at least two years in the Yoruba country. Now it looks as if I may at last be able to do so."[4]

By the time Turner corresponded with Ward, he had already conferred with Ruth C. Sloan of the Near East and African branch of the Public Affairs Overseas Program Staff, to explore his options. Sloan had also visited Turner in Chicago. After her return to Washington, D.C., she sent him an encouraging message on March 29, 1949: "I thoroughly enjoyed my visit with you in Chicago and I am looking forward to seeing you before you take off for Africa. I have talked with several people about your application for Fulbright funds and it seems to me that in due course your application should bear fruit. I will be happy if you will keep me informed of any further developments on the London side."[5]

Turner received the Fulbright award in 1950; however, in order to arrange for his multiple obligations, he requested to be allowed to postpone leaving until 1951. In mid-January 1951, after a series of letters regarding the possibility of Lois accompanying him in collaborative fieldwork, the Fulbright office concluded that only Turner would receive funds. Hence, he departed Chicago by train for New York, where he spent several days with Hugh and Mabel Smythe. The Turners and Smythes had been friends for many years, contacting each other periodically as the Smythes moved from one assignment to another, usually on the diplomatic circuit. Smythe was one of the first cohort of African American anthropologists and a graduate of Northwestern University.[6]

On the evening of January 20, Turner prepared a lengthy letter to Lois, informing her that he had visited the U.S. Health Department the day before to obtain certification of his typhoid injections. He had located the European electrical plugs he needed for his recording equipment. He reminded Lois that he valued the details that represented her care for him, as he simultaneously wished her well in managing the house and family affairs in his absence: "Well, I am certainly grateful for all the wonderful help you gave me. I couldn't possibly have gotten ready without your aid. My bags seem to be complete in every way. Take good care of yourself and take things easy. If any difficulty arises, about the house, contact Longmire and he will straighten it out. . . . Tell Lorenzo and Rani to be good boys and not give you any trouble. I will send them something from London."[7]

According to the U.S. Department of Commerce form that he completed, Turner departed, traveling tourist class, from New York on January 21, 1951, aboard the Cunard ship the *Queen Mary*. During the course of the year, he spent 20 days in England in research, 320 in West Africa, another 20 in England on his return, and 7 in France.

As soon as Turner arrived in London, he checked into the Royal Gardens Hotel and immediately dispatched a note to Lois, describing his surroundings and his circumstances. His brief stay in London was only the beginning of a series of unexpected adaptations he was required to make during the year. He wrote, "Now about this so-called Royal Gardens Hotel, I was really shocked when I arrived there. . . . The food is bad and the room is cold. . . . There was an unlighted fireplace in one corner of the [dining] room and no other facilities for heating. . . . The Fulbright man was somewhat surprised himself to see the sort of place they had sent me to. . . . Most food items in London are rationed. Each person gets one egg a week. Sugar is limited to one small lump per cup of tea or coffee. Candy is also rationed, but I seldom eat candy anyway. I shall be glad to leave London. The weather is damp and cold. It was raining when I arrived."[8]

Among the items with Turner's Fulbright papers is a business card for the Bibliophile, a bookstore specializing in "New and Second-Hand" books at 16 Little Russell Street, London. He most likely looked for books on African culture or on African languages to take with him to the African continent.

Shortly before Turner embarked, he purchased a National Excelsior diary and calendar/planner for 1951. His intention was to maintain a record of his daily field experiences. He recorded his first entry on March 5, 1951, five days after he arrived in Nigeria, and his final entry on Monday, May 21, after leaving Ibadan for the eastern provinces, among them, Onitsha. Turner's diary contains no entries thereafter, although he remained in Africa for six additional months. Once he left the urban areas for the field, his opportunities to maintain a diary became more limited. Nonetheless, the several months of glimpses into Turner's sojourn are a valuable key to his daily contacts, lectures, tape recording, filming, plans, and experiences. His introduction to Africa is detailed in his first entry:

> —After 5 days in Nigeria—My boat "The Accra" (Elder Dempster Lines) reached Lagos almost noon on February 28, after stops at Freetown, Sierra Leone (where I was shown the city by I. M. Broderick) and at Takoradi, Gold Coast (where three Africans and myself saw the towns of Takoradi and Secondi in a taxi). At Lagos, it was after six o'clock before I left the wharf. It took nearly four hours to get through the Customs. There was no duty to pay, but at one time it looked as though I would have to leave a deposit on my cameras and gramophone equaling 1/5 their cost, but a clause in the declaration sheet, stating that equipment connected with one's profession or trade was not subject to duty, relieved me of that expense.

> It took another two hours for the Africans in charge to complete arrangements for sending my large trunk by train to University College, Ibadan. Nobody seemed to know how to arrange for the trunk to be sent. It was finally weighed and a form was filled out which had to be changed several times. Then after prolonged conversations, in which at least ten different persons participated, it was decided that the trunk would be stored in a shed until the following day and sent by truck to some town nearby where it could be put on a train coming to Ibadan. They said the trunk should reach me in two days. Five days have already passed and it has not yet arrived. I was charged 8 shillings and 9 pence for its transportation, but there was another prolonged conversation among the railway employees as to how any receipt should be made out. The whole transaction took nearly three hours.
>
> An African from the College met me at the boat in a station wagon. He was able, with the help of about eight boys, each of whom I had to tip two or three times, to get the rest of my luggage in his car. Then we proceeded on the long journey to Ibadan (120 miles). The road was narrow, full of sharp curves, and otherwise bad, but the driver insisted on doing between 55 and 60 miles an hour all the way. I was greatly relieved when we reached Ibadan about 9:00 P.M.[9]

Turner immediately was initiated into the rigors and challenges of conducting research in a nontechnological society. His prior years as a self-supporting youth had accustomed him to overcoming obstacles, including deprivation. His discipline stood him in good stead. He wrote:

> There was no space available for me on the campus, so I was temporarily housed in a rest house or chalet about 1 ½ miles from the temporary campus. The permanent campus (about 5 miles away) will not be ready for occupancy for about a year. When I entered the rest house, I was greeted with this notice on the inside of the door: "Beware of thieves; visitors have frequently lost valuable articles."
>
> There are several of these chalets built in a clearing in the bush for government employees passing through the country. The forest is only a few hundred yards behind and to the side of me. Lizards, large spiders, and many other varieties of insects are everywhere—all over the house. Screens are seldom or never seen in this country. There is a dining room nearby, but the food is very bad. I have a great deal of valuable equipment which cannot be replaced in Africa or England. Consequently, I am afraid to leave the house for more than a few minutes at a time. I insisted on having a night watchman whom I have only seen twice. He carries only a small club. He was sent over by the College for my protection. I can't possibly get out to do any research as long as these conditions last. There is no hot water in the house, but a boy brings me a little in a container twice a day. He also cleans the house. I pay him £4 a month. My room and board cost—shillings and six pence a day. The weather is very hot, but there is a breeze now and then and late in the afternoon and at night.[10]

Turner's prospects for beginning his work improved when he met an English department counterpart at the newly created University of Nigeria, who opened many doors for him during his sojourn. He wrote:

Night before last (March 3) I had dinner at home of Professor Christopherson, head of the English Department. I met Mrs. Christopherson, a charming and unassuming English lady, and two guests—one a man connected with a publishing house and the other a lady who teaches at the CONS school in Ibadan—probably also from England.

I like the Christophersons very much. He is from Denmark and formerly taught English at the University of Copenhagen. He helped to complete a posthumous volume of Jesperson's 7 volume *English Grammar on Historical Principles.* Mr. Bowman is the registrar at the College and is responsible for providing housing for teachers.[11]

After a month of visiting towns and villages with the assistance of others, Turner declared his independence by purchasing a truck. It accorded him the freedom to construct his own schedule and to pursue data freely. In a March 25, 1951, letter to Lois, he detailed his plans:

In all these places, I took pictures. On my return trip, I shall take more pictures—movie and still—and make sound recordings. I have also bought some beautiful carvings, musical instruments, and other things. I shall return to Ibadan on Saturday, March 31. Before leaving Ibadan I had to buy a new car—a light truck. It cost 603 pounds and 17 shillings—about $1700. There was nothing else to do. A used car doesn't stay upon these terrible roads, even if one had been available. The original plan I had of buying a used car for 320 pounds fell through. I should be able to get about $1500 for the car when I sell it in September or October. This money I will use to go to Liberia, Sierra Leone, The Gold Coast, and probably Angola. All the Africans have been very cooperative and I am getting many varieties of materials, which I can use on my return.[12]

Turner found a number of local officials to be helpful and reliable allies. Christopher Ogum arranged his April 4, 1951, visit to Ijebu Province, one of the Yoruba areas. Turner wrote:

Wednesday
April 4, 1951
Motored to Ijebu Province. Visited General Assembly at Ijebu-Ode and spoke for about ten minutes on nature of my research and on Negroes in Brazil and solicited cooperation of members of the Assembly in obtaining informants for my research, in that Province, in Yoruba folklore. Attempted to play some Brazilian Yoruba records, but small gramophone didn't have enough volume for audience to hear. They suggested that I return and speak and play records over the radio, since in the Province there is no electricity except at the radio station. I agreed to do so.

The Ibas and the Paramount Chief (His Highness the Awujale) were eager to cooperate. There was no European to be seen anywhere. Later I met a European (Mr. H. W. Reaves) at the home of the Iba of Ijebu-Igbo, where I visited for 2 or 3 hours and was served drinks and cigarettes. The Iba was also eager to assist me. His title is Iba Joel Adeboye I of Ijebu-Igbo.

> At Ijebu-Igbo I made pictures of the shrines of Eshu, Ishu, and Ogu. Several intelligent Yorubas, including a Mr. Talabi, offered to assist me in my work. Mr. Talabi, a teacher there, will obtain for me singers of fishing and hunting songs and story tellers.
>
> This place is Christopher Ogum's home. He made all the contacts for me. The whole day was quite successful. Took photograph of the Inodo tree and many scenes of the town. Met Mr. S. A. Balogun of the Provincial Education Office at Ijebu-Ode. He offered his cooperation. I will return to the Ijebu Province in about 2 weeks.[13]

Two days later, on April 6, 1951, Turner experienced more of the beauty and dangers of the African interior. Not one to shrink from challenges, he likely reasoned that if he were to collect reliable data, he could not afford to gain a reputation for being a pampered outsider.

> Ondo Nigeria
> Friday, April 6, 1951
> Motored to Ondo today from Ibadan. Tarred road up to Ile-Ife, a distance of 3 miles. Between Ile-Ife and Ondo (42 miles), the road was terrible, said to be one of the worst in West Africa. George, driving too fast, I took over. Had to go in 2nd and frequently in 1st most of the way. Many treacherous bridges. Arrived in Ondo about 4:30 P.M., having left Ibadan at 11:00 A.M. Stayed at home of Miss Akinkugbe, 18 Oke-gbogi Street, Box 12, Ondo, Nigeria. Stayed here until 11:00 A.M. Sunday. Her father, a dispenser of drugs and medicines, is D. A. Akinkugbe. Her cousin, O. Akinkugbe, a barrister. He lives on the same street at 38 Oke-gbogi Street. Had dinner of squash, salad and sardine sandwiches Saturday night at the barrister's house. He is a law graduate of Cambridge University.

Turner made note of addresses of persons who might serve as contacts once he returned to the United States. The game hunter, J. O. Ola Ayorinbe, was one of them.

> Today I drove to a nearby mountain called Efi Rock. It was very difficult to reach. Went as far as I could in the car and then walked through the dense brush until I reached the mountain, which was very high, apparently several thousand feet. I was accompanied by George and 4 other boys. There we met a hunter with a gun. He owns the adjoining property. He hunts wild game and boa constrictors, which infest this mountain. He has built traps near the mountain to catch wild game and animals. Tigers, leopards, wild hogs, bush cows, antelopes, elephants are in this country. He showed us the traps—fences with openings over a log over which is the trap. The hunter, J. O. Ola Ayorinbe, P. O. Box 51 Ondo, Nigeria, took us to the top of the mountain. I had to remove my shoes to scale it. The hunter and the boys were already barefooted. I took several pictures of the surrounding country and of the mountain. The hunter showed us the holes in which the boa constrictors were. He frequently waits two weeks at a time at these holes to shoot them as they come out. They are easiest to shoot during the rainy season, especially in July. With great difficulty, I descended the mountain. The hunter walks down

easily, leaning back. His feet cling to the rock. I eased down in sitting position, with palm of hands flat on the rock and bare feet also on rock.

Everything is quite primitive in Indo. There is a scarcity of water and no electricity. There is a little hotel in town where there is a Frigidaire, the only one in town. There are few native arts here. European wares are sold in the little shops run by the Africans. Went to wait for the oba on Saturday, but a ceremony was in progress and we couldn't see him.[14]

At the end of the day, Turner often studied the demographics of the West African provinces in which he expected to conduct fieldwork. His special interests were the political and social organization and the arts and textiles.

In early April, Turner witnessed the reinternment of a prominent man. "[The] burial ceremony . . . took place Saturday. The body of the Canou's father had been buried too near the road and had to be removed. This necessitated a ceremony—marching, drumming and dancing, singing and sacrificing of hogs and oxen for the feast, which is to take place Monday (April 9). The new tomb will be dedicated today (April 8). . . . [Canou's father had been] the Chief Sashere Ayotilerewa Awosika, who died in 1900. The dancers were also celebrating the death of 2 other sons of his who were also sasheres. I took pictures of the revelers from the 2nd floor window of Mr. B. A. Ademodi, head master of St. Stephen's Senior Primary School, Ondo."[15]

When Turner met Rev. D. O. Togun in Ibadan, they shared materials. Rev. Togun presented "three excellent Yoruba stories" in a dramatic call and response fashion, which Turner would have recognized as the source of the style of the traditional black ministers in the United States.

Tuesday, April 10, 1951

Visited home of Rev. D. O. Togun, Baptist Mission, P. O. Box 82, Ibadan, Nigeria. Played several Yoruba records I made in Brazil. The family and a few visitors were fascinated. Then I recorded on wire three excellent Yoruba stories related by the Rev. He is a real artist. It was a pleasure to observe him as he talked. He put his whole self into his narratives—facial and bodily gestures, onomatopoetic expressions, dramatic pauses, and every detail of expression that makes for a thrilling narrative. His small audience was enthralled. Almost without realizing what they were doing, when he came to the portions of his stories that called for singing, they joined in the chorus. He related three long narratives and asked me to come back for more. I offered him 10 shillings. At first, he was inclined not to accept this, saying that he was not telling these stories for money, but rather because he enjoyed doing so and was eager to assist me in taking down such native material as I was collecting in Africa. He was aware of the great expense such work must be to me.

A paralytic Yoruba visitor got keen pleasure from all he saw there. He also joined in singing the musical portions of the stories. He showed me a written statement of his condition (in English and Yoruba), hoping that I might give him something. I gave him 5 shillings—all I had in change—and he was very grateful. I shall return there for more stories and other folk material in about 2 ½ weeks.[16]

By late April, Turner's diary entries had become briefer but still illuminating. A number of them described the series of lectures he offered through Nigerian educational institutions. Christopherson arranged the lecture tour, remaining to listen to and provide feedback on each presentation.

> Friday, April 20, 1951
> Began 1st series of 6 lectures at University College—"Africans in the New World." The first dealt with slavery in the New World and the differences of treatment accorded the slaves in the various New World areas. The lecture was well received. I spoke 50 minutes and 10–15 minutes were given over to questions. More than 50 persons attended, including approximately 15 Europeans. The questions were asked exclusively by the Africans. Prof. Christopherson took me to the lecture and back to the permanent site in his car. Mrs. Christopherson accompanied us. On reaching their home, we were served drinks and squash.
>
> Dr. Mellanby attended and introduced me—a good introduction. Christopherson said that students wanted me to speak longer.[17]

Turner then began a series of three lectures on English in America.

> Tuesday, April 24, 1951
> Today the 1st of 3 lectures on "The English Language in America." Attended largely by English majors. Only two teachers attended, Miss Cooke and Christopherson. About 20–25 Africans were present. I talked 50 minutes, about 15 minutes for questions. Lecture came off well. I talked largely about sources of American English, immigrations and migrations, etc.[18]

On April 26 Ulli Beier accompanied Turner to Abeokuta.[19] Although colonialism had influenced the traditional institutions, respect for African royalty was still a feature of Nigerian society. The Alake himself welcomed Turner, expressing his hope that Turner would return a favor.

> Thursday, April 26, 1951
> Made trip to Abeokuta with the Beiers. Took pictures; visited the Royal Palace and met the Alake who spoke with me for about 35 minutes. He was very cordial—an old man apparently in his seventies. He wanted me to assist his son in finding a college in the U.S.A. to attend. I promised to assist. He offered to assist me in my work and to allow me to record at the Palace. I took pictures of the Palace. Beier accompanied me.[20]

Back to the campus at the University of Nigeria on April 27, Turner continued his discussion of African culture in Brazil.

> Friday, April 27, 1951
> Today gave 2nd lecture in series—Africans in the New World. Topic: "Brazil's Indebtedness to the Africans." Lecture well-received. About 40 persons attended including a few Europeans.[21]

At some point after April 27 but before May 3, 1951, Turner began a "2nd series of lectures on 'English Language in the New World.' Discussed regional differences

[to] about 20–25 students at. . . ." He was apparently interrupted, as the diary entry is incomplete.[22]

Turner's experiences were not all equally fruitful. On his second trip to Abeokuta with the Beiers, his plans to photograph the Egungun met with frustration.

> Thursday, May 3, 1951
> Trip to Abeokuta with the Beiers. Would have made recordings of Egungun but left transformer in Ibadan. Sent George for it but he could not find it. Egungun disappointed. Gave them 1 £ and a few shillings for their trouble.[23]

In May 1951, Turner continued his series on Africans in Brazil.

> Friday, May 4, 1951
> Third lecture on "Africans in the New World." Very well received. Approximately 45 persons present, including a few Europeans. Spoke again on Brazil's indebtedness to Africans and played many records and showed documents. Spoke one hour. Answered questions afterwards. Mr. Coleman, an American from Utah and Harvard, doing research in Political Science in Nigeria, attended. Dr. Mellenley attended also.[24]

Turner delivered his first lecture focused exclusively on Gullah on May 8, 1951.

> Tuesday, May 8, 1951
> Third and last lecture on "English Language in America" on Gullah. About 40 attended. Lecture very well received. Spoke one hour. Several questions. I played several Gullah records.[25]

Ulli Beier did not forget that Turner wished to record the Egungun.

> Thursday, May 10, 1951
> Trip to Abeokuta with the Beiers. Made recordings of music of Egungun and students of Abeokuta Grammar School.[26]

Immediately after his return from Abeokuta to Ibadan, Turner presented a general lecture. His diary entry indicates few details of the presentation.

> Friday, May 11, 1951
> Fourth lecture on "Africans in the New World—Negroes in the U.S.A." About 40 attended. Well received. Spoke one hour. Questions for an additional 15 minutes.[27]

By mid-May 1951 the students at Ibadan were expressing interest in receiving Turner's lectures in written form. That was a tall order, given the rudimentary technology of the time and the paucity of Turner's budget.

> Tuesday, May 15, 1951
> Fifth lecture on "Africans in the New World—Negroes in the U.S.A." Especially well received. About 45 attended. Spoke one hour and 10 minutes. Many questions. Students wanted copies of all the lectures and asked whether they would be published. I told them that I would try to have a few copies mimeographed for them.[28]

Ulli Beier continued to assist Turner in traveling to Abeokuta. During his third trip, Turner visited young children.

> Thursday, May 17, 1951
> Trip to Àbeokuta with the Beiers. Made some recordings of music and speech of students of Abeokuta Grammar School.[29]

In Turner's final lecture, he discussed for the first time his data collection in Nigeria.

> Friday, May 18, 1951
> Sixth and last lecture in "Africans in the New World" series. Discussed my own research in Africa and demonstrated recordings on wire. Recorded songs by 2 No——ta (?) students. Approximately 55 persons attended, including several Europeans. Spoke one hour and 10 minutes. Questions another 15 minutes. Very well received. Professor Christopherson and Miss Cooke attended all the lectures.[30]

Turner's final diary entry was written just after he left the Ibadan area for the eastern provinces. There he met a local weaver, Mr. C. Anadu.

> Monday, May 21, 1951
> Left Ibadan at 7:30 A.M. for trip to Eastern Provinces. Arrived in Asaba Territory at 4:55 P.M., a distance of about 322 miles. George drove all the way. Left Asaba at 6:00 P.M. and reached Onitsha about 6:30. Spent night at Hotel Rainbow. Rest house had no vacancy. Took meals there, however. Visited Mr. C. Anadu, the weaver, on next morning. He demonstrated weaving. Will return there in afternoon to make still and moving picture. Will assist him in putting his cloth on the U.S. market. His address is Niger Textile Works, P.O. Box 190, Onitsha, Nigeria.[31]

On a day-to-day basis, Turner was hard at work documenting the oral traditions of the various African cultural groups he encountered. Since he had made himself a specialist on African culture from 1936 to the time of his trip in 1951, his research priorities were well conceived. Usually, he recorded data in traditional African languages. After his return to the United States, he spent thousands of hours in the translation process. Often he paid Africans attending universities in the Chicago area to serve as informants.[32]

One equipment item Turner usually transported during his travels was an 8-millimeter camera with a sound feature. His well-trained photographer's eye was the probable result of his months as a newspaper editor. His camera was equipped to process both color and black-and-white film. A viewing of Turner's fieldwork reel confirms that he consciously captured contrastive scenes from both rural areas and city life. He recorded a Nigerian woman's protest march, with all the women dressed in white; he documented various types of dances; he captured market scenes and religious ceremonies—traditional, Christian, and Islamic.

When Turner visited an Oyo village, he met a Yoruba chief who had recently converted to Islam. The conversion prompted the ruler to divest himself of his traditional, centuries-old, religious ceremonial art objects, which he placed on sale at reasonable prices. Turner, recognizing the significance of the items, purchased as many as he could. They "rank[ed] in age, authenticity and beauty with some of the best museum pieces" in America.[33] Turner had sharpened his eye for fine-quality African art at the exhibition he viewed in Mort Lake, England, during the summer of 1937. Over the years, when he lectured, he often showed some of his art to his audiences.[34]

By August, Turner had contracted malaria. After he informed Lois in a letter, she inquired regularly about his progress: "I hope you didn't have too severe an attack of malaria. Tell me more about it. Is it likely to recur? Are you all right now? Were you taking your pills every day?"[35]

As soon as Turner's health improved, he embarked on adventures beyond Nigeria, traveling briefly into Dahomey (now Benin), Togoland (now Togo), and the Gold Coast (now Ghana) in search of music and folklore. His methodology was comparable to the one from his Gullah studies years. "As he came to each village and town, he'd get in touch with tribal chiefs, a respected farmer or lawyer, explain his project, and enlist their help. Almost without exception, he found the people cooperative."[36]

Back in the United States, Lois regularly apprised Turner of his correspondences, providing the follow-up he recommended. She wrote: "A letter came here for you about two days ago about a young man in Addis Ababa. He wants to come over here to school and would like to know what financial assistance he can secure."[37]

By September, Turner had traveled thousands of miles. On one occasion, the battery in his vehicle malfunctioned, leaving him approximately fifty miles from the nearest city. He mentioned the memorable day in a draft of a letter to Kendall Taft, the Roosevelt College English department chair.

> Just before beginning the last days work in and near Nigeria, I got stranded in the thick bush of Dahomey when my car battery suddenly ceased to function. I have sent a boy to a town 50 to 60 miles away for another battery and have waited here all night for his return. I shall probably mail this letter in Badagry, an important town historically, where I shall spend two days before leaving Nigeria.[38]

After leaving Nigeria, Turner spent approximately two months in Sierra Leone collecting Krio language samples, proverbs, and folklore. Residing with the Brodericks, a prominent family in Freetown, he paid a visit to Princess Fatima Massaquoi, whom he had not seen since her student days at Fisk University in the early 1940s. He recorded her speaking in Vai.[39] From Sierra Leone, he departed for London, returning to the Royal Gardens Hotel to continue his research in London libraries.

Although the Fulbright allocation did not provide funds for Lois to join Turner as a collaborator in the field, the Turners considered the possibility of Lois joining him on his return to London. In the process, the issue of the house arose. Over the years, it continued to demand more than its share of the family resources. Its upkeep threatened to jeopardize Lois's visit to Europe. Lois wrote:

> Don't, oh, please don't begrudge me the trip in one pleasant six weeks out of the more than thirty weeks you have been away—out of the fifty two you will be away. You know how I hate this house and all it represents; you must surely remember how upset I get when I come face-to-face with a seemingly insurmountable

> financial hurdle! Have you no heart? I have tried to spare you all the details, which have arisen to cause me dismay because usually they get ironed out in the course of time but it's pretty rough bearing them alone. It's real heartbreak to me to think I'm coming out one month with a surplus of $100 only to find that I have to replace a refrigerator or pay a plumber a large sum to fix a leak or pay for the redecorating of a room in order to rent it. No surplus that month![40]

Just as Lois was concluding that the London excursion was beyond the family's means, the Fulbright office agreed to allocate funds for her European vacation. Turner wrote Lois to share the good news that they would be able to spend almost a month in London and Paris: "Just heard from Fulbright in London. They have secured passage for us on the Queen Mary leaving Southampton for New York on December 29. This will give us plenty of time for our holiday. . . . Love to the boys. With hugs and kisses. Lovingly, Dow."[41]

By November 1951 Turner's thoughts began to turn to his responsibilities in the United States. In preparation for the spring 1952 semester, he contacted Taft with plans for his courses. One of the four was new, focusing on English Language Research. Turner suggested the following course description: "Consideration of the problems involving the analysis and historical treatment of English sounds, inflections, syntax, and vocabulary. Some attention given to linguistic fieldwork."[42]

The remainder of Turner's assignment was English Language in America, Studies in the English Language, and Cultural Studies 240–B. For English Language in America, Turner requested that Taft order Kenyon's *American Pronunciation* (1945) as a text. He requested two supplementary texts, with two copies of each for the library. They were Charles Fries's *American English Grammar* (1940) and Kenneth Pike's *The Intonation of American English* (1946). For Studies in the English Language, Turner requested Bernard Bloch and George Trager's *Outline of Linguistic Analysis* (1942). For Culture Studies 240–B, Turner requested Melville Herskovits's *The Myth of the Negro Past* (1941) and his own *Africanisms in the Gullah Dialect* (1949).[43]

In early December 1951, leaving the boys behind with her parents in Louisville, Lois boarded the *Queen Mary* to London. Turner anxiously anticipated her arrival. According to Lois, "When I arrived, Dow and I engaged in a whirlwind of activity, visiting the Palace of Versailles, the Tower of London, and other attractions. We shopped. I purchased fabric to make winter coats for the boys. At the end of the vacation, we boarded the Queen Mary on December 30, 1951 for New York. To add to the allure of the interlude, we learned that Winston Churchill, the Prime Minister of England, was on board. The ocean was rocky, and I became sea sick, but the trip was otherwise a memorable adventure."[44]

Soon after Turner returned to Chicago, the treasures he had amassed during the year were delivered to him. The sculptures, musical instruments, recordings, and notebooks representing West African art, folklore, and languages filled five trunks and thirteen suitcases. A number of persons were eager to interview him. Merry O'Reilly, who prepared a story for *Say,* the alumni magazine of Roosevelt, detailed some of his triumphs and adventures. The article serves as an excellent general commentary of Turner's year, supplementing his diary and letters. It covered many of the themes Turner underscored in his lectures for the remainder of his career: "With a wire recorder and ingenuity, Dr. Turner was able to make on-the-spot recordings of stories, songs, and other folk materials never before recorded. He found the people friendly and cooperative, and technical problems were overcome by having the wire recorder connected to his car battery for ready operation under unpredictable conditions."[45]

Turner found "interesting evidence" of the original sources of African cultural survivals in the United States and Brazil, as "he was able to recognize the origins of famous American Negro spirituals and Stephen Foster melodies." Many classical folk stories of West Africa, passed orally from generation to generation, Turner found to be the counterparts of stories in Western literature such as those by Chaucer in the *Canterbury Tales*.[46]

Turner noted that tourists had seldom touched the areas he had visited, radio broadcasts were limited to British Broadcasting Company programs, and news media were largely British-controlled. The American media offerings were generally cowboy and gangster movies, accompanied by British newsreels.

Some of Turner's day-to-day experiences rivaled those in the Indiana Jones movies. After he purchased the British all-terrain vehicle, he and a hired guide adventured forth at each opportunity. He learned from experience that the local bridges, operated by men, were closed after 6:00 P.M. when the controller of the bridge left his shift for the day. If Turner arrived after 6:00 P.M., his bed for the night was the vehicle. Traveling between cities, if he found himself far from a settlement, it was wise for him and his guide to take turns sleeping so that one or the other was prepared to keep wildlife at bay with a rifle.[47]

Of Turner's numerous lectures, he presented a most unforgettable one in a mission school on a warm evening when a herd of elephants decided to forage for food. Someone peered in to announce, "Elephants are coming," prompting the audience to bolt for the door. Turner hastily packed his recording equipment, his lecture notes, and briefcase. Needless to say, the lecture was never completed. Turner's vehicle, which he drove 20,000 miles in less than twelve months, immeasurably increased his access to the most reliable original data. At the end of his fieldwork period, he sold it. By then the tires were practically worn beyond the treads.[48]

Having swum in the currents of Africa for a year, Turner was prepared to embark on a new career initiative as director of the Inter-Disciplinary Program in African Studies at Roosevelt. The courses were drawn from across the disciplines of art, English, history, anthropology, and political science. In addition to Turner, the faculty members who offered the courses were Elizabeth Balanoff, St. Clair Drake, Charles Hamilton, Peter Kellogg, Woodruff D. Smith, and Frank Untermeyer. Students could select a major or minor.

> The African Studies Program is designed to meet the needs of (a) students who have careers or career plans specifically related to business, education, mission work, or public service in the newly emergent African nations; and (b) students

who would like to secure knowledge and appreciation of African cultures and problems. A major sequence is offered to meet the needs of the first group of students, and a minor sequence for students who wish to satisfy their interest in Africa while securing competence in a specific subject-matter field.

By 1962 the major offerings were:

102 African Languages
Sociology 102 Introduction to Anthropology
Sociology 247 Peoples of Africa
301 Introduction to African Linguistics I
302 Introduction to African Linguistics II
301–309 African Art
History 328 Topics in Negro History
Sociology 332 Race and Culture Contact in West Africa
Sociology 333 Race and Culture Contact in East Africa
Sociology 334 Race and Culture Contact in South and Central Africa
340 African Culture and Its Survivals in the New World
341 African Folklore and Literature
History 370 History of Africa South of the Sahara
History 372 History of Africa
Political Science 369 The Politics of Contemporary Africa
470 Problems in Pan Africanism.[49]

After 1951, at every opportunity, Turner promoted his firsthand interpretation of continental Africa in the classroom and community. Frequently focusing on Yoruba culture, he noted a history and well-developed civilization dating to 3,000 B.C. He learned to play the talking drum and other instruments. Turner's riveting presentations often featured segments of his reel-to-reel tape, some segments in color, others in black and white. He played his African music recordings to illustrate the African origins of some of the melodies of well-known Negro spirituals and popular American secular music, among them, "I'm Climbing Up the Mountain, "A City Called Heaven" (a Marian Anderson favorite), and a number of melodies associated with Stephen Foster. He found the Foster melodies to have their origins in "lullabies and dugout canoeing songs deep in Abeokuta and in Ijebu province." The slave trade from 1530 to 1860 "brought to this hemisphere a rich [African] background."[50]

In March and April 1952, Roosevelt organized a lecture series featuring Turner's research. Funded by the Felix Frankfurter Fund and scheduled for five successive Tuesday evenings at 7:45 P.M. in Sinha Hall, Room 785, at Roosevelt, the series was open to the public but also available to students for one college credit. Entitled "Culture Conflicts and Adjustments in West Africa," the series cost two dollars. Turner began with a March 4 lecture, "Twenty Thousand Miles through British and French West Africa," illustrating it with slides, arts, and crafts. On March 11, Turner presented "Native Rhythms," highlighting various types of West African music with an exhibition of musical instruments. On March 18, he showed his sensitivity to gender issues as he spoke of "Woman's Roles in West African Life," again utilizing slides. On March 25, he turned the spotlight on "the social, political, and economic conditions among West Africans" in his lecture on "The Black Man's Burden." Finally, on April 1, Turner offered a "Pot Pourri," with "movie camera shots of his travels in West Africa."[51] Turner's fine slides and film recordings were an excellent addition to his commentary. Some of his photographs are available at his website www.lorenzodowturner.com.

Continually, Turner found opportunities to share his wealth of firsthand experiences. During spring 1953, Turner, St. Clair Drake, and Frank Untermeyer taught a five-session African Culture Institute at the Washington Park YMCA at 50th Street and Indiana Avenue. Beginning on February 4, it was sponsored by the Women's Committee, of which Etta Moton Barnett was chair.[52] On May 28–31, 1953, Turner attended a study conference on "Statesmanship in Africa" at the Kennedy School of Missions of the Hartford Seminary Foundation in Hartford, Connecticut. There he served as the discussant on May 28 for William Welmers's presentation on "The Language Question."[53] During mid-August of 1956, Turner lectured at the University of Michigan on "African Influence on Music and Folklore of the U.S."[54]

Within a few years after Turner's return from Nigeria, the worldwide quest for freedom and independence escalated among people of color.[55] One consequence of the development of the civil rights and Black Power movements in the United States and the emergence of the independent nations in Africa was the need for new data in dictionaries and encyclopedias. Turner was prepared. In 1956 he accepted an appointment to the editorial advisory board of the *Funk and Wagnall's New Practical Standard Dictionary*.[56] In the 1960s he completed etymologies for Science Research Associates and *World Book Encyclopedia*.

On February 19, 1964, Christopher Hoolihan, the special vocabularies editor of the World Publishing Company, contacted Turner requesting that he serve as "consultant for us in African languages" and for "some English words of African origin" for the *Webster's New World Dictionary*.[57] Mitford Mathews, the Americanist specialist at World Publishing Company, had recommended Turner. Turner responded on February 24, 1964: "I shall be happy to render whatever assistance I can. . . . Among all the college editions of available dictionaries, *Webster's New World* is my favorite. I think it is superior to the others in most respects."[58]

After Turner submitted the etymologies, Hoolihan replied on July 15, 1964, expressing satisfaction with them: "Thank you very much for your letter of July 10 and for the set of African language entries. We are pleased with your work, as of course we knew we would be. And we appreciated your inclusion of information on possible biographical entries. We also appreciated your remarks on the current uncertainty regarding the etymology of most African words. Your observations here will be a guide to us in handling of such entries."[59]

In his return response, Turner noted that as he labored over the definitions and etymologies, he had utilized private funds to pay informants in order to ensure accuracy. Estimating that he was able to complete approximately six etymologies per hour, he admitted that the project was a most time-consuming one.[60]

While Turner served as consultant for dictionary projects, he continued his own research initiatives. According to his circa 1955 grant proposal to the African American Institute for three hundred dollars to prepare some of his material from Nigeria and Sierra Leone for publication, he had recorded in Yoruba

> fifteen hundred stories, seven thousand proverbs, three thousand songs, several hundred riddles, and other folk materials, practically none of which has ever before been recorded. Since that time I have selected for publication and translated into English with extensive annotations what I consider the best of these materials. My selections include three hundred stories (interspersed with interesting African melodies), a thousand proverbs, a few hundred riddles, and some fascinating philosophical pieces. These materials when published will throw some light on several aspects of native West African culture and its influence on New World cultures at a time when widespread and unprecedented interest is being manifested both in sub-Saharan Africa and in the whole problem of the relations between the white and darker peoples of the world.[61]

In the document "Current Research Activities of Lorenzo D. Turner," most likely prepared for an annual report at Roosevelt College, circa 1957, Turner indicated that he had completed the translation of two volumes of folktales, which he had recorded in both Nigeria and Sierra Leone. He planned to write extensive annotations to accompany the texts. His target date for completion was fall 1958. He wrote, "I have made considerable progress on the descriptive grammar of Sierra Leone Krio and expect to complete it in early 1959."[62] Some of the Krio material found life in Turner's documents prepared for the Peace Corps. Although Turner prepared a packet of Yoruba folklore for his classes, his more lengthy Yoruba manuscripts remain unpublished.

Among the unpublished manuscripts in the Northwestern University Turner Collection are *Folklore from Brazil;* "Yorubas in Brazil"; *Dictionary of the Yoruba Language;* "The Temne Language: Grammatical Notes and Texts" (1966); "The Mende Language; Grammatical Notes" (1966); notes on Freetown Creole of Sierra Leone; a Yoruba language course; Yoruba tales in translation; Yoruba songs and stories; notes on Twi; a Krio handbook, assorted African folktales; Cameroon Creole proverbs, riddles, and stories; manuscripts entitled *Folktales from Africa;* and three separate volumes, *Chronicles of Africa: Ancient, Medieval and Modern.* Cumulatively these sixteen-plus manuscripts translated from Turner's notes and field tapes represent thousands of hours of fieldwork and translation. Had those that Turner offered to publishers been released, they would have become in some cases the first and in other cases the standard resources on the oral arts of particular regions of Africa.[63]

Why are they not in print? Turner aggressively sought publishers for a number of them. Richard Dorson at Indiana University expressed interest in the Yoruba folktales for the Folktales of the World Series. Subsequently Dorson published material of his own.[64]

Oxford University Press considered *Folktales from Africa,*[65] but on January 11, 1971, Turner received a letter from John D. Wright, the editor of the College Department, stating:

> I have recently examined your manuscript, *Folktales of Africa,* and found it quite interesting. I must tell you, however, that I cannot make an offer to publish. The reason for this regrettable decision has nothing to do with the quality or suitability of your work but rather with an internal problem here. Since receiving your manuscript I have had word from our London office that they will publish paperback editions of Whiteley, *Traditional African Prose,* which you may be familiar with. The first volume (Oral Texts) does contain a great many folktales and I feel that this will be sufficient for our list at the present time.[66]

Turner's translations were original in 1950s. After the demise of colonialism in the 1960s and 1970s, African culture was available to a number of fieldworkers. Eventually, much of the data he collected was subsequently relocated by others and has been attributed to those who followed him. Turner's plan to become a published African folklorist and cultural historian as a new stage in his career was ironically not a goal fully within his reach.

In 1956 Turner applied to the Ford Foundation for a $10,000 grant: $6,400 to replace his salary to enable him to take a leave from Roosevelt for a year; $3,000 to hire a musicologist and to pay African student assistants/translators; and $600 to purchase supplies, such as blank phonograph disks for the transcribed data.[67] The Ford Foundation acted unfavorably on the application because of Turner's age.[68] It was Turner's final grant application to a foundation as most grants were available only to researchers under the age of fifty-five. In 1956 Turner was sixty-six years of age.

Following Turner's year in Africa, he continued to prepare research for publication. "The Odyssey of a Zulu Warrior" (1955) and "The Impact of Western Education on the African's Way of Life" (1955) are cultural anthropological ethnographies. "African Survivals in the New World with Special Emphasis on the Arts" (1958) and "The Role of Folklore in the Life of the Yoruba of Southwestern Nigeria" (1958) are cross-disciplinary, combining the methodologies of linguistics and cultural anthropology.

In "The Odyssey," Turner reviewed the military history of the Zulus of South Africa, highlighting the leadership of Kings Chaka, Dingaan, and Cetewayo—all of whom strongly resisted incursions from the Boers and/or British. He then focused on one particular royal Zulu, Mngoka (also known as Richard Julian von Dickersohn), born in 1855 in Ilikenwe, Zululand. At the age of seven, Mngoka traveled with his father to Germany, where he attended a gymnasium, returning as a young adult, after the completion of his education, to Zululand. During the Zulu Wars, Mngoka was involved in several major campaigns against the British. The Zulus won the majority of them. When the Zulu King Cetewayo was captured in August 1879, Mngoka joined many other Zulus in leaving their ancestral homeland by "African Central" (on foot) to travel to Egypt. It was an arduous journey, symbolic of the permanent disruption of the Zulu way of life.[69]

The remainder of the article documented Mngoka's odyssey as a world traveler. He returned to Germany (1879), made his way to the United States (1883), returned to Zululand (ca. 1900), and want back to the United States (1906), where he remained until his death in 1924.[70]

After Mngoka's return to the United States in 1906, he settled in Kansas and later moved to Colorado, along the way marrying Sarah E. Holley, a woman of Irish and indigenous Native American ancestry. They produced ten children. In order to provide a living for their family, together they sojourned across the United States and through Central and South America on lecture tours. Over time, Mngoka held various positions in the workforce, including landscape gardener for the Denver, Colorado, Department of Parks and foreman of a steel mill. He was a gifted language learner, conversant in German, English, French, Spanish, Italian, Portuguese, Bohemian, Zulu, and several other South African languages. During the course of his lifetime, his linguistic background stood him in good stead, as he was hired to be the official interpreter for the Supreme Court of Colorado.

Turner's access to data on Mngoka was facilitated by his contact with Mngoka's daughter Philiminia M. Phillips, who had lived in Chicago since 1913.[71] From her, Turner gained access to family records and oral family history. Turner's article on Mngoka is resplendent with documents—a page from the Bible written in Zulu, the birth certificates for several of Mngoka's children and grandchildren. He died in Denver on November 9, 1924.[72]

Turner's "Odyssey of a Zulu Warrior" was a departure from the traditional articles on Africans who traveled to the Western Hemisphere before 1900, in that it traced the voluntary travels of an African under conditions of freedom. Mngoka was one of a number of Zulus who made similar journeys after the fall of the Zulu empire at the end of the nineteenth century.

Turner's "The Impact of Western Education on the African's Way of Life" evaluated the curricula offered in continental African schools, describing the effects of European educational policies on African traditions. His focus was on economics, religion, language, and literature. Selecting more than one region, Turner evaluated the impact given variations in the colonial systems from one territory to another. He concluded that the colonial economy generally disrupted the traditional economies and values; traditional African religion and Christianity had become widely syncretized; Mohammedanism (Islam) had gained ground among many Africans uncomfortable with Christianity; and as a positive outcome, Western education had assisted in the preservation of African languages and literatures.[73]

In "The Role of Folklore in the Life of the Yoruba of Southwestern Nigeria" (1958) Turner suggested that the Yoruba influence among Africans in the Western Hemisphere is greater than that of any other African cultural group since Yoruba data are "less difficult to obtain in West Africa" than that of some other groups. "The Yoruba language is still spoken in Brazil and Cuba, and many survivals from this language can be found in the United States and other [Western Hemisphere] regions."[74] Focusing his analysis on proverbs and folktales, Turner noted that older Yorubans intersperse every form of their oral speech with proverbs. Among the purposes are to convey morality, to make imaginative comments on life, to settle disputes, to offer an indirect "reply to a criticism or an insult to an elder," to ridicule, to "inspire deeds of valor," and to model correct language forms to children. He found some of the sculpture to be a manifestation of proverbs. For example, one of the Yoruban sculptures in Turner's collection that he particularly favored was called "the Greedy Hunter," whose image invoked the proverb "If you have captured an elephant, be satisfied, for you have done a good day's work." It depicted a hunter burdened with a small elephant on his head, several smaller animals in bags attached to his belt, and a nest of crickets on his right foot.[75]

Turning to the style, Turner pointed out that Yoruba proverbs are replete with the techniques of any good poetry, including metaphors ("Joy has a frail body"); parallelism ("When there are no elders, the town is ruined; when the [leader] dies, the house is desolate"); and a stanza format of two to seven lines, with at least one long line in summary or in contrast to the others. Further techniques are paronomasia (or plays on words), alliteration, assonance, internal rhyme, and end rhyme. Turner illustrated the stylistic features utilizing the Yoruba language, with English translation as the subscripts, including numerals to mark the tones.[76]

Turning to folktales, Turner pointed out that the Yoruba people value scrupulous morality, creating stories with "great subtlety and artistic skill." He outlined fourteen moral issues that figure prominently in them. Other favorite folklore types Turner located among the Yoruba were satires and etiological or origins tales. One moral tale Turner recorded was "almost identical" to Chaucer's "Pardoner's Tale," in that three friends who failed to trust each other found death at each other's hands.[77] Turner concluded that the educational value of Yoruba folklore for both children and adults is significant, noting that even the small Yoruba population with Western education has maintained a "keen" interest in its folklore.[78]

Among Turner's other publications are a number of book reviews, an interview on jazz, and "Walt Whitman and the Negro," in which Turner analyzed Whitman's attitudes toward slavery, Abraham Lincoln, and African American rights. In the latter, Turner underscored Whitman's ambivalence toward African Americans evidenced in his writings.[79]

In the classroom, Turner continued to inspire students. The contemporary historian and prolific writer Darlene Clarke Hine recalls being a student in Turner's culture courses during her junior and senior years in the 1960s. She said, "Professor Turner was in the twilight of his career when I met him. But I will never forget the aluminum records he played. . . . My own interests in linguistics and attention to language are a result of his instruction."[80]

A perusal of Turner's late career examinations indicates that he continued to stay abreast of contemporary resources and issues. In 1966 one of his English 374 final examinations focused on two major periods in African American literary history—the Harlem Renaissance and the Post–World War II period—the latter being a precursor to the Black Arts Movement. His examinations were consistently challenging in length but simultaneously allowed students a good deal of range to display their grasp of the content, analytical skills, and writing style. The 1966 examination also encouraged students to practice peer review, a process considered sound contemporary pedagogical practice.

I. Discuss the status of the Negro short story during the Harlem Renaissance (roughly between 1921 and 1931), mentioning some of the outstanding writers and indicating the nature of their contributions to the American short story.

II. Discuss each of the following Negro writers, indicating the nature and significance of their contribution to American literature exclusive of the short story: James Weldon Johnson, Langston Hughes, Richard Wright, James Baldwin, Ralph Ellison, Gwendolyn Brooks, one other contemporary writer.

III. Write an appraisal of any three term papers, other than your own, that were given in class.[81]

21

The Peace Corps Project and Public Service 1962–1966

Though for many decades Krio has been the language of oral communication for the whole of Sierra Leone and for parts of other countries nearby, and though isolated specimens of Krio writing have appeared from time to time in newspapers, typewritten manuscripts, and in some other forms, the present volume represents the first attempt to put in writing by means of a systematic phonetic alphabet any considerable body of Krio folklore and literature.

—Lorenzo Dow Turner, *An Anthology of Krio Folklore and Literature*

AFTER 1951, TURNER COORDINATED the Roosevelt University Program in African Studies while continuing to teach across the curriculum in literature, linguistics, and African Culture. Roosevelt was thrilled when, in 1962, it received the contract to train Peace Corps volunteers to Sierra Leone, where sixteen ethnic groups speak Krio. Turner was appointed as the language coordinator. Each year for a number of years, Roosevelt was abuzz with summer activities related to Peace Corps training. According to the "Fact Sheet: Sierra Leone Peace Corps Training Program 1965," the purpose was "To train secondary school teachers for service in Sierra Leone, West Africa." The dates were June 18 to August 2.[1]

Since Turner's return from Nigeria, his translated manuscripts were still awaiting publication. The Peace Corps Project, therefore, reenergized his publication activities. The contract for $54,597 made it possible for him to bring to print two Krio texts. The first was *An Anthology of Krio Folklore and Literature: With Notes and Inter-linear Translations in English* (1963). Two years later, the second was *Krio Texts: With Grammatical Notes and Translations in English* (1965).

Preparation of Krio data was especially relevant, not only for the Peace Corps, but also because of the historic relationship between Sierra Leone and the Western Hemisphere. Krio speakers are, for the most part, descendants of former enslaved Africans from the West Indies and the United States and liberated Africans from sixty ethnic groups in Africa who escaped the slave trade. They settled on the coast of Sierra Leone near the end of the eighteenth century.

Krio was of special interest to Turner as its history and structure make it a "sister creole" to Gullah. "The English of the West Indies and the American ex-slaves of the late eighteenth and early nineteenth centuries serves to form the base to which have been added important features of many differing African languages."[2] Turner's direct exposure to it was the result of his fieldwork in and around Freetown, Sierra Leone, during fall 1951. He continued to study it after his return to the United States through informants who were native speakers living in Chicago.

In *An Anthology of Krio Folklore and Literature,* Turner acknowledged the assistance of William C. Okrafosmart and Thomas Decker in the translation process. In the preface, he pointed out that most of the material in the volume was original, that is, it had not previously appeared in print. Turner expressed the hope that it would be of interest to "the people of Sierra Leone and surrounding territories," as well as to others wishing "to acquaint themselves with the life and culture of this part of West Africa." He acknowledged a number of native speaker/informants in the footnotes, as well as his wife and elder son for preparing the illustrations and drawings.

The *Anthology* encompassed 539 pages, organized around the categories of folklore (proverbs, riddles, and folktales); literature (plays, conversations, essays, letters, and poems); song lyrics; and children's material (rhymes, jingles, and catching games). It also contained some letters and a useful glossary. The short history of the Krio people in the introduction was pointed and instructive. On each page of text, the IPA transcription appeared above the Krio text, a most useful feature for those attempting accurate pronunciation of Krio.[3]

Krio Texts was developed in four chapters: "A History of Krio People in Sierra Leone"; "The Sounds of Krio"; "Grammatical Notes (including use of the major parts of speech)"; and "Krio Texts," comprised of greetings, numerals, familiar conversations, and proverbs. The final portion of the book provided English translations. Turner prepared tape recordings featuring native speakers for chapters 2, 3, and 4, with additional classroom drills. He acknowledged William C. Okrafosmart of Freetown, Sierra Leone, for assistance in the preparation of *Krio Texts*.[4]

The companion piece to Turner's volumes was to be a Krio grammar by Jack Berry from the School of Oriental and African Studies. That project was never completed. On May 10, 1963, Turner received a letter from Julia A. Petrov, a research assistant for the Language Research Section of the Division of College and University Assistance at the Department of Health, Education, and Welfare Office of Education in Washington, D.C. The purpose was to inform Turner that his Contract No. 0E-3-14–016, "providing for composition and duplication of *The Anthology of Krio Folklore and Literature* . . . is terminating on May 15, 1963." She also informed him that Jack Berry's Contract No. SAE-8906 to prepare *Krio Grammar* had already terminated on December 30, 1962.[5]

Both of Turner's Krio publications would be valuable for non-Krio speakers and would have no doubt become important reference sources had they been in wider circulation. However, the Peace Corps provided funding only for an initial printing; the available copies were soon exhausted, and Turner's request for funds for reprinting was denied. Both volumes have been out of print for forty years.

Once the Peace Corps Program was under way, Krio became a part of Turner's teaching load during more than one regular academic year. According to a May 27, 1963, letter from Turner to his dean, Otto Wirth, Turner taught a course on Krio in fall 1962 and again in spring 1963. The purpose of his letter was to request reimbursement for $99.25 he had spent on informants and for paying a Miss Julia Randolph for mimeographing texts for the Krio course.[6]

For Roosevelt's Peace Corps Training Program and his regular courses, Turner also prepared materials on other Sierra Leonean languages, among them, "The Temne Language: Grammatical Notes and Texts," twenty-two pages handwritten

(1966), and "The Mende Language: Grammatical Notes," twenty pages typed and mimeographed (1966).[7]

On other occasions, he taught Krio for Peace Corps volunteers at other universities or taught the structure of creole languages. One such occasion was the summer of 1963 at the University of Ohio, Athens. Carl Denbow, director of the Peace Corps Training Program at the Department of Education, wrote to Turner on May 17, 1963, requesting that Turner spend June 28 and 29 instructing the two professors responsible for English as a second language. Denbow wanted the professors to receive an orientation before the Peace Corps volunteers arrived. Turner was to focus on "some of the main structural differences between English and pidgin," utilize the language laboratory to "make tapes," and to lend the professors some of his. Volunteers being prepared for service in Cameroon were to arrive in early July. The actual instruction in Cameroonian pidgin was to be conducted by Reverend G. D. Schneider, his wife, and a Cameroonian, Salamon Ndikvu.[8]

In a subsequent letter of June 11, 1963, Carl Denbow requested that Turner arrive on July 5 and remain until July 7. During that time, he was to work with both the professors and the Peace Corps volunteers.[9]

Turner routinely utilized recordings from the Gullah islands, Brazil, and Africa in his lectures. It required quite an effort to mount the usual Turner presentation since he did not travel light. Among his equipment and illustrative items were a large African map, a tape recorder, recordings, one or more projectors, reel-to-reel tapes, slides and, in many cases, African artifacts, among them jewelry, drums, and masks. He utilized public transportation since his final vehicle was the one he sold before leaving Africa. In the later years, Lois Turner traveled with him to local engagements and assisted with the projection of slides and the playing of music.[10]

Turner's engaging speaking style allowed him to communicate comfortably with audiences of any age. Just as he lectured at universities, he spoke at junior high and high schools.[11]

Although teaching and research occupied much of Turner's time, he maintained relations with members of the African community at the university and in the city. Over the years, he recruited and advocated for a number of African students, some of whom possessed the skills to serve as informants for his linguistic research. One of them was Olatunde Cole Jeremy Adekoya, whom Turner met in Ibadan, Nigeria, in 1951. At that time, Adekoya was employed in a bank. Turner suggested that he relocate to the United States to continue his studies and then subsequently was instrumental in securing a four-year scholarship for him at Roosevelt University. When Adekoya arrived in the United States, he resided with the Turners for more than two years.[12]

Adekoya's story was one of both triumph and tragedy. He received a bachelor's degree with an "A" average from Roosevelt College on a four-year scholarship. In return, he served as Turner's informant for Yoruba. After graduation, he attended the University of Illinois to achieve a master's degree in city planning.[13]

Eventually, Adekoya received his doctorate in urban planning from the University of Chicago.[14] After returning in triumph to Nigeria as the city planner for West

Nigeria, he was killed in a traffic accident in a taxicab in the early 1970s while delivering the master plan for the layout of Lagos to a government office.[15] He was Turner's most prized informant, but not the only student Turner assisted.

Turner added to the list of his commitments the seeking of funds to assist in the support of African students. He manifested a humanitarian spirit by writing open letters to his friends and associates who were also humanitarians.[16]

On numerous occasions, Turner was called on to meet with dignitaries from newly freed African countries. He looked forward to the end of colonialism, availing himself of every opportunity to meet the new leaders when they traveled to Chicago. When President Kwame Nkrumah of Ghana toured Chicago in the summer of 1958, Roosevelt University hosted a reception for him at the request of Chicago mayor Richard Daley. At the July 31 event, there were thirty persons from Roosevelt University, the University of Chicago, and Northwestern University. Among them were Turner and Herskovits. They both presented to Nkrumah their best-known books, *Africanisms in the Gullah Dialect* (1949) and *The Myth of the Negro Past* (1941), respectively.[17]

Turner maintained positive relations across cultures throughout his career. At a time when black/Jewish relations did not bear the strain of the twenty-first century, groups in the Jewish community often called on him to share his research. On February 25, 1947, Turner spoke for the North Shore Branch of the Roundtable of Christians and Jews of the North Shore Citizens Council, an organization formed in 1946, after the desecration of a synagogue in Glencoe, Illinois. Turner's topic was "Brazil: An Example of Racial Tolerance." Rabbi Charles Shulman of the North Shore Temple also spoke.[18]

Turner counted Benjamin Weintroub, the editor of the *Chicago Jewish Forum,* among his friends, served on the editorial board, and on several occasions published articles in the *Forum.* In the final decade of his academic career, Turner was one of the featured presenters for the B'nai Torah Temple Forum of Highland Park, Illinois. Between November 21, 1958, and February 27, 1959, there were eight lectures, one of them Turner's presentation on "Africa in Ferment: Background and Foreground." Turner's presentation was "Illustrated with [an] Unusual Documentary Film and Original Recordings Made in Africa."[19]

Turner's public service activities spanned his entire academic career. Understandably, the demands increased sharply after each peak in his career, especially after the founding of African Studies at Fisk University (1943), the publication of *Africanisms in the Gullah Dialect* (1949), and the Fulbright year in Nigeria and Sierra Leone (1951).

22

Relations between Colleagues—Turner and Herskovits 1936–1963

> Your papers will give me some very telling ammunition in establishing the invalidity of the position of those who insist that everything in southern speech is derived from European sources, and since the results of this study will, undoubtedly, be important in giving direction to support for future projects, I think you will agree with me that it is of the utmost importance that the most forceful presentation possible be made.
>
> —Letter from Melville Herskovits to Lorenzo Dow Turner, October 17, 1939

NO OTHER COLLEGIAL RELATIONSHIP was as career-impacting for Turner as his relationship with Melville Herskovits. Turner's legitimizing of Gullah studies in linguistics and Herskovits's legitimizing of the study of African-derived cultures in anthropology were of comparable impact in American social sciences. Both men evolved as cultural relativists, believing that each culture should be measured by its own standards. That Turner and Herskovits shared scholarly interests is evident from their publications. Turner's *Africanisms in the Gullah Dialect* (1949) and Herskovits's *The Myth of the Negro Past* (1941) are often referenced in the same contexts. *The Myth* is the first study to demonstrate convincingly that many cultural patterns from Africa have been retained and reinterpreted among African people in North America, South America, and the Caribbean.

One misconception that has plagued Turner's legacy is the notion that Herskovits led him to the African retentions hypothesis. Because Herskovits's book appeared in print first and contains quotes from Turner's manuscript,[1] and for other reasons as well, it has been the prevalent assumption that Herskovits and Turner were friends, that Turner was Herskovits's student,[2] or that Herskovits exerted significant influence on Turner, but not the reverse.[3] However, a study of their correspondences and other documents reveals that they knew each other well, having developed over a period of years a long-term association that was at least as beneficial to Herskovits as to Turner.

Their lives were parallel in a number of respects: (1) Turner and Herskovits were born within five years of each other, Turner in 1890 and Herskovits in 1895, both of education-conscious parents; (2) they developed interest in Africa by the 1930s; (3) they became the leading scholars in their specialties during their lifetimes; (4) they adopted the African retentions hypothesis and developed it in their major work; (5) they served on the faculty of Howard University (Herskovits as an assistant professor of anthropology, 1925–26; Turner, 1917–28); (6) they attained higher degrees from the University of Chicago, and both later relocated to the Chicago area, Turner to Roosevelt (1946) and Herskovits to Northwestern (1927); (7) they were instrumental in the founding of African Studies (Turner as a founder at Fisk in 1943; Herskovits as founder at Northwestern in 1948); (8) they traveled and conducted research in the South (Herskovits studied African Americans for his physical anthropological research; Turner conducting Gullah research in South Carolina and Georgia in 1932, 1933, 1939, and 1942, and creole research in Louisiana in 1935); (9) they conducted research in Brazil (Turner in 1940–41; Herskovits in 1942–43); (10) they conducted research in Africa (Herskovits in Dahomey, the Gold Coast [Ghana], and Nigeria in 1931; Turner in Nigeria and Sierra Leone in 1951); (11) they were instrumental in the founding of the Negro Studies Committee (NSC) of the ACLS (1940); (12) they invited the other to make campus presentations; (13) they were invited by other groups to serve on the same panel discussions; (14) and they attended meetings of the same professional organizations, among them the conferences of the Modern Language Association and the Association for the Study of Negro Life and History.

The forces that caused Turner and Herskovits to develop interests in Africa and in African retentions in the Western Hemisphere were social, cultural, and philosophical. Both came of age during the period of World War I when America emerged as an international power. The American experience in the war caused many Americans to develop a more international perspective.

A major influence in Herskovits's intellectual development was Franz Boas, a central voice in the social sciences in the early twentieth century. In his position in anthropology at Columbia University, he and his students were well situated to develop theories and shape methodologies for generations. Boas had abandoned Europe to escape the heavy hand of anti-Semitism with its growing Nazi presence. Many of the students who gravitated to him were likewise born in Europe or were the children of immigrants. "Most were fluent in German and many were Jewish."[4] Hence, they were forced to combat marginalization in the society, a reality that played a significant role in their synthesis of theoretical paradigms. It is logical that they would have felt personally invested in supporting theories of African American acculturation "that fitted neatly into the general idea of amalgamation."[5] At the same time, "Boas used two conflicting strategies to oppose popular beliefs that immigrants and blacks were genetically inferior and 'unassimilable' to American culture: one, universalist/assimilationist, the other particularist/pluralist." From the universalist perspective, he theorized that "race" was not a category essential for analyzing any individual's emotional or mental characteristics. Looking ahead to the impact of technology, Boas concluded that "modern technology was creating a uniform culture in America to which immigrants and blacks were rapidly assimilating." Not only would they be absorbed culturally, but they would also eventually experience physical absorption into the surrounding American population.[6]

In contrast, from his particularist/pluralist perspective, Boas theorized that each culture should be appreciated for its "particular" and unique offerings to human civilization. In Europe romantic nationalism had increased appreciation for the folklore and other traditions, "and part of the mission of Boasian anthropology was to give groups that did not enjoy a sense of antiquity the equivalent of a classical past by collecting myths and folklore and by preserving artifacts."[7]

Herskovits, the only student of Boas to dedicate himself to the study of African, Caribbean, and African American culture, grappled with the tension between the competing theories. "His ethnographic studies of various Afro-American peoples also reflected tensions in American anthropology during the interwar years between the 'scientific' and 'historical' methods, between trait analysis and cultural integration, and between social criticism and applied anthropology."[8] Early on, Herskovits embraced the assimilationist perspective.

Turner and Herskovits embraced the African retentions hypothesis almost simultaneously, in Herskovits's case, several years after spending the 1925–26 academic year at Howard, at the invitation of Alain Locke, who, like Turner, was a cultural nationalist.[9] A number of other like-minded scholars, including Turner, were on the Howard faculty in 1925–26. That year Herskovits's exposure to the theories of black scholars surely prepared him to process the African retentions he observed during his travel in Suriname in 1928 and 1929, where direct observation of African culture converted him to the African retention hypothesis.

According to his wife and often collaborator, Frances Shapiro Herskovits, her husband altered his perspective after his two summers in Suriname (1928 and 1929) among Sranan and Saramaccan speakers. One particularly influential experience occurred when Herskovits traveled from Suriname to "Barbados, Antigua, St. Lucia, St. Kitts, and Dominica, where he played the African game *wari*" with the dockworkers. He had learned *wari* from the African people in the Bush of Suriname. He also relished the African dancing and drumming at the *winti* dances in the city of Paramaribo. Years later he realized that he had observed, either in the bush or in Paramaribo, "nearly all of western sub-Saharan Africa represented."[10]

Once Herskovits had experienced African retentions directly, his views began to change. They were nourished by his fieldwork and his association with other persons of similar views, one of the most influential being Turner. Another source of influence on Herskovits's perspective was contact with and use of the research of Caribbean social scientists who advocated the African retentions perspective.[11]

The Turner/Herskovits connection is evidenced through a number of types of interaction patterns, the major ones being a series of letters from each to the other; professional favors between the two often mentioned in the letters; one-on-one meetings to discuss their mutual interests; their work together on the Committee of Negro Studies of the ACLS; and their appearances together on panels and in workshops.[12] Over time, Turner and Herskovits became functioning allies but not close friends.[13] Having European ancestry and a Euro-American network accorded Herskovits the more advantaged position in the relationship.

Although there are several letters of record written between 1936 and 1939, the major correspondence indicating the sharing of information related to the African retentions hypothesis is Herskovits's letter to Turner in which Herskovits requested two papers from Turner—the one on Gullah that Turner had read at the Conference of the Modern Language Association during early December 1939; and a copy of Turner's unpublished Africanisms manuscript. These two documents became the most historic of Turner's career and a major symbol of the Turner/Herskovits relationship. Herskovits explained:

> The reason I am asking these favors is because I am now faced with the job of summarizing the work that has been done in the whole matter of African survivals in American Negro life for the study being made under the auspices of the Carnegie people. Your papers will give me some very telling ammunition in establishing the invalidity of the position of those who insist that everything in southern speech is derived from European sources. . . .
>
> Certainly, it would make me extremely happy if anything I write would further the very fruitful line of research you have been following, and I hope that it will be possible for you to cooperate with me by making available to me those materials that have appeared or are ready to appear.[14]

Herskovits had just been commissioned by the Carnegie Corporation to provide an analysis of the African background of African Americans for Gunnar Myrdal. Myrdal's contribution became *An American Dilemma: The Negro Problem and Modern Democracy* (1944). Although Herskovits was "angry" at not being selected to head the research team, he nonetheless agreed to undertake a share of the project.[15] He was an appropriate choice in that his research of the late 1930s had demonstrated his strong interest in Western Hemispheric African culture. While Turner would have also been an ideal scholar to provide a document for the series, the policy that contracts should be awarded largely to non–African American researchers resulted in his exclusion.[16]

In 1936 Herskovits had written a proposal to the Carnegie Corporation to secure funds for a massive research project on Africa. He was unaware that Frederick P. Keppel (1875–1943), the Carnegie Corporation president, had already decided to initiate a major study on black Americans. Therefore, Herskovits's proposal was rejected. From Keppel's perspective, a non-American scholar similar to Alexis de Tocqueville (1805–59) would have been ideal to prepare the proposed African American study. When Keppel sought suggestions from Herskovits, Herskovits recommended his friend the Swiss anthropologist Alfred Métraux (1902–63), urging that the researcher be from a country without a history of colonialism. Simultaneously, he lobbied to lead a United States team, suggesting that African American scholars be included. When Myrdal, the Swedish economist, was selected instead to head the team, he hired thirty-one researchers to prepare memoranda. Frazier and the African American anthropologist St. Clair Drake were among them. Turner was not. Myrdal included Herskovits "for reasons of academic politics."[17]

By the time Herskovits requested Turner's manuscript, their professional relationship had apparently resulted in enough rapport to make such a request reasonable. Turner responded by return mail, informing Herskovits that he expected to complete his book in four or five weeks and stating, "I shall be glad to have you examine it before I have it published." Turner also explained Gullah naming traditions, elaborating on the specific number of semantic items from a series of African languages he had documented in Gullah.[18]

In late November 1939, Turner visited Herskovits at Northwestern University to confer on the directions of his future research in preparation for his fieldwork in Brazil. During the visit, Herskovits entertained Turner at a luncheon with the anthropology department and some humanities faculty members interested in Africa, among them Joseph Greenberg and William R. Bascom (Turner spent time with the latter two); Turner lectured and played selected field recordings; Herskovits had made re-recordings of several of his Trinidad tapes for Turner and agreed to recommend him for a grant for the Brazil trip; and Lois Turner and Frances Herskovits met.[19]

Turner and Herskovits traveled in the same circles of linguists, anthropologists, and other intellects, many of them African American.[20] They also attended and delivered papers at a number of annual conferences of the Association for the Study of Negro Life and History. He and Herskovits were often on the same panels. Among those meetings were the 26th Annual Conference (October 31–November 2, 1941, in Columbus, Ohio); the 30th Annual Conference (October 26–28, 1945, in Columbus, Ohio); and the 39th Annual Conference (October 29–31, 1954, in St. Louis, Missouri).

On other occasions, Turner and Herskovits met in the Chicago area. When Turner organized the conference "Africa Today: A Midwestern Inquiry," it convened at Roosevelt on September 28–29, 1956. Its purpose was to acquaint the public with current issues in African Affairs. Among the topics were "America's Policy toward Africa," "The United States, the United Nations and Africa," and "Political Non-violence in Africa." Among the seven featured speakers were Turner and Herskovits.[21]

Sometimes the two were present at the same social events. Typical of this pattern was the reception held for Kwame Nkrumah, president of Ghana, on July 31, 1958. Mayor Daley of Chicago had requested that Roosevelt host the reception. Roosevelt agreed, inviting persons from the University of Chicago, Northwestern, and Roosevelt. Among the thirty guests were Herskovits and Turner.[22]

Herskovits, as the "most prominent gatekeeper of Africanist anthropology," and his Euro-American peers maintained the position that African Americans were unable to be "objective" in analyzing African culture. His own African American anthropology students, among them, Hugh Smythe, whose dissertation focused on Yoruba kinship, were forced to rely on library research.[23] In that same tradition, Herskovits agreed to recommend Turner for grants on at least two occasions but never for a grant to conduct research in Africa.

On November 7, 1955, Turner mailed a note to Herskovits informing him of his plans to apply for a Ford Foundation Fellowship in order to process his research data from his fieldwork in Nigeria and Sierra Leone. Herskovits responded on November 15, 1955, offering to recommend Turner.[24]

Their final letters of record are from May 1956, when Turner notified Herskovits that the Ford Foundation had rejected his application because of his age.[25] Herskovits responded on May 15, 1956, expressing his hope that Turner would locate another funding source and would feel free to again request a recommendation. Herskovits did not provide any leads.[26] Turner's research was delayed four years more until he received the grant to direct the language component of the Peace Corps Training Project at Roosevelt.

Turner and Herskovits were brought together by their research interests in a professional relationship that lasted for almost thirty years. During their lifetimes, their peers did not always embrace their ideas, as is evident from the transcript of the Conference on Negro Studies. Frazier's ideas provided counterpoint for those of Turner and Herskovits, as is evident in the transcript from the American Council Conference and the body of Frazier's research.[27] From his perspective, African Americans were products of the "middle passage," having been stripped of African culture and having adapted to the American context. Regarding the black family, Frazier concluded that "there is no reliable evidence that African culture has had any influence on its development."[28] The contrast between his assimilationist views and Turner's and Herskovits's African retention theories is designated as the Herskovits-Frazier debate. More accurately, it should be known as the Herskovits/Turner–Frazier debate since Turner was as strongly retentionist as Herskovits.[29] That it is not is in part attributable to the reality that Turner and Frazier did not debate their differences in a public forum. Turner's voice is fairly muted in the transcript of the discussion portion of the Conference on Negro Studies. Furthermore Turner did not challenge Frazier's perspective in his articles, most likely because of their friendship.

As the most prominent linguist and the most prominent anthropologist of the cultural retentions school, Turner and Herskovits continued for decades to travel and research and use each other's data as "ammunition" to prove that African culture was alive in the Western Hemisphere.[30] Their work complemented that of the other. Both were concerned with far more than developing an individual body of research for themselves. Rather, they committed themselves to institution-building, not only African Studies programs, but also Africanist specialties within their specific disciplines—Turner in the development of creole studies in linguistics and pan-African studies across the curriculum; Herskovits in the development of African American anthropology as a specialty in American anthropology. Both also encouraged the development of a network of scholars who could serve as the core of their disciplines.

Both were public men. Just as Turner was active in advancing his ideas to the public through schools, churches, and community organizations, Herskovits likewise spoke with frequency in similar arenas. Both argued for tolerance and democratic ideals. Turner advocated for the rights of both blacks and Jews, interacting actively with Jewish scholars and organizations. Herskovits did as well. Both joined the National Association for the Advancement of Colored People, though Herskovits somewhat reluctantly. Herskovits also joined the Council Against Intolerance in America.[31]

Contrary to earlier assumptions, Herskovits did not lead Turner to the African retentions hypothesis. Rather, documented evidence illustrates that Herskovits was influenced by Turner's research, and he and Turner were both influenced by the Caribbean and Latin American researchers, among them Jean Price-Mars of Haiti (1876–1969), Fernando Ortiz of Cuba (1881–1969), Arthur Ramos in Brazil (1903–49), and Gonzolo Aguirre Beltran in Mexico (1908–96). The Caribbean scholars arrived at the African retentions position before Turner and Herskovits.[32]

It would be misleading to suggest that the Turner/Herskovits relationship was equalitarian since Herskovits's Euro-American status accorded him greater power and influence. However, Herskovits, too, suffered disappointments at the hands of the major foundations. Early in his career, though, he was fortunate to profit from the philanthropy of Elsie Clews Parsons, also a Boas student. Parsons funded Herskovits's and Frances Herskovits's trips to Suriname and Dahomey and later paid for the publication of one of his Suriname manuscripts. Boas "obtained further financial support for both trips."[33]

For various reasons, no doubt including his Jewish ethnicity and the strength of his commitment to research on Africa, Herskovits was unable to secure large grant projects such as the Carnegie/Myrdal award.[34] On the other hand, for Turner there were neither large grants nor wealthy patrons.

During their interactions of almost thirty years, Herskovits's actions failed to insulate Turner from the slings and arrows of oppression resulting from exclusionary practices on the part of funding agencies. Funding was a major source of frustration in Turner's career, and lack of substantial fieldwork grants resulted in his publishing far fewer volumes in his lifetime than some of his colleagues in history and sociology, among them, Charles Johnson and E. Franklin Frazier.[35] His unpublished manuscripts in the Northwestern Turner Collection attest to the veracity of his research efforts.

Because Turner had contacted Herskovits on September 9, 1936, before his London trip, at Leland's suggestion, Herskovits was well aware of Turner's quest to conduct fieldwork in Africa. In his September 23, 1936, letter, Herskovits queried Turner about his interest in fieldwork, mentioning a potential Ashanti contact in Ghana, but not by name. Turner responded in the affirmative in his return letter to Herskovits on September 30, 1936. However, no correspondence of record indicates that Herskovits encouraged Turner at any point to conduct fieldwork in Africa by directing him to foundation contacts or by recommending him for grants to fund research in Africa.[36]

On at least two occasions, Turner published positive reviews of Herskovits's book *The Myth of the Negro Past* and Herskovits and Herskovits's *Dahomean Narrative: A Cross-Cultural Analysis*.[37] Herskovits did not return the favor.

On other occasions, Herskovits failed to utilize his influence or share opportunities with Turner. In 1958 and again in 1960, Herskovits was invited to provide testimony on Africa before the United States Senate Committee on Foreign Relations,[38] an opportunity that he apparently did not advocate be extended to Turner, who like Herskovits, was conversant with African affairs and could have provided valuable testimony. In fact, Turner's immersion in fieldwork in Nigeria and Sierra Leone in 1951 was twenty years more recent than Herskovits's in Dahomey.

Because of Herskovits's influence and the resources available at Northwestern, colonial officials from French and British territories and African and European scholars visited Northwestern to lead seminars and/or to confer with Herskovits. As a result of the Program in African Studies, a number of African political leaders also visited Northwestern. The latter group, in addition to Leopold Senghor (Senegal), included William Tubman (Liberia), Nnamdi Azikiwe (Nigeria), Sekou Toure

(Guinea), Eduardo Mondlane (Mozambique), Tom Mboya (Kenya), and K. A. Busia (Ghana).[39]

Ultimately, both Turner and Herskovits made a major impact in their disciplines, influencing generations of linguists and anthropologists to the present, by forcing a reevaluation of long-held assumptions about Africans in the Western Hemisphere and the loss of cultural continuities. Because Herskovits was awarded funds to travel widely and witness retentions in African-derived cultures (Dutch Guiana/Suriname in 1928 and 1929; Gold Coast/Ghana, Nigeria, and Dahomey/Benin in 1931; Haiti in 1934; Trinidad in 1939; and Brazil in 1941–42), he had the opportunity to observe the cross-cultural similarities that had survived transplantation evident in the Caribbean and the United States. Although Turner's travels were more circumscribed, he likewise observed and interpreted the retention of African-derived patterns in numerous aspects of black culture in the Western Hemisphere.

While the mid-century thrust toward integration caused some researchers to devalue retention models, suggesting that both men overstated the case, the research of Turner and Herskovits has found new life since the time of rising nationalism of the 1970s. Contemporary linguists and anthropologists in large part situate themselves at some point along the continuum of oppositions delineated by the Herskovits/Turner–Frazier debate.[40] In the process of formulating theories to account for linguistic and cultural phenomena, they utilize theoretical concepts such as universalist, substrate, creolization, acculturation, syncretism, cultural tenacity, cultural continuities, retentions, and reinterpretations.

Among the researchers influenced by Turner's and Herskovits's work and whose theories are congruent with theirs are Joseph Greenberg, Joey Dillard, William Labov, Geneva Smitherman, Winifred K. Vass, Mervyn Alleyne, Robert W. Thompson, Ian Hancock, John Rickford, Faye Harrison and Ira Harrison, and Arthur Spears. Together Turner and Herskovits have produced research that has breathed life into the African retentions hypothesis, bringing to light many issues we continue to debate today.[41]

23

Turner's Final Years 1960–1972

Thank you for the beautiful bouquet which you sent me while I was in the hospital. They certainly did much to cheer the long, tedious days of my convalescence. . . . I am at home again and expect to resume my full duties at the school next week.

—Letter from Turner to Roosevelt University president Sparling, August 30, 1960

And when I see so many Sub-Saharan African states becoming independent and so many American universities instituting African Studies programs, which we probably not even dreamed of thirty-five years ago, I can't help being thrilled.

—Lorenzo Dow Turner, "Remarks" for his retirement dinner, May 24, 1966

IN JANUARY 1952, after Turner returned from Nigeria and Sierra Leone, "he was thin and worn. The malaria had taken its toll, and there were carbuncles under his arms resulting from a tropical bacteria. Dow's physician treated them with medicated pads, which resulted in healing over time."[1]

There were, however, still a number of productive years ahead. While Turner was abroad, Lois had pursued the credentials to enter public school teaching. Her employment as a high school English teacher and subsequent tenure as an elementary school teacher greatly relieved the family tensions over finances. The Victorian house on Ellis Avenue continued to be an albatross. Hence when new houses began to spring up in Hyde Park near the University of Chicago, the Turners contracted for the purchase of one on East 56th Street. After they relocated in 1961, they rented the Ellis Avenue house to others.[2]

As Lorenzo Dow Jr. and Rani Meredith grew, the Turner household bustled with activity. Lois continued to serve as the primary caregiver, taking the boys to social activities and enrichment classes. Lorenzo Jr. studied ballroom dancing and became expert. He took piano lessons and spent many hours in the basement on the piano. Among his most cherished memories are of the few occasions when he was twelve or thirteen and Turner took him to Chicago Cubs and Chicago White Sox baseball games. Later Turner followed up by spending hours in the backyard teaching Lorenzo Jr. baseball strategies and playing Ping-Pong with Rani Meredith. When Lorenzo Jr. was in high school, his father sometimes assisted him with his homework, while they both burned midnight oil over coffee, Campbell's soup, and melted cheese on crackers.[3]

As Turner ripened in age, he experienced occasional episodes of physical travail. In June 1954, when he was sixty-four, he was involved in an automobile accident that required his hospitalization for several days.[4] He and Lois became aware that he had developed hypertension when, on one Sunday a few years later, Lorenzo

Jr. summoned Lois from church because Turner had suffered a severe nosebleed. At the doctor's office, he was diagnosed with hypertension.[5]

During the summer of 1957, when Lorenzo Jr. was fourteen and Rani Meredith was nine, the family embarked on a rare train trip to visit relatives in Atlantic City, Philadelphia, New York, and New Bedford, Massachusetts. On that occasion Turner collapsed during an outing in a park in Philadelphia. Lois assumed that the cause was fish that did not agree with him. He recovered and the family continued its trip.[6]

The beginning of Turner's physical decline became evident when, in the summer of 1960, the ache that had nagged his lower abdomen since the week of his mother's funeral became a full-blown bleeding ulcer. Lois remembers, "It took a great deal from him. By the time the problem was diagnosed, we learned that he had developed a perforation the size of a silver dollar near his liver." His physician, the prominent African American surgeon Dr. Leonidas H. Berry, had invented one of the first methods of viewing the interior of the abdomen, creating an endoscope consisting of a metal rod with a light and mirror.[7] Dr. Berry successfully repaired the perforation. Turner remained in the hospital for several weeks. Since he had been scheduled to teach summer school, he found it difficult to rest. Consequently Lois agreed to teach his course on black culture. She did so expertly, utilizing her own background along with guest lecturers, audiovisual aids, and notes that Turner had prepared.[8]

Back home, in somewhat fragile condition but improving, Turner composed a long handwritten note to Roosevelt's President Sparling on August 30, 1960. It was in part a thank you and in part a missive to assure Dr. Sparling of his readiness to return to work: "I am at home again and expect to resume my full duties at the school next week."[9] Because of his commitment to his work, Turner was routinely resistant to the idea of allocating time for doctor's visits. "He absolutely refused to stay in bed." His health, Lois thought, was amazingly good, considering his lack of sleep and limited exercise. Periodically she would convince him to keep a doctor's appointment, especially a dental appointment, and "he had a significant amount of dental work and eventually a bottom plate."[10]

Into the 1960s, Turner continued to work at a brisk pace. On January 25, 1961, he delivered an address at the AMVETS seminar at Georgetown University, "What Ought to Be the Long-Range Intentions of the United States with Respect to Race Relations." The final version was twenty-nine pages.[11] According to the *Chicago Defender,* in May 1963 he accepted an award of merit from the Howard University Alumni Club at its annual scholarship awards dinner. He and Chicago attorney George Leighton were the honorees.[12]

By 1966, according to Turner's personnel records at Roosevelt, he had reached the retirement age of seventy. On the occasion of his official retirement, Lucy Ann Marx, the director of the Division of Continuing Education and Extension at Roosevelt, began to contact Turner's colleagues, some from a list he provided, to announce the occasion and to request testimonial letters. A number of colleagues and former students from around the country responded. In addition several well-wishers from Africa sent telegrams. Marx collected the letters for a commemorative notebook to present to Turner. Among the written testimonials were those from officials from Nigeria and Kenya; retired dean of the faculties Wayne A. R. Leys; Dorothy B. Porter, the former Howard student and curator of the Moorland-Spingarn Research Center; John Hope Franklin, Turner's most-prized student at Fisk; Arna Bontemps, the Fisk poet/librarian; the linguists Joseph Greenberg, Frederic G. Cassidy, Raven and Virginia McDavid, Alan P. Merriam, and Alan Walker Read; Richard Dorson, the folklorist; Mitford Mathews and Christopher Hoolihan, the lexicographers; Benjamin Weintroub, the editor of the *Chicago Jewish Forum;* Frances Herskovits, the widow of Melville Herskovits; Marion Koenigseder, the director of Informal Adult Education for the Central YMCA Community College; and the superintendents of several Illinois school districts where Turner had offered presentations for middle and secondary schools. Turner's retirement dinner was held on Sunday, April 24, 1966.[13]

In the lengthiest of the testimonials, Richard Waterman of the Department of Sociology and Anthropology at Wayne State University captured the sentiment of most, noting the determination Turner possessed that enabled him to persevere against the tide and subsequently resulted in his momentous contribution. Waterman carefully contextualized the era and attitudes under which Turner labored. He underscored that some persons, who having learned only stereotypes about the African experience, looked forward to the day when, they hoped, the African heritage would be forgotten. He reminded people, "Much of what Lorenzo Turner worked so hard to establish seems now but simple common sense. For example, if you wish to investigate the extent to which West African languages have provided materials for Sea Island Negro dialects you had better learn something about West African languages. Yet this reasonable proposition, when Turner first propounded it, was denied, excoriated, or simply ignored by most of the experts, who had already made up their minds that African languages had nothing to do with the American dialects. We must remember that when Lorenzo Turner started his work the image of Africa in the minds of most Americans was a compound of gorillas, jungles and naked, cultureless savages."[14]

In closing, Waterman commented that, fortunately, Turner had survived long enough to see a resurgence of interest in Africa, in and out of academia: "Now, times have changed, and Lorenzo Turner has made his point. What was once his revolutionary linguistic document is now a standard reference work. Africa has once again come into its place in the sun; the African component of the heritage of the American Negro is a matter for pride. The pioneering work of Dr. Turner has been so completely vindicated that one feels tempted to wonder how anyone could possibly have disagreed with him."[15]

The image that emerges from the Turner testimonials is of a pioneer, of a man who was a committed, creative researcher, a challenging teacher who was firm but gentle, an innovator who was committed to the African diaspora but was also a lover of languages and literature, a lifelong learner, and a gentlemanly scholar and role model. The dinner and testimonials were a fitting crescendo for a career well spent. In his golden years, Turner's memories of his sacrifices and disappointments but even more of his triumphs and successes must have enlivened his days. A painful footnote to the chapters of his life was that, even though he was a notable alumnus situated geographically in the Hyde Park community that bordered the University of Chicago, he was never invited by his colleagues, among them Raven McDavid, to teach for the Department of English at the University of Chicago. The loss was surely theirs.

When Turner was informed that Roosevelt was organizing a retirement party for him in 1966, he prepared a response, a single page with nine talking points. He expressed his pleasure in seeing or hearing from "many of my friends . . . including several of my former pupils." He spoke of how rewarding his work had been, asserting, "My contacts over the years, not only with Africans, many of whom have in recent years become distinguished heads of state, but also my contacts with Africanists in Europe . . . and with Africanists in North and South America, as well as in the Caribbean, have all been highly stimulating; and my travels to and within these countries have greatly enriched my life."[16]

He admitted that he was thrilled to see "so many Sub-Saharan African states becoming independent and so many American universities instituting African Studies programs." His remarks turned to his publications. Looking forward to the blocks of time ahead, he noted, "So far I have had time to publish only a limited portion of the valuable African materials I have collected, but I hope to begin doing so before very long."[17]

Turner then added a touch of humor to his remarks by underscoring the challenges of conducting fieldwork. He said, "Of course, not all of my experiences in the different areas where I did field work were pleasant; but as I look back on them now they don't seem so bad after all. . . . High tides on Edisto Island, S.C., and being left in a row boat at the bottom of the river. Finding myself eating at the table with a big snake on another island. Snakes falling from trees onto my truck while I'm having my lunch, on the Sea Islands as well as in West Africa. Being stuck in the mud for twelve hours during the rainy season throughout the night, without being able to get help—in Northern Dahomey. Finding six lizards in my hotel room in the interior of Brazil."[18]

At the banquet, President Sparling encouraged Turner to continue teaching by stating that he was welcome at Roosevelt for as long as he wished to serve.[19] Therefore, Turner accepted yearly teaching contracts until 1970. In the meantime, beginning in 1968, he was also appointed to teach African American Literature and Culture courses at the University of Illinois, Chicago Circle campus, where he assisted in the creation of a grant-funded Institute for Advanced Study of Negro History. The major goal of the institute was the generation of research to result in new curricula on the black experience for secondary schools. Although Turner was already seventy-eight years of age by 1968, he was current in his preparation and utilization of resources. He continued to favor essay examinations.

Time, however, was taking its toll. By 1966 Lois recalls, "Dow found it quite stressful to maintain his traditional pace. At the same time, it was difficult for him to say no. He continued to work far into the night to prepare his research for publication, with exhaustion causing him to experience many unproductive hours.

Returning student papers was more and more a chore. On many occasions, he fell asleep on the couch early in the evening and did not awaken before dawn."[20]

By 1970 Lois knew that retirement was the best solution; while Turner's colleagues assumed that he was several years past seventy, "I knew that he was approximately eighty and required more rest than his expectations allowed him to experience. I prepared and submitted his letter of resignation."[21]

Turner retired completely from Roosevelt in May 1970, suffering a stroke that same year. Although his physician, Dr. Quinton Young, utilized state-of-the-art procedures to effect improvement, Turner "slowly declined for the next two years. The condition left him most frustrated. His desire to advance his research was pronounced. In contrast, his concentration and stamina were much diminished." Lois continued to answer his correspondences and seek publishers for his work.[22]

On February 10, 1972, Turner died of hypertensive heart failure at Michael Reese Hospital of Chicago. In a final irony for a proud man who spent his life exploring and illuminating the cultural experiences of blacks, the person who completed the death certificate listed his race as "white."[23] It remains uncorrected to this day.

When the news of Turner's death spread, cards, telegrams, and floral arrangements overran the family home. Visitation and prayers were held for him on Monday, February 14, 1972, at 10:00 A.M. His final rites were handled by the Griffin Funeral Home at 3232 Martin Luther King Drive, Chicago, Illinois, with Rev. Kenneth Smith and Rev. G. Hamilton Martin presiding. The inhumation was in the Lincoln Cemetery.[24]

Immediately after Turner's death, Alderman William Cousins of the Eighth Ward of the Chicago City Council proposed a resolution commemorating his life. It was adopted and appears in the *Journal of the Chicago City Council* of February 24, 1972.[25]

24

Conclusions

ONE CANNOT MENTION GULLAH STUDIES without referring to their father, Lorenzo Dow Turner. He was a pioneer, toiling alone, continuing to persevere, even against a tide of naysayers who believed his research was inconsequential, returning repeatedly to the Sea Islands between 1932 and 1942 until his analysis was complete. The effort bore exemplary fruit. *Africanisms in the Gullah Dialect* is a classic work and remains the most important in the field.

Because of the strength of interest in Gullah, coupled with the limited distribution of his Krio and other materials, Turner's other contributions to linguistics are relatively unrecognized. According to Herskovits, Turner was the first American with a background in linguistics to conduct field research in Brazil.[1] He was the first to transcribe Sierra Leone Krio phonetically and to offer courses in Krio.[2] He was also the first to collect and translate a number of the traditional Yoruba folktales to English, and the first to offer courses on linguistics at an HBCU.[3]

Turner poured nearly all his time, talent, and influence into the accomplishment of his goals, reserving few moments for leisure. By the 1940s he had relinquished his personal social life, putting aside activities with Alpha Phi Alpha fraternity and other groups, as well as his own Rooks family reunions.[4] One mantra Turner offered to his sons was, "If you want to do something well, you must set aside time to do it a little every day."[5]

Although Turner had a keen eye for politics, the arts, and sports, he limited the hours he spent away from his research. He was an early advocate of multitasking, listening to sports on the radio as he read newspapers and magazines. Among his favorite personalities were Ralph Bunche, Winston Churchill, Langston Hughes, Etta Moten, Josephine Baker, Lena Horne, Joe Louis, Franklin D. Roosevelt, Eleanor Roosevelt, and Queen Elizabeth II, all pioneers like Turner.

Just as he was inspired by the emerging nations of Africa, he was likewise invigorated by the civil rights movement in the United States, realizing that the changes it promised were long overdue and would bring greater opportunities for African Americans attempting to break through the ceiling of segregation and institutionalized discrimination. Among the form letters Turner retained is a 1962 photocopied message from Dr. Martin Luther King Jr., soliciting funds for the work of the Southern Christian Leadership Conference.

Turner surely did not maintain his punishing schedule for a half-century only for himself. Rather, the record of his speaking engagements and other public service and humanitarian activities leads to the conclusion that Turner was a civic-minded scholar who took seriously his role in advancing scholarship while improving the status of persons of African ancestry by documenting the contributions of African people in the Western Hemisphere and throughout the diaspora.

He brought inspiration to others to pursue the study and analysis of African languages and creole languages, as well as other forms of African diasporic culture, using paradigms not generally available during his lifetime. He is one of a cohort of men and women of similar conviction and dedication.

One symbol of a scholar's enduring legacy is the students he or she inspires. A number of them have become prominent: the anthropologist Zora Neale Hurston (1895–1960), Romance linguist Raleigh Morgan (1917–98), historian John Hope Franklin (1915–), bibliophile Dorothy Porter Wesley (1908–91), and historian Darlene Clarke Hine (1947–).

By the time of his death, Turner had made significant strides in his ambitious research agenda.[6] Efforts to collect data in the Caribbean did not come to fruition, but his research in Brazil yielded much material. His original manuscripts on Brazilian Yoruba, Nigerian Yoruba, African-language dictionaries, and African folklore still hold much promise for future researchers.

The full range of Turner's manuscripts, published and unpublished, defines his intellectual legacy as a literary scholar, linguist, pan-African creolist, African folklorist, and cultural historian. If one considers the body of articles he published in the *Washington Sun* on cultural, political, and economic topics, his legacy as a cultural historian becomes even more apparent.[7]

Among the finest assessments of Turner's legacy are those by Michael Montgomery and David DeCamp. According to Montgomery, "[One should not] underplay the drama of Turner's migration from the field of literature to that of linguistics. It is a rare person who has the capacity to completely retrain and retool in mid-career, as he had to do to learn phonetics, fieldwork methods, and so on. I cannot think of another case of someone doing this so well."[8] He has also noted, "It would be difficult to calculate creolists' debt to Turner or to say how much we may still learn from this scholar," and that "Turner's achievement in breaking through the barriers of professional prejudice and undertaking a one-man comparison of several dozen African languages with his Gullah data, despite the few resources he had at hand, is matched only, perhaps, by the similar efforts of Herskovits in the field of cultural anthropology."[9] DeCamp describes Turner as a scholar who "brought about his own little revolution" when he "convince[d] his academic peers that at least in Gullah, and perhaps also in Black English generally, the black American has a genuine and continuous linguistic history leading back to Africa."[10]

Looking toward the future, Turner's intellectual children and grandchildren have inherited a number of productive research possibilities. Lorenzo Dow Turner Jr. is editing a volume of Turner's photographs from Brazil and Africa and another volume featuring sixteen of the folktales from Africa that Turner collected in Nigeria.[11] Herb Frazier, a journalist with the *Charleston Post and Courier,* is completing *Crossing the Sea on a Sacred Song,* a volume on the saga of Amelia Dawley's Mende song and its Sierra Leone counterpart. The volumes will increase appreciation for usually overlooked dimensions of Turner's accomplishments. On the international scene Pol Briand of Paris is preparing a study of Brazilian music with reference to Turner's music recordings in Brazil.[12] Livio Sansone has prepared a virtual archive on Afro-Brazilian heritage at the Centro de Estudos Afro-Orientais of the Universidade Federal da Bahia, where he is a professor of anthropology. Simultaneously, he is writing a book on E. Franklin Frazier's, Turner's, and Herskovits's research in Brazil.[13]

A festschrift, a conference on Turner's unpublished work, analysis of his contribution to the *Washington Sun* and of his public lectures, essays on his unpublished grammars and dictionaries, studies of his contributions to the colleges to which he dedicated his academic career, and analyses of his research beyond Gullah are all topics that await future researchers. The Northwestern University Turner Collection and other Turner collections contain the data to support these and other studies. Future scholarship, properly contextualized, will continue to tease out the nuances of Turner's life, a life dedicated to the advancement of the American tradition in linguistics and the development of a canon on African diasporan culture.

Epilogue CONTEMPORARY RELEVANCE OF TURNER'S CONTRIBUTION TO LINGUISTICS

THE PUBLICATION OF *Africanisms in the Gullah Dialect* (1949) is a singular achievement, as the first and still the most important book on African retentions in speech varieties of the United States. Although a full review of the research directions stimulated by Turner's volume is beyond the scope of this analysis, it is relevant to mention some of the synchronic and diachronic research issues since Turner's *Africanisms in the Gullah Dialect.* As a result of its continuing immediacy, the book has been reissued periodically over the last fifty years, most recently, with a new introduction, by the University of South Carolina Press.[1]

Maintaining a committed following over the decades, "Turner's partial account of Gullah laid a secure foundation on which others would build,"[2] influenced subsequent thinking about African retentions in American culture, and stimulated the writing of a number of dissertations, articles, and other projects on Gullah and its relation to Caribbean creoles and to African American Vernacular English (AAVE).

In the light of modern research, Turner's achievement continues to be extraordinary. Without the benefit of contemporary linguistic methods and insights, he utilized his intuitions to shatter prevailing assumptions and create respect for a severely stigmatized community. Confronting the prevailing wisdom that Gullah was "broken English," with little or no structure, Turner was the first to collect the data to demonstrate that it was in fact rule governed and systematic.[3]

Had Turner's recommendation that other geographic areas in the Deep South—including Euro-American communities with significant contact with African American communities[4]—be mined for Africanisms in the 1940s transpired, a more nuanced geography of dialects would have been documented. Linguistic Atlas data often contained only a limited number of interviews from African Americans.[5] By now, substantial language change has obliterated some of the pre–World War II linguistic retentions. Consistent with the Linguistic Atlas approach, Turner interviewed elders living in relative isolation. Further studies during the 1930s and 1940s by Turner or others of younger Gullah speakers would have added different patterns of variation to his corpus.

Although Turner referred to Gullah as a "dialect" in the title of his book, he pointed to a more distinct linguistic variety in his commentary, referring to it as "a creolized form of English." He meticulously documented phonological and morpho-syntactic similarities between some West African languages, particularly of the Kwa group, and Gullah, demonstrating that "Gullah is indebted to African sources."[6] He then further propelled the specialty of creole studies forward by identifying a number of the concepts and patterns central to creole languages. In the process Turner illustrated how rich and complex the language variety of a stigmatized and oppressed group can be. His analysis made a strong case at a time when little had been written in English about creole languages.

When considering the scope of Turner's research, it is important to underscore that Gullah is unique in the United States rather than representative of the speech of the entire African American community.[7] On the United States mainland, greater contact between speakers of African languages and speakers of English resulted in more substantial decreolization of Black English.

Turner advanced linguistic scholarship substantially by providing "a fresh way of looking at any variety of American English," whether Black English/Ebonics, Spanish/English code-switching, or Appalachian English. Significantly, his research legitimized the study of a nonstandard variety of English spoken by working-class members in the African American population, challenging the prevailing assumption that low-prestige varieties were unworthy of detailed attention and analysis.[8]

Beyond linguistics, "*Africanisms* is indispensable to understanding the early development of Afrocentric thinking in this country."[9] Turner was far ahead of his times, as "Afrocentricity" and Afrocentric scholarship did not achieve full development until the advent of the Black Studies movement of the 1970s and 1980s. He was true to the Linguistic Atlas methodology, which sought to find a correlation between British semantic items and their American English counterparts, in the process documenting immigration patterns and settlement. Turner studied Elizabeth Donnan's books and other historical documents on the slave trade and then, after mastering aspects of the languages that were spoken by the largest groups of Africans brought to the United States, traced their linguistic history in Gullah. By establishing the roots of Gullah in African languages, he reconstructed a Gullah past that both scholars and interested observers could respect, helping to lay the groundwork for related research approaches that are central to Black Studies and modern African Studies. Had there been as many sources on settlement history available in the 1940s as have appeared since *Africanisms in the Gullah Dialect,* Turner's research process would have been less labor intensive.[10]

Those who maintain that Turner's *Africanisms in the Gullah Dialect* simply presents one plausible theory to explain the contrasts between Gullah and American English varieties may wish to consider the many levels of fieldwork inquiry Turner undertook on three continents over almost two decades to construct a well-conceived and well-executed analysis. His year in London at the School of Oriental Studies (1936–37) solidified his competence in African languages. His semester at Yale with Edward Sapir (fall 1938) introduced him to Arabic and opened the possibilities of lexical items from Arabic into his work. His study of Native American languages there also assisted him in ruling out Native American lexical retentions in Gullah. His year in Brazil (1940–41) resulted in his immersion in Brazilian Yoruba, in which he located many lexical items, tones, and morphophonemic patterns also evident in Gullah. His summer weeks in 1935 collecting creole data in Louisiana provided corroborating evidence from another creolized variety in the United States. During Turner's return visits to the Sea Islands, he expanded his research and reassessed and clarified his data. Although he was modest in his claims, no other individual project has been as comprehensive or as detailed as *Africanisms in the Gullah Dialect.*

The development of creolistics has been greatly stimulated by *Africanisms in the Gullah Dialect* and has focused in several productive directions, such as the origins and history of creoles and their characteristics and structure. John P. Thomas, Richard S. Dunn, Peter Wood, Daniel C. Littlefield, and Jack P. Greene have documented the connection between Barbados and South Carolina, indicating that Charleston, South Carolina, was first settled in 1670 by both Africans and Europeans from the Caribbean, particularly Barbados. Until the end of the seventeenth century, most South Carolina Africans arrived from the Caribbean rather than directly from Africa. As a result, it is possible that their speech was already creolized when they arrived in South Carolina.[11] Ian Hancock has established that one form of the Gullah Creole (Gullah West) was transplanted to Texas with the forced migration of the Afro-Seminole population.[12]

As enslavement and colonialism began to result in the rapid displacement of massively large populations, especially from Africa, several nineteenth-century theorists began to grapple with the significance of creole languages. In so doing, several researchers of the 1880s planted the seeds for the two major theoretical positions—the substrate and the universal hypotheses—that would later animate discussions of creoles. In 1884 J. W. Harrison produced the first known study of Black American English; in 1889 P. Grade, the first known study of West African Pidgin; and in 1880–81 Adolfo Coëlho, the first known study of African-derived Portuguese creoles.[13] Hugo Schuchardt, a German linguist who wrote more widely than any other early theorist, prepared approximately forty articles between 1880 and 1914, although many remained unpublished during his lifetime. He utilized the term *creole* to refer to any language of European origin strongly altered phonologically, morphologically, syntactically, and semantically by a non-Indo-European language.[14] His position was neither clearly universalist nor substratist. Generally, he accounted for features of creole languages individually. He, like a number of others after him, tended to minimize the African-language component.

Other theorists continued inquiries into the recent language varieties. Lucien Adam, a French philologist who lived in French Guiana for three years, utilized documents of several other writers to establish comparisons between Trinidadian Creole, the creole of Guiana, and several languages of West Africa. He concluded that while the lexicons were largely French, the phonology, morphology, and syntax were largely African: "The Guinea Negroes, transported to [the Caribbean] colonies, took words from French but retained as far as possible the phonology and grammar of their mother tongues."[15] His position was substratist.

Addison Van Name prepared the first comparative study of creoles. He stated in his introduction that "the creole dialects which have grown out of European languages grafted on African stock, though inferior in general interest to even the rudest languages of native growth, are in some respects well worth attention."[16] His position is in agreement with the current main trend in creolistics; that is, creolization is a special case of language contact and change, and that while "the changes . . . are not essentially different in kind, and hardly greater in extent than those . . . which separate the French from the Latin, but from the greater violence of forces at work they have been far more rapid . . . two or three generations have sufficed for a complete transformation."[17]

He raised an issue that continues to be debated by contemporary creolists: how much of any particular creole is African and how much is European? His conclusion was that the European component far outweighed the African component, with African influence being most evident in the phonology.[18]

The publication of *Africanisms in the Gullah Dialect* was the first in a series of studies that established an entirely new direction in linguistics. One central debate has been the issue of how pidgins and creoles develop. The "baby talk" theory of Turner's era assumed that pidgins resulted from imperfect imitation of European speakers on the part of Africans, with Europeans communicating with Africans as one would to babies, either because of the "undeveloped" nature of African languages or the genetic and/or socioeconomic limitations of African speakers.[19] Rooted in racial prejudices and stereotypes, the baby talk theory is no longer considered scientifically sound.

Several decades later the monogenesis theory evolved. It postulates that a Portuguese-based pidgin that developed on the west coast of Africa might have been the source of many pidgins and creoles. Since the Portuguese established numerous trading ports and slave outposts on the West African coasts by 1500, this putative Portuguese pidgin would have developed in the early generations.[20] Based on this theory, pidgins and creoles are assumed to be descendants of a "proto pidgin," the antecedent to the English, French, and Dutch pidgins that took root in the Western Hemisphere as the enslavement of Africans spread. Differences among various pidgins and creoles are accounted for by "relexification." According to William A. Stewart and Robert A. Hall Jr., the putative Portuguese pidgin lost African-language lexical items and gained or was relexified with the vocabularies of English, French, and Dutch, while maintaining a constant syntactic base.[21] Peter Bakker and many other creolists have come to believe that the monogenesis hypothesis should be abandoned. One of the major arguments in support of it had been that the Portuguese-derived vocabulary in Saramaccan had an African source, but it now appears that the Portuguese influence entered Saramaccan later than the English influence.[22]

Existing along with the *substrate* and the *universal* views is the *superstrate* hypothesis.[23] The superstrate hypothesis appears in the research of dialectologists who maintain that the major features of creoles lie in the lexifier languages from which they gained vocabulary.[24] By the 1950s Raven I. McDavid and Virginia McDavid, while advocating the superstrate hypothesis, had agreed with Samuel G. Stoney and Gertrude M. Shelby that a limited number of lexical items in Gullah were traceable to African languages.[25] Among the more recent superstratists are Edgar W. Schneider and Shana Poplack.[26] The superstrate hypothesis assumes that even though the Africans were in the majority during the decades of the pidgin/creole genesis, that is, they constituted the majority in South Carolina and almost half the populations of several other southern states, they neither impacted southern English in a significant manner nor retained significant aspects of the African languages among themselves.

A number of substratists, like Turner, have maintained that African languages underlie Atlantic pidgins and creoles (those resulting from the collision between African and European languages). Among them are Suzanne Comhaire-Sylvain, who in 1936 was the first to make a strong case for this position, Jules Faine, Beryl Bailey, Mervyn Alleyne, Margaret Wade-Lewis, and John Holm.[27] Salikoko S. Mufwene, who has called for a more sophisticated set of "selection principles" to account for substrate influence, maintains that one major account of pidgin/creole origins is inadequate. Mufwene, Philip Baker and Chris Corne, and Ian Hancock are among those who have suggested that the "complementary hypothesis" is a good alternative to a single genetic theory. Much research remains to be accomplished to articulate the conditions under which the competing theories converge.[28]

One of the theorists of the 1980s who stimulated substantial debate is Derek Bickerton, the strongest proponent of the universal hypothesis. Bickerton's model proposes a bioprogram—that is, genetic universals operating in children account for creole origins: "because the grammatical structures of creole languages are more similar to one another than they are to the structures of any other language, it is reasonable to suppose most if not all creoles were invented by children of pidgin-speaking immigrants. Moreover, since creoles must have been invented in isolation, it is likely that some general ability, common to all people, is responsible for the linguistic similarities."[29] A number of unresolved issues include the question of how to explain origins in territories where few children have been present and whether or not the bioprogram operates in adults. Gillian Sankoff and Peter Mühlhäusler have concluded that it can.[30]

There is general agreement that pidgins and creoles are recent language varieties that have emerged from conditions of war, enslavement, or trade when contact groups with no language in common must communicate. Rudimentary in that they have "fewer words, less morphology, and a more restricted range of phonological and syntactic options," they developed around the Atlantic, Indian, and Pacific Oceans between the seventeenth and the nineteenth centuries.[31] For the conquered or colonized, they have often become the major language; they serve as a lingua franca for speakers who utilize an Indo-European language in other contexts. An unresolved contradiction is that the terms *pidgin* and *creole* are associated with speech varieties of the formerly colonized, whereas the term *dialect* is associated with nonstandard varieties of Portuguese, Spanish, and French spoken by Europeans with similar linguistic histories in areas such as Quebec.

One major assumption has been that pidgins develop into creoles when they gain native speakers and stable norms, the native speakers being the children of pidgin speakers who have themselves become adults and utilize the pidgin as a native language. In the process, the developing creole gains an extended social role and a more complex lexical and grammatical structure than a pidgin.[32]

Recently some researchers have postulated that there are exceptions in Africa, around the Indian Ocean, and in the Caribbean where "abrupt creolization" has taken place before a pidgin has had years to become well established. They cite as examples the creole Sango, spoken in the Central African Republic, and Tok Pisin, spoken in New Guinea.[33]

The explosion in pidgin/creole studies following *Africanisms in the Gullah Dialect* was stimulated in part by the rise in the number of non-Western nations moving from colonialism to independence, which focused substantial attention on the linguistic heritages of the formerly colonized and on the need for changes in language policy, in some cases from an insider perspective. In the 1950s two master's-level linguists from Caribbean countries signaled the dramatic increase in interest in creole languages. Beryl Loftman (later Bailey) of Jamaica examined a number of them in 1953 in "Creole Language of the Caribbean Area: A Comparison of the Grammar of Jamaican Creole with Those of the Creole Languages of Haiti, the Antilles, the Guianas, the Virgin Islands, and the Dutch West Indies." Arguing for an African syntactic substrate, she concluded that these creoles were related through their Niger-Congo backgrounds and relexified in the Western Hemisphere by Romance and Germanic languages: "These languages belong to a single group, and their relationship to each other cannot be denied. . . . It would seem, therefore, on the basis of their grammar, that [. . . they] form an independent linguistic group, though with roots going back to both West African and West European languages, and that the name Creole could well be used to cover such languages."[34]

Bailey then identified in the Caribbean creoles the "outstanding traits" that are among those characteristics now associated with creoles worldwide, such as noninflected endings; single gender pronouns to designate masculine, feminine, and neuter; zero copula; use of aspect with verb tense; reduplication for comparative and superlative; and the use of repetition as a derivational process to create nouns and adjectives from verbs.

Noting that most have been lexified by Romance languages (principally French and Spanish) or Germanic languages (principally English and Dutch), Bailey recommended that they be categorized into one family called Afro-European, with an Afro-Romance branch and an Afro-Germanic branch: "By Afro-European languages, therefore, we would mean those languages that have resulted from the thorough mixture of some West-European language or languages with those of West Africa."[35]

Bailey's Afro-European construct is a valid approach to acknowledge the African language influence in the Atlantic pidgins and creoles, as languages should be classified by their syntactic structures. However, the linguistic community has not adopted it. Because her master's thesis remains unpublished, and because she died at midlife, most scholars are unaware of how many ideas presently accepted in pidgin and creole linguistics originated in her work.[36]

After the completion of her master's thesis, Bailey continued her examination of creoles by focusing on Jamaican. She prepared *A Language Guide to Jamaica* (1962) for the Peace Corps, then published her 1964 dissertation as *Jamaican Creole Syntax* in 1966. It was the first full-length analysis of Jamaican Creole, made more innovative by its use of the syntactic theoretical framework developed by Noam Chomsky in *Syntactic Structures* (1957). Although Chomsky's "ideal speaker/hearer" construct seems incongruous when utilized to describe the fluid nature of a creole, Bailey viewed it as the most appropriate model to delineate many of the syntactic subtleties of Jamaican Creole.[37]

Richard Allsopp completed his University of London master's thesis, "Pronominal Forms in the Dialect of English Used in Georgetown (British Guiana) and Its Environs by People Engaged in Nonclerical Occupations" in 1958.[38] Like Turner, he referred to the creole as a dialect. At the same time, he clearly delineated a number of systematic characteristics of Guyanese Creole, establishing a framework that became a point of departure for later theorists, among them John R. Rickford.[39]

Turner must have been gratified to observe the growth of pidgin and creole linguistics in his lifetime. The year 1953 was stellar for the advancement of creole studies as Robert A. Hall, Suzanne Comhaire-Sylvain, H. O. McConnell, and Albert Métraux expanded the analysis of Romance creoles in *Haitian Creole: Grammar, Texts, Vocabulary*.[40] By 1958 Robert B. Le Page raised pidgin/creole studies to a new organizational level when he convinced three foundations—Rockefeller, Carnegie, and Ford—to fund the first conference on creole languages at the University College in Mona, Jamaica, March 28–April 4, 1959. Representatives arrived from the School of Oriental and African Studies in London and from universities in the United States, Amsterdam, Suriname, Dominica, and British Guiana. The response to the conference indicated that a body of researchers was prepared to pursue pidgin/creole linguistics as a scholarly specialty.

Le Page then undertook the organization of a second Mona conference that convened nine years later, April 9–12, 1968. The Social Science Research Council was the funding source. Thirty-six of the forty participants presented papers, most of which were published three years later in a volume edited by Dell Hymes as a set of essays essential to an understanding of the specialty.[41] Many of the contributors are now well-established voices in pidgin/creole linguistics.

Until the 1970s, the conversations focused primarily on Atlantic creoles, namely, those emerging from displaced Africans, the most massively displaced group. However, in 1973 the University of Papua, New Guinea, hosted a conference and focused attention on Pacific creoles, those emerging from Asian languages. A second conference in 1975 in Honolulu, Hawaii, likewise focused on Pacific pidgins and creoles.

As the specialty continued to take root, another breakthrough was the publication in 1966 of the first textbook designed for undergraduates, Hall's *Pidgin and Creole Languages*. A year later Frederic G. Cassidy and Robert B. Le Page published the first full-length dictionary of a creole, *Dictionary of Jamaican English*. Among the most recent creole dictionaries are John Holm and Alison Shilling, *Dictionary of Bahamian English;* Richard Allsopp, ed., with Jeannette Allsopp, *Dictionary of Caribbean English Usage;* and Albert Valdman, ed., *Dictionary of Louisiana Creole*.[42]

In 1975 the first comprehensive bibliography appeared. John E. Rienecke and Stanley M. Tsuzaki, with Ian Hancock, David DeCamp, and Richard E. Wood, produced *Bibliography of Pidgin and Creole Languages*, which brought together in one source a list of the publications in the specialty.[43] A revised version, covering publications from 1975 to the present, would be a welcome addition to the literature, though there are now several on-line distribution points for research papers and bibliographies, among them the Pidgin and Creole Archives supported by the University of Siegen, Germany.

The continued expansion and institutionalization of any specialty requires the development of learned societies and journals. In 1972 the Society for Caribbean Linguistics was founded in St. Augustine, Trinidad. A few years later, the Society of Pidgin and Creole Linguistics, which meets biennially, was established. Among the related academic societies is the Associacáo de Crioulos de Base Léxica Portuguesa e Espanhola. In 1972 the newsletter/journal the *Carrier Pidgin,* proposed at a Georgetown University on Languages and Linguistics Roundtable, took flight, serving as a forum for issues, presenting profiles of scholars, and announcing publications and conferences. The year 1977 saw both the founding and demise of the *Journal of Creole Studies,* but with its reincarnation as the *Journal of Pidgin and Creole Languages* in 1986, it was clear that the pidgin/creole linguistics had become mainstream. Among the journals in Romance creoles are *Études Créoles, Créolica,* and *Papia: Revista de Associacão Brasileira de Estudos Crioulos e Similares.*

In 1971 Ian Hancock created a map of the world's one-hundred-plus pidgins and creoles, seventy-five of which have been created by African populations, the largest group of rapidly and involuntarily displaced speakers. It has found broad circulation, appearing in Hymes's *Pidginization and Creolization of Language* (1971), in Valdman's *Pidgin and Creole Linguistics* (1977), and on the masthead of the *Carrier Pidgin.*[44]

By 1971 David DeCamp had proposed the notion of a "creole continuum," resulting from the "decreolization" of a creole in contact with a standard variety, where the creole gradually loses many of its features or gains other features as it moves in the direction of the standard variety. Researchers have identified Guyana, Jamaica, and Hawaii as being representative. In these situations there are a number of intermediate varieties of the creole or *mesolects* between the *basilect* (the most creolized variety) and the *acrolect* (the standard language), terminology that William Stewart introduced in his 1965 description of Black English.[45]

The same year, Mervyn Alleyne postulated that another process can also unfold. In Jamaica the creole continuum may have developed during the earliest years of contact between Africans and Europeans, with the consistent influx of speakers of African languages, and with social class divisions resulting from the house slave/field slave dichotomy being set in motion. The nuanced nature of the speech continuum depended on the relations and nature of contacts between particular groups of Africans and Europeans—older arrivals vs. newly arrived, house workers vs. field workers, skilled craftspersons vs. unskilled laborers.[46]

Others have postulated that a creole continuum may also develop backward, with the first groups of Africans learning Standard or near-Standard English. When the earliest groups have been of limited numbers, resulting in a smaller ratio of Africans to Europeans, a context conducive to the spread of a standard variety has pertained. As the numbers increased in subsequent generations, the Africans acquired "restructured" or creolized English, having more limited access to the standard varieties.[47]

Hancock raised the question of whether the African pidgin developed on the African continent or later on plantations in the Western Hemisphere. His research demonstrates that a pidgin, which he designates as Guinea Coast Creole English, was generated by Africans and Europeans on the Guinea coast as a result of trade and war before the settlement of plantations in North America. It became the precursor to both Krio and the Western Hemisphere Anglophone creoles.[48] Cassidy, however, maintains that the number of speakers was so small that it is more reasonable to assume that the pidgin developed in the Caribbean as Africans were separated from family and cultural groups, and he emphasizes Barbados as the matrix for Jamaican, Suriname Djuka, Gullah, and other creoles as Barbados was utilized as a major distribution site and trading center.[49] In 1980 Alleyne postulated a putative West African substratum that has survived decreolization and is predominately influenced by Kwa languages. The differences between "Afro-American" dialects throughout the Western Hemisphere, he maintains, lies in the nature and extent of linguistic "continuity" they have maintained.[50]

Hancock and Mufwene advocate analysis of genesis from multiple sources. Hancock's theory of componentiality suggests that the "social and linguistic matrix" for "Atlantic" pidgins and creoles grows from a convergence of different proportions of "ingredients" or "components under different circumstances." These components are "(a) the African languages, (b) the various dialects of metropolitan English, (c) the West African creole component, and (d) other languages." Eight parameters must also be considered, among them the migration and settlement dates, the point of origins and proportion of various linguistic groups converging during the first twenty-five years, the social relations within the linguistic context, "the changing ratio of locally born to those arriving as adults," and migration in and out of the community, along with the changing ratios within the population over time.[51]

Mufwene's parallel concept of "ecology" suggests that the variation in the structural features of creoles lexified by the same language must be correlated with the sociolinguistic history of the language. Hence a combination of factors, including interactions between various population groups and rates of population growth comprise the "ecology" of a creole.[52]

While the majority or body of creolistic research has focused on issues of origins, an increasing body of data since the 1990s has dealt with structural features, including morpho-syntax, phonology, semantics, and pragmatics; see, for example, John V. Singler on tense, mood, and aspect and Susanne M. Mühleisen and Bettina Migge on politeness and face in creoles. Within the past several years, studies of creoles have increased in geographic variety. Among them are Winford James and Valerie Youssef's analysis of the language of Tobago; Thomas Klinger's study of Louisiana creole; I. H. W. Wellens's dissertation on Nubi, an African-Arabic creole; Kent Sakoda and Jeff Siegel's grammar of Hawaiian creole; and Terry Crowley's grammar of Bislama of Hawaii.[53]

During the 1960s and 1970s, researchers on language variation focusing on speech in the United States, particularly in the South, increased in number and generally could be categorized into two groups: dialect geographers/dialectologists and sociolinguists. Dialectologists analyzed systematic variation in pronunciation and the lexicon, while sociolinguists pursued systematic variation in phonology, syntax, and semantics. The two groups utilized different methodologies, with the dialect geographers operating within the Linguistic Atlas framework to examine variation between blacks and whites across a region and the sociolinguists developing quantitative analyses to examine the speech of a social class in a specific community. This dialectologist position has been referred to as Anglicist for its assumption that black dialect descends from British sources. Each group believed its approaches were the most effective for producing salient answers.[54]

Since the 1960s more research has focused on black American speech than on any other American English variety, the majority of it on the historical development, sociolinguistic variation, and language policy/education implications.[55] The study of Gullah gave rise to the theory that Black English was a sister creole of Gullah (the creolist position) that decreolized because of sustained contact with speakers of English. William Stewart noted that if educators viewed Black English as having creole roots, they would be more willing to embrace it as valid and distinct, rather than as incorrect, English and more likely to incorporate it into language arts pedagogy. Stewart and Joey L. Dillard found that African American speech in the eighteenth and nineteenth centuries was more similar to Caribbean creoles than it is today. A number of additional researchers have concluded that when copula absence and other features of Black English are examined, its creole origins become more evident. Although there is not a consensus between Anglicists and creolists relating to the origins of Black English, currently many would concede that both positions are valid. See, for example, Walter Wolfram and Erik Thomas.[56]

With the integration of U.S. schools in the wake of the civil rights movement, educators who had not been exposed to the linguistic differences between the speech of African American children and that of Euro-American children now encountered them in the classroom. Attempts to address the issues in reading and testing, in particular, resulted in a proliferation of studies on black speech behavior, as well as reading and testing issues. Grant funding accelerated the development of research.

Ralph Fasold and Roger Shuy's *Teaching Standard English in the Inner City* and Geneva Smitherman's studies of Black English and education, among them, *Talkin and Testifyin: The Language of Black America* and *Black English and the Education of Black Children and Youth,* led to new interpretations of the competencies of black youth as well as to methods of maximizing their reading, writing, and testing performances. During the 1970s Stewart and other researchers at the Center for Applied Linguistics, in Washington, D.C., produced innovative research, including textbooks to enrich teaching pedagogy and encourage the teaching of Standard English to Black English speakers through a "bridge" or English-as-a-second-language approach.[57]

In 1972, at the height of the civil rights movement, Dillard authored *Black English: Its History and Usage in the United States,* the first full-length textbook providing a context in which the African American dialect could expect serious attention from trained language specialists. That same year William Labov published *Language in the Inner City* while encouraging his students at the University of Pennsylvania to undertake fieldwork projects leading to dissertations on urban speech of black youths. The Labov approach of examining a number of speech variables utilizing mostly youthful speakers was a departure from the traditional process of analyzing the speech of older, rural African Americans.

Since the 1960s the dialect has generally been referred to as Black English. More recently a number of researchers have preferred African American Vernacular English (AAVE) or African American English (AAE).[58] Though Williams coined the term *Ebonics* in 1973, it was not popularized until the Oakland debate of 1996.[59]

Black English reached a legal milestone in 1979, when an Ann Arbor case judge, Charles Joiner, ruled that attitudes toward the dialect, rather than the dialect itself, hamper the educational achievement of black children and youths. Smitherman organized a conference to further explore this topic, which resulted in the volume *Black English and the Education of Black Children and Youth,* edited by Smitherman.

The Ebonics-in-the-schools debate is rekindled periodically as a result of examination of language in education policy, most recently in 1996 in California. Black English became headline news, capturing public attention during December 1996 and spring 1997 with the "Oakland Debate." The Oakland school district's attempts to improve the performance of speakers of Black English by providing a "bridge" or bilingual approach to the teaching of Standard English were grossly misinterpreted and denounced in the media. The school board, referring to African American speech as a language, utilized the term *Ebonics.* A resolution from the Linguistic Society of America in support of using Ebonics as a bridge to Standard English did not deter the United States Senate in 1997 from holding hearings, led by Senator Arlen Specter, to deny the allocation of funds for the Oakland project and for similar projects. The backlash against Ebonics combined larger oppositions to affirmative action, bilingual education, and "any measure that seemed to offer special 'advantages'" to people of color.[60] In the wake of the national debate, a number of states have passed English-only laws.

Several recent analyses have increased the number of resources available to serve as textbooks. Mufwene, Rickford, Bailey, and Baugh compiled ten essays that update the data on the history, structure, discourse, and legal issues; Rickford and Rickford have provided a user-friendly resource for both the classroom and the informed public; and Green has authored a text/research resource that outlines the structure of the grammar as a holistic rule-governed system. Spears, Baugh, and Morgan have provided major treatments on topics of language and power.[61]

Several dictionaries provide substantial information on the lexicon of Black English, the most extensive being those published by Dillard in 1977, Major in 1970 and 1994, and Smitherman in 1994. A rapidly expanding body of resources examines rap music and hip-hop culture, both of which are inexorably bound to Ebonics. In recent dissertations, Mary Bucholtz has addressed the embracing of black culture by white youth; Halifu Osumare, the spread of hip-hop culture beyond America.[62]

A number of scholars have examined the historic connections between Gullah and AAVE. Among them are Dillard, Rickford, Baugh, Holm, and Tracy L. Weldon. The extensive body of research on AAVE/Ebonics and education includes work by Baugh; Perry and Delprit, eds.; Adger, Christian, and Taylor, eds.; Wolfram, Adger, and Christian eds.; and Smitherman.[63]

A number of landmark dissertations have been stimulated by Turner's work, each important for expanding the body of data on the grammar. The 1970 dissertation by Irma Aloyce Ewing Cunningham presented the first transformational syntactic analysis of Gullah (revised and published in 1992 as *A Syntactic Analysis of Sea Island Creole*). Patricia Causey Nichols's 1976 dissertation analyzed male/female linguistic strategies and styles. Patricia Jones-Jackson made the case that Gullah was decreolizing through convergence with Standard English in her 1978 work. Katherine Wyly Mille demonstrated that while the number of Gullah speakers is diminishing, there is "stable variation" in the tense-mood-aspect systems. More recently, two comparative studies examined Gullah and other "Afro-Creoles." Tometro Hopkins analyzed Gullah and Afro-Cuban, while Tracy Weldon examined the copula in both Gullah and AAVE. Mary Twining's 1977 dissertation provided the most exhaustive study of cultural forms, in material culture, expressive behavior, and social institutions.[64]

In recent years several studies of the Gullah language and culture have appeared, among them works by Margaret Creel, Twining, Cunningham, Michael Montgomery, Marquetta Goodwine, and William Pollitzer. Joseph Holloway produced the most recent interdisciplinary collection of essays on African retentions.[65] Hundreds of published articles and thousands of web sites reference *Africanisms in the Gullah Dialect.*

In 1995 the Wycliffe Bible Translators collaborated with a dozen or more native speakers of Gullah on the Sea Island Literacy and Translation Team to produce *De Good Nyews Bout Jedus Christ Wa Luke Write: The Gospel according to Luke.* It rapidly became a collector's item among church groups, including those in northern cities with large numbers of members from South Carolina. In 2003 *The Gospel of John* appeared. An entire Bible in Gullah is in preparation.[66]

The complete grammar of Gullah that Turner had originally envisioned is realized in large part in Cunningham's *A Syntactic Analysis of Sea Island Creole.* Additional pieces are found in the research of other scholars. A comprehensive Gullah dictionary is overdue. The late Virginia Geraty of Charleston was in the process of completing one.[67]

The majority of Turner scholars have been inspired by his research, never having met him before his death. When Cunningham was a graduate student, she contacted Turner about the possibility of borrowing some of his field recordings. Since he and her dissertation adviser recommended that she conduct fieldwork on the Sea Islands, she did. Cunningham introduced the term *Sea Island Creole.* Her dissertation became the first in a series of grammatical studies of Gullah after 1970.[68]

Patricia Nichols's introduction to Turner's work was a logical outgrowth of her own cultural legacy.

> I never met Turner. I became interested in Gullah when I went away to graduate school at the U of Minnesota and a professor of Old English asked me about it. I had grown up in Conway, S.C., just north of where the Sea Islands begin. I had never heard that name because we used the term "Geechee" up in my county, and of course I had heard the language. I was cared for daily between the ages of 1 ½

> & 3 1/2 by a young woman who grew up in Little River, whose great-grandmother had been one of the last slaves to come from Africa. She spoke African American English, which I learned as a second dialect. When I was about 12, my dad ran for attorney general and took me to every county in the state for the stump speeches at the courthouse—on that trip I heard the full range of speech in the state from coast to mountains. (He lost but I gained lots!) Later as a teenager, I worked in the local department store of my small town on Saturdays (when the country folks came to town for supplies) and heard lots of country speech, both black and white, as I interacted with customers—a wide range then, because some of them came to town in horse and wagon. When I went to undergraduate college in Rock Hill, S.C., I was always begged to do African American parts in theatrical productions (white, segregated women's college in 1955) because my dialect was so good.
>
> Then when I took my first course in Linguistics here in California during the 60s, it all came together. My professor, Edith Trager, lent me Turner's book to read for some paper or other she had assigned. From there, I was off.[69]

Among the most compelling contemporary issues are concerns for the stability of Gullah Creole and the diminution of land and property rights of native Gullah citizens. The individual most actively involved in the formation of an "ethnonationalist movement" to gain political autonomy for them is Marquetta Goodwine from St. Helena Island, a mathematician/computer scientist/social activist who is a descendant of two Gullah families. In 1996 she founded the Gullah/Geechee Coalition with the threefold mission to participate in the preservation of Gullah "history, heritage, culture and language"; to work toward "Sea Island land re-acquisition and maintenance"; and to celebrate Gullah/Geechee "cultures through artistic and educational means."[70]

Goodwine's authority was first legitimized in 1999, when she presented by teleconference for the UN Conference on the Right to Self-Determination held in Geneva, Switzerland. That same year she and other members of the coalition succeeded in lobbying Representative James E. Clyburn from South Carolina to sponsor the bill that authorized the *Low Country Gullah Culture Special Resource Study* (SRS) from the United States Parks Service. One ultimate goal of the coalition is to secure National Historic Landmark status for certain Gullah territories.[71]

In order to achieve the authority to represent the Gullah nation, Goodwine was "enstooled" as Queen Quet, Chieftess of the Gullah/Geechee nation, in July 2000. In January 2003 she briefed to press at the U.S. State Department in Washington, D.C.[72]

According to Goodwine, Turner's contribution inspires respect among the Sea Islanders who know of him:

> Many Gullah/Geechee people have never heard of Mr. Lorenzo Dow Turner because those who live something do not usually study it. However, those of us who are familiar with his groundbreaking work appreciate the chance he took to stand and declare that we have kept our African heritage through language and through deeds. We are sure that if he had lived longer, he would have come to

state that we have our own language, which is Gullah and not simply a dialect. It is his work on which many linguists who study "creoles" stand today. Thus, he is to be honored for being a trailblazer who respected our people.

If you are interested in accurate information concerning the Gullah/Geechee Nation and/or would like to conduct research at the only archive in the world that is totally dedicated to Gullah/Geechee history, heritage, and culture, contact:

Gullah/Geechee Sea Island Coalition
Post Office Box 1207
St. Helena Island SC 29920
(843) 838-1171
GullGeeCo@aol.com
or
GullGeeCo@officialgullahgeechee.info[73]

As public interest and Gullah scholarship have increased, Gullah has connected America and Africa. In the 1980s the Fourah Bay College in Freetown, Sierra Leone, established the Gullah Research Center. President Joseph Momoh and Joseph Opala arranged a state visit to the Sea Islands. By 1990 approximately a dozen South Carolinians visited Sierra Leone for two weeks to visit sites related to the history of enslavement and to examine the relationship between Krio and Gullah. The visit was the focus of the documentary film *Family across the Sea* (1990), initiated by Joseph Opala and produced by South Carolina Educational Television. The film focuses on the parallels between Gullah and Sierra Leonean cultural lifestyles. A number of recent sources provide broad coverage of creole studies issues.[74]

Among the additional movies and documentaries that feature Gullah and/or Black English are "Black on White" (1986), from the *Story of English* series, produced for PBS, which traces the development of the Afro-European creole that became Gullah, the Caribbean creoles, and the African American Vernacular English; and *Daughters of the Dust* (1991), written and produced by Julie Dash to present Gullah traditions to a popular audience. The most recent documentary, *The Language You Cry In* (1998), from California Newsreel, produced by Opala, is especially pertinent as a follow-up to Turner's work in that it documents the present-day retention of the Mende funeral chant sung to Turner by Amelia Dawley in 1933 and the meeting in the 1990s of Dawley's daughter Mary Moran, her grandson Wilson Moran, and several other Sea Islanders who have retained the song with a Sierra Leone family that has done the same. In April 2005 Wilson Moran paid a return visit to Sierra Leone head woman Baindu Jabati. Moran was accompanied by the journalist Herb Frazier.[75]

At the level of popular culture, Gullah Studies continues to inspire interest. The PBS television series for children called *Gullah, Gullah Island* has been augmented by a number of children's books, videos, and music cassettes. Black English has become a part of the national consciousness as a result of the media, in particular movies, hip-hop culture, spoken word poetry, and rap music.

The preservation of Gullah culture is well under way on the Sea Islands. The Penn Center on St. Helena serves as a clearinghouse for Gullah culture, bus tours are available, and annual Gullah festivals emanate from the Penn Center and elsewhere. A number of books, cassettes, and photographs are available for youths and adults.

In the past three decades several conferences have focused on the Sea Islands, Gullah, or Africanisms in general, the first at Atlanta University in 1972 by Richard Long. In 1985 the Ninth Annual Language and Culture in South Carolina Symposium convened at the University of South Carolina, Columbia. A number of the essays from the symposium that explore the connections between Gullah language and culture and African or Caribbean languages appear as *Crucible of Carolina: Essays in the Development of Gullah Language and Culture.* In 1988 Salikoko Mufwene convened an international conference at the University of Georgia. The proceedings appear as *Africanisms in Afro-American Language Varieties.* The University of San Francisco hosted a summer symposium, "Issues in the African Diaspora: Connections and Continuity in the Americas," in June 1998. Organized by Anita DeFrantz and sponsored by the School of Education's Department of International Multicultural Education, it featured John Rickford, Wade Nobles, Joseph Opala, Asa Hilliard, and several other scholars. On February 17, 1999, National Geographic sponsored a conference, "Crossing the Sea on a Song: A Gullah Family Finds Its Roots in Sierra Leone," to profile the documentary *The Language You Cry In.* The conference featured Joseph Opala, Cynthia Schmidt, Mary Moran, her son Wilson Moran, and Lois Turner Williams. On November 3, 2000, Paul Fallon convened a conference at Howard University that focused on the fiftieth anniversary of Turner's *Africanisms in the Gullah Dialect.* Among the featured presenters were John Rickford, Margaret Wade-Lewis, Salikoko Mufwene, Patricia Causey Nichols, and John V. Singler. In 2002 the conference "Pidgin and Creole Linguistics in the Twenty-First Century" resulted in a cutting-edge volume of the same name, edited by Gilbert.[76] The eleven papers in the Gilbert volume cut across the central debates in creolistics today—issues in the lives of creole speakers, applied creolistics in education, creole formation as a historical process (relexification, reanalysis, and dialect leveling), the absence of research on African language retentions populations in Latin America among Spanish and Portuguese populations—among them Ecuador and Uruguay—the dearth of research on Spanish- and Portuguese-lexified creoles, universals of language acquisition and language shift, and the ways in which creole studies must be distinct from other language contact analyses.

Judging from the brisk level of activity related to Gullah language and culture, to creolistics and Black English studies, the future holds much promise.

APPENDIX

Lorenzo Dow Turner Family

This is a preliminary genealogy for Lorenzo Dow Turner, born October 21, 1890, in Elizabeth City, North Carolina.* The use of asterisks in this genealogy indicates data sources as follows:

Lorenzo Dow Turner's List	*
U.S. Census for North Carolina, 1870	†
U.S. Census for North Carolina, 1880	‡
U.S. Census for Massachusetts, 1880	§
U.S. Census for North Carolina, 1900	#

Beginnings in America

Joseph Rooks (family patriarch—Scots-Irish) married ——— (best evidence based on 1790 U.S. Census for North Carolina). This marriage produced a daughter, Sally Rooks (Scotch-Irish), who married James Brady (enslaved African). They had four daughters: Polly, Julia, Sarah (Sally), and Margaret (Peggy). The descendants have been free since 1799.

Polly Rooks (b. 1799) married David Rooks on October 19, 1824 (North Carolina Marriage Bond #000052134). They had six children.

Nancy Rooks (b. 1814)—married William Burke on December 18, 1843
Joseph Rooks (b. 1818)—married Sarah Hare on June 6, 1941
Joanna Rooks (b. 1826)—married William Burk(e) on February 5, 1847
James Rooks (1829–1906), blacksmith—married Elizabeth Burke (1837–1900)
Mary A. Rooks (b. 1836)—married Thomas Butler on October 16, 1856
John Rooks (1836–1910), carpenter—married Cassandra Burke (1840–1907)

Julia Rooks (b. 1802) married Micajah Reid/Mik Reed on February 28, 1826 (North Carolina Marriage Bond #000052002). They had six children, three of whom lived to adulthood.

William Reid (b. 1826), preacher—married Jane Jones on September 11, 1845
Asbury Reid (1827–1901), farmer, elected justice of the peace, Republican politician—married Clarissa (b. 1838)
Mary Reid (b. 1828)—married William Jones (b. 1820), a painter

Sarah (Sally) Rooks (b. 1805) married Jethro (Jet) Martin (North Carolina Marriage Bond not found). The exact number of their offspring is unknown.

Jethro Martin (b. 1820), farmer—married Lydia (b. 1825), housewife
Margaret Martin (b. 1824), relative?
Sarah Ann Martin (b. 1845)
Virginia Ann Martin (b. 1848)

(1850 U.S. Census, Gates County, North Carolina, Roll M32-631: 53)

Margaret (Peggy) Rooks (b. 1812) married Daniel Turner (1804–January 1880) on April 17, 1828 (North Carolina Marriage Bond 000052554). They had twelve children.

See also Cornelia Reid Jones, "The Four Rooks Sisters," *Negro History Bulletin* 16, no. 1 (October 1952): 3–8; State of North Carolina, *An Index to Marriage Bonds Filed in the North Carolina State Archives* (Raleigh: North Carolina Division of Archives and History, 1977); U.S. Bureau of the Census, Department of Commerce and Labor, *Heads of Families at the First Census of the United States Taken in the Year 1790: North Carolina* (Washington, D.C.: U.S. Government Printing Office, 1908).

The Children of (Margaret) Peggy Rooks and Daniel Turner

Except for Julia, Elisha, Isaiah, John, and Samuel, the children of Daniel and (Margaret) Peggy (Rooks) Turner appear with them on the 1860 census rolls. (See 1860 U.S. Federal Census, Nixonton Township, Pasquotank County, North Carolina, Roll M6532–909: 365.)

Julia/Juley/Juliann Turner (b. 1829), housewife, married Jeffry/Jeffrey Overton (b. 1798), farmer.

Jeffry Overton (b. 1840)*
Haywood Overton (b. 1842)*
Wiley Overton (b. 1848)*
Rubin Overton (b. 1850)*
Margaret Overton (b. 1851)* †
Mary A. Overton (b. 1854)* †
John Paul Overton (b. 1856)* †
George Overton (b. 1858)* †
Wiley/Wesley Overton (b. 1859)†
Eliza Overton (b. 1861)†
Alpiere Overton (b. 1864)†
Joseph C. Overton (b. 1865)†
Juliann Overton (b. 1867)†

(1860 U.S. Federal Census, Mount Hermon Township, Pasquotank County, Elizabeth City, North Carolina, Roll M653-909: 365; and 1870 U.S. Federal Census, Mount Hermon Township, Pasquotank County, Elizabeth City, North Carolina, Roll M593-1154: 359)

Alfred Turner (b. 1830), farmer (also worked on the railroad), married Sophia (b. 1835), housewife; no children.

(1880 U.S. Federal Census, District 109, Pasquotank County, Elizabeth City, North Carolina, Roll T9-976: 334C)

Elisha Turner (b. 1832), carpenter, no children.
(Elisha resided with various relatives. He appears in the Rooks and Elizabeth Turner household on the 1880 U.S. Federal Census for North Carolina.)

(1880 U.S. Federal Census, District 109, Pasquotank County, Elizabeth City, North Carolina, Roll T9-976: 335B)

Isaiah Turner (b. 1835), laborer and farmer; married Charlotte (b. 1840), housewife.

William Henry Turner (b. 1861)* † ‡
James Monroe Turner (b. 1861)* † ‡

Liston F. Turner (b. 1863)* † ‡
Sansbury Turner*
Ella Turner (b. 1867)*
Mary Turner (b. 1868)* ‡
Martha Turner (b. 1868)*—married John Bell; children:
Charlotte
Martha
John
Betty Turner (twin with Sally)*
Sally Turner*
Isaiah Turner Jr.*
Charlotte Turner (b. 1872)* ‡
Sarah Frances Turner (b. 1872)* ‡
Tolson Turner*
Ella Turner (b. 1877)* ‡
(Two additional children)*

(1870 U.S. Federal Census, New Hope Township, Perquimans County, North Carolina, Roll M593-1154: 496; and 1880 U.S. Federal Census, District 119, Perquimans County, North Carolina, Roll T9-977: 62C)

Mary Adeline/Adaline Turner (b. 1838), housewife, married John Reid/Reed (b. 1837), farmer/carpenter, on November 2, 1866 (North Carolina Marriage Bond # 000104030).
William Henry Reid/Reed (b. 1862)† §
James Edward Reid/Reed (b. 1864)* † §
John Edward Reid/Reed (b. 1873)* §
(The Reids/Reeds moved to New Bedford, Massachusetts.*)

(1870 U.S. Federal Census, Parkville, Perquimans County, North Carolina, Roll M593-1154: 528; and 1880 U.S. Federal Census, District 117, New Bedford, Massachusetts, Roll T9-525: 279.3000)

John Turner (b. 1839), farmer and fisherman, married Mary Jane (b. 1840), housewife.
Elisha Turner (b. 1858)* †
Martha Jane Turner (b. 1860)†
Alice A. Turner (b. 1861)† ‡
William Miller Turner (b. 1862)† ‡
Mary Jane (Ann) Turner (b. 1862)*
John W. Turner Jr. (b. 1864)* † ‡
Nathanial Haywood Turner (b. 1866)* † ‡
Margaret Turner (b. 1868)† ‡
Camilla Turner (b. 1871)*
Daniel E. Turner (b. 1872)‡
Elexander/Alexander Turner (b. 1873)‡
Dora T. Turner (b. 1876)‡
Julia J. Turner (b. 1878)‡
Willard C. Turner (b. 1880)‡

(1870 U.S. Federal Census, New Hope Township, Perquimans County, North Carolina, Roll M593-1154: 511; and 1880 U.S. Federal Census, District 119, Perquimans County, North Carolina, Roll T9-977: 74C)

Margaret Turner (b. 1841), domestic
(Margaret has been located only on the 1860 U.S. Federal Census. She was nineteen years old and resided in the family home with Daniel, Peggy, and her younger siblings. Lorenzo Dow Turner indicated that he had no information on her.)

(1860 U.S. Federal Census, Pasquotank County, North Carolina, Roll M653-909: 365)

Sarah A. Turner (b. 1843), housewife, married Nathaniel/Nathanuel Bowe/Bow/Baw (b. 1846), farmer.

Ida Willa Bowe (b. 1868)* †
Sarah Bowe (b. 1870)* †
Arbillia Bowe (b. 1871)* ‡
Timothy Bowe (b. 1872)* ‡
Willie Bowe (b. 1874)* ‡
Omediant Bowe (b. 1876)* ‡
Margaret Bowe (b. 1877)* ‡
Nathaniel Bowe (b. 1878)‡

(The Bowes moved to Montgomery County, Maryland, circa 1900.*)

(1870 U.S. Federal Census, Mount Hermon Township, Pasquotank County, North Carolina, Roll 593-1154: 360; and 1880 U.S. Federal Census, District 111, Mount Hermon Township, Pasquotank County, North Carolina, Roll T9-976: 352B)

Rooks Turner (October 24, 1844–July 22, 1926), teacher, married Elizabeth Sessoms Freeman (March 12, 1861–November 23, 1931) in 1880.

Shelby Turner (1881–1883)*
Rooks Turner Jr. (1883–1912)* #—married Aquilla (b. 1885)
Sedgwick Turner (b. 1909)

(Aquilla Turner and Sedgwick Turner appear on the 1930 U.S. Federal Census for District 7, Rockville, Montgomery County, Maryland, Roll 876: 14A.)

Arthur Turner (1885–1972)* #—married (1) Nellye, (2) Zephra, (3) Essie; no children

Lorenzo Dow Turner (October 21, 1890–February 10, 1972)* #—married (1) Geneva Calcier Townes on September 16, 1919, (2) Lois Morton on September 1, 1938; children:

Lorenzo Dow Turner Jr. (b. July 1, 1943)
Rani Meredith Turner (May 13, 1948–September 12, 2003)

(1880 U.S. Federal Census for Elizabeth City, District 109, Pasquotank County, North Carolina, Roll T9-976: 335B; and 1900 U.S. Federal Census, District 75, Pasquotank County, Elizabeth City, North Carolina, Roll T623-1210: 3B)

Eliza(h) Turner (b. 1846), housewife, married Benjamin Lamb (b. 1841) on March 4, 1875.

Thomas Lamb (b. 1877)* ‡
Benny (Benjamin) Lamb (b. 1879)* ‡

Elizah Lamb (b. 1880)‡
Pauline Lamb (b. 1882)#
Peter Lamb (b. 1885)#

(1880 U.S. Federal Census, Mount Hermon Township, District 111, Pasquotank County, North Carolina, Roll T9-976: 351B; and 1900 U.S. Census, Parkville District 87, Perquimans County, North Carolina, Roll T623-1211: 12B)

Daniel Francis (Frank) Turner (b. 1848) married Catharine (b. 1868), of European ancestry.
William B. (Willie) Turner (b. 1900)*
Frank Turner Jr. (b. 1903)*
Lloyd Turner (b. 1906)*

(1860 U.S. Federal Census, Nixonton Township, Pasquotank County, North Carolina, Roll M653-909: 365; and 1910 U.S. Federal Census, District 31, Galloway County, Atlantic, New Jersey, Roll T624-867: 4-B)

Elmira/Alvira Turner (b. 1851) married Joseph Savage (b. 1836).
Lela/Aurilla Savage (b. 1868)*
Lewis Savage (b. 1870)
Clarence Savage (b. 1875)*
Carrie (b. 1875)
Eugene (b. 1877)
Kate (b. 1880)

(Elmira Turner appears at age nine on the 1860 U.S. Federal Census, Nixonton Township, Pasquotank County, North Carolina, Roll M653-909: 365. However, since she has not been definitively located as the adult Elmira Savage, the genealogy for her family is speculative. She and her family possibly became members of white society. See, for example, 1880 U.S. Census, District 242, Antioch, Lake, Illinois, Roll T9-221: 635.2000.)

NOTES

Introduction

1. *Newsletter of the American Dialect Society* 33, no. 1 (January 2001): 4.

1. Sally Rooks, Jacob Brady, and the Origins of the Rooks/Turner Clan: 1799

1. Cornelia Reid Jones, "The Four Rooks Sisters," *Negro History Bulletin* 16, no. 1 (October 1952): 3.

2. Since only family heads were listed by name, circumstantial evidence must suffice. Ten men with the Rooks surname resided in North Carolina, with only two living in Gates County by the time of the U.S. Census of 1790, namely, Joseph and Dempsey. There were no Africans on the Dempsey Rooks plantation. Joseph Rooks had three. Jacob Brady was likely one of them. Only one free white female, probably Sally, appears on the Joseph Rooks plantation. See U.S. Bureau of the Census, *Heads of Families at the First Census of the United States Taken in the Year 1790: North Carolina* (Washington, D.C.: Government Printing Office, 1908), 23–24.

3. "Black" and "African American" are both used in this narrative, with "black" being the more general term for persons of African ancestry. See Walter Clark, ed., *State Records of North Carolina* (Winston, N.C.: For the General Assembly, 1905), 23:65; and John Hope Franklin, *The Free Negro in North Carolina, 1790–1860* (Chapel Hill: University of North Carolina Press, 1943), 10.

4. Franklin, *Free Negro,* 7.

5. Jones, "Four Rooks Sisters," 3.

6. 1860 U.S. Census, Perquimans County, N.C., 2.

7. Thomas R. Butchko, *Forgotten Gates: The Historical Architecture of a Rural North Carolina County* (Gatesville, N.C.: Gates County Historical Society, 1991), 237; Franklin, *Free Negro,* 35.

8. Hugh Talmage Lefler, *North Carolina History Told by Contemporaries* (Chapel Hill: University of North Carolina Press, 1965), 280–82.

9. Jones, "Four Rooks Sisters," 3–4; 1860 U.S. Census, Pasquotank County, N.C., 76.

10. Jones, "Four Rooks Sisters," 3–4.

11. Sandra Lee Almasy, *Gates County, North Carolina Marriage Bonds, 1741–1868* (Joliet, Ill.: Kensington Glen Publishing, 1987), 76.

12. Jones, "Four Rooks Sisters," 3–4.

13. Almasy, *Gates County, North Carolina Marriage Bonds* (bond #000052554), 92.

14. Lorenzo Dow Turner Questionnaire, circa 1933, from the E. Franklin Frazier Papers, Manuscript Division, Moorland-Spingarn Research Center, Howard University, Washington, D.C., Collection 131, Folder 8, No. 1588 (cited hereafter as Frazier Papers, HU, with collection and folder locators).

E. Franklin Frazier taught from 1929 to 1934 at Fisk University, where he collected empirical data through "A Study of the Negro Family" survey, which he mailed to members of the black community, especially those of the middle class. The purpose was to amass data on the family backgrounds of African Americans. Some became grist for one of Frazier's best-known books, *Black Bourgeoisie: The Rise of the New Middle Class* (Glencoe, Ill.: Free Press, 1957), a sociological analysis. The original surveys are archived in the Frazier Papers, HU. Turner's Questionnaire No. 2588, though sketchy, provides valuable details about his parents and grandparents.

15. Pasquotank County Office of Register of Deeds, Elizabeth City, N.C., Book 6 (1885), 572.

16. The 1860 Pasquotank County Census lists the members of the immediate family:

Alfred Turner, age 31, male, mulatto (farmhand)
Mary Turner, age 22, female, mulatto
Margaret Turner, age 19, female, mulatto (domestic)
Sarah Turner, age 17, female, mulatto (domestic)
Rooks Turner, age 16, male, mulatto (farmhand)
Eliza Turner, age 14, female, mulatto
Francis (Frank) Turner, age 12, male, mulatto
Elmira Turner, age 9, female, mulatto
Trecia Robins, age 80, female, mulatto
Moses Overton, age 17, male, black

(1860 U.S. Census, Pasquotank County, N.C., 76).

The census does not account for the three children Lorenzo Dow Turner identified as John, Isaiah, and Elisha. They were among the older siblings. By 1860 two of them may have moved to another county or died. Elisha appears in the 1880 North Carolina Federal Census as the forty-eight-year-old brother of Rooks residing in the household of Rooks and his wife, Elizabeth (1880 U.S. Census for North Carolina, Pasquotank County, Roll 79-976, 3358, District 109, Image 0396). Turner indicated that he had no information about Margaret (age nineteen in 1860) and that Alfred and Elisha had no children (Personal Collection of Lois Turner Williams, Chicago, Ill.).

17. Jeffrey J. Crow, Paul D. Escott, and Flora J. Hatley, *A History of African Americans in North Carolina* (Raleigh: Division of Archives and History, North Carolina Department of Cultural Resources, 1992), 84–85.

2. Rooks Turner: 1844–1926

1. Lorenzo Dow Turner, "Rooks Turner Biography," Personal Collection of Lois Turner Williams. Shortly after his father's death, Turner prepared a two-page biographical sketch on his father's life to compensate for the loss of his father's autobiography in progress. It contains details about Rooks Turner that are important to an understanding of his life and contribution.

2. Pasquotank County Office of Register of Deeds, Elizabeth City, N.C., Book 6 (1885), 572.

3. Jones, "Four Rooks Sisters," 4.

4. Turner, "Rooks Turner Biography."

5. Ibid.

6. Michele Valerie Ronnick, "Wiley Lane (1852–1855): The First Professor of Greek at Howard University," *Classical Outlook* 79, no. 3 (Spring 2002): 108–9.

7. Turner, "Rooks Turner Biography."

8. Leonard R. Ballou, *Pasquotank Pedagogues and Politicians: Early Educational Struggles* (Elizabeth City, N.C.: Elizabeth City State College, 1966), 30–31.

9. Pasquotank County, Office of Register of Deeds, Elizabeth City, N.C., Book 2 (1879), 78.

10. Frenzies A. Logan, *The Negro in North Carolina, 1876–1894* (Chapel Hill: University of North Carolina Press, 1964), 147.

11. Cited in Ballou, *Pasquotank Pedagogues and Politicians,* 34.

12. Ibid.

13. From the October 28, 1890, *North Carolinian,* reported in Ballou, *Pasquotank Pedagogues and Politicians,* 37.

14. Ibid., 58.

15. Ibid., 70.

16. Harold Harvey Murrill, "A History of the Roanoke Missionary Baptist Association 1866–1886" (master's thesis, Shaw University Divinity School, 1979), 91–92.

17. 1880 U.S. Census for North Carolina, Elizabeth City, Pasquotank County, Roll 79-976, 335B, Image 0396. The 1880 Census shows that Rooks and Elizabeth were already married. Her age is listed as nineteen. His age is erroneously listed as twenty-eight, with an estimated birth year of 1852. It is possible that Rooks chose to list himself as younger than he actually was; the actual year of his birth was 1844.

18. Lois Turner Williams, interview by author, June 22, 1989, Chicago, Ill.

19. Ibid.

20. 1900 U.S. Census for North Carolina, Elizabeth City, Pasquotank County, Roll T623 1210, 3B.

21. Charlotte Bell, interview by author, June 2, 1989, Philadelphia.

22. 1880 U.S. Census for North Carolina, Elizabeth City, Pasquotank County, Roll 79-976, 326C, Image 0377.

23. Murrill, "Roanoke Missionary Baptist Association," 92.

24. Ballou, *Pasquotank Pedagogues and Politicians,* 43.

25. Correspondence from John Green to author, September 3, 2002; Turner Questionnaire, circa 1933, from the Frazier Papers, HU.

26. Crow et al., *History of African Americans,* 96–97.

27. Pasquotank County Office of Register of Deeds, Elizabeth City, N.C., Book 8 (1886), 43.

28. Turner, "Rooks Turner Biography."

29. Pasquotank County Office of Register of Deeds, Elizabeth City, N.C., Book 13 (1892), 369–70.

30. Thomas R. Butchko, *On the Shores of the Pasquotank: The Architectural Heritage of Elizabeth City and Pasquotank County, North Carolina* (Elizabeth City, N.C.: Museum of the Albermarle, 1989), 336n191.

31. *Elizabeth City State University Strategic Plan 1998–2003* (Elizabeth City, N.C.), 2.

32. Ibid.; Ballou, *Pasquotank Pedagogues and Politicians,* 58–62; Butchko, *On the Shores of the Pasquotank,* 272.

33. Lou N. Overman and Edna M. Shannonhouse, eds., *Yearbook: Pasquotank Historical Society, Elizabeth City, North Carolina* (Baltimore: Gateway Press, 1975), 3:11.

34. Pasquotank County Office of the Register of Deeds, Elizabeth City, N.C., Book 13 (1892), 373.

35. Glenda Elizabeth Gilmore, *Gender and Jim Crow: Women and the Politics of White Supremacy in North Carolina, 1896–1920* (Chapel Hill: University of North Carolina Press, 1996), 1–2.

36. Ibid.

37. Kate Tuttle, "*Plessy v. Ferguson,*" in *Africana: The Encyclopedia of the African and African American Experience,* ed. Kwame Anthony Appiah and Henry Louis Gates Jr. (New York: Perseus Books, 1999), 1531–32.

38. Lois Turner Williams, interview by author, June 22, 1989, Chicago, Ill.

39. Pasquotank County, Office of Register of Deeds, Elizabeth City, N.C., Book 20 (1899): 588–89.

40. Turner, "Rooks Turner Biography."

41. Frederick D. Wilkinson, *Howard University Directory of Graduates 1870–1980* (White Plains, N.Y.: Bernard Harris Publishing Company, 1982), 449; Lois Turner Williams, interview by author, May 26, 1986, Chicago, Ill.; Charlotte Bell, interview by author, June 2, 1989, Philadelphia.

42. Nina H. Clarke and Lillian B. Brown, *History of the Black Public Schools of Montgomery County, Maryland—1872–1961* (New York: Vantage Press, 1978), 178–88.

43. Vinson was a twenty-eight-year-old farm laborer, born in Maryland in July 1871. His wife, Jemina, born in Maryland in February 1881, was nineteen years of age. They were the parents of a two-year-old daughter (1900 U.S. Census, Potomac District, Montgomery County, Md., #129).

44. 1900 U.S. Census, Potomac District, Montgomery County, Md., #129.

45. Richard M. Ralston, "An Independence Gift for Sierra Leone: A Krio Dictionary," *FREE: A Roosevelt University Magazine* 1, no. 1 (Spring 1962): 7; Brenda Frazier, introduction to *Folktales from Africa,* ed. Lorenzo Dow Turner Jr. (Chicago: Nyala Press, forthcoming 2007).

46. "Rockville, Md., Sept. 8—The annual institute for the colored public school teachers of Montgomery County adjourned today, after an interesting session. The programme to-day included a talk on 'School Gardens,' by Matthew M. Morton; a discussion of 'Manual Training in Rural Schools,' by Rooks Turner[,] and an address on 'How to Lengthen the School Term,' by W. B. Evans, Principal of the McKinley Manual Training School, Washington" ("Negro Teachers Conclude Session," *Washington Post,* September 9, 1905, 5).

47. Clarke and Brown, *Black Public Schools of Montgomery County,* 20–26.

48. Ibid., 26, 190.

49. Turner, "Rooks Turner Biography."

50. Personal Collection of Lois Turner Williams.

51. Jones, "Four Rooks Sisters," 5.

52. *Winton, North Carolina History* (Winton, N.C.: Hertford County Tourist Bureau, 2004).

53. 1920 U.S. Census, Montgomery County, Md., Roll 625-671, 6A, Ed. 130, Image 769.

54. Lois Turner Williams, interview by author, September 25, 2001; Sarah Turner Bowe, 1930 U.S. Census, Washington, D.C., Roll T626-293, 13A, Image 0225. By 1926 Daniel Francis (Frank) Turner was Rooks's last surviving brother (Turner, "Rooks Turner Biography").

3. Elizabeth Sessoms Freeman Turner: 1861–1931

1. Lois Turner Williams, interview by author, September 25, 2001, Chicago, Ill.

2. Turner Questionnaire, circa 1933.

3. Turner, "Elizabeth Turner Obituary, 1931," Personal Collection of Lois Turner Williams.

4. Ibid.

5. Lorenzo Dow Turner Collection, Anacostia Museum, Smithsonian Institution, Washington, D.C.

6. Turner Questionnaire, circa 1933.

7. Benjamin Griffith Brawley, "Lorenzo Dow," *Journal of Negro History* 1, no. 3 (July 1916): 265–75; Emily S. Gilman, "Lorenzo Dow," *New England Magazine* 20, no. 4 (June 1899): 411–17.

8. Lois Turner Williams, interview by author, October 2, 2003, Chicago, Ill.

9. Lorenzo Dow Turner Collection, Anacostia Museum.

10. Howard N. Rabinowitz, "A Comparative Perspective on Race Relations in Southern and Northern Cities, 1860–1900, with Special Emphasis on Raleigh," in *Black Americans in North Carolina and the South,* ed. Jeffrey J. Crow and Flora J. Hatley (Chapel Hill: University of North Carolina Press, 1984), 145.

11. Pasquotank County Office of Register of Deeds, Elizabeth City, N.C., Book 16 (1895), 116; Turner, "Elizabeth Turner Obituary, 1931."

12. Ralston, "Independence Gift," 7; Lois Turner Williams, interview by author, October 2, 2003, Chicago, Ill.

13. In 1957, when Turner and his own nuclear family visited Rockville, Maryland, he was photographed in front of the house of his youth (Lois Turner Williams, interview by author, June 22, 1989, Chicago, Ill.).

14. Wilkinson, *Howard University Directory of Graduates,* 447.

15. Elizabeth Turner's Bible in Lorenzo Dow Turner Collection, Anacostia Museum.

16. Rooks Turner Jr. postcard to Elizabeth Turner, 1911, Personal Collection of Lois Turner Williams.

17. Rooks Turner Jr. postcard to Elizabeth Freeman Turner, September 30, 1911, Personal Collection of Lois Turner Williams.

18. Rooks Turner Jr. correspondence to Elizabeth Freeman Turner, December 1911, Personal Collection of Lois Turner Williams.

19. Turner Questionnaire, circa 1933.

20. Ibid.

21. See Logan, *Negro in North Carolina,* 199. A survey of causes of deaths of African Americans in North Carolina in 1893 points out the major causes of death by disease as tuberculosis, diarrheal diseases, brain diseases, heart diseases, pneumonia, malarial fever, and typhoid fever. The immense death rate from tuberculosis resulted from "insufficient clothing during the winter months; the lack of fire wood in winter; the want of the abundance of good, nutritious food; the lack of proper care in sickness; and overcrowding in the most unhealthy parts of the towns and cities" (*North Carolina, Fifth Biennial Report of the Board of Health, 1893–1894* [Raleigh, N.C., 1894], 91, 105).

22. Lois Turner Williams, interview by author, June 22, 1989, Chicago, Ill.; Jean Evans, telephone interview by author, September 6, 2002.

23. Wilkinson, *Howard University Directory of Graduates,* 447.

24. Turner, "Rooks Turner Biography."

25. Lois Turner Williams, telephone interview by author, June 25, 2003.

26. Personal Collection of Lois Turner Williams.

27. Ibid.

28. Ibid.

29. Turner, "Obituary of Elizabeth R. Freeman Turner."

4. Childhood: 1890–1910

1. Turner's July 19, 1949, Fulbright application confirms his birth date as August 21, 1890. The 1900 U.S. Census likewise lists 1890 (Elizabeth City, Pasquotank County, N.C., Roll T62 1210, 3B). On numerous other documents Turner listed his birth year as 1893, 1894, or 1895, depending on the requirements of the situation (in Personal Collection of Lois Turner Williams). Birth certificates were not usually filed for African Americans in southern states until well into the twentieth century. Lois Turner Williams was informed of Turner's actual birth year by Arthur's third wife, Effie, after Lois and Turner had been married for some years (Lois Turner Williams, interview by author, May 26, 1986, Chicago, Ill.). As early as 1933 Turner had begun listing his birth year as 1893 (see Turner Questionnaire, circa 1933). Intellects of his era sometimes shaved years from their lives in an attempt to maintain eligibility for grants and fellowships, which until the 1960s generally limited eligibility to those fifty-five years of age or younger.

2. Brawley, "Lorenzo Dow," 265–75; Gilman, "Lorenzo Dow," 411–17.

3. Lois Turner Williams, interview by author, October 2, 2003, Chicago, Ill.

4. Ralston, "Independence Gift," 7.

5. In the tradition of the African griot, Turner relayed such stories to his sons to teach them appropriate social behavior and the importance of planning ahead. Lorenzo Turner Jr. remembers the fun and laughter generated at the dinner table whenever his father told the story of the open mouth and the apple core (from Lois Turner Williams, telephone interview by author, August 5, 2002; and Lorenzo Dow Turner Jr., telephone interview by author, January 5, 2003).

6. Turner's savings passbook, Personal Collection of Lois Turner Williams.

7. Lorenzo Dow Turner Transcript, Howard University Academy, 1906–10, Office of the General Counsel, Howard University, Washington, D.C.

8. Ralston, "Independence Gift," 7.

9. Ibid.

10. Lorenzo Dow Turner, Howard University Transcript, 1910–14, Office of the General Counsel, Howard University, Washington, D.C.

5. Howard University: 1910–1914

1. Turner Questionnaire, circa 1933.

2. See Michele Valerie Ronnick, ed., *The Autobiography of William Sanders Scarborough: An American Journey from Slavery to Scholarship* (Detroit: Wayne State University Press, 2005), 2–5.

3. While Booker T. Washington, one of the influential Howard University trustees, is known for championing industrial education and shaping Tuskegee Institute as a vocational college, it is also a matter of record that his philosophy was more nuanced than is usually suggested. In his role as a Howard University trustee, Washington advocated that the board take the steps to obtain $200,000 to be "used in proper buildings for the Medical and Allied Departments." The trustees' favorable vote on September 4, 1909, resulted in the construction of the Howard University Medical School, the first at a Historically Black College and University (HBCU). See Rayford Logan, *Howard University: The First Hundred Years* (New York: New York University Press, 1969), 156.

4. Logan, *Howard University,* 115–18, 154–56; W. E. B. Du Bois, "Of Mr. Booker T. Washington and Others," in his *The Souls of Black Folk* (New York: McClurg, 1903), 79–108; David Levering Lewis, *When Harlem Was in Vogue* (New York: Alfred A. Knopf, 1981), 6–8, 156–58; Meyer Reinhold, *Classica Americana: The Greek and Roman Heritage in the United States* (Detroit: Wayne State University Press, 1984), 35–36, 63, 72.

5. Joy James, *Transcending the Talented Tenth: Black Leaders and American Intellectuals* (New York: Routledge, 1997), 1–11.

6. Logan, *Howard University,* 50, 140; *NIKH: Howard University Yearbook,* Moorland-Spingarn Research Center, Howard University, Washington, D.C., 1914, 12–13.

7.

Courses	*Credits*
Academic Year 1910–1911	
General Inorganic Chemistry	6
English Composition	6
Elementary German	6
History of Western Europe	6
Cicero, Levy, and Latin Prose Composition	6
Plane Trigonometry	3
Spherical Trigonometry	3

Academic Year 1911–1912	
Studies in English Prose Style	3
Argumentation and Debating	6
Elementary French	6
Second-Year German	6
Commercial Law	3
International Law	3
College Algebra	3
Academic Year 1912–1913	
English Literature I	6
English Literature II	6
Scientific and Historical German	6
American History	6
General Zoology	6
Academic Year 1913–1914	
English Literature III	6
Ethics	3
Conversation and Advanced Composition	6
History of Philosophy	6
Logic	3
Political Science	6
Educational Psychology	6

(Lorenzo Dow Turner, Howard University Transcript, 1910–14)

8. Lorenzo Dow Turner, Howard University Transcript, 1910–14.

9. Lorenzo Dow Turner Collection, Africana Manuscripts 23, Melville J. Herskovits Library, Northwestern University Archives, Box 52, Folder 5 (cited hereafter as NU with box and folder locators).

10. Ibid.

11. *NIKH,* 44.

12. Lois Turner Williams, interview by author, June 14, 2000, Chicago, Ill.

13. Lorenzo Dow Turner Collection, Anacostia Museum.

14. *NIKH,* 45.

15. Lorenzo Dow Turner Passport, 1936, Personal Collection of Lois Turner Williams.

16. Lois Turner Williams, interview by author, September 25, 2001, Chicago, Ill.

17. Deborah Willis, "African American Photography," in *Africana: The Encyclopedia of the African and African American Experience,* ed. Kwame Anthony Appiah and Henry Louis Gates Jr. (New York: Perseus Books, 1999), 1519, 1683.

18. Lois Turner Williams, interview by author, June 22, 1989, Chicago, Ill. Photographs are in the Personal Collection of Lois Turner Williams.

19. Geneva Townes Turner, "Biographical Sketch," 1964, Personal Collection of Eugene Townes, Bryans Road, Md.

20. Ibid.

21. *NIKH,* 44; Lorenzo Dow Turner, Howard University Transcript, 1910–14.

22. *NIKH,* 44.

23. Ibid.

24. Ibid., 46.

25. Ibid.

26. Logan, *Howard University,* 152–53.

27. David DeCamp, foreword to *Africanisms in the Gullah Dialect,* by Lorenzo Dow Turner (Ann Arbor: University of Michigan Press, 1974), v. In his foreword to the 1974 edition, DeCamp indicates that Turner graduated from Howard University at the age of nineteen and from the University of Chicago at age thirty-one. Turner actually graduated at ages twenty-four and thirty-six, respectively.

28. Geneva Townes to Edlow Townes, August 1914, Personal Collection of Eugene Townes.

29. Minor Normal School Diploma, 1916; Geneva Townes Turner, "Biographical Sketch," 1964.

6. Chicago: 1914–1915

1. In the 1940s, by the time the Turners made Chicago their permanent home, Turner's cousin Anthony Overton was the owner of Overton's Cosmetics. The Overtons had founded their business by 1914. They were cousins on Turner's father's family line from Juley Turner, Rooks's oldest sibling, who was born in 1829 and married Jeffry Overton, born in 1798. Their twelve children, Turner's first cousins, migrated to various regions, particularly Philadelphia and Chicago. See the Turner family tree in the appendix.

2. David Anderson, "He Worked His Way through This College," *Chicago Sun Times,* May 19, 1969, 48.

3. Lois Turner Williams, interview by author, June 15, 2002, Chicago, Ill.

4. Ibid.

5. Lorenzo Dow Turner's "Harvard University Application for Admission to Candidacy for a Degree in Arts or Philosophy," February 6, 1915, Lorenzo Dow Turner File, Harvard University Archives, Pusey Library, Cambridge, Mass., UAV 161.201.10, Box 109.

6. Ibid.

7. Ibid.

7. Harvard University: 1915–1917

1. Randall Kennedy, "Introduction: Blacks and the Race Question at Harvard," in *Blacks at Harvard: A Documentary History of African American Experience at Harvard and Radcliffe,* ed. Werner Sollors, Caldwell Titcomb, and Thomas A. Underwood (New York: New York University Press, 1993), xix.

2. Ibid., xix–xxi.

3. Lorenzo Dow Turner, Harvard University Notebooks, Turner Collection, NU, Box 9, Folder 10. During various decades Harvard did not welcome African American students into its residence halls. Off-campus housing opportunities were limited as well since some "white families who rented lodgings to white students" did not rent to African Americans (Kennedy, "Introduction: Blacks and the Race Question at Harvard," xxi). Because Turner was familiar with the area as a result of his travels occasioned by his work on the steamboat, he was able to locate housing in the community. It is also likely that he could live more frugally in a rented room off campus.

4. Lois Turner Williams, interview by author, June 22, 1989, Chicago, Ill.

5. Ralston, "Independence Gift," 7.

6. Oscar Handlin, "A Small Community," in *Glimpses of the Harvard Past,* ed. Bernard Bailyn, Donald Fleming, Oscar Handlin, and Stephan Thernstrom (Cambridge, Mass.: Belknap Press of Harvard University Press, 1986), 97–113.

7. Turner Collection, NU, Box 9, Folders 1, 2, 4, 5, and 10.

8. Donald Fleming, "Some Notable Harvard Students," in *Glimpses of the Harvard Past,* 133–46.

9. Turner to President Thomas Elsa Jones of Fisk University, January 4, 1929, in Thomas Elsa Jones Collection, Fisk University Archives, Nashville, Tenn., Box 42, Folder 9 (hereafter designated as Jones Collection).

10. The courses listed with the professors who usually taught them are as follows:

Academic Year 1915–1916		
English 1	Chaucer	Profs. William Neilson and F. N. Robinson
English 3a (½ course)	Anglo Saxon (1st half)	Asst. Prof. K. G. T. Webster
English 14	The Drama in England from 1590 to 1642	Prof. George Baker
English 25 (½ course)	Anglo-Saxon Poetry	Prof. F. N. Robinson
English 67	English Composition	Prof. C. N. Greenough
Academic Year 1916–1917		
Comparative Literature 6b (½ course)		Prof. Bliss Perry
Comparative Literature 32	Lyric Poetry	Prof. Bliss Perry
English 4	Early English Literature from 1200 to 1450	Profs. G. L. Kittridge and F. N. Robinson
English 11b (½ course)	Milton (2nd half)	Asst. Prof. K. G. T. Webster
English 19 (½ course)	Historical English Grammar (2nd Half)	Prof. F. N. Robinson
English 54 (½ course)	Carlyle (1st half)	Prof. Bliss Perry
German 12a (½ course)	Gothic: Intro. to the Study of Germanic Philology (1st half)	Prof. von Jageman

(*Official Register of Harvard University, 1917,* 27–39; Lorenzo Dow Turner Transcript, 1915–17, Harvard University Archives, UAV 161. 272.5, File 1, Box 14).

11. Lorenzo Dow Turner, "Harvard Handbook, 1915–1916," Personal Collection of Lois Turner Williams.

12. Ibid.

13. Turner Collection, NU, Box 52, Folder 4.

14. The Harlem Renaissance initiated a period of cultural nationalism. The cultural nationalist philosophy maintains that for blacks to thrive as whole people in America and the Western Hemisphere, it is imperative for them to embrace their African roots, defining their own intellectual traditions and culture. In so doing, they are able to maintain a strong common identity as they participate in the American society. Simultaneously, other Americans will develop respect for the black experience because of enhanced understanding, the result being a diminution of racism and oppression. Cultural nationalists view the cultural arts as a major vehicle for fostering intercultural understanding in that as others are exposed to their beauty, variety, and vitality, attitudes toward blacks will undergo positive transformation. In short, cultural nationalists define the arts and culture as the key to both enhanced identity and societal acceptance (see Lewis, *When Harlem Was in Vogue,* 155–58).

15. Charles Wesley, *The History of Alpha Phi Alpha: A Development in College Life,* 14th ed. (Washington, D.C.: Foundation Publishers, 1981), 98. Turner's name is erroneously listed as J. D. Turner. See also the history of the Sigma Chapter maintained by the chapter at Harvard University.

16. Ibid., 15.

17. Alexa B. Henderson, *Atlanta Life Insurance Company: Guardian of Black Economic Dignity* (Tuscaloosa: University of Alabama Press, 1990); Carole Merritt, *The Herndons: An Atlanta Family* (Athens: University of Georgia Press, 2002). Atlanta Life Insurance Company was founded by Norris Herndon's father, Alonzo Herndon, in 1905. A few years after Norris Herndon's Harvard graduation, and after the 1927 death of his father, he assumed the reins of the presidency for four decades. Today the company is the leading African American stock-owned insurance company in the United States.

18. Logan, *Howard University,* 140.

19. "Profile of a Scholar: Lorenzo Dow Turner," *Negro History Bulletin* 21, no. 2 (November 1957): 26, 47.

20. The envelope of the September 16, 1919, letter from Turner to Elizabeth indicates that the letter was mailed in care of Victorine Williams of Rockville, Maryland (in Personal Collection of Lois Turner Williams).

21. Lewis, *When Harlem Was in Vogue,* 157–58.

22. According to Connie Jones, the Rooks family descendants have been well represented in professions such as medicine, law, and teaching for generations. See Connie Jones, "The Rooks Family Reunion: Famous North Carolina Family Observes Its 153st Anniversary in Old Homestead in Gates County," *Color,* March 1953, 12–17.

8. Professor Lorenzo Dow Turner: 1917–1926

1. Alain LeRoy Locke, ed., *The New Negro: An Interpretation* (New York: Albert and Charles Boni, 1925), 3.

2. Lewis, *When Harlem Was in Vogue,* 157–58.

3. Turner to Dr. Thomas Elsa Jones, January 4, 1928, Jones Collection, Box 42, Folder 9.

4. David A. Lane Jr. to Turner, April 18, 1923, Turner Collection, NU, Box 2, Folder 7.

5. Howard University Honors Day Program, December 15, 1926, Turner Collection, NU, Box 2, Folder 7.

6. Keith Gilyard, "African American Contributions to Composition Studies," *College Composition and Communication* (*CCC*) 50, no. 4 (June 1999): 626–28.

7. *Howard University Catalogue,* 1917–18 (Washington, D.C.: Howard University), 38.

8. Personal Collection of Lois Turner Williams.

9. Scott Zaluda, "Lost Voices of the Harlem Renaissance: Writing Assigned at Howard University, 1919–31," *CCC* 50, no. 2 (December 1998): 232–57.

10. Michael R. Winston, *The Howard University Department of History, 1913–1973* (Washington, D.C.: Department of History, Howard University, 1973), 51.

11. Montgomery Gregory, "A Chronology of Negro Theater," in *Plays for Negro Life: A Source Book of Native American Drama,* ed. Alain Locke and Montgomery Gregory (New York: Harper, 1927), 409–23.

12. Zaluda, "Lost Voices of the Harlem Renaissance," 232–57.

13. Logan, *Howard University,* 219.

14. Jacqueline Goggin, *Carter G. Woodson: A Life in Black History* (Baton Rouge: Louisiana State University Press, 1993), 50–51.

15. J. Stanley Durkee to Thomas Elsa Jones, March 2, 1929, Jones Collection, Box 42, Folder 9.

16. Geneva, too, shared the vision, writing a series on the source of the names for the black public schools in Washington, D.C., for the *Negro History Bulletin* and serving as coauthor of two juvenile books featuring black heroes, both published by Associated Publishers. See Elise Palmer Derricotte, Geneva Calcier Turner, and Jessie Hailstalk Roy, *Word Pictures of Great Negroes* (Washington, D.C.: Associated Publishers, 1941); and Jessie Hailstalk Roy

and Geneva Calcier Turner, *Pioneers of Long Ago* (Washington, D.C.: Associated Publishers, 1951).

17. Goggin, *Carter G. Woodson,* 355–75.

18. Ibid., 67–80.

19. Porter is the author of bibliographic articles and useful full-length bibliographies, among them *The Negro in the United States: A Selected Bibliography* (Washington, D.C.: U.S. Government Printing Office, 1970). See Dorothy Porter to Turner, April 19, 1966, Personal Collection of Lois Turner Williams.

20. Logan, *Howard University,* 188–89.

21. Nathan Huggins, *The Harlem Renaissance* (New York: Oxford University Press, 1971), 6–7.

22. Ambrose E. Gonzales, *The Black Border: Gullah Stories of the Carolina Coast* (Columbia, S.C.: The State Company, 1922); Elsie Clews Parsons, *Folklore of the Sea Islands, South Carolina* (Cambridge, Mass.: American Folklore Society, 1923); Charles Colcock Jones Jr., *Negro Myths from the Georgia Coast* (Columbia, S.C.: The State Company, 1925); DuBose Heyward, *Porgy* (New York: George H. Doran Company, 1925); DuBose Heyward, *Mamba's Daughters* (New York: Doubleday Doran, 1927); Guy B. Johnson, *Folk Culture on St. Helena Island, South Carolina* (Chapel Hill: University of North Carolina Press, 1930).

9. The University of Chicago: 1919–1926

1. Goggin, *Carter G. Woodson,* 64, 89.

2. Lorenzo Dow Turner, preface to his *Anti-Slavery Sentiment in American Literature prior to 1865* (Washington, D.C.: Association for the Study of Negro Life and History, 1929), v.

3. Richard J. Storr, *Harper's University: The Beginning—History of the University of Chicago* (Chicago: University of Chicago Press, 1966).

4. Anthony Grafton, "The Public Intellectual and the American University: Robert Morss Lovett Revisited," *American Scholar* 70, no. 4 (Autumn 2001): 45.

5. Ibid., 46–47.

6. "A Brief History," University of Chicago News Office Press Kit, 2006.

7. Werner Sollors, Caldwell Titcomb, and Thomas A. Underwood, eds., *Blacks at Harvard: A Documentary History of African-American Experience at Harvard and Radcliffe* (New York: New York University Press, 1993), 3–4.

8. "The Presidents of The University of Chicago: A Centennial View," *The University of Chicago Centennial Catalogues,* Special Collections of the University of Chicago Library, 1990.

9. Henrietta Crews Meredith, Mellie's daughter, a child of approximately nine years old, was raised by both women. After the Turners returned to Chicago in 1946, the Crews often provided child care for Turner's sons when Turner and Lois fulfilled social obligations. Over the years the two families maintained contact. On one occasion Lois painted a landscape for Henrietta. In 1970 several members of the family attended Turner's eightieth birthday party. See Lois Turner Williams, interview by author, June 15, 2002, Chicago, Ill.

10. Lorenzo Dow Turner, University of Chicago library card, 1924–25, Personal Collection of Lois Turner Williams.

11. Lois Turner Williams, interview by author, June 22, 1989, Chicago, Ill.

12. Richard Robbins, *Sidelines Activist: Charles S. Johnson and the Struggle for Civil Rights* (Jackson: University Press of Mississippi, 1996), 34. The report of the Chicago Commission on Race Relations is *The Negro in Chicago* (Chicago: University of Chicago Press, 1922).

13. Ralston, "Independence Gift," 7.

14. "Profile of a Scholar," 26, 47.

15. "Building for a Long Future: The University of Chicago and Its Donors, 1889–1930," in *The University of Chicago Centennial Catalogue,* Special Collections Research Center, University of Chicago, 1992.

16. Lorenzo Dow Turner, University of Chicago Transcript, University of Chicago Office of Registrar, Chicago, Ill., 1926.

17. Turner to Elizabeth Turner, September 16, 1919, Personal Collection of Lois Turner Williams.

18. Ibid.

19. Eugene Townes, interview by author, April 24, 2003, Washington, D.C.; Certificate of Marriage #93370, Washington, D.C., Personal Collection of Eugene Townes.

20. Geneva Townes Turner's passport of February 13, 1937, documents her height (in Personal Collection of Eugene Townes). Lorenzo Dow Turner's passport of 1936 documents his height (in Personal Collection of Lois Turner Williams). James Van Der Zee was the prominent African American photographer of the Harlem Renaissance. See Eric Bennett, "James Augustus Van Der Zee," in *Africana: The Encyclopedia of the African and African American Experience,* ed. Kwame Anthony Appiah and Henry Louis Gates Jr., 1934–35 (New York: Perseus Books, 1999).

21. 1920 U.S. Census for Washington County, Washington, D.C., Roll 625-210, 2B, Ed. 185.

22. Eugene Townes, interview by author, April 24, 2003, Washington, D.C.

23. Lorenzo Dow Turner, University of Chicago Transcript, University of Chicago Office of Registrar, Chicago, Ill., 1926.

24. Eugene Townes, telephone interview by author, November 12, 2002; Millard A. Dorsey, "Biographical Statement for Geneva Townes Turner's Retirement Dinner, June 17, 1954," in Geneva Townes Turner Collection, Moorland-Spingarn Research Center, Howard University, Washington, D.C., June 17, 1954.

25. Several of Turner's Howard University colleagues and friends from Washington, D.C., published articles in Alain Locke's *The New Negro* (1925), including Gwendolyn Bennett, Sterling Brown, and Kelly Miller at Howard; Melville Herskovits; Jessie Redmond Fauset and Angelina Grimké, who taught at the prestigious Dunbar High School in Washington, D.C.; and Georgia Douglas Johnson and Willis Richardson, both practicing writers in the Washington, D.C., community. As a literary scholar and head of the Department of English, Turner would have been a logical contributor. The absence of an article by him is most likely the result of his sense of urgency to complete his dissertation research and Ph.D. examinations. It is worth noting that Turner may have come to national public attention more than twenty years sooner than he did had he written an article for the historic volume, which has been much quoted and much cited since its release more than eighty years ago. See Locke, *New Negro,* 415–20.

26. Ralston, "Independence Gift," 7.

27. Turner, *Anti-Slavery Sentiment,* v.

28. Dr. John Manley to George E. Haynes, August 17, 1927, in Lorenzo Dow Turner Correspondences, Papers of the English Department of the University of Chicago, Joseph Regenstein Library Special Collections Research Center, Box 16, Folder 14, Chicago, Ill. Immediately after he completed his doctorate, Turner began to seek research grants. The Harman Foundation request was his first grant application of record. The purpose may have been to begin Gullah research. His request was denied.

29. C. R. Baskering to President Jones, March 29, 1929, Jones Collection, Box 42, Folder 9.

30. Rooks Turner to Metropolitan Life Insurance Company, August 16, 1924, and November 15, 1924; Metropolitan Life Insurance Company to Rooks Turner, November 28, 1924, Personal Collection of Lois Turner Williams.

31. Frederick Douglass, "The Significance of Emancipation in the West Indies: An Oration, August 2 1857," in *Frederick Douglass Papers, Series One: Speeches, Debates and Interviews,* ed. John Blassingame (New Haven, Conn.: Yale University Press, 1985), 3 (1855–63): 204.

32. "85, No Higher, Forecast for Today . . . ," *Washington Post,* July 23, 1926, 1.

33. Ibid.

34. Telegram, Geneva Turner to Turner, July 22, 1926, Personal Collection of Lois Turner Williams.

35. Telegram, Turner to Geneva Turner, July 23, 1926, Personal Collection of Lois Turner Williams.

36. Telegram, Arthur Turner to Turner, July 24, 1926, Personal Collection of Lois Turner Williams. Turner and Geneva arranged for his father's burial in Woodland Cemetery, Plot #135-A-20, Washington, D.C. The McGuire Funeral Home of 1820 Ninth Street, North West, completed the arrangements. On Saturday, July 24, Turner paid one hundred dollars toward the process. A few days later, on Tuesday, July 27, he paid the final two hundred dollars (receipts from McGuire Funeral Home to Turner, July 24 and 27, 1926, Personal Collection of Lois Turner Williams).

37. Turner Transcript, University of Chicago, 1926.

38. Turner, *Anti-Slavery Sentiment,* 153–82.

39. Ibid., 153.

40. Ralston, "Independence Gift," 8.

41. Goggin, *Carter G. Woodson,* 55, 94.

42. Ibid.

43. Carter Woodson to Turner, February 23, 1930; invoice from Woodson to Turner, February 25, 1930; Woodson to Turner, March 3, 1930, Turner Collection, NU, Box 2, Folder 7.

44. Turner, preface to *Anti-Slavery Sentiment,* v.

45. See Newberry Library Web site http://www.newberry.org/collections/africanam.html, March 20, 2006, African American Studies page.

46. Aubrey Bowser, "Book Review: Ink Turns to Blood," *New York Amsterdam News,* May 21, 1930.

47. Ibid.

48. Ibid.

49. Turner, *Anti-Slavery Sentiment,* 126.

50. Ibid., 141.

51. Turner, "Appendix," in his *Anti-Slavery Sentiment,* 123–52.

52. Arthur C. Cole, review of *Anti-Slavery Sentiment,* by Turner, *Mississippi Valley Historical Review* 17, no. 4 (1930): 624–25.

53. Eugene Townes, interview by author, April 24, 2003, Washington, D.C.

10. Howard University: Turner's Final Two Years: 1926–1928

1. *Annual Catalogue 1927–28, Howard University* (Washington, D.C., 1927), 46.

2. Ibid., 15–32.

3. Logan, *Howard University,* 250.

4. Ibid.

5. Dr. John Manley of the University of Chicago wrote to George E. Haynes of the Harmon Foundation to recommend Turner for a grant: "I can think of no better candidate for the Harmon Awards, if their purpose is to recognize and encourage the most representative young men" (John Manley to George E. Haynes, August 17, 1927, Turner Correspondences, Papers of the English Department of the University of Chicago, Joseph Regenstein Library Special Collections Research Center, Box 16, Folder 14).

6. Logan, *Howard University,* 251.

7. Ibid., 248–58.

8. *Howard University Alumni Magazine,* Winter 1937, 4–5; Logan, *Howard University,* 284–94, 338–39.

9. Logan, *Howard University,* 445–46.

11. The *Washington Sun*—A Venture in Entrepreneurship: September 1928–January 1929

1. Turner Collection, Anacostia Museum.

2. The Turner brothers organized the receipts systematically in the following categories: Deposits, Advertisements, Subscriptions, Newsboys, News Stands, Counter Sales, Payments in Stock, Miscellaneous (Cuts/Refunds), Overage in Cash.

3. Account Ledgers for *The Washington Sun,* Turner Collection, Anacostia Museum.

4. Lorenzo Dow Turner, "65,000 Spectators Line Pennsylvania Avenue Day Parade . . . ," *Washington Sun,* September 5, 1928, 1, 8.

5. Ibid.

6. Ibid., 1, 7.

7. Lorenzo Dow Turner, "The Knots," *Washington Sun,* September 5, 1928, 8.

8. Ibid.

9. Ibid., 6.

10. Account Ledgers for the *Washington Sun,* Turner Collection, Anacostia Museum.

12. Fisk University: 1929–1932

1. Joe M. Richardson, *A History of Fisk University, 1865–1946* (Tuscaloosa: University of Alabama Press, 1980), 9.

2. *Fisk University Bulletin* (April 1942): 11.

3. Ibid., 12.

4. Rodney T. Cohen, *Fisk University* (Charleston, S.C.: Arcadia Publishing, 2001), 7–8. See also Richardson, *History of Fisk University,* 118–20.

5. Richardson, *History of Fisk University,* 84.

6. Ibid., 95.

7. Ibid.

8. Ibid., 100, 110.

9. Ibid., 102–3.

10. Turner to President Thomas Elsa Jones, January 4, 1929, Jones Collection, Box 42, Folder 9.

11. Charles Wesley to Jones, March 1, 1929, Jones Collection, Box 42, Folder 9.

12. Goggin, *Carter G. Woodson,* 51–52.

13. Durkee to Jones, March 2, 1929, Jones Collection, Box 42, Folder 9.

14. Jones to President Mordecai Johnson, March 3, 1929, Jones Collection, Box 42, Folder 9.

15. Johnson to Jones, March 8, 1929, Jones Collection, Box 42, Folder 9.

16. Jones to Turner, April 3, 1929, Jones Collection, Box 42, Folder 9.

17. Turner to Jones, April 7, 1929, Jones Collection, Box 42, Folder 9.

18. Turner to Jones, July 20, 1929, Jones Collection, Box 42, Folder 9.

19. Evidence from Turner photographs; Bill of Sale from Steuart Motor Company, Sixth and New York Avenue, North West, Washington, D.C., Personal Collection of Lois Turner Williams.

20. Lorenzo Dow Turner Jr., telephone interview by author, December 22, 2002.

21. Personal Collection of Lois Turner Williams.

22. Richardson, *History of Fisk University,* 116.

23. Harry W. Greene, "The Ph.D. and the Negro," *Opportunity* 6, no. 9 (September 1928): 267–69; Harry W. Greene, "The Number of Negro Doctorates," *School and Society* 38 (September 16, 1933): 375; Lewis, *When Harlem Was in Vogue,* 158.

24. Richardson, *History of Fisk University,* 116.

25. Ibid., 117.

26. *Howard University Alumni Directory—1880–1919* (Washington, D.C.: Howard University, 1920), 147; Robbins, *Sidelines Activist,* 65.

27. Turner to Elizabeth Turner, July 9, 1929, Personal Collection of Lois Turner Williams.

28. Eugene Townes, interview by author, April 24, 2002, Washington, D.C.

29. Ibid.

30.

Name	*Relation*	*Race*	*Gender*	*Age*	*Employment*	*Marital*
Edlow A. Townes	Head	Black	Male	Age 68	Clerk U.S.Gov't	Married
Letitia P. Townes	Wife	Black	Female	Age 65	Housewife	Married
Justine O. Maloney	Daughter	Black	Female	Age 30	Teacher	Married
Geneva C. Turner	Daughter	Black	Female	Age 29	Teacher	Married
A. R. Jackson	Lodger	Black	Male	Age 33	Waiter Hotel	Single
Thomas Jerrigan	Lodger	Black	Male	Age 42	Laborer U.S. Gov't	Single
Elizabeth Turner	Lodger	Black	Female	Age 60		Widowed

(1930 U.S. Census for District of Columbia, District 77, Roll 294, 22B).
It appears that someone other than Geneva, Justine, and Elizabeth listed their ages, as each is inaccurate, based on their birth dates of record. Geneva was born in 1893, Justine in 1891, and Elizabeth in 1861, making them ages 37, 39, and 69, respectively.

31. Turner to Elizabeth Turner, January 10, 1930, Personal Collection of Lois Turner Williams.

32. Ibid.

33. Richardson, *History of Fisk University,* 119.

34. *Fisk University Bulletin* 5, no. 1 (June 1930): 82, 87–89; Personal Collection of Lois Turner Williams.

35. *Fisk University Bulletin* 5, no. 1 (June 1930): 87–89.

36. Ibid., 88–89.

37. Jean P. Evans, telephone interview by author, September 6, 2002.

38. Turner to Jones, November 8, 1930, Jones Collection, Box 42, Folder 10.

39. Goggin, *Carter G. Woodson,* 78–80.

40. President Jones to Henry Moe, November 13, 1930, Jones Collection, Box 42, Folder 10.

41. Turner to Jones, June 6, 1931, Jones Collection, Box 42, Folder 10.

42. Logan, *Howard University,* 50.

43. Ibid.

44. Mary Louise Strong, "*Readings from Negro Authors for Schools and Colleges,* by Otelia Cromwell, Lorenzo Dow Turner, and Eva B. Dykes." *Journal of Negro History* 17, no. 3 (July 1932): 384.

45. Ibid.

46. Ibid., 386.

47. "Dr. Eva Dykes Co-Author of Text Book, Book on Negro Literature," *Hilltop,* November 26, 1931, 1.

48. Turner to Robert J. Sailstad, March 20, 1943, Turner Collection, NU, Box 4, Folder 1.

49. Telegram from Zephra Turner to Turner, November 24, 1931, Personal Collection of Lois Turner Williams.

50. Nellye Turner to Turner, November 25, 1931, Personal Collection of Lois Turner Williams.

51. Ibid.

52. James Edward Reed to Turner, November 26, 1931, Personal Collection of Lois Turner Williams.

53. Telegrams, Personal Collection of Lois Turner Williams.

54. Personal Collection of Lois Turner Williams.

13. The Beginnings of Gullah Research: 1932–1942

1. Julie Tetel Andresen, *Linguistics in America, 1969–1924: A Critical History* (London: Routledge, 1990), 14–16.

2. Archibald A. Hill, "History of the Linguistic Institute," *ACLS* [American Council of Learned Societies] *Newsletter* 15, no. 3 (March 1964): 2–3.

3. Ibid.

4. Ibid.

5. Ralston, "Independence Gift," 5.

6. Ibid.

7. Lois Turner Williams, interview by author, May 26, 1986, Chicago, Ill.

8. Thomas Wentworth Higginson, *Army Life in a Black Regiment* (1870; reprint, East Lansing: Michigan State University, 1960).

9. Lorenzo Dow Turner, "Notes on the Sounds and Vocabulary of Gullah," *Publications of the American Dialect Society* 3 (May 1945): 13.

10. Turner, *Africanisms in the Gullah Dialect,* 4.

11. Peter Wood, *Black Majority: Negroes in South Carolina from 1670 through the Stono Rebellion* (New York: Alfred A. Knopf, 1974), xiv, 36.

12. Michael Montgomery, ed., *The Crucible of Carolina: Essays in the Development of Gullah Language and Culture* (Athens: University of Georgia Press, 1994), 5, 10–12; Frederic G. Cassidy, "Gullah and the Caribbean Connection," in ibid., 16–22.

13. Turner, *Africanisms in the Gullah Dialect,* 4.

14. Wood, *Black Majority,* 170; Ian F. Hancock, "A Provisional Comparison of the English-based Atlantic Creoles," *African Language Review* 8 (1969): 11.

15. H. L. Mencken, *The American Language: Supplement II* (New York: Alfred A. Knopf, 1948), 101.

16. Joey L. Dillard, *Black English: Its History and Usage in the United States* (New York: Random House, 1972), 189.

17. Raven I. McDavid Jr., review of *Africanisms in the Gullah Dialect,* by Turner, *Language* 26, no. 2 (April–June 1950): 324.

18. Turner, *Africanisms in the Gullah Dialect,* 5–8.

19. Reed Smith, *Gullah,* Bulletin of the University of South Carolina Press, No. 190 (Columbia: University of South Carolina Press, 1926).

20. Gonzales, *Black Border,* 10, 17–18.

21. H. P. Johnson, "Who Lost the Southern R?," *American Speech* 3, no. 4 (June 1928): 377–83.

22. DeCamp, foreword to *Africanisms in the Gullah Dialect,* by Turner (1974), iv.

23. George Philip Krapp, *The English Language in America* (New York: Century Company for the Modern Language Association of America, 1925), 252.

24. Lorenzo Dow Turner, "A Descriptive Grammar of the Gullah Dialect: Statement of the Project," circa 1930, Papers of the English Department, University of Chicago, Box 16, Folder 14.

25. John H. Stanfield, *Philanthropy and Jim Crow in American Social Science* (Westport, Conn.: Greenwood Press, 1985), 68; Richardson, *History of Fisk University*, 81–82, 112–13.

26. Hill, "History of the Linguistic Institute," 2–3.

27. Roland Kent, "Record of the Linguistic Institute, Third Session, July 7–August 15, 1930," *Language* 6, no. 3 (September 1931): 8–12.

28. Hans Kurath, *A Word Geography of the Eastern United States* (Ann Arbor: University of Michigan Press, 1949), v.

29. Kurath adopted the linguistic atlas project as his life work, directing it himself for thirty years. Because of three decades of work, the series of volumes known as *The Linguistic Atlas of the United States* was published. Kurath died in 1992. See also Richard Bailey, "Hans Kurath: Obituary," *Language* 68, no. 4 (December 1992): 797–808.

30. Turner to John Manley, November 14, 1930, Papers of the English Department of the University of Chicago, Joseph Regenstein Library Special Collections Research Center, Box 16, Folder 14. In Turner's "Profile of a Scholar" and his Fulbright Application (1949), he indicated that he attended the Linguistic Institute of 1931 and 1932. A range of letters from 1930 and 1931 and several of Turner's early grant applications verify that the years were 1930 and 1931.

31. Manley to Turner, November 17, 1930, Papers of the English Department of the University of Chicago, Joseph Regenstein Library Special Collections Research Center, Box 16, Folder 14.

32. Ibid.

33. Hans Kurath to Turner, December 11, 1930, Turner Collection, NU, Box 2, Folder 7.

34. Ibid.

35. "Professor Jud" was Jakob Jud, a Professor of Romance Philology from the University of Zurich. At the 1931 Linguistic Institute, he and Paul Scheuermeier of Bern "trained the prospective workers . . . ensuring up-to-date knowledge among them of the methods of German dialectology as carried out in Italy and Switzerland" (Bailey, "Hans Kurath: Obituary," 802). Jud and Scheuermeier's course was Les Problèmes de la Préparation d'un Atlas Linguistique.

36. Turner to Kurath, December 24, 1930, Turner Collection, NU, Box 2, Folder 7.

37. Ibid.

38. Turner mentioned to Dean W. T. B. Williams of Tuskegee Institute, in a letter of March 8, 1938, that he had taught at Tuskegee in the summer of 1931 (Turner to Dean W. T. B. Williams, March 8, 1938, Turner Collection, NU, Box 3, Folder 4).

39. Kent, "Record of the Linguistic Institute," 8–11.

40. Hill, "History of the Linguistic Institute," 2–3.

41. Miles L. Hanley, "Progress of the Linguistic Atlas and Plans for the Future Work of the Dialect Society," *Dialect Notes: Publications of the American Dialect Society* 6, part 3 (1931): 92–93.

42. Hill, "History of the Linguistic Institute," 2–3.

43. Harold B. Allen, "Regional Dialects, 1945–1974," *American Speech* 52, no. 3/4 (Autumn/Winter 1977): 167–68.

44. Ibid., 224.

45. Turner is the most prominent of the first cohort of five black linguists. See Wade-Lewis, "Joseph Applegate," "Beryl Loftman Bailey," "Raleigh Morgan," "Mark Hanna Watkins," and "Lorenzo Dow Turner," in *African American National Biography*, ed. Henry Louis Gates Jr. and Evelyn Higginbotham (New York: Oxford University Press, forthcoming 2008).

46. DeCamp, foreword to *Africanisms in the Gullah Dialect,* by Turner (1974), vi.

47. A. D. Parkinson to Turner, May 18, 1932, Turner Collection, NU, Box 2, Folder 7.

48. "Colorful Dialect Is Saved from Oblivion: Young Couple in Providence Has Recorded Picturesque Tongue of Islanders off South Carolina Coast," *Providence (R.I.) Evening Bulletin,* August 13, 1934.

49. Telegram, Donald Goodchild to Turner, March 5, 1932, Personal Collection of Lois Turner Williams.

50. Telegram, Turner to Geneva Turner, March 5, 1932, Personal Collection of Lois Turner Williams.

51. Goodchild to Turner, March 18, 1932, Turner Collection, NU, Box 2, Folder 7.

52. Goodchild's March 9 letter confirmed an earlier telegram stating that the Committee on Fellowships had "voted to approve your application for a grant of $1,000 in aid of research." It was the first of several grants and the beginning of a new era in linguistic history. See Goodchild to Turner, March 9, 1932; Goodchild to Turner, March 15, 1932, Turner Collection, NU, Box 2, Folder 7.

53. "Professor Studies Dialect: Lorenzo D. Turner," *Nashville Journal and Guide,* April 2, 1932.

54. See "Fisk Professor Gets Grant to Study," *Afro-American,* March 19, 1932; "English Head to Study Gullah Negro Dialect," *New York Amsterdam News,* March 30, 1932; and "Teacher to Study Dialect of Gullahs," *Washington Times,* March 22, 1932.

55. Turner to Manley, November 14, 1930, Papers of the English Department of the University of Chicago, Joseph Regenstein Library Special Collections Research Center, Box 16, Folder 14.

56. Ibid.

57. Parkinson to Turner, April 18, 1932, Turner Collection, NU, Box 2, Folder 7.

58. Ralston, "Independence Gift," 5.

59. "Magnetic Wire Recorder Preserves Running Account of Observation Flight Battle Description on Steel Wire," *Life* 15 (November 1, 1943): 49–50; David Lindsay Morton Jr., "The History of Magnetic Recording in the United States, 1888–1978" (Ph.D. diss., Georgia Institute of Technology, 1995), 340–79. In 1951 during Turner's fieldwork in Africa, he continued to utilize the wire recorder as there are references in his letters to Lois indicating his need for more wire (Turner to Lois Turner, Wednesday, May 2, 1951, Personal Collection of Lois Turner Williams). Later, when Turner returned from the field, he would have the wire recording transferred to aluminum or acetate 78-rpm recordings. Whenever possible, he commissioned duplicates of his most valuable data to ensure that they would never be lost. On some occasions he allowed other colleagues to borrow some of his field recordings.

60. Parkinson to Turner, April 18, 1932, Turner Collection, NU, Box 2, Folder 7.

61. In Turner's attempts to elicit natural speech, he applied the Linguistic Atlas approach with sensitivity to the context. William Labov would later refer to this approach as "Observer's Paradox." See William Labov, *Sociolinguistic Patterns* (Philadelphia: University of Pennsylvania Press, 1972), 61–62, 69, 209.

62. Turner to Kurath, September 4, 1934, Turner Collection, NU, Box 2, Folder 8.

63. "Colorful Dialect Is Saved from Oblivion."

64. Ibid. See also Lydia Parrish, *Slave Songs of the Georgia Sea Islands* (New York: Creative Age Press, 1942).

65. Turner, *Africanisms in the Gullah Dialect,* 308n4; Parrish, *Slave Songs of the Georgia Sea Islands,* vi, 49.

66. Turner, *Africanisms in the Gullah Dialect,* xv.

67. Kurath, *Word Geography,* v.

68. Turner, "Appendix I," in his *Africanisms in the Gullah Dialect,* 291–92; Turner to Melville Herskovits, October 4, 1942, Turner Collection, NU, Box 4, Folder 1.

69. Turner to Kurath, September 4, 1934, Turner Collection, NU, Box 2, Folder 8.

70. Raven I. McDavid Jr., William A. Kretzschmar Jr., and Gail J. Hankins, eds., *Gullah: The Linguistic Atlas of the Middle and South Atlantic States and Affiliated Projects; Basic Materials,* Microfilm Manuscripts on Cultural Anthropology 71.378, Joseph Regenstein Library, University of Chicago, 1982.

71. Personal correspondence, Michael Montgomery to author, February 17, 2005.

72. Disc 46. While the Dawley song is listed without a date, it was most likely recorded during the summer of 1933 since Turner conducted his Georgia fieldwork between June 23 and August 26, 1933. See Turner Collection, NU.

73. Turner, *Africanisms in the Gullah Dialect,* 292.

74. Joseph Opala, *The Language You Cry In,* VHS (Los Angeles: California Newsreel, 1998).

75. Ibid.

76. Ibid.

77. Turner, *Africanisms in the Gullah Dialect,* 257.

78. Ibid.

79. Ibid., 271–73.

80. Ibid., 283.

81. Ibid., 283–85.

82. Ibid.

83. Ibid., 285–89, 309.

84. Ralston, "Independence Gift," 5.

85. Lorenzo Dow Turner, "Statement of Work" for Research in Brazil, February 17, 1940, Turner Collection, NU, Box 3, Folder 7.

86. One of the presentations at the Yale session of the MLA held concurrently with that of the American Dialect Society was William F. Kamman's paper on "English Loan Words in Low German" of Dubois County, Indiana (see "Records in Gullah Heard by Linguists: Dialect of Coastal Negroes of South Carolina Is Presented at Yale Session [Unique Study Described]," *New York Times,* January 1, 1933, 16, col. 3), which would have been of special interest to Turner. See also Steven M. Benjamin and Luanne von Schneidemesser, "German Loanwords in American English: A Bibliography of Studies, 1872–1978," *American Speech* 54, no. 2 (Autumn 1979): 210–15, for a detailed bibliography of research on Pennsylvania Dutch, including articles dating to the nineteenth century, among them Lee L. Grumbine, "Provincialisms of the 'Dutch' Districts of Pennsylvania," *Transactions of the American Philological Association* (1886): Appendix17, xii–xiii; W. H. Allen, "Pennsylvania," *Dialect Notes* 4, part 2 (1914): 157–58; and Samuel S. Halderman, *Pennsylvania Dutch: A Dialect of South German with an Infusion of English* (Philadelphia: Reformed Church Publication Board, 1872).

87. Kurath to Turner, June 1, 1933; July 28, 1933; November 6, 1934, Turner Collection, NU, Box 2, Folder 8.

88. Turner, *Africanisms in the Gullah Dialect,* 12.

89. Kurath to Turner, September 6, 1932, Turner Collection, NU, Box 2, Folder 7; January 27, 1933, March 22, 1933, June 1 and June 14, 1933, July 28, 1933, November 23, 1933, ibid., Box 2, Folder 8.

90. McDavid, review of *Africanisms in the Gullah Dialect,* by Turner, 330n33.

91. Kurath to Turner, September 6, 1932, Turner Collection, NU, Box 2, Folder 7.

92. Kurath to Turner, November 6, 1934, Turner Collection, NU, Box 2, Folder 8.

93. Miles Hanley, "Progress of the Linguistic Atlas," *Dialect Notes: Publications of the American Dialect Society* 6, part 5 (1932): 281–82.

94. Miles Hanley to American Dialect Society Members, December 10, 1932, Turner Collection, NU, Box 2, Folder 7.

95. *Fisk News,* January 1933, 14.

96. Katherine Wyly Mille and Michael B. Montgomery, introduction to *Africanisms in the Gullah Dialect,* by Lorenzo Dow Turner (Columbia: University of South Carolina Press, 2002), xii.

97. "Records in Gullah Heard by Linguists," 16, col. 3.

98. David DeCamp, "Social and Geographical Factors in Jamaican Dialects," in *Proceedings of the Conference on Creole Language Studies Held at the University College of the West Indies, March 28–April 4, 1959,* ed. Robert Le Page (London: Macmillan, 1961), 61–84, quote on 82.

99. "Records in Gullah Heard by Linguists," 16, col. 3.

100. "Topics of the Times: Gullah," *New York Times,* January 2, 1933, 22, col. 5.

101. Ibid.

102. "Gullah: South Carolina Dialect Studied by Linguists," *Washington Sentinel,* January 14, 1933.

103. "Records of Strange Gullah Dialect Made for Scientists," *Pittsburgh Courier,* January 14, 1933.

104. Goodchild to Turner, April 13, 1933, Turner Collection, NU, Box 2, Folder 8.

105. Adele Abel to Turner, July 11, 1933, Turner Collection, NU, Box 2, Folder 8.

106. "Colorful Dialect Is Saved from Oblivion." By 1949, when *Africanisms in the Gullah Dialect* was published, Turner and Geneva Townes Turner had parted. Her contribution to the research that resulted in *Africanisms in the Gullah Dialect* is not acknowledged in the volume. In a letter from Turner to President Jones of Fisk University dated February 7, 1946, Turner mentioned the June 18 to September 8, 1934, session in Rhode Island in which he participated in "a series of conferences on the methodology of dialect investigation" (Turner Collection, NU, Box 4, Folder 4).

Although history is now silent on this detail, it is possible that Turner and his Fisk colleague Mark Hanna Watkins encouraged each other in the pursuit of African linguistic studies. Watkins, an anthropologist who completed a doctorate at the University of Chicago in 1933, joined the Fisk faculty in the fall of 1934 and remained until 1947. Watkins was the second known African American to receive a Ph.D. in anthropology and the first American to write a grammar of an African language: *A Grammar of Chichewa: A Language of Central Africa* (1933) (Washington, D.C.: Linguistic Society of America, 1937). See Margaret Wade-Lewis, "A Bridge over Many Waters: Mark Hanna Watkins, Linguistic Anthropologist," *Dialectical Anthropology* 28, no. 2 (June 2004): 147–202; and Regna Darnell, *Edward Sapir: Linguist, Anthropologist, Humanist* (Los Angeles: University of California Press, 1990). Laurence Foster was the first known African American anthropologist with a Ph.D., which was from the University of Pennsylvania in 1931. See Yolanda Moses, "Laurence Foster: Anthropologist, Scholar, and Social Advocate," in *African American Pioneers in Anthropology,* ed. Ira E. Harrison and Faye V. Harrison (Urbana: University of Illinois Press, 1999), 87–88.

107. "Colorful Dialect Is Saved from Oblivion."

108. "Linguists from All Parts of Country Meet at Brown University," *Providence Journal,* July 21, 1934.

109. Hans Kurath, "Progress of the Linguistic Atlas," *Dialect Notes* 6, no. 8 (July 1934): 392.

110. Turner to Waldo Leland, December 3, 1934, Turner Collection, NU, Box 2, Folder 8.

111. Eric Hamp, "Guy Summer Lowman, Jr.," in *Lexicon Grammaticorum: Who's Who in the History of World Linguistics,* ed. Harro Stammerjohan (Tübingen: Max Niemeyer, 1996), 588.

112. Turner to Leland, December 3, 1934, Turner Collection, NU, Box 2, Folder 8.

113. Ibid.

114. Turner, "Statement of Work" for Research in Brazil, February 17, 1940, Turner Collection, NU, Box 3, Folder 8.

115. Professor Luella F. Norwood of Spelman College was a representative of the Association of Teachers of English in Negro Colleges. Turner notified her on March 10, 1938, that he expected to spend ten days on the Sea Islands from March 13 to 23, 1938. On March 12, 1938, Turner informed Dean Alrutheus A. Taylor of Fisk of his plans to have other faculty members and graduate students teach his classes. See Turner to Luella F. Norwood, March 10, 1938; Turner to Alrutheus A. Taylor, March 12, 1938, Turner Collection, NU, Box 3, Folder 4.

116. Turner to Herskovits, October 4, 1942, Turner Collection, NU, Box 4, Folder 1.

117. "Records in Gullah Heard by Linguists," 16, col. 3. Turner joined the American Dialect Society in 1931 but apparently not as its first African American member. According to Ronnick, that distinction belongs to William Sanders Scarborough, a scholar of Greek and Latin, who joined in the 1880s and whose published textbook was *First Lessons in Greek* (1881). During his productive career as a faculty member and president of Wilberforce University (1908–20), Scarborough published articles on linguistic/language issues. See Ronnick, *Autobiography of William Sanders Scarborough;* and Ronnick, "William Sanders Scarborough: The First African American Member of the Modern Language Association," *PMLA Journal* 115, no. 7 (December 2000): 1787–93.

118. Turner's summers between 1932 and 1942 can be accounted for as follows. He spent April to September 1932 initiating the data collection on the Sea Islands. He and Geneva spent the summer of 1933 together in fieldwork on the Sea Islands and the summer of 1934 at Brown University. During summer 1935 Turner taught at Alcorn College in Mississippi, after which he collected data on Louisiana creole around New Orleans in order to compare Afro-French creole with an Afro-English version (Gullah). He spent the summer of 1936 in preparation for his 1936–37 year at the University of London. In the summer of 1937, he interviewed continental Africans in London and Paris before returning to the United States. In the summer of 1938, he pursued romantic interests. In the summer of 1939, he returned to the Sea Islands for further data collection; his second wife, Lois, and her mother, Myrtle, accompanied him. In the summers of 1940 and 1941, Turner collected data among Yoruba speakers in Brazil. In the summer of 1942, when he collected data in the Sea Islands for the final time, he was convinced that his corpus contained all the evidence he needed to construct a strong case for his African retentions hypothesis.

119. Lorenzo Dow Turner, "Linguistic Research and African Survivals," in *The Inter-disciplinary Aspects of Negro Studies,* ed. Melville J. Herskovits, special issue, *American Council of Learned Societies Bulletin* 32 (September 1941): 69–70.

120. Turner, "Linguistic Research and African Survivals," 71.

121. Ibid.

122. Ibid.

123. Ibid., 71–72.

124. Ibid., 72.

125. Ibid., 73.

126. Ibid.

127. Ibid., 76–77.

128. The typewritten versions of the "Slave Narratives" are available as Microfilm 1448 in the Van Pelt Library, Washington, D.C.

129. Kurath, *Word Geography,* 6.

130. Raven I. McDavid and Lawrence M. Davis, "The Dialects of Negro Americans," in *Studies in Linguistics in Honor of George L. Trager,* ed. M. Estellie Smith (The Hague: Mouton, 1972), 303–12.

131. Michael Montgomery and Guy Bailey, eds., *Language Variety in the South: Perspectives in Black and White* (Tuscaloosa: University of Alabama Press, 1986), 8–9.

132. See Walter Wolfram, "The Relationship of White Southern Speech to Vernacular Black English," *Language* 50, no. 3 (September 1974): 498–527; Walter Wolfram and Donna Christianson, *Sociolinguistics in Appalachian Dialects* (Washington, D.C.: Center for Applied Linguistics, 1976); Ralph W. Fasold et al., "Are Black and White Vernaculars Diverging?," papers from the NWAVE XIV Panel Discussion, *American Speech* 62, no. 1 (Spring 1987): 3–80.

133. Turner, "Notes on the Sound and Vocabulary of Gullah," 13–28, esp. 18–23.

134. Ibid., 23–27.

135. Ibid., 13–28.

136. Lorenzo Dow Turner, "Problems Confronting the Investigator of Gullah," *Publications of the American Dialect Society* 9 (November 1948): 74–84.

137. Ibid.

138. Ibid.

139. Joseph Greenberg, *Essays in Linguistics* (Chicago: University of Chicago Press, 1957), 45.

140. Turner, *Africanisms in the Gullah Dialect,* 31–208.

141. Mille and Montgomery, introduction to *Africanisms in the Gullah Dialect,* by Turner, liii*n*40. See also John Reinecke, "Marginal Language: A Sociological Survey of the Creole Languages," 2 vols. (Ph.D. diss., Yale University, 1937).

142. Turner, *Africanisms in the Gullah Dialect,* v.

143. Ibid., 219–38.

144. See Stow Persons, ed., *Ethnic Studies at Chicago—1905–45* (Urbana: University of Illinois, 1987); and James B. McKee, *Sociology and the Race Problem: The Failure of a Perspective* (Urbana: University of Illinois Press, 1993).

145. *Fisk University Brochure on African Studies,* 1943, Turner Collection, NU, Box 18, Folder 5; Robbins, *Sidelines Activist,* 32–34.

146. E. Franklin Frazier, a committed proponent of "the Chicago School" for his entire professional career, was, like Turner, a graduate of the University of Chicago. Their interactions were more than casual (see chap. 16).

147. Turner to Jones, July 4, 1935, Jones Collection, Box 42, Folder 10.

148. Discs 127–36, Turner Collection, NU.

149. In the past fifty years, Turner's insistence on studying stigmatized creoles and bringing them into the center of linguistic interest has born much fruit. For a treatment of research since *Africanisms in the Gullah Dialect,* see epilogue.

14. The University of London: 1936–1937

1. C. H. Phillips, *The School of Oriental and African Studies University of London 1917–1967: An Introduction* (London: School of Oriental and African Studies, n.d.), 24.

2. Ralston, "Independence Gift," 6.

3. *Report of the Governing Body and Statement of Accounts for the Year Ending July 31, 1932, School of Oriental Studies, London Institution* (London: Waterlow and Sons, 1932), 7.

4. The donor organizations often were corporations and government offices, among them Barclay's Bank, the Corporation of the City of London, the Standard Bank of South Africa and the United Africa Company, the British and Foreign Bible Society, the Bibliothèque Égyptienne of Cairo, the Cloth Worker's Company, La Société Royale de Géographie, the Foreign Office, the governor of the Gold Coast, the Harvard Yenching Institute, the Institute of Historical Research, and the London School of Economics (*Report of the Governing Body* [1932], 13–15).

5. Turner to Jones, February 7, 1936, Turner Collection, NU, Box 3, Folder 2.

6. Turner's assignment was three courses—S103: Composition and Rhetoric (3 credits) at 10:00 A.M.; S208: Survey of American Literature from William Cullen Bryant to Walt Whitman (3 credits) at 1:30 P.M.; S209: Negro Poets from Phillis Wheatley to the Present (3 credits) at 9:30 A.M. (Turner Collection, NU, Box 2, Folder 1).

7. Turner to Jones, July 4, 1935, Jones Collection, Box 42, Folder 10.

8. In December 1935 Moe contacted Turner requesting three additional copies of his "Plan of Work." On January 6, 1936, Moe thanked Turner for the copies. On February 19, 1936, he contacted Turner again, this time requesting copies of his publications. Turner sent an unpublished Gullah manuscript a week later on February 24. On February 27, 1936, Moe acknowledged its receipt. On March 13, 1936, he returned Turner's materials. See Turner to Moe, Fall 1935, Moe to Turner, December 1935, Turner Collection, NU, Box 3, Folder 1; Moe to Turner, January 6, 1936, Moe to Turner, February 19, 1936, Moe to Turner, February 27, 1936, Moe to Turner, March 13, 1936, Moe to Turner, March 14, 1936, Moe to Turner, March 30, 1936, ibid., Box 3, Folder 2).

9. Moe to Turner, March 30, 1936, Turner Collection, NU, Box 3, Folder 2. See also Stanfield, *Philanthropy and Jim Crow,* 8.

10. Hurston did not disappoint the Guggenheim Foundation. Her research funded by the grant led to a trip to Haiti and Jamaica, to exploration of Afro-Caribbean folk life and spiritual beliefs, and to the publication of *Mules and Men* (Philadelphia: Lippincott, 1935), as well as *Tell My Horse* (Philadelphia: Lippincott, 1938), a book of Caribbean folktales. She was one of the earliest African Americans to be awarded a Guggenheim Fellowship. The first, in 1925, was Isaac Fisher, a faculty member at Fisk University, for a study of race relations outside the United States. See Richardson, *History of Fisk University,* 102.

11. Goggin, *Carter G. Woodson,* 80.

12. Turner to Leland, March 30, 1936, Turner Collection, NU, Box 3, Folder 2.

13. Turner to Jones, April 6, 1936, Turner Collection, NU, Box 3, Folder 2.

14. Bailey, "Hans Kurath: Obituary," 803.

15. Guy Summer Lowman to Turner, early 1936, Turner Collection, NU, Box 3, Folder 2.

16. Turner to Lowman, June 21, 1936, Personal Collection of Lois Turner Williams.

17. Ibid.

18. Turner to Herskovits, September 30, 1936, Turner Collection, NU, Box 3, Folder 3.

19. *Report of the Governing Body* (1932), 5–6.

20. Ibid.

21. Turner to G. W. Rossetti, August 11, 1936, Personal Collection of Lois Turner Williams.

22. Ibid.

23. "Profile of a Scholar," 26, 47.

24. Leland to Turner, August 21, 1936, Personal Collection of Lois Turner Williams.

25. Leland to Turner, August 21, 1936; Waldo Leland, "To Whom It May Concern," August 21, 1936, Personal Collection of Lois Turner Williams.

26. Ibid.

27. Kurath to Firth, August 29, 1936, Personal Collection of Lois Turner Williams.

28. Ibid.

29. Letters and Forms re: Turner's 1936 University of London enrollment, Personal Collection of Lois Turner Williams.

30. Turner to Herskovits, September 9, 1936, Turner Collection, NU, Box 3, Folder 3.

31. Ibid.

32. Herskovits to Turner, September 23, 1936, Turner Collection, NU, Box 3, Folder 3.

33. Ibid.

34. Ibid.

35. Turner to Herskovits, September 30, 1936, Turner Collection, NU, Box 3, Folder 3.

36. Personal Collection of Lois Turner Williams.

37. Receipts to Turner from the University of London, Fall 1936, Personal Collection of Lois Turner Williams.

38. See Louis Nnamdi Oraka, *The Foundations of Igbo Studies* (Onitsha, Nigeria: University Publishing Company, 1983), 32–35.

39. Ibid.

40. "Proposal by Lorenzo Turner for a Study of Speech in Brazil," January 1940, 1, Turner Collection, NU, Box 3, Folder 7.

41. Turner to Jones, November 15, 1936, Jones Collection, Box 42, Folder 10.

42. Ibid.

43. Ibid.

44. Ibid.

45. Jones to Turner, December 18, 1934 [*sic*], Jones Collection, Box 42, Folder 10.

46. W. Ofari Atta to Turner, March 18, 1937, Turner Collection, NU, Box 3, Folder 3.

47. Turner to Jones, November 15, 1936, Jones Collection, Box 42, Folder 10.

48. Ralston, "Independence Gift," 6; Howard Cohen, "Lorenzo Turner: Professor, Linguist, Author," *Oracle* (Roosevelt University) 1, no. 10 (December 1962): 2.

49. Turner to Jones, November 15, 1936, Jones Collection, Box 42, Folder 10; Lorenzo Dow Turner, "Statement of Work" for Research in Brazil, February 17, 1940, Turner Collection, NU, Box 3, Folder 7.

50. Cohen, "Lorenzo Turner," 2; Ralston, "Independence Gift," 6.

51. See Martin Duberman, *Paul Robeson: A Biography* (New York: New Press, 1989), 169–70, 623.

52. Ibid.

53. Paul Robeson, "The Culture of the Negro," *Spectator* (London), June 15, 1934, 916–17.

54. *SOAS* [School of Oriental and African Studies] *Alumni Newsletter,* 17 (Winter 1998): 15.

55. Students numbering 122 were studying Phonetics and Linguistics. Of the latter group, 29 were enrolled in Swahili, 1 in Yoruba, and 1 in Yao. By 1928, "There [had] been a considerable increase in the number of students for African languages generally, the total number being 111." See *Report of the Governing Body and Statement of Accounts, School of Oriental Studies, London Institution (University of London)* (Hertford: Stephen Austin and Sons, Ltd., 1928), 6.

56. *Report of the Governing Body* (1932), 7; *Report of the Governing Body and Statement of Accounts for the Year Ending 31st July, 1936, School of Oriental Studies, London Institution* (Hertford: Stephen Austin and Sons, Ltd., 1936), 13–15.

57. Eugene Townes lived with Mrs. Harvey, a care giver of whom he has fond memories. Her residence was at 437 Manhattan Avenue. Justine lived elsewhere in New York. See Eugene Townes, interview by author, April 24, 2003, Washington, D.C.

58. European Scrapbook of Geneva Turner, 1937, in Geneva Townes Turner Collection.

59. Ibid.

60. Ibid.

61. During the eighteen years of their marriage, there had also been lengthy absences necessitated by Turner's career trajectory. Turner had spent the summers of 1919, 1920 (Geneva accompanied him in 1920), and 1922; the academic year 1924–25; and summer 1926 at the University Chicago in pursuit of his doctorate. He had spent the seven academic years from 1929 to 1936 in Nashville teaching at Fisk University. He had spent April to September 1932 on the Sea Islands, the summer of 1935 in Louisiana teaching summer school and collecting data, and the entire academic year 1936–37 at the University of London.

The now fashionable long-distance lifestyle of the American jet-set couple has been a historic reality for black families since 1619 and the beginning of African enslavement. It continued after freedom in 1865 because of the distribution of employment opportunities in cities and rural areas for African American men and women of all social classes. In large measure, the social conditions causing black married couples to reside in separate cities has for generations resulted in a higher rate of dissolution of black marriages than of white ones. See Lawrence Gary, "A Social Profile," in *Black Men,* ed. Gary (Beverly Hills, Calif.: Sage Publications, 1981), 21–45; and Robert Staples, "Race and Marital Status: An Overview," in *Black Families,* ed. Harriette Pipes McAdoo (Beverly Hills, Calif.: Sage Publications, 1981), 175.

15. Lois Gwendolyn Morton: 1918–1938

1. Bill of Sale, Steuart Motor Company, Washington, D.C., Personal Collection of Lois Turner Williams; Lorenzo Dow Turner Jr., telephone interview by author, December 22, 2002.

2. Lois Turner Williams, interview by author, June 15, 2002, Chicago, Ill.

3. Kalibala subsequently returned to the United States to join the faculty of Lincoln University in Missouri. After the founding of the United Nations, he joined its staff as area specialist in the trustee department. See Lois Turner Williams, interview by author, January 15, 2003, and October 1, 2003, Chicago, Ill. See also "Contributors," *Midwest Journal* 1 (Winter 1948): iii.

4. Lois Turner Williams, interview by author, June 15, 2002, Chicago, Ill.

5. Ibid.

6. Yerby is the author of popular historical novels. See Bruce A. Glasrud and Laurie Champion, "The Fishes and the Poet's Hands: Frank Yerby, a Black Author in White America," *Journal of American and Comparative Cultures* 23, no. 4 (Winter 2000): 15–21.

7. Lois Turner Williams, interview by author, June 15, 2002, Chicago, Ill.

8. Lois Morton to Turner, circa Easter 1938, Personal Collection of Lois Turner Williams.

9. Eugene Townes, interview by author, April 24, 2003, Washington, D.C.

10. Ibid.; Geneva Townes Turner, "Biographical Statement," circa 1964, Personal Collection of Eugene Townes.

11. Paid and unpaid leaves of absence with guaranteed return for women became legal as a result of Title VII amended (the Pregnancy Discrimination Act in 1978). See Herma H. Kay, *Sex-Based Discrimination: Text, Cases and Materials* (St. Paul, Minn.: West Publishing Company, 1981), 494–95.

12. Eugene Townes, interview by author, April 24, 2003, Washington, D.C.; telegram from Geneva Townes Turner to Turner, November 2, 1967, Personal Collection of Lois Turner Williams.

13. Lois Turner Williams, interview by author, January 15, 2003, Chicago, Ill.

14. Telegram from Morton to Turner, April 10, 1938, Turner Collection, NU, Box 3, Folder 4.

15. Over the years, Turner and Geneva continued to correspond, exchange photographs, and communicate about the house at 1621 S Street, North West, which they owned jointly until 1967, when Geneva sought a loan utilizing the house as collateral. The purpose was to gain funds so that Eugene Townes, married by then and the father of three daughters, could acquire funds to purchase his own residence.

According to Eugene Townes, Geneva never spoke of the divorce. In fact, he learned of it on one occasion when he inquired about the absence of Turner from their lives during holidays. As a child, he remembered a period when Turner had come and "stayed awhile," perhaps during intersession of December 1937–January 1938 as Turner and Geneva were negotiating the divorce. The divorce was initiated when Townes was five years old. He was in high school or the military when he inquired and learned of it. See Eugene Townes, telephone conversation with author, November 12, 2002.

According to an October 16, 1976, letter from Geneva Turner to Julian B. Wilkins, the attorney handling Turner's estate after Turner's demise, Geneva and Turner were civil when she visited Nashville to confer over the divorce papers. See letter from Julian B. Wilkins to Geneva Turner, September 29, 1976, and letter from Geneva Turner to Wilkins, October 16, 1976, Personal Collection of Eugene Townes; telegram from Geneva Turner to Turner, November 2, 1967, and letter from Turner to Geneva Turner, November 5, 1967, Personal Collection of Lois Turner Williams.

After 1938 Geneva did not remarry. She taught public school until her retirement in 1954, after which she led an active life as a board member and contributor to the *Negro History Bulletin,* the clerk at the Nineteenth Street Baptist Church, and a member of Zeta Phi Beta Sorority. One of her most important roles was as the moving force behind the Washington Conservatory of Music and School of Expression, an African American school of the arts, for which she served as a member of the board of trustees and then as president. See "Geneva Turner," in *Who's Who among Black Americans* (Northbrook, Ill.: Who's Who among Black Americans Inc. Publishing Company), 1:631. She died June 10, 1983, in a retirement home in Washington, D.C., just weeks short of her ninetieth birthday (Geneva Townes Turner, "Death Certificate," Washington, D.C., Personal Collection of Eugene Townes).

16. Lois Turner Williams, interview by author, June 15, 2002, Chicago, Ill.

17. Ibid.

18. Ibid.

19. Ibid.

20. Richardson, *History of Fisk University,* 117–18.

21. "Miss Lois Gwendolyn Morton Received Her Master of Arts Degree in English from Fisk University," *Pittsburgh Courier,* July 9, 1938, 1. During the heyday of the independent black newspapers, between the 1920s and the 1960s, some papers maintained bureau offices and impressive circulations in large cities in states such as Florida, Kentucky, and Illinois. The *Pittsburgh Courier* was among them.

22. Lois Turner Williams, interview by author, January 15, 2003, Chicago, Ill.

23. Lois Turner Williams, interviews by author, June 15, 2002, and January 15, 2003, Chicago, Ill.

24. Ibid.

25. Ibid.

26. "Miss Morton in Pretty Marriage to Fisk Instructor," *Louisville Defender,* September 1, 1938.

27. Lois Turner Williams, interview by author, June 15, 2002, Chicago, Ill.

28. Turner Williams's basket name for Turner was Dow. See Lois Turner Williams, interview by author, June 15, 2002, Chicago, Ill.

29. Lois Turner Williams, interview by author, June 15, 2002, Chicago, Ill.

30. Ibid.

16. Yale University: Fall 1938

1. Lois Turner Williams, interview by author, June 15, 2002, Chicago, Ill.; Lorenzo Dow Turner, Deed, October 6, 1944, Personal Collection of Lois Turner Williams.

2. Wade-Lewis, "Bridge over Many Waters," 147–202; Margaret Wade-Lewis, "Mark Hanna Watkins: African American Linguistic Anthropologist," in *Histories of Anthropology Annual,* ed. Regna Darnell and Frederic W. Gleach (Lincoln: University of Nebraska Press, 2005), 1:180, 210.

3. Darnell, *Edward Sapir,* 299–30, 234.

4. Fred W. Voget, *A History of Ethnology* (New York: Holt, Rinehart and Winston, 1975), 368–69.

5. See George Wilson Pierson, *Yale: The University College—1921–1937* (New Haven, Conn.: Yale University Press, 1955), 675.

6. Darnell, *Edward Sapir,* 366–70.

7. Dell Hymes and John Fought, "American Structuralism," in *Current Trends in Linguistics,* vol. 13, *Historiography of Linguistics,* ed. Thomas Sebeok (The Hague: Mouton, 1975), 903–1176.

8. Carl F. Voegelin, "Edward Sapir," in *Portraits of Linguists: A Biographical Source Book for the History of Western Linguistics, 1746–1963,* ed. Thomas A. Sebeok (Bloomington: Indiana University Press, 1966), 2:489–92.

9. Not all of Sapir's students of African ancestry found him as supportive as Turner and Watkins did. The case of Charles Blooah, a Christianized Liberian, is one tragedy illustrating the disparity in treatment. According to Stanfield in *Philanthropy and Jim Crow,* the Laura Spelman Rockefeller Memorial, one funding agency emblematic of many, "gave scholarships only to blacks who were admitted into a graduate program in one of the social sciences. Once they were admitted, they were at the mercy of white social scientists, who used the scholarship program to get blacks to do their research, often 'dropping' their students after they had ceased to be useful." Sapir and his colleague Fay-Cooper Cole described Blooah, a Gweabo speaker from Liberia, as a "rare gem" when he arrived at the University of Chicago at their invitation, a transfer from Wooster College in Ohio. After Blooah completed his bachelor's degree in anthropology, Sapir was anxious for him to serve as a fieldworker in Liberia for George Herzog but unwilling to support his application for a fellowship to gain an advanced degree in anthropology so that he could become an independent field anthropologist. Blooah and Herzog, a musicologist, spent 1929–30 on a Rockefeller Fellowship in Liberia studying Gweabo ethnology and music. Sapir subsequently described Blooah's work with his own culture as less than satisfactory, a notion imbedded in the assumption stated by both foundation boards and academics at major research institutions that persons of African ancestry were too close to material about African culture and African diasporic culture to maintain "objectivity." Finding himself without financial support, Blooah subsequently disappeared from anthropological history. See Stanfield, *Philanthropy and Jim Crow,* 84–86. See also Darnell, *Edward Sapir,* 229–30; and Wade-Lewis, "Bridge over Many Waters," 194–95.

10. Ralston, "Independence Gift," 6.

11. *School of Fine Arts Bulletin of Yale University for the Academic Year 1938–1939,* Personal Collection of Lois Turner Williams.

12. "Mr. and Mrs. Lorenza [*sic*] D. Turner Studying at Yale," *Nashville Defender,* September 23, 1938, Jones Collection, Box 42, Folder 11.

13. *Graduate School Bulletin of Yale University for the Academic Year 1938–1939,* 66. Besides examining his Gullah data for evidence of Arabic influence, Turner also was determined to ascertain whether or not Gullah contained lexical items from Native American languages, since the African and Native American experiences often intersected in the southern states. He found none. In contrast, one researcher who documented some Africanisms in a Native American language is Daniel G. Denton, "On Certain Supposed Nanticoke Words Shown to Be of African Origin," *American Antiquarian* 9, no. 6 (1887): 350–54.

14. *School of Fine Arts Bulletin of Yale University,* 1938–1939, 10.

15. Ibid., 29–30.

16. Lois Turner Williams, interview by author, September 26, 2001, Chicago, Ill.

17. Ibid.

18. Turner to Jones, December 17, 1938, Jones Collection, Box 42, Folder 11. Turner's translation of the diary is not in print. One thirteen-page Arabic manuscript appears as Joseph Greenberg, "The Decipherment of the 'Ben-ali Diary': A Preliminary Statement," *Journal of Negro History* 25, no. 3 (July 1940): 372–75. The same manuscript is discussed in Harold Courlander, ed., "The Bilali Document," in *A Treasury of Afro-American Folklore* (New York: Crown, 1975), 289–90.

19. Turner, *Africanisms in the Gullah Dialect,* 4.

20. Turner to Jones, December 17, 1938, Jones Collection, Box 42, Folder 11; Darnell, *Edward Sapir,* 409, 414–15.

21. Darnell, *Edward Sapir,* 409, 414–15.

22. Turner to Jones, December 17, 1938, Jones Collection, Box 42, Folder 11.

23. Ibid.

24. "Education," *Newsweek,* January 9, 1939, 39.

25. Turner to Jones, December 17, 1938, Jones Collection, Box 42, Folder 11.

26. Lois Turner Williams, interview by author, January 14, 2003, Chicago, Ill.

27. Ibid.; Personal Collection of Lois Turner Williams.

28. Lois Turner Williams, interview by author, January 14, 2003, Chicago, Ill.

29. Ibid.

17. Brazil and Back: 1940–1941

1. Lorenzo Dow Turner, "Statement of Work" for Research in Brazil, February 17, 1940, Turner Collection, NU, Box 3, Folder 7.

2. Among the more recent sources are Judith Wragg Chase, *Afro-American Arts and Crafts* (New York: Van Nostrand, 1971); Robert Farris Thompson, *Flash of the Spirit* (New York: Random House, 1982); and Muriel Branch, *Fine Arts and Crafts: African American Arts* (New London, Conn.: Twenty-First Century, 2001).

3. George M. Reynolds to Turner, April 12, 1939, Turner Collection, NU, Box 3, Folder 5.

4. Turner suggested the preparation of a series of monographs when the scholarly study of African languages was in its infancy. After studying in London, he became increasingly aware of the limitations of the available scholarship, i.e., few written grammars of African languages and few scholars with depth and breath in the languages of Africa. Therefore, preparing separate monographs had not become a practical alternative. Turner subsequently treated aspects of each element in *Africanisms in the Gullah Dialect.*

5. Turner to Herskovits, May 24, 1939, Turner Collection, NU, Box 3, Folder 5.

6. Turner to Herskovits, October 17, 1939, Turner Collection, NU, Box 3, Folder 6.

7. Turner to Herskovits, October 24, 1939, Turner Collection, NU, Box 3, Folder 6.

8. Ibid.

9. Leland to Herskovits, March 6, 1940, Herskovits Collection, NU, Turner Folder, Box 25, Folder 2.

10. Ibid.

11. Ibid.

12. Herskovits to Leland, March 12, 1940, Herskovits Collection, NU, Turner Folder, Box 25, Folder 2.

13. Ibid.

14. Ibid.

15. Herskovits to Leland, March 12, 1940, Herskovits Collection, NU, Turner Folder, Box 25, Folder 2. Gilberto Freyre is the author of *Sobrados e mucambos* (São Paulo: Boizoi Books of Alfred A. Knopf, 1936) and *Casa-grande e senzala,* 3rd ed. (Rio de Janeiro: Schmidt, 1938).

16. Herskovits to Leland, March 12, 1940, Herskovits Collection, NU, Turner Folder, Box 25, Folder 2.

17. Ibid.

18. Ibid.

19. Robbins, *Sidelines Activist,* 77.

20. Turner to E. Franklin Frazier, July 9, 1940, Frazier Papers, HU, Collection 131, Folder 16.

21. Ibid.

22. Turner to Frazier, July 9, 1940, Frazier Papers, HU, Collection 131, Folder 16; David J. Hollwig, "E. Franklin Frazier's Brazil," in *Proceedings of the Conference on the Black Image in Latin American Culture,* ed. Elba Birmingham Porkornoy (Slippery Rock, Pa.: Slippery Rock State University, 1990), 2:252–69.

23. Turner to Frazier, July 9, 1940, Frazier Papers, HU, Collection 131, Folder 16.

24. Turner to Frazier, July 26, 1940, Frazier Papers, HU, Collection 131, Folder 16.

25. Ibid.

26. Inscriptions on photographs Turner collected in Brazil, Personal Collection of Lois Turner Williams.

27. Turner Inventory of Brazilian Recordings in Archives of Traditional Music, Indiana University, Bloomington.

28. Lois Turner Williams donated some of Turner's acetate discs from his research in Brazil to the Indiana University Archives of Traditional Music in 1987 and the remaining ones to the Anacostia Museum of the Smithsonian Institution in the summer of 2003.

29. Ralston, "Independence Gift," 6.

30. A substratum consists of the vestiges of languages maintained by less powerful groups as they influence the superstrate, or languages of more powerful groups when the languages reside in the same contact situation.

31. Lois Turner Williams, interview by author, January 14, 2003, Chicago, Ill.

32. Lois Turner to Turner, September 17, 1940, Personal Collection of Lois Turner Williams.

33. Ibid.

34. Turner to Lois Turner, October 14, 1940, Personal Collection of Lois Turner Williams.

35. Ibid.

36. Ibid.

37. Lois Turner to Turner, January 20, 1941, Personal Collection of Lois Turner Williams.

38. Turner to Frazier, July 9, 1940, and July 26, 1940, Frazier Papers, HU.

39. Hollwig, "E. Franklin Frazier's Brazil," 252–69.

40. Turner to Herskovits, February 4, 1941, Turner Collection, NU, Box 3, Folder 8.

41. Ibid.

42. Ibid.

43. Herskovits to Turner, February 17, 1941, Turner Collection, NU, Box 3, Folder 8.

44. Turner to Lois Turner, April 6, 1941, Personal Collection of Lois Turner Williams.

45. Ibid.

46. Turner, *Africanisms in the Gullah Dialect,* 302n29.

47. Turner Collection, Anacostia Museum.

48. Lois Turner Williams, interview by author, January 14, 2003, Chicago, Ill.

49. J. Raymundo, *O Elemento Afro-Negro na lingua Portuguesa* (Rio de Janeiro: Renascença Editora, 1933); J. Raymundo, *O Negro Brasileiro* (Rio de Janeiro: Record, 1936); Edison Carneiro, *Negros Bantús: Notas de Ethnographia Religiosa e de Folclore* (Rio de Janeiro: Editora Civilização, Brasileira, 1937); J. Ribeiro, *O Elemento Negro: História-Folclore-Linguistica* (Rio de Janeiro: Record, 1939); Nelson de Senna, *Africanos no Brasil* (Belo Horizonte, Brazil: Oficinas

Gráficas Queiroz Breyner Limitada, 1940); R. Méndonça, *A influencia Africana no Portugués do Brasil,* 3rd ed. (Porto: Livraria Figueirinhas, 1948).

50. While it is a valuable research resource, it rarely indicates specific African languages in which the semantic items occur, or their breadth of distribution in African languages, often documenting the source from a region, rather than from specific languages. In contrast, *Africanisms in the Gullah Dialect* systematically documents breadth of distribution in African languages, indicating variations in connotation, tones, and orthographic form. As important as it is, Schneider's *Dictionary* stands as one contrasting testament to the massiveness of the achievement of *Africanisms in the Gullah Dialect* forty years earlier. See John T. Schneider, *Dictionary of African Borrowings in Brazilian Portuguese* (Hamburg: Helmut Buske, 1991).

51. Lorenzo Dow Turner, "Some Contacts of Brazilian Ex-Slaves with Nigeria, West Africa," *Journal of Negro History* 27, no. 1 (January 1942): 58.

52. Ibid., 67.

53. Lorenzo Dow Turner, "The Negro in Brazil," *Chicago Jewish Forum,* 15, no. 4 (Summer 1957): 232–36.

54. Ibid., 233–34.

55. Ibid., 236.

56. Lorenzo Dow Turner, "African Survivals in the New World with Special Emphasis on the Arts," in *Africa from the Point of View of American Negro Scholars* (Paris: American Society of African Culture/*Presence Africaine,* 1958), 101–16.

57. Ibid., 116.

58. Ibid., 107; Turner Collection, Anacostia Museum.

59. Turner Collection, NU, Box 4, Folder 4.

60. "Negroes Not Naturally Submissive—Dr. L. Turner," *Louisville Defender,* June 6, 1942.

61. Ibid.

62. Ibid.

63. Richardson, *History of Fisk University,* 132–33.

64. Jones to Turner, December 28, 1936, Jones Collection, Box 42, Folder 10.

65. Ibid.

66. Richardson, *History of Fisk University,* 132–33.

67. Turner to Jones, July 23, 1941, Jones Collection, Box 42, Folder 11.

68. Ibid.

69. Ibid.

70. Jones to Turner, July 28, 1941, Jones Collection, Box 42, Folder 11.

71. Allen, "Regional Dialects," 168.

72. Hamp, "Guy Summer Lowman, Jr.," 588.

73. Sailstad to Turner, February 2, 1943; Turner to Sailstad, undated, mid-February 1943, Turner Collection, NU, Box 4, Folder 1.

74. Turner to Sailstad, March 20, 1943, Turner Collection, NU, Box 4, Folder 1.

75. Ibid.

76. "Fisk Professor Concludes Colorful Lecture Series," *Chicago Defender,* August 7, 1943.

18. Fisk University and the Founding of African Studies: 1943–1946

1. Wade-Lewis, "Bridge over Many Waters," 175–77.

2. *Fisk University Brochure on African Studies,* 1943, Turner Collection, NU, Box 18, Folder 5.

3. Ibid.

4. Founded in 1961 by President John F. Kennedy, the Peace Corps has three general goals to "make friends of strangers" through (1) helping the people of interested countries in meeting their needs for trained men and women; (2) helping to promote a better understanding

of Americans on the part of peoples served; and (3) helping promote a better understanding of other peoples on the part of all Americans. See Joseph F. Kauffman, "A Report on the Peace Corps: Training for Overseas Service," *Journal of Higher Education* 33, no.7 (October 1962): 361–66.

5. Seminar on Africa Brochure, April 14–16, 1943, Watkins Collection; *Fisk University Brochure on African Studies,* 1943, Turner Collection, NU, Box 18, Folder 5.

6. Ibid.

7. Comhaire-Sylvain was a valued contact for Turner as her thesis related to African retentions in Haitian creole was similar to his thesis related to Gullah creole. "Si l'influence du français se reconnait à beaucoup de details, celle de l'africain est, en general, preponderante. . . . Nous sommes en presence d'un français coule dan la moule dela syntax africains ou, comme on classe generalement les langues d'apres leur parente syntaxique, d'une langue ewe a vocabulaire français" (Suzanne Comhaire-Sylvain, *Le Créole haïtien: Morphologie et syntaxe* [Wetteren, Belgium: Imprimerie de Meester; Port-Au-Prince, Haiti: Chez L'Auteur, 1936], 177–78).

8. Seminar on Africa Brochure, April 14–16, 1943, Watkins Collection.

9. Lois Turner Williams, interview by author, January 15, 2003, Chicago, Ill.

10. "Society," *Louisville Defender,* July 8, 1944, 12+.

11. Lois's Singer sewing machine was manufactured in the early 1940s, before the days of planned obsolescence. She continues to utilize it for sewing projects. See Lois Turner Williams, interview by author, January 14, 2003, Chicago, Ill.

12. Lois Turner Williams, interview by author, October 1, 2003, Chicago, Ill.

13. Historically, one symbol of arrival at solid black middle-class status has been the ability of a family to maintain a comfortable existence with the husband as the sole breadwinner. Since Turner's father had insisted on having his wife, Elizabeth, serve as a full-time homemaker as long as the family was intact, Turner idealized the two-parent, male breadwinner model. Though the pattern collapsed in the case of the family of his childhood, he intended to make it work for his own nuclear family. See Lois Turner Williams, telephone interview by author, September 2, 2003; and Lois Turner Williams, interview by author, October 1, 2003, Chicago, Ill.

14. Wade-Lewis, "Bridge over Many Waters," 178–81.

15. Ibid.

16. Jones to Turner, September 29, 1944, Jones Collection, Box 42, Folder 11.

17. Jones to Turner, December 27, 1944, Jones Collection, Box 42, Folder 11.

18. Lois Turner Williams, interview by author, September 26, 2001, Chicago, Ill.

19. Robbins, *Sidelines Activist,* 67–68.

20. Ibid.

21. Ibid., 68–70.

22. Dr. Halfdan Gregerson to Thomas Elsa Jones, March 6, 1945, Personal Collection of Lois Turner Williams.

23. Turner to Daniel Wilson, April 9, 1945, Turner Collection, NU, Box 4, Folder 3.

24. Ibid.

25. Turner to Howard H. Long, June 2, 1944, Personal Collection of Lois Turner Williams.

26. Mrs. William Haygood to Turner, April 25, 1945, Turner Collection, NU, Box 4, Folder 3.

27. Fulbright Application, July 19, 1949, Turner Collection, NU, Box 2, Folder 4.

28. Gregerson to Jones, March 6, 1945; Johnson to Gregerson, March 19, 1945, Personal Collection of Lois Turner Williams. On multiple grant proposals Turner requested to have Lois serve as his collaborative researcher, as Francis Herskovits often did with Melville Herskovits.

Had that goal been accomplished, both Turners would no doubt have achieved a more voluminous publication record.

29. Roger Dorsinville to Turner, August 1, 1945, Personal Collection of Lois Turner Williams.

30. Johnson to Turner, September 18, 1945; Max Bond to Johnson, September 19, 1945, Personal Collection of Lois Turner Williams. After leaving Haiti, Watkins published "Race, Class and Caste in Haiti," *Midwest Journal* 1, no. 1 (Winter 1948): 6–15; and "The Social Role of Color in Haiti: Some Facts and Impressions," *A Monthly Summary of Events and Trends in Race Relations* 3, no. 8 (March 1946): 250–51, two of the most important social anthropological articles of his career. See Wade-Lewis, "Bridge over Many Waters."

31. Mrs. William Haygood to Turner, April 25, 1945, Turner Collection, NU, Box 4, Folder 3.

32. Cohen, "Lorenzo Turner," 2.

33. Ibid.

34. Turner to the American Philosophical Society, January 8, 1946, Turner Collection, NU, Box 4, Folder 4.

35. Turner contacted Wilt after he received a letter inviting him to join the faculty at Roosevelt College. He thanked Wilt for "helping me to obtain the appointment." See Turner to James Napier Wilt, Spring 1946, Turner Collection, NU, Box 4, Folder 4.

36. Richardson, *History of Fisk University*, 97, 132–36; Goggin, *Carter G. Woodson*, 51–52.

37. Robbins, *Sidelines Activist*, 138–39.

38. Turner to Jones, April 22, 1946, Turner Collection, NU, Box 4, Folder 4.

19. Roosevelt College and the Publication of *Africanisms in the Gullah Dialect*: 1946–1966

1. President Edward J. Sparling to Turner, March 26, 1946, Turner Collection, NU, Box 4, Folder 4.

2. Turner to Wilt, circa Spring 1946, Turner Collection, NU, Box 4, Folder 4.

3. Lois Turner Williams, interview by author, October 2, 2003, Chicago, Ill.

4. Turner to I. A. Johnson of Irvin Jacobs and Company, June 19, 1948, Personal Collection of Lois Turner Williams.

5. Lois Turner Williams, interview by author, October 2, 2003.

6. Ibid.

7. Ibid.

8. Ibid.; John Wilson to Turner, February 12, 1958, Personal Collection of Lois Turner Williams.

9. "Editorial," *Chicago Defender*, May 25, 1946. According to Theodore Cross, the first full-time faculty member at a Euro-American university was actually Richard Greener, who "was named professor of metaphysics at the University of South Carolina" in 1872. In the twentieth century Turner was apparently the first, followed by the psychologist W. Allison Davis, hired by the University of Chicago in 1947. See Theodore Cross, "The Black Faculty Count at the Nation's Most Prestigious Universities," *Journal of Blacks in Higher Education* 19 (Spring 1998): 109–10. Cross does not mention Turner as Cross's focus is on long-established universities. He lists W. Allison David as the first hired after Greener.

10. Lorenzo Dow Turner, "Roosevelt College: Democratic Haven," *Opportunity* 25 (October 1947): 223–25.

11. Ibid., 224.

12. Ibid., 225.

13. Ibid.

14. Gail Frazier-Clemons, telephone interview by author, May 28, 2002.

15. Gloria Stewart and Lois Turner Williams, interview by author, June 15, 2002, Chicago, Ill.

16. Lois Turner Williams, interview by author, October 2, 2002, Chicago, Ill.

17. "Dr. Lorenzo Turner to Speak Sunday," *Chicago Defender,* March 22, 1947.

18. "African Safari," *Visitor* (Bulletin of the First English Evangelical Church of Chicago), March 1953, 7.

19. "Dr. Lorenzo Turner Named Adult Education Lecturer," *Chicago Defender,* May 11, 1946.

20. "Meharry Alumni Association," *Chicago Defender,* May 31, 1947.

21. "Poet Wins Award," *Chicago Defender,* February 8, 1947.

22. Lorenzo Dow Turner Jr., telephone interview by author, January 5, 2003.

23. Among Turner's offerings over his twenty-year tenure were:

Culture Studies (a Three-Course Sequence)
Phonetics
A series of English Literature courses, among them Chaucer and Shakespeare
History of the English Language
Early English Literature
American Literature 1608–1860
American Literature 1860–1900
American Literature since 1890
African Linguistics—Swahili
African Linguistics—Yoruba
Krio
The Negro in American Literature
The Novel I and II
Poetry
19th Century Poetry
Journalism
The Political and Cultural Emergence of Sub-Saharan Africa

(Course materials in Turner Collection, NU, Boxes 12–15; Box 16, Folder 10; Box 17, Folder 8; Box 18, Folder 2).

24. For the most part, Turner was his own secretary, typing the examinations two or three times on the same sheet. He utilized as many sheets of carbon paper as would result in legible copies. After completing the typing, he cut each sheet apart, the result being sufficient copies for the entire class, each receiving one-third to one-half page, depending on the length of the examination.

25. Personal Collection of Lois Turner Williams.

26. Kurath to Turner, January 17, 1945, Turner Collection, NU, Box 4, Folder 2.

27. "Faculty Notes," *Progress: A Report from Roosevelt College,* 2, no. 3 (June 1948): 8.

28. Joseph Greenberg later elaborated on these criteria in *Essays in Linguistics* (Chicago: University of Chicago Press, 1957), 45. His treatment has become the standard.

29. Turner to Daniel Wilson, April 9, 1945, Turner Collection, NU, Box 4, Folder 2.

30. J. M. Cowan to Turner, February 7, 1946, Turner Collection, NU, Box 4, Folder 4.

31. Cowan to Turner, May 21, 1946, Turner Collection, NU, Box 4, Folder 4.

32. Donald Young to Turner, July 3, 1946, Turner Collection, NU, Box 4, Folder 4.

33. Ibid.

34. Elizabeth L. Titus to Turner, August 15, 1947, Personal Collection of Lois Turner Williams.

35. George Wilson, "Secretary's Report: The Detroit Meeting," *Publications of the American Dialect Society* 9 (November 1947): 85.

36. Goodchild to Turner, January 13, 1948, Turner Collection, NU, Box 4, Folder 6.

37. Turner to Goodchild, February 17, 1948, Turner Collection, NU, Box 4, Folder 6.

38. "Notification of Award" to Turner, May 18, 1948, Turner Collection, NU, Box 4, Folder 6.

39. *Africanisms in the Gullah Dialect* was first published by the University of Chicago Press and subsequently reissued by Arno Press (1969), the University of Michigan Press (1974), and the University of South Carolina Press (2002).

40. Turner to Herskovits, October 24, 1939, Turner Collection, NU, Box 3, Folder 8; Turner to Daniel Wilson, April 9, 1945, Turner Collection, NU, Box 4, Folder 3.

41. Turner, *Africanisms in the Gullah Dialect,* v.

42. Melville Herskovits, *The Myth of the Negro Past* (New York: Harper, 1941), 37, 191, 276–79, 316.

43. W. D. W., "Gullah Use of African Names Is Cited in Mencken's Volume," *Charleston Post and Courier,* August 20, 1948. Mencken had gathered his material on Turner's research from "outlines of lectures [Turner] gave before the American Dialect Society at Columbia University in Dec. 1938," from Turner's presentation for the Linguistic Club before he left Yale in Fall 1938, and from Turner's July 1943 University of Wisconsin lectures. See H. L. Mencken, *The American Language: An Inquiry into the Development of English in the United States,* Supplement I (New York: Alfred A. Knopf, 1945), 199.

44. Mille and Montgomery, introduction to *Africanisms in the Gullah Dialect,* by Turner, xxi.

45. James Ivy, review of *Africanisms in the Gullah Dialect,* by Turner, *Crisis* 57 (April 1950): 263–64.

46. Mel Most, "Negro Professor Traces Gullah and Geechee Dialects to Africa," *Charleston Post and Courier,* October 16, 1949.

47. Ibid.

48. John Bennett, "Gullah Called Mostly English, Only 100 African Words Left," *Charleston Post and Courier,* November 13, 1949.

49. Herbert Aptheker, "Africanisms in America: *Africanisms in the Gullah Dialect* by Lorenzo D. Turner," *Masses and Mainstream* 2, no. 12 (December 1949): 76–78.

50. Robert Hall, "The African Substratum in Negro English," *American Speech* 25, no. 1 (April 1950): 51–54.

51. George Wilson, review of *Africanisms in the Gullah Dialect,* by Turner, *Quarterly Journal of Speech* 36, no. 2 (April 1950): 261–62.

52. Ibid.

53. Ibid.

54. Morris Swadesh, review of *Africanisms in the Gullah Dialect,* by Turner, *Word* 7, no. 1 (April 1951): 82–84.

55. Mark Hanna Watkins, "*Africanisms in the Gullah Dialect,*" *American Anthropologist* 52, no. 2 (April–June 1950): 259; Mark Hanna Watkins, "Africanisms in New World Speech," *Journal of Negro Education* 19, no. 4 (Autumn 1950): 485–86.

56. Turner, *Africanisms in the Gullah Dialect,* 17, 246, 268; Watkins, "Africanisms in New World Speech," 486.

57. Watkins, "Africanisms in New World Speech," 486.

58. Ibid.

59. McDavid, review of *Africanisms in the Gullah Dialect,* by Turner, 326.

60. Ibid.

61. Ibid., 330.

62. They are William E. Welmers and Zellig Harris, "The Phonemes of Fanti," *Journal of the American Orientat Society* (*JOAS*) 62, no. 4 (December 1942): 318–33; Joseph H. Greenberg, "Some Problems in Hausa Phonology," *Language* 17, no. 4 (October–December 1941): 316–23; C. T. Hodge and Helen E. Hause, "Hausa Tone," *JOAS* 64, no. 2 (April–June 1944): 51–52; George L. Trager and Bernard Bloch, "The Syllabic Phonemes of English," *Language* 17, no. 3 (July–September 1941): 223–46; Bernard Bloch and George Trager, *Outline of Linguistic Analysis* (Baltimore: Linguistic Society of America, 1942); Kenneth L. Pike, *The Intonation of American English* (Ann Arbor: University of Michigan Press, 1945); R. S. Wells, "The Pitch Phonemes of English," *Language* 21, no. 1 (January–March 1945): 27–39; Eugene Nida, *Morphology: The Descriptive Analysis of Words* (Ann Arbor: University of Michigan Press, 1949); Kenneth L. Pike, *Tone Languages* (Ann Arbor: University of Michigan Press, 1948); William E. Welmers, *A Descriptive Grammar of Fanti,* Language Dissertation 39 (Baltimore: Linguistic Society of America, 1946; published as a supplement to *Language* 22, no. 3 [July–September 1946]): 1–78; and Carlton T. Hodge, *An Outline of Hausa Grammar,* Language Dissertation 41 (Baltimore: Linguistic Society of America, 1947; published as a supplement to *Language* 23, no. 4 [October–December 1947]): 1–61. McDavid was unnecessarily harsh, except in the case of Welmers and Hodge, in that Turner had well utilized his limited bibliographic space for the following categories: "Grammars and Dictionaries of African Languages," "Other Works on Africa," "Studies Related to the Slave Trade," "Works Related to the Gullah and Their Dialect," "Works on Language" (Turner included only books here), and "Works Related to Africanisms in Latin America and the Caribbean." Given Turner's thorough approach to research, he had most likely consulted these works.

63. McDavid, review of *Africanisms in the Gullah Dialect,* by Turner, 332.

64. Ibid., 329.

65. Raven I. McDavid to Turner, August 18, 1949, Turner Collection, NU, Box 4, Folder 8.

66. McDavid to Turner, November 13, 1949, Turner Collection, NU, Box 5, Folder 1.

67. McDavid to Turner, November 28, 1949, Turner Collection, NU, Box 5, Folder 1.

68. Raleigh Morgan to Turner, August 13, 1950, Turner Collection, NU, Box 5, Folder 3.

69. Turner to Morgan, September 12, 1950, Turner Collection, NU, Box 5, Folder 4.

70. Those for which she had not received duplicates were the *San Francisco Chronicle,* January 11, 1950; the *Anderson, South Carolina Mail,* December 14, 1949; the *Chicago Defender,* November 5, 1949; the *Rochester Democrat and Chronicle,* October 16, 1949; and the *Book Exchange,* November 1949. See Elizabeth Wright to Turner, May 3, 1950, Turner Collection, NU, Box 5, Folder 3.

71. L. D. Reddick to Turner, September 27, 1949, Turner Collection, NU, Box 5, Folder 1.

72. Woodson to Ralph Linton, December 28, 1949, Turner Collection, NU, Box 5, Folder 2.

73. Ibid.

74. Turner to Paul Corbett, October 3, 1949, Turner Collection, NU, Box 5, Folder 1.

75. Mille and Montgomery, introduction to *Africanisms in the Gullah Dialect,* by Turner, xxi.

76. Turner to G. James Fleming, May 11, 1949, Turner Collection, NU, Box 4, Folder 8.

77. Ibid.

78. Ibid.

79. Ibid.

80. Woodson to Turner, April 23, 1949, Carter G. Woodson Papers and Papers of the Association for the Study of Negro Life and History 1915a–1950, Lorenzo Dow Turner Letters,

Manuscript Division, Library of Congress, UPA microfilm, Reel 8, folder entitled "*Encyclopedia Africana,* Miscellaneous Correspondence."

81. Turner to Woodson, October 11, 1949, in ibid.

82. Woodson's review is "*Africanisms in Gullah Dialect* by Lorenzo D. Turner," *Journal of Negro History* 3, no. 4 (October 1949): 477–79.

83. Kate Tuttle, "William Edward Du Bois," in *Encyclopedia Africana: The Encyclopedia of the African and African American Experience,* ed. Kwame Anthony Appiah and William Henry Gates Jr. (New York: Perseus Books, 1999), 635–36.

84. Kwame Anthony Appiah and William Henry Gates Jr., eds., *Encyclopedia Africana: The Encyclopedia of the African and African American Experience* (New York: Perseus Books, 1999).

85. Rayford W. Logan to Turner, May 18, 1950, Turner Collection, NU, Box 5, Folder 3.

86. Ibid.

87. Turner to Logan, June 15, 1950, Turner Collection, NU, Box 5, Folder 3.

88. Ibid.

20. Africa at Last! 1951

1. "Fulbright Plan of Work," July 19, 1949, Turner Collection, NU, Box 2, Folder 4.

2. Ibid.

3. Ibid. Turner made significant progress toward his goals. See the translated, annotated manuscripts in the Turner Collection at the Northwestern University Archives.

4. Turner to Ida Ward, March 18, 1949, Turner Collection, NU, Box 4, Folder 7.

5. Ruth C. Sloan to Turner, March 29, 1949, Personal Collection of Lois Turner Williams.

6. Ira E. Harrison and Faye V. Harrison, eds., *African American Pioneers in Anthropology* (Urbana: University of Illinois Press, 1999), 8–9.

7. Turner to Lois Turner, January 20, 1951, Personal Collection of Lois Turner Williams.

8. Turner to Lois Turner, January 26, 1951, Personal Collection of Lois Turner Williams.

9. Turner, Entry 1, March 5, 1951, Personal Collection of Lois Turner Williams.

10. Ibid.

11. Ibid.

12. Turner to Lois Turner, March 25, 1951, Personal Collection of Lois Turner Williams.

13. Turner, Entry 2, April 4, 1951, Personal Collection of Lois Turner Williams.

14. Turner, Entry 3, April 6, 1951, Personal Collection of Lois Turner Williams.

15. Turner, Entry 4, April 8, 1951, Personal Collection of Lois Turner Williams.

16. Turner, Entry 5, April 10, 1951, Personal Collection of Lois Turner Williams.

17. Turner, Entry 6, April 20, 1951, Personal Collection of Lois Turner Williams.

18. Turner, Entry 7, April 24, 1951, Personal Collection of Lois Turner Williams.

19. Ulli Beier arrived in Nigeria in 1950 to teach English Phonetics at the then two-year University College, Ibadan. During his illustrious multidecade career in Nigeria, he founded and edited the journal *Black Orpheus,* immersed himself in Yoruba culture, edited numerous anthologies on African literature, and authored books on African art and culture. See Wole Ogundele, *Omuluabi: Ulli Beier, Yoruba Society and Culture* (Trenton, N.J.: Africa World Press, 1998).

20. Turner, Entry 8, April 26, 1951, Personal Collection of Lois Turner Williams.

21. Turner, Entry 9, April 27, 1951, Personal Collection of Lois Turner Williams.

22. Turner, Entry 10, late April 1951, Personal Collection of Lois Turner Williams.

23. Turner, Entry 11, May 3, 1951, Personal Collection of Lois Turner Williams.

24. Turner, Entry 12, May 4, 1951, Personal Collection of Lois Turner Williams.

25. Turner, Entry 13, May 8, 1951, Personal Collection of Lois Turner Williams.

26. Turner, Entry 14, May 10, 1951, Personal Collection of Lois Turner Williams.

27. Turner, Entry 15, May 11, 1951, Personal Collection of Lois Turner Williams.

28. Turner, Entry 16, May 15, 1951, Personal Collection of Lois Turner Williams.

29. Turner, Entry 17, May 17, 1951, Personal Collection of Lois Turner Williams.

30. Turner, Entry 18, May 18, 1951, Personal Collection of Lois Turner Williams.

31. Turner, Entry 19, May 21, 1951, Personal Collection of Lois Turner Williams.

32. "U.S. Profs Instilled Dream . . . ," *Jet* 28, no. 6 (October 20, 1960): 16–19. The majority of his field recordings from West Africa are housed in the Archives of Traditional Music at Indiana University, having been donated by Turner Williams in 1986 and 2003. There are 267 sound discs featuring numerous informants performing stories, proverbs, and songs and participating in discussions. They were originally recorded on wire and transferred to 78 rpm, mono. The majority are in Yoruba, the Ondo, Itsekiri and Iworo dialects; Mande (Susu, Vai); Shebro and Temne, Ewe, Igbo, Plateau Benue-Congo languages (Rukuba and Iregwe); Cross River Benue-Congo languages (Efik and Ibibio); Edo languages (Kukuruku and Ishan) and dialects (Isoko and Otwa); and Tiv. While most were recorded in Africa, some were recorded from African students in the United States.

33. Ralston, "Independence Gift," 8.

34. In 2000 Lois Turner Williams donated the majority of the art objects to the DuSable Museum in Chicago, Ill.

35. Lois Turner to Turner, August 9, 1951, Personal Collection of Lois Turner Williams.

36. Norman Sklarewitz, "Dr. Turner's African Odyssey," *Pittsburgh Courier,* August 16, 1952, "Courier Magazine Section," 3.

37. Lois Turner to Turner, August 9, 1951, Personal Collection of Lois Turner Williams.

38. Turner to Kenneth Taft, September 26, 1951, Personal Collection of Lois Turner Williams.

39. Fatima Massaquoi completed a master's degree in sociology at Fisk in 1942 while serving as an informant for Watkins's anthropology courses. She subsequently completed twenty-three courses toward a doctorate from Boston University, but when the opportunity arose to return to Liberia in 1946, she did so. There she became a professor at the University of Liberia, wrote her autobiography, and emerged as the most prominent Vai woman in Liberia. See blue books containing her unpublished autobiography, Archives of Traditional Music, Indiana University. See also Wade-Lewis, "Bridge over Many Waters," 175–76; and Massaquoi's Boston University transcript, Howard Gotlieb Archival Research Center, Boston University.

40. Lois Turner to Turner, August 9, 1951, Personal Collection of Lois Turner Williams.

41. Turner to Lois Turner, November 6, 1951, Personal Collection of Lois Turner Williams.

42. Turner to Taft, November 29, 1951, Personal Collection of Lois Turner Williams.

43. Ibid.

44. Lois Turner Williams, interview by author, October 14, 2003, Chicago, Ill.

45. Gladys Priddy, "Roosevelt College Professor Collects Native Art on Study Trips to Africa: Latin American Music Traced to Origin—Africa," *Chicago Daily Tribune,* May 1, 1952, part 5, W10; Merry O'Reilly, "Dr. Turner Returns: 20,000 Miles through West Africa," *Say: Roosevelt University Alumni Magazine* 5 (Spring 1952): 5.

46. O'Reilly, "Dr. Turner Returns," 5.

47. Ibid., 5, 13.

48. Ibid.

49. "The African Studies Program at Roosevelt University," circa 1962, Turner Collection, NU, Box 2, Folder 1; other documents in Turner Collection, NU.

50. Sklarewitz, "Dr. Turner's African Odyssey," 3.

51. "Cultural Conflicts . . . ," Lecture Series Announcement, March–April 1952, Turner Collection, NU.

52. "African Culture Institute," *Chicago Defender,* January 31, 1953, 21.

53. Program from the Hartford Seminary Foundation, Personal Collection of Lois Turner Williams.

54. Martha Munck and Catherine Kinch, "West African Rhythms Influence Modern American Music, Dance," *Forecast of the University of Michigan,* August 17, 1956, 1; "Faculty Notes," *Progress: A Report from Roosevelt University* 11, no. 1 (December 1956): 8.

55. Though Turner was anxious to return to Africa and to participate in the independence celebrations of the emerging nations, beginning with Ghana in 1958, funds did not permit him to do so. His 1951 African odyssey was his only trip to the continent. See Lois Turner Williams, interview by author, March 26, 2006.

56. "Faculty Notes," *Progress: A Report from Roosevelt University,* 11, no. 1 (December 1956): 8.

57. Turner to Christopher Hoolihan, February 19, 1964, Turner Collection, NU, Box 7, Folder 10.

58. Turner to Hoolihan, February 24, 1964, Turner Collection, NU, Box 7, Folder 10.

59. Hoolihan to Turner, July 15, 1964, Turner Collection, NU, Box 7, Folder 10.

60. Turner to Hoolihan, July 21, 1964, Turner Collection, NU, Box 7, Folder 10.

61. "Grant Proposal . . . ," circa 1955, Turner Collection, NU, Box 9, Folder 2.

62. Turner, "Annual Report," circa 1957, Turner Collection, NU, Box 9, Folder 2.

63. Turner Collection, NU, Boxes 33–42.

64. Richard Dorson to Turner, May 20, 1963, Turner Collection, NU, Box 7, Folder 8.

65. Brenda Ludwig to Turner, December 21, 1970, Turner Collection, NU, Box 8, Folder 7. During the 1960s, *Encyclopaedia Britannica* converted five of the folktales into an illustrated sound film strip recording, Series 6557K.

66. John D. Wright to Turner, January 11, 1971, Turner Collection, NU, Box 8, Folder 7.

67. Ford Foundation "Plan of Work on West African Folklore," 1956, Turner Collection, NU, Box 2, Folder 4.

68. Turner to Herskovits, May 6, 1956, Turner Collection, NU, Box 6, Folder 5.

69. "Denver's Zulu, Who Has Fought Briton and Boer, Talks of South African Affairs," *Denver Republican,* February 25, 1900, 30.

70. Lorenzo Dow Turner, "The Odyssey of a Zulu Warrior," *Journal of Negro History* 40, no. 4 (July 1955): 305–17.

71. *Bulletin,* August 22, 1963.

72. Turner, "Odyssey of a Zulu Warrior," 305–17.

73. Lorenzo Dow Turner, "The Impact of Western Education on the African's Way of Life," in *Africa Today,* ed. Charles Grove (Baltimore: Johns Hopkins University Press, 1955), 147–71.

74. Lorenzo Dow Turner, "The Role of Folklore in the Life of the Yoruba of South-western Nigeria," in *Report of the Ninth Annual Round Table Meeting on Linguistics and Language Study,* ed. William M. Austin (Washington, D.C.: Institute of Languages and Linguistics, Edmund A. Walsh School of Foreign Service, Georgetown University, 1958), 43–56.

75. Ibid., 46–48.

76. Ibid., 48–50.

77. Ibid., 52.

78. Ibid., 56.

79. Lorenzo Dow Turner, "Walt Whitman and the Negro," *Chicago Jewish Forum* 15, no. 1 (Fall 1956): 5–11.

80. Correspondence from Clarke Hine to author, September 24, 2002.

81. Turner Examination, 1966, Turner Collection, NU, Box 8, Folder 3.

21. The Peace Corps Project and Public Service: 1962–1966

1. "Fact Sheet: Sierra Leone Peace Corps Training Program 1965," Turner Collection, NU, Box 18, Folder 9.

2. See Lorenzo Dow Turner, preface to his *Krio Texts: With Grammatical Notes and Translations in English* (Chicago: Roosevelt University, 1965), 8. The first known written version of Krio appears in Florence M. Cronise and Henry W. Ward, *Cunnie Rabbit, Mr. Spider and the Other Beef: West African Folk Tales* (New York: Dutton and Company, 1903).

3. Lorenzo Dow Turner, *An Anthology of Krio Folklore and Literature: With Notes and Interlinear Translations in English* (Chicago: Roosevelt University, 1963), Turner Collection, NU, Box 37, Folder 4.

4. Turner, 1965, Turner Collection, NU, Box 37, Folder 4.

5. Julia A. Petrov to Turner, May 10, 1963, Turner Collection, NU, Box 7, Folder 8.

6. Turner to Otto Wirth, May 27, 1963, Turner Collection, NU, Box 7, Folder 8.

7. Turner Collection, NU, Box 27, Folder 4.

8. Carl Denbow to Turner, May 17, 1963, Turner Collection, NU, Box 7, Folder 8.

9. Denbow to Turner, June 11, 1963, Turner Collection, NU, Box 7, Folder 8.

10. Lois Turner Williams, interview by author, June 22, 1989, Chicago, Ill.

11. Margaret Wade-Lewis, "Lorenzo Dow Turner: Beyond Gullah Studies," *Dialectical Anthropology* 26, no. 3/4 (November 2001): 235–66.

12. "Open Solicitation Letter" from Turner to friends, circa 1951, Turner Collection, NU, Box 7, Folder 5; Lois Turner Williams, telephone interview by author, June 22, 1989.

13. Ibid.; Lois Turner Williams, interview by author, September 25, 2001, Chicago, Ill.

14. Turner to B. Hackett, March 14, 1964, Turner Collection, NU, Box 7, Folder 10.

15. Lois Turner Williams, interview by author, May 26, 1986, Chicago, Ill.

16. Turner, "Open Letter 1963," Turner Collection, NU, Box 7, Folder 10. See also Wade-Lewis, "Lorenzo Dow Turner: Beyond Gullah Studies," 253–54.

17. "Faculty Notes," *Progress: A Report from Roosevelt University* 13 (November 1958): 2.

18. "Lorenzo Dow Turner Forum Speaker," *Chicago Defender,* March 1, 1947, 6. The audience of five hundred persons gathered at the Winnetka Community Center in Winnetka, Illinois.

19. Brochure from the 1958–59 B'nai Torah Temple Forum Lecture Series, Lincoln School, Highland Park, Ill., Turner Collection, NU.

22. Relations with Colleagues—Turner and Herskovits: 1936–1963

1. Herskovits, *Myth of the Negro Past,* 37, 191, 276–79, 316.

2. Joseph E. Holloway, ed., *Africanisms in American Culture* (Bloomington: Indiana University Press, 1990), xi.

3. John A. Holm, *Pidgins and Creoles,* vol. 1, *Theory and Structure* (Cambridge: Cambridge University Press, 1988), 43.

4. Regna Darnell, *And Along Came Boas: Continuity and Revolution in American Anthropology* (Amsterdam: John Benjamins, 1998), 271.

5. E. L. Cerroni-Long, "Benign Neglect? Anthropology and the Study of Blacks in the United States," *Journal of Black Studies* 17, no. 4 (June 1987): 441.

6. Walter Jackson, "Melville Herskovits and the Search for Afro-American Culture," in *Malinowski, Rivers, Benedict and Others,* ed. George W. Stocking Jr. (Madison: University of Wisconsin Press, 1986), 96–97.

7. Ibid.

8. Ibid.

9. Ibid., 101–2.

10. Frances Shapiro Herskovits, introduction to *The New World Negro: Selected Papers in Afro American Studies by Melville J. Herskovits,* ed. Frances Shapiro Herskovits (Bloomington: Indiana University Press, 1966), vii–viii.

11. See Kevin Yelvington, "The Anthropology of Afro-Latin America and the Caribbean: Diasporic Dimensions," *Annual Review of Anthropology* 30, no. 1 (2001): 227–60; and Kevin Yelvington, "The Invention of Africa and Latin America in the Caribbean: Political Discourse and Anthropological Praxis, 1920–1940," in *Afro-Atlantic Dialogues: Anthropology in the Diaspora,* ed. Yelvington (Santa Fe, N.Mex.: School of American Research Press, 2006), 35–86.

12. See Margaret Wade-Lewis, "The Impact of the Turner/Herskovits Connection on Anthropology and Linguistics," *Dialectical Anthropology* 17, no. 4 (November 1992): 391–412.

13. Lois Turner Williams, interview by author, June 22, 1989, Chicago, Ill.

14. Herskovits to Turner, October 17, 1939, Turner Collection, NU, Box 3, Folder 7.

15. Kevin Yelvington, "Melville J. Herskovits and the Institutionalization of Afro-American Studies," presentation for the International Colloquium on Brazil, UNESCO, January 12–14, 2004, 5.

16. The 1938 *Annual Report* of the president of the Carnegie Corporation described its priorities:

> The Corporation has for some time felt the need for a general study of the Negro in the United States, not only as a guide to its own activities, but for broader reasons. It appeared to be essential that such a study be made under the direction of a person who would be free from the presuppositions and emotional charges which we all share to a greater or less degree on this subject, and the Corporation, therefore, looked outside the United States for a distinguished student of the social sciences who would be available to organize and direct the project. It is a pleasure to announce that Dr. Karl Gunnar Myrdal has been granted a leave of absence from the University of Stockholm to enable him to accept the invitation of the Trustees to undertake this work. (Melville Herskovits, "Foreword," in his *Myth of the Negro Past,* ix)

17. Yelvington, "Melville J. Herskovits and the Institutionalization of Afro-American Studies," 5. The black scholars commissioned to prepare monographs included Sterling Brown, Ralph Bunche, Allison Davis, St. Clair Drake, E. Franklin Frazier, Charles S. Johnson, Ira de A. Reid, and Doxey Wilkerson. See Stanfield, *Philanthropy and Jim Crow,* 181.

18. Turner to Herskovits, October 24, 1939, Turner Collection, NU, Box 3, Folder 7.

19. Herskovits to Turner, November 22, 1939; Turner to Herskovits, December 9, 1939, Turner Collection, NU, Box 3, Folder 7.

20. "Faculty Notes," *Progress: A Report from Roosevelt University* 3 (April 1949): 8.

21. "Faculty Notes," *Progress: A Report from Roosevelt University* 11, no. 1 (December 1956): 7.

22. "Faculty Notes," *Progress: A Report from Roosevelt University* 13 (November 1958): 2.

23. Harrison and Harrison, *African American Pioneers in Anthropology,* 28n16; Jackson, "Melville Herskovits and the Search for Afro-American Culture," 95–226. Fortunately, by the end of World War II, this perspective was giving way to the view that African Americans should also have the option to conduct fieldwork in Africa. Consequently, Johnetta Cole, one of Herskovits's students of the early 1960s and currently president of Bennett College in North Carolina, was able to collect data in Liberia. By the late 1950s and early 1960s, the Ford and Rockefeller Foundations provided funding opportunities for some African Americans to pursue in fieldwork in Africa.

24. Turner to Herskovits, November 7, 1955, Turner Collection, NU, Box 6, Folder 5; Herskovits to Turner, November 15, 1955, Turner Collection, NU, Box 6, Folder 5.

25. Turner to Herskovits, May 6, 1956, Turner Collection, NU, Box 6, Folder 5.

26. Herskovits to Turner, May 15, 1956, Turner Collection, NU, Box 6, Folder 5.

27. See the *American Council of Learned Societies Bulletin* 32 (September 1941): 85–89.

28. E. Franklin Frazier, *The Negro Family in the United States* (Chicago: University of Chicago Press, 1939), 12.

29. Frazier and Herskovits are widely viewed as belonging to competing camps as a result of the debate on their contrasting philosophies that played out in the *American Sociological Review.* The focus was their divergent analyses of the structure and status of the black family in Brazil. See E. Franklin Frazier, "The Negro Family in Bahia, Brazil," *American Sociological Review* 7, no. 4 (August 1942): 465–78; E. Franklin Frazier, "Rejoinder," *American Sociological Review* 8, no. 4 (August 1943): 402–4; and Melville Herskovits, "The Negro in Bahia, Brazil: A Problem in Method," *American Sociological Review* 8, no. 4 (August 1943): 394–404.

30. Herskovits to Turner, October 17, 1939, Turner Collection, NU, Box 3, Folder 6.

31. James W. Fernandez, "Tolerance in a Repugnant World and Other Dilemmas in the Cultural Relativism of Melville J. Herskovits," *Ethos* 18, no. 2 (June 1990): 147, 150–51.

32. Wade-Lewis, "Impact of the Turner/Herskovits Connection," 391–412; Yelvington, "Anthropology of Afro-Latin America and the Caribbean," 227–60.

33. George Eaton Simpson, *Melville J. Herskovits* (New York: Columbia University, 1973), 9; Rosemary Levy Zumwalt, *Wealth and Rebellion: Elsie Clews Parsons, Anthropologist and Folklorist* (Urbana: University of Illinois Press, 1992), 7.

34. Simpson, *Melville J. Herskovits,* 7.

35. Among their major books are Charles S. Johnson's *The Negro in American Civilization* (New York: Henry Holt, 1930) and *The Shadow of the Plantation* (Chicago: University of Chicago Press, 1934); and Frazier's *Negro Family in the United States* and *Black Bourgeoisie.*

36. Turner letters to Herskovits and Herskovits letters to Turner, Turner Collection, NU, Box 3, Folder 3.

37. Lorenzo Dow Turner, "The Negro's African Past: Review of *The Myth of the Negro Past* by Melville Herskovits," *Journal of Negro Education* 11, no. 2 (April 1942): 185–87; Lorenzo Dow Turner, review of *Dahomean Narrative: A Cross-Cultural Analysis,* by Melville J. Herskovits and Frances S. Herskovits, *Journal of Negro History* 43, no. 4 (October 1958): 321–23.

38. Fernandez, "Tolerance in a Repugnant World," 163.

39. Simpson, *Melville J. Herskovits,* 20.

40. Yelvington, "Anthropology of Afro-Latin America and the Caribbean," 227–28, 232.

41. See also Salikoko Mufwene, "The Linguistic Significance of African Proper Names," *De Nieuwe West-Indische Gids* 59, no. 3/4 (1985): 149–66; Montgomery and Bailey, *Language Variety in the South;* Pieter Muysken and Norval Smith, eds., *Substrata versus Universals in Creole Genesis* (Amsterdam: John Benjamins, 1986); Faye Vaughn-Cooke, "Lexical Diffusion: Evidence from a Decreolizing Variety of Black English," in *Language Variety in the South,* ed. Montgomery and Bailey, 101–30; Ron Butters, "Linguistic Convergence in a North Carolina Community," in *Variation in Language,* ed. K. M. Denning et al. (Stanford, Calif.: Department of Linguistics, Stanford University, 1989), 52–60; and Guy Bailey and Natalie Maynor, "The Divergence Controversy," *American Speech* 64, no. 1 (Spring 1989): 12–39.

23. Turner's Final Years: 1966–1972

1. Lois Turner Williams, interview by author, January 14, 2003, Chicago, Ill.

2. Ibid.

3. Lorenzo Dow Turner Jr., interview by author, January 15, 2003, Chicago, Ill.

4. Turner to C. Grove Haines, June 7, 1954; Haines to Turner, June 11, 1954, Turner Collection, NU, Box 6, Folder 2.

5. Lois Turner Williams, interview by author, September 25, 2001, Chicago, Ill.

6. Ibid.

7. Quotation, ibid. Dr. Berry's pioneering endoscope and other instruments are preserved in the Smithsonian Institution's National Museum of American History. Born in 1902, and receiving an M.D. from Rush Medical College at the University of Chicago, Dr. Berry is remembered for his distinguished multifaceted contributions. In the fullness of his career he was affiliated with the Michael Reese Hospital, the Provident Hospital, and the University of Illinois Medical School. In 1965–66 he served as president of the National Medical Association. Over the years he published articles on gastroenterology and other issues, and a family history/autobiography, *I Wouldn't Take Nothin' for My Journey* (1981). Like Turner, he was a social activist. See Leonidas H. Berry Papers, 1907–82, Collection MS C 423, in the United States National Library of Medicine of the National Institutes of Health, History of Medicine Division, Washington, D.C.

8. Lois Turner Williams, interview by author, October 2, 2003, Chicago, Ill.

9. Turner to President Sparling, August 30, 1960, Turner Collection, NU, Box 7, Folder 3.

10. Lois Turner Williams, interview by author, October 2, 2003, Chicago, Ill.

11. Personal Collection of Lois Turner Williams.

12. "Howard Alumni Meet," *Chicago Defender,* May 18–24, 1963.

13. Personal Collection of Lois Turner Williams.

14. Richard Waterman to Turner, April 13, 1966.

15. Ibid.

16. Turner Retirement Remarks, May 24, 1966, Personal Collection of Lois Turner Williams.

17. Ibid.

18. Ibid.

19. Lois Turner Williams, interview by author, October 2, 2003, Chicago, Ill.

20. Ibid.

21. Ibid.

22. Ibid.

23. Lois Turner Williams, interview by author, October 2, 2003, Chicago, Ill.; Death Certificate for Lorenzo Dow Turner, February 10, 1972, Chicago, Ill., Personal Collection of Lois Turner Williams.

24. Program for the "In Remembrance" Ceremony for Lorenzo Dow Turner, February 14, 1972, Chicago, Ill., Personal Collection of Lois Turner Williams.

25. "Tribute Paid to the Late Lorenzo Dow Turner," *Journal of the Chicago City Council,* February 24, 1972, 2636.

24. Conclusions

1. Herskovits to Leland, March 12, 1940, Herskovits Collection, NU, Turner Folder, Box 25, Folder 2.

2. Turner, 1963, Turner Collection, NU, Box 37, Folder 4.

3. "Grant Proposal . . . ," circa 1955, Turner Collection, NU, Box 9, Folder 2; Ford Foundation "Plan of Work on West African Folklore," 1956, Turner Collection, NU, Box 2, Folder 4.

4. Lois Turner Williams, interview by author, October 2, 2003, Chicago, Ill.

5. Lorenzo Dow Turner Jr., interview by author, October 1, 2003, Chicago, Ill.

6. Turner was relentless in pursuit of grants to fund his data collection activities. He applied for a Harmon Foundation Award in 1927, unsuccessfully; for two Guggenheim

Fellowships, one in 1930 and one in 1936, both unsuccessfully; for two Rosenwald Fellowships (1940, 1945 successful); various grants from the American Council of Learned Societies (1936 unsuccessful, 1932, 1933, 1937, 1940, 1949, 1951 successful); an American Philosophical Society Fellowship (1945–46 successful); a Fulbright Fellowship (1949 successful); a grant from the African American Institute for $300 (1955 unsuccessful); a Ford Foundation Fellowship of $10,000 (1956 unsuccessful); and grants from Fisk University and Roosevelt University (usually successful). Turner's grants were generally small. The smallest was the $300 American Council award for the summer of 1933 in the Georgia Sea Islands. The American Philosophical Society Fellowship was $750 for the three volumes on Brazilian folklore. The American Council grant for the initial work on Gullah in 1932 was $1,000 for the year. The grant from the Rosenwald Fund for his 1940 research in Brazil was $3,100 for the year.

Turner's heavy teaching load, the lack of funds for regular clerical assistance for typing and manuscript preparation, the limited funds for recording devices and other equipment, the limited funds to pay informants, the limited leave time to focus on phonetic transcription of data, and limited publication opportunities resulting from the politics of the first half of the twentieth century all took their toll. These difficulties were compounded by the demands on his schedule as English department head and coordinator of African Studies for most of his academic career. See "Profile of a Scholar," 26, 47; and Wade-Lewis, "Lorenzo Dow Turner: Beyond Gullah Studies." Moreover, the academic, social, and political engagements resulting from his status as the most prominent African American linguist, though enticing, served to limit his manuscript preparation time. The most devastating constraint of his generation, however, was the assumption that persons of African ancestry were not imbued with the "objectivity" to analyze their own experiences and therefore should not be funded to do so.

7. Until the advent of the Black Studies movement, when an explosion of departments and courses required a steady supply of textbooks, publication options for black scholars were limited. Usually if a publisher issued one title on a topic related to the black experience, it considered its offerings sufficient. Herskovits, with strong ties to Alfred A. Knopf, Inc., and university presses, met with a more favorable reception. Herskovits and Herskovits's *Dahomean Narrative: A Cross Cultural Analysis,* music and folklore based on Herskovits's fieldwork in 1931, for example, was released when there was rising interest in Africa twenty-seven years after Herskovits's fieldwork in Dahomey.

8. Montgomery to author, February 17, 2005.

9. Montgomery, *Crucible of Carolina,* 3, 170–71.

10. DeCamp, foreword to *Africanisms in the Gullah Dialect,* by Turner, xi.

11. Both of the volumes will be published by Nyala Press. *Folktales from Africa* will appear in 2007. Lorenzo Dow Turner Jr. is a free-lance artist in Chicago, Ill. Rani Meredith Turner died on September 12, 2003.

12. Correspondence from Pol Briand to author, February 28, 2005.

13. Correspondence from Livio Sansone to author, March 2, 2006.

Epilogue: Contemporary Relevance of Turner's Contribution to Linguistics

1. Mille and Montgomery, introduction to *Africanisms in the Gullah Dialect,* by Turner.

2. Ibid., xxviii.

3. Turner, *Africanisms in the Gullah Dialect,* chap. 4.

4. Turner, "Linguistic Research and African Survivals," 68–89.

5. Montgomery and Bailey, *Language Variety in the South,* 2–5.

6. Turner, *Africanisms in the Gullah Dialect,* xiii, 5, 254.

7. Mille and Montgomery, introduction to *Africanisms in the Gullah Dialect,* by Turner, xxix.

8. Ibid., xxviii.

9. Ibid., xxv.

10. See Peter Wood, "'More Like a Negro Country': Demographic Patterns in Colonial South Carolina, 1700–1740," in *Race and Slavery in the Western Hemisphere: Quantitative Studies,* ed. Stanley L. Engerman and Eugene D. Genovese (Princeton, N.J.: Princeton University Press, 1975), 131–71; Daniel C. Littlefield, *Rice and Slaves: Ethnicity and the Slave Trade in Colonial South Carolina* (Baton Rouge: Louisiana State University Press, 1981); Charles W. Joyner, *Down by the Riverside: A South Carolina Slave Community* (Urbana: University of Illinois Press, 1984); Charles W. Joyner, *Shared Traditions: Southern History and Folk Culture* (Urbana: University of Illinois Press, 1999); and William Pollitzer, *The Gullah People and Their African Heritage* (Athens: University of Georgia Press, 1999).

11. John P. Thomas, "The Barbadians in Early South Carolina," *South Carolina Historical Magazine* 31, no. 2 (April 1930): 75–92; Richard S. Dunn, "The English Sugar Islands and the Founding of South Carolina," *South Carolina Historical Magazine* 72, no. 3 (July 1971): 81–93; Wood, *Black Majority;* Daniel C. Littlefield, "Continuity and Change in Slave Culture: South Carolina and the West Indies," *Southern Studies* 27 (Fall 1987): 202–16; and Jack P. Greene, "Colonial South Carolina and the Caribbean Connection," *South Carolina Historical Magazine* 88, no. 4 (1987): 192–210.

12. Ian Hancock, "Texas Gullah: The Creole English of the Brackettville Afro-Seminoles," in *Perspectives on American English,* ed. J. L. Dillard (The Hague: Mouton, 1980), 305–33.

13. J. W. Harrison, "Negro English," *Anglia* 7 (1884): 232–79; P. Grade, "Bemerkungen über das Negerenglisch an der West-Küste von Afrika," *Archiv für das Studium der neueren Sprachen* 83 (1889): 261–72; Adolfo Coelho, "Os dialectos românicos ou neolatinos na África, Ásia, e América," *Bolletim do Sociedade de Geografia de Lisboa: Estudos linguisticos crioulos* 2 (1880–81): 193.

14. Hugo Schuchardt, *Pidgin and Creole Languages: Selected Essays,* ed. and trans. Glenn G. Gilbert (Cambridge: Cambridge University Press, 1980), 85.

15. Lucien Adam, *Les idioms négro-aryen et maléo-aryen: Essai d'hybridologie linguistique* (Paris: Maisonneuve, 1883), 4–7.

16. Addison Van Name, "1869–1870: Contributions to Creole Grammar," *Transactions of the American Philological Association* 1 (1869–70): 123–67.

17. Ibid., 123.

18. Ibid., 124, 129.

19. Gonzales, *Black Border,* 10, 17–18; Krapp, *English Language in America,* 192–93;

20. Robert W. Thompson, "A Note on Some Possible Affinities between the Creole Dialects of the Old World and Those of the New," in *Creole Language Studies II: Proceedings of the Conference on Creole Language Studies Held at the University College of the West Indies, March 28–April 4, 1959,* ed. Robert Le Page (London: Macmillan, 1961), 107–13.

21. William A. Stewart, "Creole Languages of the Caribbean," in *Study of the Role of Second Languages in Asia, Africa and Latin America,* ed. F. A. Rice (Washington, D.C.: Center for Applied Linguistics, 1962), 34–53; Robert A. Hall Jr., *Pidgin and Creole Languages* (Ithaca, N.Y.: Cornell University Press, 1966), 183.

22. Peter Bakker, "Future Challenges for Pidgin and Creole Studies," in *Pidgin and Creole Linguistics in the Twenty-first Century,* ed. Glenn Gilbert (New York: Peter Lang, 2002), 69–92.

23. Salikoko S. Mufwene, "The Ecology of Gullah's Survival," *American Speech* 72, no. 1 (Spring 1997): 69–83; Salikoko S. Mufwene, *The Ecology of Language Evolution* (Cambridge: Cambridge University Press, 2001).

24. Hans Kurath, "The Origin of Dialectal Differences in Spoken American English," *Modern Philology* 25, no. 4 (May 1928): 385–95; Johnson, *Folk Culture on St. Helena Island,* 49, 53.

25. McDavid, review of *Africanisms in the Gullah Dialect,* by Turner, 323–33; Raven I. McDavid Jr. and Virginia McDavid, "The Relationship of the Speech of American Negroes to the Speech of Whites," *American Speech* 26, no. 1 (February 1951): 3–17; Samuel G. Stoney and Gertrude M. Shelby, *Black Genesis* (New York: Macmillan, 1930), xv.

26. Edgar W. Schneider, *American Early Black English: Morphological and Syntactic Variables* (Tuscaloosa: University of Alabama Press, 1989); Shana Poplack, ed., *The English History of African American English* (Oxford: Basil Blackwell, 1999).

27. Comhaire-Sylvain, *Le Créole haïtien;* Jules Faine, *Philologie créole: Études historiques et étymologiques sur la langue créole d'Haïti* (Port-au-Prince: Imprimerie de l'Etat, 1937); Beryl Loftman [Bailey], "Creole Language of the Caribbean Area: A Comparison of the Grammar of Jamaican Creole with Those of the Creole Languages of Haiti, the Antilles, the Guianas, the Virgin Islands, and the Dutch West Indies" (master's thesis, Columbia University, 1953); Beryl Loftman Bailey, *Jamaican Creole Syntax: A Transformational Approach* (London: Oxford University Press, 1966); Mervyn Alleyne, *Comparative Afro-American: An Historical-Comparative Study of English-based Afro-American Dialects of the New World* (Ann Arbor, Mich.: Karoma Press, 1980); Mervyn Alleyne, *Syntaxe historique créole* (Paris: Karthala, 1996); Margaret Wade-Lewis, "The African Substratum in American English" (Ph.D. diss., New York University, 1988); Holm, *Pidgins and Creoles;* John A. Holm, "Phonological Features Common to Some West African and Atlantic Creole Languages," in *Africanisms in Afro-American Language Varieties,* ed. Salikoko S. Mufwene (Athens: University of Georgia Press, 1993), 317–27.

28. Salikoko S. Mufwene, ed., *Africanisms in Afro-American Language Varieties* (Athens: University of Georgia Press, 1993); Mufwene, *Ecology of Language Evolution;* Philip Baker and Chris Corne, "Universals, Substrata and the Indian Ocean Creoles," in *Substrata versus Universals in Creole Genesis,* ed. Pieter Muysken and Norval Smith (Amsterdam: John Benjamins, 1986), 163–83; Ian F. Hancock, "The Domestic Hypothesis, Diffusion, and Componentiality: An Account of Atlantic Anglophone Creole Origins," in *Substrata versus Universals in Creole Genesis,* ed. Muysken and Smith, 71–102.

29. Derek Bickerton, "Creole Languages," *Scientific American* 249, no. 3 (1983): 116–22.

30. Gillian Sankoff, "The Genesis of Language," in *The Genesis of Language,* ed. Kenneth C. Hill (Ann Arbor, Mich.: Karoma, 1979), 23–47; Peter Mühlhäusler, "The Development of the Category of Number in Tok Pisin," in *Generative Studies on Creole Languages,* ed. Pieter Muysken (Dordrecht: Foris, 1981), 35–84.

31. John R. Rickford, "Pidgins and Creoles," in *International Encyclopedia of Linguistics,* ed. William Bright (Oxford: Oxford University Press, 1992), 3:224–32; John R. Rickford, "The Creole Origins of African-American Vernacular English: Evidence from Copula Absence," in *African American English: Structure, History and Use,* ed. Salikoko S. Mufwene et al. (London: Routledge, 1998), 155–56.

32. Hall, *Pidgin and Creole Languages.*

33. Sarah G. Thomason and Thomas Kaufman, *Language Contact, Creolization, and Genetic Linguistics* (Berkeley: University of California Press, 1988), 147–66.

34. Loftman [Bailey], "Creole Language of the Caribbean Area," 74.

35. Ibid., 74–75.

36. John A. Holm, "Focus on Creolists: Beryl Loftman Bailey," *Carrier Pidgin* 10, no. 3 (September 1982): 1–3; Margaret Wade-Lewis, "Beryl Loftman Bailey: Africanist Woman Linguist in New York State," *Afro-Americans in New York Life and History* 17, no. 1 (Spring 1993): 7–15.

37. Beryl Loftman Bailey, *A Language Guide to Jamaica* (New York: Research Institute for the Study of Man, 1962); Bailey, *Jamaican Creole Syntax,* 10–11.

38. Richard Allsopp, "Pronominal Forms in the Dialect of English Used in Georgetown (British Guiana) and Its Environs by Persons Engaged in Nonclerical Occupations" (master's thesis, University of London, 1958).

39. John R. Rickford, *Dimensions of a Creole Continuum: History, Texts and Linguistic Analysis of Guyanese Creole* (Stanford, Calif.: Stanford University Press, 1987); John R. Rickford, "Variation in a Creole Continuum: Quantitative and Implicational Approaches" (Ph.D. diss., University of Pennsylvania, 1979).

40. Robert A. Hall Jr. et al., *Haitian Creole: Grammar, Texts, Vocabulary,* Memoir 74 of the American Anthropological Association and Memoir 43 of the American Folklore Society (Philadelphia: American Folklore Society, 1953).

41. Dell Hymes, ed., *Pidginization and Creolization of Languages* (Cambridge: Cambridge University Press, 1971).

42. Hall, *Pidgin and Creole Languages;* Frederic G. Cassidy and R. B. Le Page, eds., *Dictionary of Jamaican English* (Cambridge: Cambridge University Press, 1967); John A. Holm and Alison Shilling, *Dictionary of Bahamian English* (Cold Spring, N.Y.: Lexik House, 1982); Richard Allsopp, ed., with Jeannette Allsopp, *Dictionary of Caribbean English Usage* (Oxford: Oxford University Press, 1996); Albert Valdman, ed., *Dictionary of Louisiana Creole* (Bloomington: Indiana University Press, 1998).

43. John E. Reinecke et al., eds., *A Bibliography of Pidgin and Creole Languages* (Honolulu: University Press of Hawaii, 1975).

44. Ian F. Hancock, "A Survey of the Pidgins and Creoles of the World," in *Pidginization and Creolization of Language,* ed. Dell Hymes (Cambridge: Cambridge University Press, 1971), 509–23; Ian F. Hancock, "Appendix: Repertory of Pidgin and Creole Languages," in *Pidgin and Creole Linguistics,* ed. Albert Valdman (Bloomington: Indiana University Press, 1977), 362–91.

45. Daniel DeCamp, "Toward a Generative Analysis of a Post-creole Speech Continuum," in *Pidginization and Creolization of Language,* ed. Dell Hymes, 349–70; William A. Stewart, "Urban Negro Speech: Sociolinguistic Factors Affecting English Teaching," in *Social Dialects and Language Learning,* ed. Roger W. Shuy (Champaign, Ill.: National Council of Teachers of English, 1965), 10–18.

46. Mervyn Alleyne, "Acculturation and the Cultural Matrix of Creolization," in *Pidginization and Creolization of Language,* ed. Dell Hymes, 169–86.

47. Philip Baker, "Column: Causes and Effects," *Journal of Pidgin and Creole Languages* 6, no. 2 (1991): 267–78; Derek Bickerton, "Column: Beyond Roots—The Five Year Test," *Journal of Pidgin and Creole Languages* 1, no. 2 (1986): 225–32; Salikoko S. Mufwene, "The Founder Principle in Creole Genesis," *Diachronica* 13 (1996): 83–134.

48. Hancock, "Domestic Hypothesis," 71–102; Ian F. Hancock, "Creole Language Provenance and the African Component," in *Africanisms in Afro-American Language Varieties,* ed. Salikoko S. Mufwene (Athens: University of Georgia Press, 1993), 182–91.

49. Frederic Cassidy, "The Place of Gullah," *American Speech* 55, no. 1 (Spring 1980): 3–16; Hancock, "Domestic Hypothesis"; Hancock, "Creole Language Provenance"; Alleyne, *Comparative Afro-American,* 126.

50. Alleyne, *Comparative Afro-American,* 140.

51. Hancock, "Creole Language Provenance," 182–84.

52. Mufwene, "Ecology of Gullah's Survival," 69–83; Mufwene, *Ecology of Language Evolution.*

53. John V. Singler, ed., *Pidgin and Creole Tense-Mood-Aspect Systems* (Amsterdam: John Benjamins, 1990); Susanne M. Mühleisen and Bettina Migge, eds., *Politeness and Face in Caribbean Creoles* (Amsterdam: John Benjamins, 2005); Winford James and Valerie Youssef, *The Languages of Tobago: Genesis, Structure and Perspectives* (St. Augustine: University of the West Indies SOCS, 2002); Thomas Klinger, *If I Could Turn My Tongue Like That: The Creole Language of Pinta Coupee Parish, Louisiana* (Baton Rouge: Louisiana State University Press, 2003); I. H. W. Wellens, "An Arabic Creole in Africa: The Nubi Language of Uganda" (Ph.D. diss.,

University of Nijmegen, 2003); Kent Sakoda and Jeff Siegel, *Pidgin Grammar: An Introduction to the Creole Language of Hawai'i* (Honolulu: Bess Press, 2003); Terry Crowley, *Bislama Reference Grammar* (Honolulu: University of Hawaii Press, 2004).

54. Montgomery and Bailey, *Language Variety in the South,* 2–4.

55. John R. Rickford, foreword to *African American English: A Linguistic Introduction,* by Lisa J. Green (Cambridge: Cambridge University Press, 2002), ix, 6.

56. William Stewart, "Toward a History of American Negro Dialect," in *Language and Poverty: Perspectives on a Theme,* ed. Frederick Williams (Chicago: Markham, 1970), 351–79; Dillard, *Black English.* See also Beryl Bailey, "Toward a New Perspective on Negro English Dialectology," *American Speech* 40, no. 3 (October 1965): 171–77; John R. Rickford, "The Question of Prior Creolization in Black English," in *Pidgin and Creole Linguistics,* ed. Albert Valdman (Bloomington: Indiana University Press, 1977), 190–221; John Baugh, "A Re-examination of the Black English Copula," in *Locating Language in Time and Space,* ed. William Labov (New York: Academic Press, 1980), 83–106; John Holm, "Variability of the Copula in Black English and Its Creole Kin," *American Speech* 59, no. 4 (Winter 1984): 291–309; Donald Winford, "Back to the Past: The BEV/Creole Connection Revisited," *Language Variation and Change* 4, no. 3 (1992): 311–57; and Walter Wolfram and Erik Thomas, *The Development of African American English* (Oxford: Basil Blackwell, 2002).

57. Ralph W. Fasold and Roger W Shuy, eds., *Teaching Standard English in the Inner City* (Washington, D.C.: Center for Applied Linguistics, 1970); Geneva Smitherman, *Talkin' and Testifyin': The Language of Black America* (Boston: Houghton Mifflin, 1977); Geneva Smitherman, ed., *Black English and the Education of Black Children and Youth: Proceedings of the Education of the National Invitational Symposium of the King Decision* (Detroit: Center for Black Studies, Wayne State University, 1981).

58. Lisa J. Green, *African American English: A Linguistic Introduction* (Cambridge: Cambridge University Press, 2002), 6.

59. Robert Williams, ed., *Ebonics: The True Language of Black Folks* (St. Louis, Mo.: Institute of Black Studies, 1975).

60. John R. Rickford and Russell John Rickford, *Spoken Soul: The Story of Black English* (New York: John Wiley and Sons, 2000), 8.

61. Salikoko S. Mufwene et al., eds., *African American English: Structure, History, and Use* (London: Routledge, 1998); Rickford and Rickford, *Spoken Soul;* Green, *African American English;* Arthur K. Spears, ed., *Race and Ideology: Language, Symbolism, and Popular Culture* (Detroit: Wayne State University Press, 1999); John Baugh, *Beyond Ebonics: Linguistic Pride and Racial Prejudice* (Oxford: Oxford University Press, 2000); Marcyliena Morgan, *Language, Power and Discourse in African American Culture* (Cambridge: Cambridge University Press, 2002).

62. J. L. Dillard, *Lexicon of Black English* (New York: Seabury Press, 1977); Clarence Major, *From Juba to Jive: A Dictionary of Afro-American Slang* (New York: Penguin, 1994); Geneva Smitherman, *Black Talk: Words and Phrases from the Hood to the Amen Corner* (New York: Houghton Mifflin, 1994; revised, 2000); Mary Bucholtz, "Borrowed Blackness: Language, Racialization, and White Identity in an Urban High School" (Ph.D. diss., University of California, Berkeley, 1997); Halifu Osumare, "African Aesthetics, American Culture: Dancing towards a Global Culture" (Ph.D. diss., University of Hawaii, Manoa, 1999).

63. Dillard, *Black English;* Rickford, "Question of Prior Creolization in Black English," 190–221; Baugh, "Re-examination of the Black English Copula," 83–106; Tracy L. Weldon, "Exploring the AAVE-Gullah Connection: A Comparative Study of Copula Variability (African American Vernacular English, South Carolina, Georgia Gullah)" (Ph.D. diss., Ohio State University, Columbus, 1998); John Baugh, *Out of the Mouths of Slaves: African American Language and Educational Malpractice* (Austin: University of Texas Press, 1999); Theresa Perry

and Lisa Delpit, eds., *The Real Ebonics Debate: Power, Language, and the Education of Black Children* (Boston: Beacon Press, 1998); Carolyn Temple Adger, Donna Christian, and Orlando Taylor, eds., *Making the Connection: Language and Academic Achievement among African American Students* (Washington, D.C.: Center for Applied Linguistics; McHenry, Ill.: Delta Systems, 1999); Walter Wolfram, Carolyn Temple Adger, and Donna Christian, eds., *Dialects in Schools and Communities* (Mahwah, N.J.: Erlbaum, 1999); Geneva Smitherman, *Talkin' That Talk: Language, Culture and Education in African America* (London: Routledge, 1999).

64. Irma Aloyce Ewing Cunningham, "A Syntactic Analysis of Sea Island Creole (Gullah)" (Ph.D. diss., University of Michigan, Ann Arbor, 1970); Irma Aloyce Cunningham, *A Syntactic Analysis of Sea Island Creole,* Publications of the American Dialect Society (PADS) 75 (Tuscaloosa: For American Dialect Society by the University of Alabama Press, 1992); Patricia Causey Nichols, "Linguistic Change in Gullah: Sex, Age, and Mobility" (Ph.D. diss., Stanford University, 1976); Patricia Jones-Jackson, "The Status of Gullah: An Investigation of Convergent Processes" (Ph.D. diss., University of Michigan, Ann Arbor, 1978); Katherine Wyly Mille, "A Historical Analysis of Tense-Mood-Aspect in Gullah Creole: A Case of Stable Variation" (Ph.D. diss., University of South Carolina, 1990); Tometro Hopkins, "Issues in the Study of Afro-Creoles: Afro-Cuban and Gullah" (Ph.D. diss., Indiana University, Bloomington, 1992); Tracy L. Weldon, "Exploring the AAVE-Gullah Connection: A Comparative Study of Copula Variability (African American Vernacular English, South Carolina, Georgia Gullah)" (Ph.D. diss., Ohio State University, Columbus, 1998); Mary A. Twining, "An Examination of African Retentions in the Folk Culture of the South Carolina and Georgia Sea Islands," 2 vols. (Ph.D. diss., Indiana University, Bloomington, 1977).

65. Margaret Washington Creel, *A Peculiar People: Slaves, Religion, and Community-Culture among the Gullahs* (New York: New York University Press, 1988); Mary A. Twining and Keith E. Baird, eds., *Sea Island Roots: African Presence in the Carolinas and Georgia* (Trenton, N.J.: Africa World Press, 1991); Montgomery, *Crucible of Carolina;* Marquetta L. Goodwine, *Gullah/Geechee: Seeds in the Winds of the Diaspora,* vol. 2, *Gawd Dun Smile Pun We: Beaufort Isles* (New York: Kinship Publications, 1997); Marquetta L. Goodwine, ed., *The Legacy of Ibo Landing: Gullah Roots of African American Culture* (Atlanta: Clarity Press, 1998); Marquetta L., Goodwine, ed. *Gullah/Geechee: Africa's Seed in the Winds of the Diaspora,* vol. 3, *Frum Wi Soul Tuh De Soil: Cotton, Rice and Indigo* (New York: Kinship Publications, 1999); William Pollitzer, *The Gullah People and Their African Heritage* (Athens: University of Georgia Press, 1999); Holloway, *Africanisms in American Culture.*

66. For more information, see http://www.seaislandcreole.org (accessed January 10, 2006).

67. Eric Frazier, "She Who Guards Gullah: Virginia Geraty," *Charlotte Observer,* September 12, 2004, E1, E10.

68. Montgomery, *Crucible of Carolina,* 14n2; Irma Aloyce Cunningham, telephone interview by author, November 6, 2004.

69. Correspondence from Patricia Causey Nichols to author, October 20, 2004.

70. GullGeeCo@officialgullahgeechee.info.

71. United States Park Service, *Low Country Gullah Culture: Special Resource Study and Final Environmental Impact Statement* (Washington, D.C.: Department of the Interior, 2003).

72. Joko Sengova, "My Mother Dem Nyus to Plan' Reis': Reflections of Gullah/Geechee Creole Communication, Connections, and the Construction of Cultural Identity," in *Afro-Alantic Dialogues: Anthropology in the Diaspora,* ed. Kevin A. Yelvington (Santa Fe, N.Mex.: School of American Research Press, 2006), 35–82.

73. Correspondence from Queen Quet to author, March 2, 2006.

74. Jacques Arends et al., *Pidgins and Creoles: An Introduction* (Amsterdam: John Benjamins, 1994); Arthur K. Spears and Donald Winford, eds., *The Structure and Status of Pidgins and*

Creoles: Including Selected Papers from the Meetings of the Society for Pidgin and Creole Linguistics (Amsterdam: John Benjamins, 1997); Sarah Thomason and Thomas Kaufman, *Language Contact, Creolization and Genetic Linguistics* (Berkeley: University of California Press, 1988); John A. Holm, *An Introduction to Pidgins and Creoles* (Cambridge: Cambridge University Press, 2000); Robert Chaudenson and Salikoko S. Mufwene, *Creolization of Language and Culture,* trans. Michelle Aucoin et al. (London: Routledge, 2001); Glenn Gilbert, ed., *Pidgin and Creole Linguistics in the Twenty-first Century* (New York: Peter Lang, 2002); John Holm, *Languages in Contact: The Partial Restructuring of Vernaculars* (Cambridge: Cambridge University Press, 2004).

75. Herb Frazier, telephone interview by author, April 28, 2005.

76. Gilbert, *Pidgin and Creole Linguistics.*

BIBLIOGRAPHY

PRIMARY SOURCES

Archives and Collections

Berry, Leonidas H., Papers. Collection MS C 423. United States National Library of Medicine of the National Institutes of Health, History of Medicine Division, Washington, D.C.

Frazier, E. Franklin, Papers. Moorland-Spingarn Research Center, Collection 131. Lorenzo Dow Turner Correspondence in Folders 8 and 16. Howard University, Washington, D.C.

Personal Collection of Eugene Townes, Bryans Road, Md.

Personal Collection of Lois Turner Williams, Chicago, Ill.

Turner, Geneva Townes, Collection. Manuscript Division. Moorland-Spingarn Research Center, Howard University, Washington, D.C.

Turner, Lorenzo Dow, Collection. Africana Manuscripts 23. Melville J. Herskovits Library. Northwestern University Archives, Evanston, Ill.

Turner, Lorenzo Dow, Collection. Anacostia Museum of the Smithsonian Institution, Washington, D.C.

Turner, Lorenzo Dow, Correspondence. Melville Jean Herskovits Collection, Box 25, Folder 2, and Box 73, Folder 33. Africana Manuscripts 6, Series 35/6. Melville J. Herskovits Library. Northwestern University Archives, Evanston, Ill.

Turner, Lorenzo Dow, Correspondence. Papers of the English Department of the University of Chicago. Joseph Regenstein Library Special Collections Research Center, Box 16, Folder 14, Chicago, Ill.

Turner, Lorenzo Dow, Correspondence. Roosevelt University Archives, Chicago, Ill.

Turner, Lorenzo Dow, Correspondence. Thomas Elsa Jones Collection, Box 42, Folders 9–12. Fisk University Archives, Nashville, Tenn.

Turner, Lorenzo Dow, Files. Pusey Library. Harvard University Archives, Cambridge, Mass. Turner Official Student Folder UAV 161.201. 10, Box 109. Turner Graduate Student Record UAV 161.272.5, File 1, Box 14.

Turner, Lorenzo Dow, Folder. Howard University Archives, Washington, D.C.

Turner, Lorenzo Dow, Sound Recordings. Archives of Traditional Music. Indiana University, Bloomington.

Watkins, Mark Hanna, Collection. Archives of Traditional Music. Indiana University, Bloomington.

Woodson, Carter G., Papers, and Papers of the Association for the Study of Negro Life and History 1915a–1950. Lorenzo Dow Turner Letters. Manuscript Division. Library of Congress. UPA microfilm, Reel 8. Folder entitled "*Encyclopedia Africana,* Miscellaneous Correspondence."

Books and Articles by Lorenzo Dow Turner (in order of date of publication)

Turner, Lorenzo Dow. "G. O. P. Chieftains Plan Vigorous Campaign: To Recruit Unprecedented Registration of Negro Voters. . . . " *Washington Sun,* September 5, 1928, 1, 8.

———. "The Knots." *Washington Sun,* September 5, 1928, 7.

———. "65,000 Spectators Line Pennsylvania Avenue Day Parade: Colored Company Makes Brilliant Showing Wins 5th Prize—Four States Take Part—Has High Efficiency Rating Says George Watson, Fire Chief." *Washington Sun,* September 5, 1928, 1, 8.

———. "Two More Negroes Shot by Officers . . . No Guns Found on Men or at Scene of Chase." *Washington Sun*, September 5, 1928, 1, 7.

———. *Anti-Slavery Sentiment in American Literature prior to 1865*. Washington, D.C.: Association for the Study of Negro Life and History, 1929.

Cromwell, Otelia, Lorenzo Dow Turner, and Eva Dykes, eds. *Readings from Negro Authors for Schools and Colleges*. New York: Harcourt, Brace, 1931.

Turner, Lorenzo Dow. "Linguistic Research and African Survivals." In *The Inter-disciplinary Aspects of Negro Studies*, ed. Melville J. Herskovits, special issue, *American Council of Learned Societies Bulletin* 32 (September 1941): 68–89.

———. "Some Contacts of Brazilian Ex-Slaves with Nigeria, West Africa." *Journal of Negro History* 27, no. 1 (January 1942): 55–67.

———. "Some Problems Involved in the Teaching of Spoken English." *Bulletin of the Middle Tennessee Colored Teachers' Association*. Nashville, Tenn., October 1942.

———. "Comments on Word Lists from the South." *Publications of the American Dialect Society* 3 (May 1945): 7–12.

———. "Notes on the Sounds and Vocabulary of Gullah." *Publications of the American Dialect Society* 3 (May 1945): 13–28.

———. "Roosevelt College: Democratic Haven." *Opportunity* 25 (October 1947): 223–25.

———. "Problems Confronting the Investigator of Gullah." *Publications of the American Dialect Society* 9 (November 1948): 74–84.

———. *Africanisms in the Gullah Dialect*. Chicago: University of Chicago Press, 1949.

———. "New Directions in Jazz Research—Symposium" (Interview). *Record Changer* (July–August 1953): 14–17, 48–49.

———. "The Impact of Western Education on the African's Way of Life." In *Africa Today*, ed. Charles Grove, 147–71. Baltimore: Johns Hopkins University Press, 1955.

———. "The Odyssey of a Zulu Warrior." *Journal of Negro History* 40, no. 4 (July 1955): 305–17.

———. "Walt Whitman and the Negro." *Chicago Jewish Forum* 15, no. 1 (Fall 1956): 5–11.

———. "Our African Heritage." *Say: Roosevelt University Alumni Magazine*, Spring 1957, 15–19.

———. "The Negro in Brazil." *Chicago Jewish Forum* 15, no. 4 (Summer 1957): 232–36.

———. "African Survivals in the New World with Special Emphasis on the Arts." In *Africa from the Point of View of American Negro Scholars*, 101–16. Paris: American Society of African Culture/*Presence Africaine*, 1958.

———. "The Role of Folklore in the Life of the Yoruba of South-western Nigeria." In *Report of the Ninth Annual Round Table Meeting on Linguistics and Language Study*, ed. William M. Austin, 43–56. Washington, D.C.: Institute of Languages and Linguistics, Edmund A. Walsh School of Foreign Service, Georgetown University, 1958.

———. *An Anthology of Krio Folklore and Literature: With Notes and Inter-linear Translations in English*. Chicago: Roosevelt University, 1963.

———. *Krio Texts: With Grammatical Notes and Translations in English*. Chicago: Roosevelt University, 1965.

Turner, Lorenzo Dow, et al. "Fiftieth Anniversary of the Journal of Negro History." *Journal of Negro History* 52, no. 2 (April 1966): 75–97.

Book Reviews by Lorenzo Dow Turner

Turner, Lorenzo Dow. "The Negro's African Past: Review of *The Myth of the Negro Past*, by Melville Herskovits." *Journal of Negro Education* 11, no. 2 (April 1942): 185–87.

———. Review of *The Negro Caravan: Writings by American Negroes*, by Sterling Brown, Arthur P. Davis, and Ulysses Lee. *Journal of Negro History* 27, no. 2 (April 1942): 219–22.

———. Review of *Some Sources of Southernisms,* by Mitford M. Mathews. *Language* 26, no. 1 (January 1950): 167–70.

———. Review of *The Negro in Northern Brazil: A Study in Acculturation,* by O. da Costa Eduardo. *Journal of American Folklore* 63, no. 250 (October 1950): 490–92.

———. Review of *The Sin of the Prophet,* by Truman Nelson. *Journal of Negro History* 37, no. 4 (October 1952): 466–68.

———. Review of *The Outsider,* by Richard Wright. *Journal of Negro History* 39, no.1 (January 1954): 77–80.

———. Review of *The Palm-Wine Drinkard,* by Amos Tutuola. *Midwest Folklore* 5, no. 3 (1955): 189–91.

———. Review of *Dr. Dan: Pioneer in American Surgery,* by Helen Buckler. *Journal of Negro History* 40, no. 3 (April 1955): 191–93.

———. "Words for a Vast Music." Review of *Libretto for the Republic of Liberia,* by Melvin Tolson. *Poetry* 86, no. 3 (June 1955): 174–76.

———. Review of *The Negro in American Culture,* by Margaret Just Butcher. *Chicago Jewish Forum* 16, no. 1 (Fall 1957): 56–57.

———. Review of *Dahomean Narrative: A Cross-Cultural Analysis,* by Melville J. Herskovits and Frances S. Herskovits. *Journal of Negro History* 43, no. 4 (October 1958): 321–23.

———. Review of *Lucretia Mott,* by Otelia Cromwell. *Journal of Negro History* 44, no. 2 (April 1959): 186–87.

SECONDARY SOURCES

Interviews

Ballou, Leonard (archivist at Elizabeth City State University, Elizabeth City, N.C.). Telephone interviews by the author, May 9, June 1, and September 6, 2002; January 20 and June 14, 2003; and April 16, 2004.

Bell, Charlotte (second cousin of Lorenzo Turner on her mother's and his father's family line). Interview by the author, June 2, 1989, Philadelphia, Pa.

Cunningham, Irma Aloyce. Telephone interviews by the author, November 6, 2004, and March 10, 2005.

Evans, Jean P. (cousin of Lorenzo Turner on her mother's and his father's family line). Telephone interview by the author, September 6, 2002.

Ferguson, Teresa (archivist, the Family Research Society of Northeastern North Carolina, Elizabeth City, N.C.). Telephone interviews by the author, May 1 and September 4, 2002.

Frazier, Herb (senior reporter, *Charleston Post and Courier*). Telephone interviews by the author, December 20, 2004; April 28, 2005; and April 2, 2006.

Frazier-Clemons, Gail (cousin of Lorenzo Dow Turner through Burke family line). Telephone interview by the author, May 28, 2002.

Morgan, Raleigh (former Turner student and Romance linguist). Interview by the author, May 28, 1986, Ann Arbor, Mich.

Stewart, Gloria Morton (sister of Lois Turner Williams). Interviews by the author, June 15, 2002, and January 15, 2003, Chicago, Ill.

Townes, Eugene (nephew of Geneva Townes Turner). Interview by the author, April 24, 2003, Washington, D.C. Telephone interviews by the author, November 12, 2002, and December 20, 2003.

Turner, Lorenzo Dow, Jr. (son of Lorenzo Dow Turner). Interviews by the author, January 15 and October 1, 2003, Chicago, Ill. Telephone interviews by the author, December 22, 2002; January 5, 2003; January 26 and August 10, 2004; and January 2, 2005.

Turner Williams, Lois (widow of Lorenzo Dow Turner). Interviews by the author, May 26, 1986; June 22, 1989; June 14, 2000; September 25–26, 2001; June 15, 2002; January 14–15 and October 1–2, 2003, Chicago, Ill. Telephone interviews by the author, June 25, 1986; August 28, 1989; May 16 and August 5, 2002; May 24, June 25, and September 2, 2003; March 20 and August 10, 2004; April 10, 2005; and March 26, 2006.

Books and Articles

Abrahams, Roger. *Deep Down in the Jungle: Negro Narrative Folklore from the Streets of Philadelphia.* New York: Aldine Press, 1963.

Adam, Lucien. *Les idioms négro-aryen et maléo-aryen: Essai d'hybridologie linguistique.* Paris: Maisonneuve, 1883, 4–7.

Adger, Carolyn Temple, Donna Christian, and Orlando Taylor, eds. *Making the Connection: Language and Academic Achievement among African American Students.* Washington, D.C.: Center for Applied Linguistics; McHenry, Ill.: Delta Systems, 1999.

"African Culture Institute." *Chicago Defender,* January 31, 1953, 21.

"African Safari." *Visitor* (Bulletin of the First English Evangelical Church of Chicago), March 1953, 7.

Allen, Harold B. "Regional Dialects, 1945–1974." *American Speech* 52, no. 3/4 (Autumn/Winter 1977): 163–261.

Allen, W. H. "Pennsylvania." *Dialect Notes* 4, part 2 (1914): 157–58.

Alleyne, Mervyn. "Acculturation and the Cultural Matrix of Creolization." In *Pidginization and Creolization of Languages,* ed. Dell Hymes, 169–86. Cambridge: Cambridge University Press, 1971.

———. *Comparative Afro-American: An Historical-Comparative Study of English-based Afro-American Dialects of the New World.* Ann Arbor, Mich.: Karoma Press, 1980.

———. *Syntaxe historique créole.* Paris: Karthala, 1996.

Allsopp, Richard, ed., with Jeanette Allsopp. *Dictionary of Caribbean English Usage.* Oxford: Oxford University Press, 1996.

Almasy, Sandra Lee. *Gates County, North Carolina Marriage Bonds, 1741–1868.* Joliet, Ill.: Kensington Glen Publishing, 1987.

Anderson, David. "He Worked His Way through This College." *Chicago Sun-Times,* May 19, 1969, 48.

Anderson, Eric. *Race and Politics in North Carolina, 1872–1901: The Black Second.* Baton Rouge: Louisiana State University Press, 1981.

Anderson, Eric, and Alfred Moss Jr. *Dangerous Donations: Northern Philanthropy and Southern Black Education, 1902–1930.* Columbia: University of Missouri Press, 1999.

Andresen, Julie Tetel. *Linguistics in America, 1769–1924: A Critical History.* London: Routledge, 1990.

Appiah, Kwame Anthony. "James Amos Porter." In *Africana: The Encyclopedia of the African and African American Experience,* 1541. New York: Perseus Books, 1999.

Appiah, Kwame Anthony, and Henry Louis Gates Jr., eds. *Africana: The Encyclopedia of African and African American Experience.* New York: Perseus Books, 1999.

Aptheker, Herbert. "Africanisms in America: *Africanisms in the Gullah Dialect* by Lorenzo D. Turner." *Masses and Mainstream* 2, no. 12 (December 1949): 76–78.

Arends, Jacques, John Victor Singler, Pieter Muysken, and Norval Smith, eds. *Pidgins and Creoles: An Introduction.* Amsterdam: John Benjamins, 1995.

Bailey, Beryl Loftman. *Jamaican Creole Syntax: A Transformational Approach.* London: Oxford University Press, 1966.

———. *A Language Guide to Jamaica.* New York: Research Institute for the Study of Man, 1962.

———. "Toward a New Perspective in Negro English Dialectology." *American Speech* 40, no. 3 (October 1965): 171–77.

Bailey, Guy, and Natalie Maynor. "The Divergence Controversy." *American Speech* 64, no. 1 (Spring 1989): 12–39.

Bailey, Richard. "Hans Kurath: Obituary." *Language* 68, no. 4 (December 1992): 797–808.

Bailyn, Bernard, Donald Fleming, Oscar Handlin, and Stephan Thernstrom, eds. *Glimpses of the Harvard Past.* Cambridge, Mass.: Harvard University Press, 1986.

Baker, Philip. "Column: Causes and Effects." *Journal of Pidgin and Creole Languages* 6, no. 2 (1991): 267–78.

Baker, Philip, and Chris Corne. "Universals, Substrata and the Indian Ocean Creoles." In *Substrata Versus Universals in Creole Genesis,* ed. Pieter Muysken and Norval Smith, 163–83. Amsterdam: John Benjamins, 1986.

Bakker, Peter. "Future Challenges for Pidgin and Creole Studies." In *Pidgin and Creole Linguistics in the Twenty-first Century,* ed. Glenn Gilbert, 69–92. New York: Peter Lang, 2002.

Ballou, Leonard R. *Pasquotank Pedagogues and Politicians: Early Educational Struggles.* Elizabeth City, N.C.: Elizabeth City State College, 1966.

Barksdale, Richard, and Keneth Kinnamon, eds. *Black Writers of America: A Comprehensive Anthology.* New York: Macmillan, 1972.

Bascom, William R. "Acculturation among the Gullah Negroes." *American Anthropologist* 43, no. 1 (January–March 1941): 43–50.

Bastide, Roger. *The African Religions of Brazil.* Baltimore: Johns Hopkins University Press, 1978.

Batista, Marlyse. *The Syntax of Cape Verdean Creole: The Sotavento Varieties.* Amsterdam: John Benjamins, 2002.

Baugh, John. *Beyond Ebonics: Linguistic Pride and Racial Prejudice.* Oxford: Oxford University Press, 2000.

———. *Black Street Speech: Its History, Structure and Survival.* Austin: University of Texas Press, 1983.

———. *Out of the Mouths of Slaves: African American Language and Educational Malpractice.* Austin: University of Texas Press, 1999.

———. "A Re-examination of the Black English Copula." In *Locating Language in Time and Space,* ed. William Labov, 83–106. New York: Academic Press, 1980.

Beltrán, Gonzalo Aguirre. "La Ethnohistoria y el Estudio del Negro en Mexico." In *Acculturation in the Americas,* ed. Sol Tax, 161–68. New York: Cooper Square Publishers, 1967.

———. *La Población negra de México, Estudio Ethnohistorico (1519 1810).* Mexico City: Ediciones Fuente Cultural, 1946a.

———. "Tribal Origins of Slaves in Mexico." *Journal of Negro History* 31, no. 3 (July 1946): 269–89.

Benjamin, Steven M., and Luanne von Schneidemesser. "German Loanwords in American English: A Bibliography of Studies, 1872–1978." *American Speech* 54, no. 2 (Autumn 1979): 210–15.

Bennett, Eric. "James Augustus Van Der Zee." In *Africana: The Encyclopedia of the African and African American Experience,* ed. Kwame Anthony Appiah and Henry Louis Gates Jr., 1934–35. New York: Perseus Books, 1999.

Bennett, John. "Gullah Called Mostly English, Only 100 African Words Left." *Charleston (S.C.) Post and Courier,* November 13, 1949.

Berry, Leonidas H. *I Wouldn't Take Nothin' for My Journey: Two Centuries of an American Minister's Family.* Chicago: Johnson Publishing Company, 1979.

Bickerton, Derek. "Column: Beyond Roots—The Five Year Test." *Journal of Pidgin and Creole Languages* 1, no. 2 (1986): 225–32.

———. "Creole Languages." *Scientific American* 249, no. 3 (1983): 116–22.

———. "The Language Bioprogram Hypothesis." *Behavioral and Brain Sciences* 7 (1984): 173–221.

———. *Roots of Language*. Ann Arbor, Mich.: Karoma, 1981.

Bloch, Bernard, and George L. Trager. *Outline of Linguistic Analysis*. Baltimore: Linguistic Society of America, 1942.

Blok, H. P. "Annotations to Mr. Turner's *Africanisms in the Gullah Dialect*." *Lingua* 8 (1959): 306–21.

Bloomfield, Leonard. *Language*. New York: Holt, Rinehart and Winston, 1933.

Bowser, Aubrey. "Book Review: Ink Turns to Blood." *New York Amsterdam News*, May 21, 1930.

Branch, Muriel. *Fine Arts and Crafts: African American Arts*. New London, Conn.: Twenty-First Century, 2001.

Brawley, Benjamin Griffith. "Lorenzo Dow." *Journal of Negro History* 1, no. 3 (July 1916): 265–75.

"Building for a Long Future: The University of Chicago and Its Donors, 1889–1930." In *The University of Chicago Centennial Catalogue*. Chicago: Special Collections Research Center, University of Chicago, 1992.

Butchko, Thomas R. *Forgotten Gates: The Historical Architecture of a Rural North Carolina County*. Gatesville, N.C.: Gates County Historical Society, 1991.

———. *On the Shores of the Pasquotank: The Architectural Heritage of Elizabeth City and Pasquotank County, North Carolina*. Elizabeth City, N.C.: Museum of the Albermarle, 1989.

Butters, Ron. "Linguistic Convergence in a North Carolina Community." In *Variation in Language*, ed. K. M. Denning, S. Inkelas, F. C. McNair-Knox, and John Rickford, 52–60. Stanford, Calif.: Department of Linguistics, Stanford University, 1989.

Carneiro, Edison. *Negros Bantús: Notas de Ethnographia Religiosa e de Folclore*. Rio de Janeiro: Editora Civilização, Brasileira, 1937.

"The Case against Dr. Mordecai Johnson." Special issue of *Howard University Alumni Magazine*, Winter 1937.

Cassidy, Frederic G. "Gullah and the Caribbean Connection." In *The Crucible of Carolina: Essays in the Development of Gullah Language and Culture*, ed. Michael Montgomery, 16–22. Athens: University of Georgia Press, 1994.

———. "The Place of Gullah." *American Speech* 55, no. 1 (Spring 1980): 3–16.

———. "Sources of the African Element on Gullah." In *Studies in Caribbean Language: Papers from the Third Biennial Conference of the Society of Creole Languages*, 1980, ed. Lawrence Carrington, D. R. Craig, and R. Todd Dandare, 75–81. St. Augustine, Trinidad: Society for Caribbean Linguistics, 1983.

Cassidy, Frederic G., ed. *Dictionary of American Regional English*. Vol. 1., A–C. Cambridge, Mass.: Belknap Press of Harvard University Press, 1985.

Cassidy, Frederic G., and R. B. Le Page, eds. *Dictionary of Jamaican English*. Cambridge: Cambridge University Press, 1967.

"A Celebration of the Life of Paul Robeson." *SOAS* [School of Oriental and African Studies] *Alumni Newsletter* 17 (Winter 1998): 6.

Cerroni-Long, E. L. "Benign Neglect? Anthropology and the Study of Blacks in the United States." *Journal of Black Studies* 17, no. 4 (June 1987): 439–59.

Chase, Judith Wragg. *Afro-American Arts and Crafts*. New York: Van Nostrand, 1971.

Chaudenson, Robert, and Salikoko S. Mufwene. *Creolization of Language and Culture*. Translated by Michelle Aucoin, Sabrina Billings, Salikoko S. Mufwene, and Sheri Pargman. London: Routledge, 2001.

Chicago Commission on Race Relations. *The Negro in Chicago.* Chicago: University of Chicago Press, 1922.

Clarke, Nina H., and Lillian B. Brown. *History of the Black Public Schools of Montgomery County, Maryland—1872–1961.* New York: Vantage Press, 1978.

Coelho, F. Adolfo. "Os dialectos românicos ou neolatinos na África, Ásia, e América." *Bolletim da Sociedade de Geografia de Lisboa* 2 (1880–81): 129–96.

———. "Os dialectos românicos ou neolatinos na África, Ásia, e América. Notas complementares." *Bolletim da Sociedade de Geografia de Lisboa* 3 (1882): 451–78.

———. "Os dialectos românicos ou neolatinos na África, Ásia, e América. Notas complementares." *Bolletim da Sociedade de Geografia de Lisboa, Terceiro artigo, Novas notas supplementares* 6, no. 12 (1886): 705–55.

Cohen, Howard. "Lorenzo Turner: Professor, Linguist, Author." *Oracle* (Roosevelt University) 1, no. 10 (December 1962): 2.

Cohen, Rodney T. *Fisk University.* Charleston, S.C.: Arcadia Publishing, 2001.

Cole, Arthur C. Review of *Anti-Slavery Sentiment in American Literature prior to 1865,* by Lorenzo Dow Turner. *Mississippi Valley Historical Review* 17, no. 4 (1930): 624–25.

Collins, L. M. *One Hundred Years of Fisk University Presidents, 1875–1975.* Nashville, Tenn.: Hemphill Creative Printing, 1989.

"Colorful Dialect Is Saved from Oblivion: Young Couple in Providence Has Recorded Picturesque Tongue of Islanders off South Carolina Coast." *Providence (R.I.) Evening Bulletin,* August 13, 1934.

"Contributors." *Midwest Journal* 1 (Winter 1948): iii.

Corbitt, David Leroy. *The Formation of the North Carolina Counties, 1663–1943.* 5th printing. Raleigh: State Department of Archives and History; North Carolina Department of Cultural Resources, 1996.

Courlander, Harold, ed. "The Bilali Document." In *A Treasury of Afro-American Folklore,* 289–90. New York: Crown, 1975.

Creel, Margaret Washington. *A Peculiar People: Slaves, Religion, and Community-Culture among the Gullahs.* New York: New York University Press, 1988.

Cronise, Florence M., and Henry W. Ward. *Cunnie Rabbit, Mr. Spider and the Other Beef: West African Folk Tales.* New York: Dutton and Company, 1903.

Cross, Theodore, "The Black Faculty Count at the Nation's Most Prestigious Universities." *Journal of Blacks in Higher Education* 19 (Spring 1998): 109–15.

Crow, Jeffrey J., Paul D. Escott, and Flora J. Hatley. *A History of African Americans in North Carolina.* Raleigh: Division of Archives and History, North Carolina Department of Cultural Resources, 1992.

Crow, Jeffrey J., and Flora J. Hatley, eds. *Black Americans in North Carolina and the South.* Chapel Hill: University of North Carolina Press, 1984.

Crowley, Terry. *Bislama Reference Grammar.* Honolulu: University of Hawaii Press, 2004.

Cunningham, Irma Aloyce Ewing. *A Syntactic Analysis of Sea Island Creole.* Publications of the American Dialectic Society (PADS) 75. Tuscaloosa: For the American Dialect Society by the University of Alabama Press, 1992.

Darnell, Regna. *And Along Came Boas: Continuity and Revolution in American Anthropology.* Amsterdam: John Benjamins, 1998.

———. *Edward Sapir: Linguist, Anthropologist, Humanist.* Los Angeles: University of California Press, 1990.

Davis, Alva L., Raven I. McDavid Jr., and Virginia G. McDavid. *A Compilation of the Work Sheets of the Linguistic Atlas of the United States and Canada and Associated Projects.* 2nd ed. Chicago: University of Chicago Press, 1969.

Davis, Arthur P. "E. Franklin Frazier (1894–1962): A Profile." *Journal of Negro Education* 31, no. 4 (Autumn 1962): 429–35.

DeCamp, David. Foreword to *Africanisms in the Gullah Dialect,* by Lorenzo Dow Turner, v–xi. Ann Arbor: University of Michigan Press, 1974.

———. "Social and Geographical Factors in Jamaican Dialects." In *Proceedings of the Conference on Creole Language Studies Held at the University College of the West Indies, March 28–April 4, 1959,* ed. Robert Le Page, 61–84. London: Macmillan, 1961.

DeCamp, David, and Ian F. Hancock, eds. *Pidgins and Creoles: Current Trends and Prospects.* Washington, D.C.: Georgetown University Press, 1974.

Denton, Daniel G. "On Certain Supposed Nanticoke Words Shown to Be of African Origin." *American Antiquarian* 9, no. 6 (1887): 350–54.

"Denver's Zulu, Who Has Fought Briton and Boer, Talks of South African Affairs." *Denver Republican,* February 25, 1900, 30.

Derricotte, Elise Palmer, Geneva Calcier Turner, and Jessie Hailstalk Roy. *Word Pictures of Great Negroes.* Washington, D.C.: Associated Publishers, 1941.

de Senna, Nelson. *Africanos no Brasil.* Belo Horizonte, Brazil: Oficinas Gráficas Queiroz Breyner Limitada, 1940.

Dillard, Joey L. *Black English: Its History and Usage in the United States.* New York: Random House, 1972.

———. *Lexicon of Black English.* New York: Seabury Press, 1977.

Donnan, Elizabeth. *Documents Illustrative of the History of the Slave Trade to America.* 4 vols. Washington, D.C.: Carnegie Institution, 1930–35.

Douglass, Frederick. "The Significance of Emancipation in the West Indies: An Oration, August 2, 1857." In *Frederick Douglass Papers, Series One: Speeches, Debates and Interviews,* ed. John Blassingame, vol. 3 (1855–63). New Haven, Conn.: Yale University Press, 1985.

Dow, Lorenzo. *The Dealings of God, Man and the Devil, as Exemplified in the Life, Experience and Travels of Lorenzo Dow.* Cincinnati: Appleton, 1858.

"Dr. Eva Dykes Co-author of Text Book, Book on Negro Literature." *Hilltop,* November 26, 1931, 1.

"Dr. Lorenzo Turner Named Adult Education Lecturer." *Chicago Defender,* May 11, 1946.

"Dr. Lorenzo Turner to Speak Sunday." *Chicago Defender,* March 22, 1947.

Duberman, Martin. *Paul Robeson: A Biography.* New York: New Press, 1989.

Du Bois, William E. B. *The Autobiography of W. E. B. Du Bois: A Soliloquy on Viewing My Life from the Last Decade of Its First Century.* New York: International Publishers, 1979.

———. "Negroes in College." *Nation,* March 3, 1926, 228–30.

———. "Of Mr. Booker T. Washington and Others." In *The Souls of Black Folk,* by Du Bois, 79–108. Chicago: A. C. McClurg, 1903.

———. *The Souls of Black Folk.* Chicago: A. C. McClurg, 1903.

Dunn, Richard S. "The English Sugar Islands and the Founding of South Carolina." *South Carolina Historical Magazine* 72, no. 3 (July 1971): 81–93.

"Editorial." *Chicago Defender,* May 25, 1946.

"Education." *Newsweek,* January 9, 1939, 39.

"85, No Higher, Forecast for Today; Heat Kills 2; 1 Drowns; 9 Prostrated." *Washington Post,* July 23, 1926, 1.

Elizabeth City State University Strategic Plan: 1998–2003. Elizabeth City, N.C.: Elizabeth City State University, 1998.

"English Head to Study Gullah Negro Dialect." *New York Amsterdam News,* March 30, 1932.

"Executive Council: 'Lorenzo Dow Turner T-Shirt.'" *Newsletter of the American Dialect Society* 33, no. 1 (January 2001): 4, col. 2, item 11.

"Faculty Notes." *Progress: A Report from Roosevelt College* 2, no. 3 (June 1948): 8.

"Faculty Notes." *Progress: A Report from Roosevelt University* 3 (April 1949): 8.

"Faculty Notes." *Progress: A Report from Roosevelt University* 11, no. 1 (December 1956): 7–8.

"Faculty Notes." *Progress: A Report from Roosevelt University* 13 (November 1958): 2.

Faine, Jules. *Philologie créole: Études historiques et étymologiques sur la langue créole d'Haïti.* Port-au-Prince: Imprimerie de l'État, 1937.

Fasold, Ralph W., William Labov, Fay Boyd Vaughn-Cooke, Guy Bailey, Walt Wolfram, Arthur K. Spears, and John Rickford. "Are Black and White Vernaculars Diverging?" Papers from the NWAVE XIV Panel Discussion. *American Speech* 62, no. 1 (Spring 1987): 3–80.

Fasold, Ralph W., and Roger W. Shuy, eds. *Teaching Standard English in the Inner City.* Washington, D.C.: Center for Applied Linguistics, 1970.

Fernandez, James W. "Tolerance in a Repugnant World and Other Dilemmas in the Cultural Relativism of Melville J. Herskovits." *Ethos* 18, no. 2 (June 1990): 140–64.

"Fisk Professor Concludes Colorful Lecture Series." *Chicago Defender,* August 7, 1943.

"Fisk Professor Gets Grant to Study." *Afro-American,* March 19, 1932.

Fisk University Brochure on African Studies, 1943. Turner Collection. Northwestern University. Box 18, Folder 5.

Fisk University Bulletin. Nashville, Tenn. 1930, 1940–41, 1942–43, 1943–44, 1944–45, 1946–47.

Fleming, Donald. "Some Notable Harvard Students." In *Glimpses of the Harvard Past,* ed. Bernard Bailyn, Donald Fleming, Oscar Handlin, and Stephan Thernstrom, 133–46. Cambridge, Mass.: Belknap Press of Harvard University Press. 1986.

Franklin, John Hope. *The Free Negro in North Carolina, 1790–1860.* Chapel Hill: University of North Carolina Press, 1943.

———. *From Slavery to Freedom.* New York: Alfred A. Knopf, 1947.

Frazier, Brenda. Introduction to *Folktales from Africa,* edited by Lorenzo Dow Turner Jr. Chicago: Nyala Press, forthcoming 2007.

Frazier, E. Franklin. *Black Bourgeoisie: The Rise of the New Middle Class.* Glencoe, Ill.: Free Press, 1957.

———. "The Negro Family in Bahia, Brazil." *American Sociological Review* 7, no. 4 (August 1942): 465–78.

———. *The Negro Family in the United States.* Chicago: University of Chicago Press, 1939.

———. "Rejoinder." *American Sociological Review* 8, no. 4 (August 1944): 402–4.

Frazier, Eric. "She Who Guards Gullah: Virginia Geraty." *Charlotte Observer,* September 12, 2004, E1, E10.

Frazier, Herb. "Interest Remains in '32 Findings of Gullah Researcher." *Charleston (S.C.) Post and Courier,* February 16, 1997, edition PC, section B1.

———. "Sisters in Song Musical Roots Run under an Ocean and across Time to Bind Two Women with Oral History." *Chicago Tribune,* May 9, 1997, Tempo section, 1.

Freyre, Gilberto. *Casa grande e senzala.* Rio de Janeiro: Schmidt, 1938. American translation by Samuel Putnam published as *The Masters and the Slaves.* New York: Alfred A. Knopf, 1946.

———. *Sobrados e mucambos.* São Paulo: Boizoi Books of Alfred A. Knopf, 1936.

Fries, Charles C. *American English Grammar.* New York: Irvington Publishers, 1940.

Gary, Lawrence. "A Social Profile." In *Black Men,* ed. Lawrence Gary, 21–45. Beverly Hills, Calif.: Sage Publications, 1981.

"Geneva Turner." In *Who's Who among Black Americans,* 1975–76, 1:631. Northbrook, Ill.: Who's Who among Black Americans Inc. Publishing Company, 1976.

Geraty, Virginia Mixson. *Gullah fuh Oonuh (Gullah for You): A Guide to the Gullah Language.* Orangeburg, S.C.: Sandlapper, 1997.

———. *Gullah Night before Christmas*. Gretna, La.: Pelican Publishing Company, 1998.

———. *A Teacher's Guide to the Gullah Language*. Charleston, S.C.: (Self-published) Wyrick and Company, 1990.

Gilbert, Glenn. "Hugo Schuchardt and the Atlantic Creoles: A Newly Discovered Manuscript 'On the Negro English of West Africa.'" *American Speech* 60, no. 1 (Spring 1985): 31–63.

———, ed. *Pidgin and Creole Linguistics in the Twenty-first Century*. New York: Peter Lang, 2002.

Gilman, Emily S. "Lorenzo Dow." *New England Magazine* 20, no. 4 (June 1899): 411–17.

Gilmore, Glenda Elizabeth. *Gender and Jim Crow: Women and the Politics of White Supremacy in North Carolina, 1896–1920*. Chapel Hill: University of North Carolina Press, 1996.

Gilyard, Keith. "African American Contributions to Composition Studies." *College Composition and Communication (CCC)* 50, no. 4 (June 1999): 626–44.

Glasrud, Bruce A., and Laurie Champion, "The Fishes and the Poet's Hands: Frank Yerby, a Black Author in White America." *Journal of American and Comparative Cultures* 23, no. 4 (Winter 2000): 15–21.

Goggin, Jacqueline. *Carter G. Woodson: A Life in Black History*. Baton Rouge: Louisiana State University Press, 1993.

———. "Countering White Racist Scholarship: Carter G. Woodson and the Journal of Negro History." *Journal of Negro History* 48, no. 4 (Autumn 1983): 355–75.

Gonzales, Ambrose E. *The Black Border: Gullah Stories of the Carolina Coast*. Columbia, S.C.: The State Company, 1922.

———. *Two Gullah Tales: The Turkey Hunter and At the Crossroads Store*. Columbia, S.C.: The State Company, 1926.

———. *With Aesop Along the Black Border*. Columbia, S.C.: The State Company, 1924.

Goodspeed, Thomas Wakefield. *History of the University of Chicago*. 1916. Chicago: University of Chicago Press, 1972.

Goodwine, Marquetta L., ed. *Gullah/Geechee: Africa's Seed in the Winds of the Diaspora*. Vol. 2, *Gawd Dun Smile Pun We: Beaufort Isles*. New York: Kinship Publications, 1997.

———. *Gullah/Geechee: Africa's Seed in the Winds of the Diaspora*. Vol. 3, *Frum Wi Soul Tuh De Soil: Cotton, Rice and Indigo*. New York: Kinship Publications, 1999.

———. *The Legacy of Ibo Landing: Gullah Roots of African American Culture*. Vol. 1. Atlanta: Clarity Press, 1998.

Grade, P. "Bermerkungen über das Negerenglisch an de West-Küste von Afrika." *Archiv für das Studium der neueren Sprachen* 83 (1889): 261–72.

Grafton, Anthony. "The Public Intellectual and the American University: Robert Morss Lovett Revisited." *American Scholar* 70, no. 4 (Autumn 2001): 41–55.

Green, Lisa J. *African American English: A Linguistic Introduction*. Cambridge: Cambridge University Press, 2002.

Greenberg, Joseph H. "The Decipherment of the 'Ben-ali Diary': A Preliminary Statement." *Journal of Negro History* 25, no. 3 (July 1940): 372–75.

———. *Essays in Linguistics*. Chicago: University of Chicago Press, 1957.

———. *The Languages of Africa*. Bloomington: Indiana University Press/The Hague: Mouton, 1966.

———. *Studies in African Linguistic Classification*. New Haven, Conn.: Compass Publishing Company, 1955.

Greene, Harry W. "The Number of Negro Doctorates." *School and Society* 38 (September 16, 1933): 375.

———. "The Ph.D. and the Negro." *Opportunity* 6, no. 9 (September 1928): 267–69.

Greene, Jack P. "Colonial South Carolina and the Caribbean Connection." *South Carolina Historical Magazine* 88, no. 4 (1987): 192–210.

Gregory, Montgomery. "A Chronology of Negro Theater." In *Plays for Negro Life: A Source Book of Native American Drama,* ed. Alain Locke and Montgomery Gregory, 409–23. New York: Harper, 1927.

Grumbine, Lee L. "Provincialisms of the 'Dutch' Districts of Pennsylvania." *Transactions of the American Philological Association* (1886): Appendix 17, xii–xiii.

"Gullah: South Carolina Dialect Studied by Linguists." *Washington Sentinel,* January 14, 1933.

Hailstalk Roy, Jessie, and Geneva Calcier Turner. *Pioneers of Long Ago.* Washington, D.C.: Associated Publishers, 1951.

Hair, P. E. H. "Sierra Leone Items in the Gullah Dialect of American English." *African Language Review* 4 (1965): 79–84.

Halderman, Samuel S. *Pennsylvania Dutch: A Dialect of South German with an Infusion of English.* Philadelphia: Reformed Church Publication Board, 1872.

Hall, Robert A., Jr. "The African Substratum of Negro English." *American Speech* 25, no. 1 (April 1950): 51–54.

———. *Pidgin and Creole Languages.* Ithaca, N.Y.: Cornell University Press, 1966.

Hall, Robert A., Jr., Suzanne Comhaire-Sylvain, H. O. McConnell, and Albert Métraux. *Haïtian Creole: Grammar, Texts, Vocabulary.* Memoir 74 of the American Anthropological Association and Memoir 43 of the American Folklore Society. Philadelphia: American Folklore Society, 1953.

Hamp, Eric P. "Guy Summer Lowman, Jr." In *Lexicon Grammaticorum: Who's Who in the History of World Linguistics,* ed. Harro Stammerjohann, 588. Tübingen: Max Niemeyer, 1996.

Hancock, Ian F. "Appendix: Repertory of Pidgin and Creole Languages." In *Pidgin and Creole Linguistics,* ed. Albert Valdman, 277–90. Bloomington: Indiana University Press, 1977.

———. "Creole Language Provenance and the African Component." In *Africanisms in Afro-American Language Varieties,* ed. Salikoko S. Mufwene, 182–91. Athens: University of Georgia Press, 1993.

———. "The Domestic Hypothesis, Diffusion, and Componentiality: An Account of Atlantic Anglophone Creole Origins." In *Substrata versus Universals in Creole Genesis,* ed. Pieter Muysken and Norval Smith, 71–102. Amsterdam: John Benjamins, 1986.

———. "Gullah and Barbadian: Origins and Relationships." *American Speech* 55, no. 1 (Spring 1980): 17–35.

———. "On the Origin of the Term Pidgin." In *Readings in Creole Studies,* ed. Ian F. Hancock, Edward Polomé, Morris Goodman, and B. Heine, 81–88. Ghent: E. Story-Scientia, 1979.

———. "A Provisional Comparison of the English-based Atlantic Creoles." *African Language Review* 8 (1969): 7–72.

———. "A Survey of the Pidgins and Creoles of the World." In *Pidginization and Creolization of Language,* ed. Dell Hymes, 509–25. Cambridge: Cambridge University Press, 1971.

———. "Texas Gullah: The Creole English of the Brackettville Afro-Seminoles." In *Perspectives on American English,* ed. J. L. Dillard, 305–33. The Hague: Mouton, 1980.

Handlin, Oscar. "A Small Community." In *Glimpses of the Harvard Past,* ed. Bernard Bailyn, Donald Fleming, Oscar Handlin, and Stephan Thernstrom, 97–113. Cambridge, Mass.: Belknap Press of Harvard University Press, 1986.

Hanley, Miles L. "Progress of the Linguistic Atlas." *Dialect Notes: Publications of the American Dialect Society* 6, part 5 (1932): 281–82.

———. "Progress of the Linguistic Atlas and Plans for the Future Work of the Dialect Society." *Dialect Notes: Publications of the American Dialect Society* 6, part 3 (1931): 91–98.

Harris, Joel Chandler. *Free Joe and Other Georgia Sketches.* New York: Scribners, 1887.

———. *Nights with Uncle Remus.* Boston: Houghton Mifflin, 1883.

———. *Uncle Remus, His Songs and Sayings: The Folklore of the Plantation.* New York: D. Appleton, 1881.

Harris, Robert L., Jr. "Segregation and Scholarship: American Council of Learned Societies' Committee on Negro Studies, 1941–1950." *Journal of Black Studies* 12, no. 3 (March 1982): 315–31.

Harrison, Faye V., and Ira E. Harrison. "Introduction: Anthropology, African Americans, and the Emancipation of Subjugated Knowledge." In *African American Pioneers in Anthropology,* ed. Faye V. Harrison and Ira E. Harrison, 1–36. Urbana: University of Illinois Press, 1999.

Harrison, J. A. "Negro English." *Anglia* 7 (1884): 232–79.

Harvard University. *Official Register of Harvard University, 1917.* Cambridge, Mass.: Harvard University, 1917.

Henderson, Alexa B. *Atlanta Life Insurance Company: Guardian of Black Economic Dignity.* Tuscaloosa: University of Alabama Press, 1990.

Herskovits, Frances S., ed. *The New World Negro: Selected Papers in AfroAmerican Studies by Melville J. Herskovits.* Bloomington: Indiana University Press, 1966.

Herskovits, Melville J. "Acculturation and the American Negro." *Southwestern Political and Social Science Quarterly* 8, no. 3 (December 1927): 212–24.

———. *The American Negro: A Study in Racial Crossing.* New York: Alfred A. Knopf, 1928.

———. *The Myth of the Negro Past.* New York: Harper, 1941.

———. "The Negro in Bahia, Brazil: A Problem in Method." *American Sociological Review* 8, no. 4 (August 1943): 394–404.

———. "The Negro's Americanism." In *The New Negro: An Interpretation,* ed. Alain Locke, 353–60. New York: Albert and Charles Boni, 1925.

———. "The Significance of West Africa for Negro Research." *Journal of Negro History* 21, no. 1 (January 1936): 15–30.

Herskovits, Melville J., and Frances S. Herskovits. *Dahomean Narrative: A Cross Cultural Analysis.* Evanston, Ill.: Northwestern University Press, 1958.

———. "A Footnote on the History of American Slaving." *Opportunity* 11 (June 1933): 178–81.

Hesseling, D. C. "Hoe ontstond de Eigenaardige vorm van het Kreools?" *Neophilologus* 18 (1933): 209–15. Reprinted as "How Did Creoles Originate?" In Hesseling's *On the Origin and Formation of Creoles: A Miscellany of Articles,* ed. and trans. T. L. Markey and P. T. Roberge, 62–70. Ann Arbor, Mich.: Karoma, 1979.

Heyward, DuBose. *Mamba's Daughters.* New York: Doubleday Doran, 1927.

———. *Porgy.* New York: George H. Doran Company, 1925.

Higginson, Thomas Wentworth. *Army Life in a Black Regiment.* 1870. East Lansing: Michigan State University Press, 1960.

Hill, Archibald A. "History of the Linguistic Institute." *ACLS* [American Association of Learned Societies] *Newsletter* 15, no. 3 (March 1964): 1–12.

Hodes, Martha. *White Women, Black Men: Illicit Sex in the Nineteenth Century South.* New Haven, Conn.: Yale University Press, 1997.

Holloway, Joseph E., ed. *Africanisms in American Culture.* Bloomington: Indiana University Press, 1990.

Holloway, Joseph E., and Winifred K. Vass. *The African Heritage of American English.* Bloomington: Indiana University Press, 1993.

Hollwig, David J. "E. Franklin Frazier's Brazil." In *Proceedings of the Conference on the Black Image in Latin American Culture,* ed. Elba Birmingham Porkornoy, 2:252–69. Slippery Rock, Pa.: Slippery Rock State University, 1990.

Holm, John A. "Focus on Creolists: Beryl Loftman Bailey." *Carrier Pidgin* 10, no. 3 (September 1982): 1–3.

———. *An Introduction to Pidgins and Creoles.* Cambridge: Cambridge University Press, 2000.

———. *Languages in Contact: The Partial Restructuring of Vernaculars.* Cambridge: Cambridge University Press, 2004.

———. "On the Relationship of Gullah and Bahamian." *American Speech* 58, no. 4 (Winter 1983): 303–18.

———. "Phonological Features Common to Some West African and Atlantic Creole Languages." In *Africanisms in Afro-American Language Varieties,* ed. Salikoko S. Mufwene, 317–27. Athens: University of Georgia Press, 1993.

———. *Pidgins and Creoles.* Vol. 1, *Theory and Structure.* Cambridge: Cambridge University Press, 1988.

———. *Pidgins and Creoles.* Vol. 2, *Reference Survey.* Cambridge: Cambridge University Press, 1989.

———. "Variability of the Copula in Black English and Its Creole Kin." *American Speech* 59, no. 4 (Winter 1984): 291–309.

Holm, John A., and Alison Shilling. *Dictionary of Bahamian English.* Cold Spring, N.Y.: Lexik House, 1982.

Howard University. *Howard University Alumni Directory: 1870–1919.* Washington, D.C.: Howard University, 1920.

———. *Howard University Annual Catalogues,* 1917–18, 1927–28, 1928–29. Washington, D.C.: Trustees of Howard University.

———. *Howard University Yearbook.* Howard University, Washington, D.C., 1917.

Huggins, Nathan. *The Harlem Renaissance.* New York: Oxford University Press, 1971.

Hurston, Zora Neale. *Mules and Men.* Philadelphia: Lippincott, 1935.

———. *Tell My Horse.* Philadelphia: Lippincott, 1938.

Hymes, Dell, ed. *Pidginization and Creolization of Languages.* Cambridge: Cambridge University Press, 1971.

Hymes, Dell, and John Fought. "American Structuralism." In *Current Trends in Linguistics.* Vol. 13, *Historiography of Linguistics,* ed. Thomas Sebeok, 903–1176. The Hague: Mouton, 1975.

Ivy, James. Review of *Africanisms in the Gullah Dialect,* by Lorenzo Dow Turner. *Crisis* 57 (April 1950): 263–64.

Jackson, Walter. "Melville Herskovits and the Search for Afro-American Culture." In *Malinowski, Rivers, Benedict and Others,* ed. George W. Stocking Jr., 95–126. Madison: University of Wisconsin Press, 1986.

James, Joy. *Transcending the Talented Tenth. Black Leaders and American Intellectuals.* New York: Routledge, 1997.

James, Winford, and Valerie Youssef. *The Languages of Tobago: Genesis, Structure and Perspectives.* St. Augustine: University of the West Indies SOCS, 2002.

Johnson, Charles S., ed. *Ebony and Topaz.* New York: National Urban League, 1927.

———. *Growing Up in the Black Belt: Negro Youth in the Rural South.* New York: American Council on Education, 1941.

———. *The Negro in American Civilization.* New York: Henry Holt, 1930.

———. *The Shadow of the Plantation.* Chicago: University of Chicago Press, 1934.

Johnson, Evelyn Adelaide. *History of Elizabeth City State University: A Story of Survival.* New York: Vantage Press, 1980.

Johnson, Guion G. *A Social History of the Sea Islands with Special Reference to St. Helena Island, South Carolina.* Chapel Hill: University of North Carolina Press, 1930.

Johnson, Guy B. *Folk Culture on St. Helena Island, South Carolina.* Chapel Hill: University of North Carolina Press, 1930.

Johnson, H. P. "Who Lost the Southern R?" *American Speech* 3, no. 5 (June 1928): 377–83.

Johnson, J. F., Jr. "C. E. M. Joad, Richard Weaver and the Decline of Western Civilization." *Modern Age* 44, no. 3 (Summer 2002): 226–34.

Jones, Charles Colcock, Jr. *Negro Myths from the Georgia Coast.* Columbia, S.C.: The State Company, 1925.

Jones, Connie. "The Rooks Family Reunion: Famous North Carolina Family Observes Its 153st Anniversary in Old Homestead in Gates County." *Color,* March 1953, 12–17.

Jones, Cornelia Reid. "The Four Rooks Sisters." *Negro History Bulletin* 16, no. 1 (October 1952): 3–8.

Jones-Jackson, Patricia. *When Roots Die: Endangered Traditions on the Sea Islands.* Athens: University of Georgia Press, 1987.

Joyner, Charles W. *Down by the Riverside: A South Carolina Slave Community.* Urbana: University of Illinois Press, 1984.

———. *Shared Traditions: Southern History and Folk Culture.* Urbana: University of Illinois Press, 1999.

Kauffman, Joseph F. "A Report on the Peace Corps: Training for Overseas Service." *Journal of Higher Education* 33, no. 7 (October 1962): 361–66.

Kay, Herma H. *Sex-Based Discrimination: Text, Cases and Materials.* St. Paul, Minn.: West Publishing Company, 1981.

Kay, Marvin L. Michael, and Lorin Lee Cary. *Slavery in North Carolina, 1748–1775.* Chapel Hill: University of North Carolina Press, 1995.

Keesing, Roger M. *Melanesian Pidgins and Oceanic Substrate.* Stanford, Calif.: Stanford University Press, 1988.

Kennedy, Randall. "Introduction: Blacks and the Race Question at Harvard." In *Blacks at Harvard: A Documentary History of African American Experience at Harvard and Radcliffe,* ed. Werner Sollors, Caldwell Titcomb, and Thomas A. Underwood, xvii–xxxiv. New York: New York University Press, 1993.

Kent, Roland. "Record of the Linguistic Institute: Third Session, July 7–August 15, 1930." *Language* 6, no. 3., Bulletin no. 6 (September 1930): 3–17.

Kenyon, John Samuel. *American Pronunciation.* Ann Arbor, Mich.: George Wahr Publisher, 1945.

Klingler, Thomas. *If I Could Turn My Tongue Like That: The Creole Language of Pinte Coupee Parish, Louisiana.* Baton Rouge: Louisiana State University Press, 2003.

Kochman, Thomas, ed. *Rappin' and Stylin' Out: Communication in Urban Black America.* Champaign: University of Illinois Press, 1972.

Krapp, George Philip. *The English Language in America.* New York: Century Company for the Modern Language Association of America, 1925.

———. "The English of the Negro." *American Mercury* 2, no. 5 (June 1924): 190–95.

Kurath, Hans. "The Origin of Dialectal Differences in Spoken American English." *Modern Philology* 25, no. 4 (May 1928): 385–95.

———. "Progress of the Linguistic Atlas." *Dialect Notes: Publications of the American Dialect Society* 6, part 8 (July 1934): 391–92.

———. *Studies in Area Linguistics.* Bloomington: Indiana University Press, 1972.

———. *A Word Geography of the Eastern United States.* Ann Arbor: University of Michigan Press, 1949.

Labouret, Henri. *Les Manding et leur langue.* Paris: Larose, 1934.

Labouret, Henri, and Ida C. Ward. "Quelques observations sur la langue mandingue." *Africa* 6, no. 1 (1933): 38–50.

Labov, William. "Are Black and White Dialects Diverging?" Papers from NWAVE XIV Panel Discussion. *American Speech* 62, no. 1 (Spring 1987): 5–12.

———. *Language in the Inner City: Studies in the Black English Vernacular.* Philadelphia: University of Pennsylvania Press, 1972.

———. *Sociolinguistic Patterns.* Philadelphia: University of Pennsylvania Press, 1972.

Laird, Marilyn Poe, Vivian Poe Jackson, and Judith Krause Reid. *Gates County, North Carolina Land Deeds.* Vol. 1, *1776–1795.* Calumet Park, Ill.: Poe Publishers, 1977.

Laye, Camera. *The Dark Child.* London: Collins, 1955.

Lefebvre, Claire. *Creole Genesis and the Acquisition of Grammar: The Case of Haitian Creole.* Cambridge: Cambridge University Press, 1998.

Lefler, Hugh Talmage. *North Carolina History Told by Contemporaries.* Chapel Hill: University of North Carolina Press, 1965.

Lefler, Hugh Talmage, and Albert Ray Newsome. *The History of a Southern State.* Chapel Hill: University of North Carolina Press, 1973.

Lewis, David Levering. *W. E. B. Du Bois: The Fight for Equality and the American Century, 1919–1963.* New York: Henry Holt and Company, 2000.

———. *When Harlem Was in Vogue.* New York: Alfred A Knopf, 1981.

"Linguists from All Parts of Country Meet at Brown University." *Providence Journal,* July 21, 1934.

"Linguist Traces English Words to Negroes." *Oneonta Star,* November 11, 1948, 5.

Littlefield, Daniel C. "Continuity and Change in Slave Culture: South Carolina and the West Indies." *Southern Studies* 27 (Fall 1987): 202–16.

———. *Rice and Slaves: Ethnicity and the Slave Trade in Colonial South Carolina.* Baton Rouge: Louisiana State University Press, 1981.

Locke, Alain Leroy, ed. *The New Negro: An Interpretation.* New York: Albert and Charles Boni, 1925.

Logan, Frenzies A. *The Negro in North Carolina, 1876–1894.* Chapel Hill: University of North Carolina Press, 1964.

Logan, Rayford. *Howard University: The First Hundred Years.* New York: New York University Press, 1969.

Lomax, Alan. *Folksongs of North America.* New York: Doubleday, 1960.

"Lorenzo Turner Forum Speaker. . . . " *Chicago Defender,* March 1, 1947, 6.

"Magnetic Wire Recorder Preserves Running Account of Observation Flight Battle Description on Steel Wire." *Life* 15 (November 1, 1943): 49–50.

Major, Clarence. *From Juba to Jive: A Dictionary of Afro-American Slang.* New York: Penguin, 1994.

Mathews, Mitford M. *A Dictionary of Americanisms on Historical Principles.* Chicago: University of Chicago Press, 1956.

Matney, William C., and Ann Wolk Krouse, eds. "Geneva C. Turner." In *Who's Who among Black Americans,* 1975–76. 1st ed., 631. Northbrook, Ill.: Who's Who among Black Americans, 1976.

McDavid, Raven I., Jr. Review of *Africanisms in the Gullah Dialect,* by Lorenzo Dow Turner. *Language* 26 (April–June 1950): 323–33.

McDavid, Raven I., Jr., and Lawrence M. Davis. "The Dialects of Negro Americans." *In Studies in Linguistics in Honor of George L. Trager,* ed. M. Estellie Smith, 303–12. The Hague: Mouton, 1972.

McDavid, Raven I., Jr., and Virginia McDavid. "The Relationship of the Speech of American Negroes to the Speech of Whites." *American Speech* 26, no. 1 (February 1951): 3–17.

McKee, James B. *Sociology and the Race Problem: The Failure of a Perspective.* Urbana: University of Illinois Press, 1993.

McWhorter, John H. *The Missing Spanish Creoles: Recovering the Birth of Plantation Contact Languages*. Berkeley: University of California Press, 2000.

"Meharry Alumni Association." *Chicago Defender,* May 31, 1947.

Mencken, H. L. *The American Language: An Inquiry into the Development of English in the United States*. Supplement I. New York: Alfred A. Knopf, 1945.

———. *The American Language*. Supplement II. New York: Alfred A. Knopf, 1948.

Méndonça, R. *A influencia Africana no Portugués do Brasil.* 3rd ed. Porto: Livraria Figueirinhas, 1948.

Merritt, Carole. *The Herndons: An Atlanta Family.* Athens: University of Georgia Press, 2002.

Mille, Katherine Wyly, and Michael B. Montgomery. Introduction to *Africanisms in the Gullah Dialect,* by Lorenzo Dow Turner, xi–lvii. Columbia: University of South Carolina Press, 2002.

"Miss Lois Gwendolyn Morton . . . Received Her Master of Arts Degree in English from Fisk University." *Pittsburgh Courier,* July 9, 1938, 1.

"Miss Morton in Pretty Marriage to Fisk Instructor." *Louisville Defender,* September 1, 1938.

Mitchell-Kernan, Claudia. *Language Behavior in a Black Urban Community.* Monographs of the Language-Behavior Laboratory 2. Berkeley: University of California, 1971.

Montgomery, Michael. "The Linguistic Value of the Ex-slave Recordings." In *The Emergence of Black English: Text and Commentary,* ed. Guy Bailey, Natalie Maynor, and Patricia Cukor-Avila, 173–89. Amsterdam: John Benjamins, 1991.

Montgomery, Michael, ed. *Crucible of Carolina: Essays in the Development of Gullah Language and Culture.* Athens: University of Georgia Press, 1994.

Montgomery, Michael, and Guy Bailey, eds. *Language Variety in the South: Perspectives in Black and White.* Tuscaloosa: University of Alabama Press, 1986.

Morgan, Marcyliena. *Language, Power and Discourse in African American Culture.* Cambridge: Cambridge University Press, 2002.

Morison, Samuel Eliot. *The Founding of Harvard College.* Cambridge: Harvard University Press, 1935.

Moses, Yolanda. "Laurence Foster: Anthropologist, Scholar, and Social Advocate." In *African American Pioneers in Anthropology,* ed. Ira E. Harrison ad Faye V. Harrison, 85–100. Urbana: University of Illinois Press, 1999.

Most, Mel. "Negro Professor Traces Gullah and Geechee Dialects to Africa." *Charleston Post and Courier,* October 16, 1949.

"Mr. and Mrs. Lorenza [*sic*] D. Turner Studying at Yale." *Nashville Defender,* September 23, 1938.

Mufwene, Salikoko S., ed. *Africanisms in Afro-American Language Varieties.* Athens: University of Georgia Press, 1993.

———. "Africanisms in Gullah: A Re-Examination of the Issues." In *Old English and New: Studies in Language in Honor of Frederic G. Cassidy,* ed. Joan H. Hall, Dick Wrangler, and Nick Doan, 156–82. New York: Garland Press, 1992.

———. "The Ecology of Gullah's Survival." *American Speech* 72, no. 1 (Spring 1997): 69–83.

———. *The Ecology of Language Evolution.* Cambridge: Cambridge University Press, 2001.

———. "The Founder Principle in Creole Genesis." *Diachronica* 13 (Spring 1996): 83–134.

———. "Gullah's Development: Myths and Sociohistorical Evidence." In *Language Variety in the South Revisited,* ed. Cynthia Bernstein, Robin Sabino, and Tom Nunally, 113–22. Tuscaloosa: University of Alabama Press, 1997.

———. "The Linguistic Significance of African Proper Names." *De Nieuwe West-Indische Gids* 59, no. 3/4 (1985): 149–66.

———. "On Decreolization: The Case of Gullah." In *Language and the Social Construction of Identity in Creole Situations,* ed. Marcyliena Morgan, 63–99. Los Angeles: UCLA Center for Afro-American Studies, 1994.

———. "The Universalist and Substrate Hypothesis Complement One Another." In *Substrata versus Universals in Creole Genesis,* ed. Pieter Muysken and Norval Smith, 129–62. Amsterdam: John Benjamins, 1986.

———. "Why Study Pidgins and Creoles?" *Journal of Pidgin and Creole Languages* 3, no. 2 (1988): 265–76.

Mufwene, Salikoko S., John R. Rickford, Guy Bailey, and John Baugh, eds. *African American English: Structure, History, and Use.* London: Routledge, 1998.

Mühleisen, Susanne M., and Bettina Migge, eds. *Politeness and Face in Caribbean Creoles.* Amsterdam: John Benjamins, 2005.

Muhlhausler, Peter. "The Development of the Category of Number in Tok Pisin." In *Generative Studies on Creole Languages,* ed. Pieter Muysken, 35–84. Dordrecht: Foris, 1981.

Munck, Martha, and Catherine Kinch. "West African Rhythms Influence Modern American Music, Dance." *Forecast of the University of Michigan,* August 17, 1956, 1.

Muysken, Pieter, and Norval Smith, eds. *Substrata versus Universals in Creole Genesis.* Amsterdam: John Benjamins, 1986.

Myers, Aaron. "Moorland-Spingarn Research Collection." In *Africana: The Encyclopedia of the African and African American Experience,* ed. Kwame Anthony Appiah and Henry Louis Gates Jr., 1332–33. New York: Perseus Books, 1999.

Myrdal, Gunnar. *An American Dilemma: The Negro Problem and Modern Democracy.* New York: Harper, 1944.

NADS: Newsletter of the American Dialect Society 33, no. 1 (January 2001): 4.

National Park Service. *Low Country Gullah Culture: Special Resource Study and Final Environment Impact Statement.* Washington, D.C.: Department of the Interior, 2003.

The Negro in Chicago: A Study in Race Relations and a Race Riot. Chicago: University of Chicago Press, 1922.

"Negroes Not Naturally Submissive—Dr. L. Turner." *Louisville Defender,* June 6, 1942.

"Negro Teachers Conclude Session." *Washington Post,* September 9, 1905, 5.

Newberry Library Web site: http://www.newberry.org/collections/africanam.html (African American Studies page, March 20, 2006).

NIKH: Howard University Yearbook. Moorland-Spingarn Research Center, Howard University, Washington, D.C., 1914.

O'Cain, Raymond K. "Linguistic Atlas of New England." *American Speech* 54, no. 4 (Winter 1979): 243–78.

Odum, Howard, and Guy Johnson. *The Negro and His Songs: A Study of Typical Negro Songs in the South.* Chapel Hill: University of North Carolina Press, 1925.

Ogundele, Wole. *Omuluabi: Ulli Beier, Yoruba Society and Culture.* Trenton, N.J.: Africa World Press, 1998.

Opala, Joseph A. *The Gullah: Rice, Slavery, and the Sierra Leone American Connection.* Freetown, Sierra Leone: U.S. Information Service, 1987.

Oraka, Louis Nnamdi. *The Foundations of Igbo Studies.* Onitsha, Nigeria: University Publishing Company, 1983.

O'Reilly, Merry. "Dr. Turner Returns: 20,000 Miles through West Africa." *Say: Roosevelt University Alumni Magazine* 5 (Spring 1952): 13.

Overman, Lou N., and Edna M. Shannonhouse, eds. *Yearbook: Pasquotank Historical Society, Elizabeth City, North Carolina.* Vol. 3. Baltimore: Gateway Press, 1975.

Parrish, Lydia. *Slave Songs of the Georgia Sea Islands.* New York: Creative Age Press, 1942.

Parsons, Elsie Clews. *Folklore of the Sea Islands, South Carolina.* Cambridge, Mass.: American Folklore Society, 1923.

Perry, Theresa, and Lisa Delpit, eds. *The Real Ebonics Debate: Power, Language, and the Education of Black Children.* Boston: Beacon Press, 1998.

Persons, Stow, ed. *Ethnic Studies at Chicago—1905–1945.* Urbana: University of Illinois Press, 1987.

Peterkin, Julia. *Black April.* Indianapolis: Bobbs-Merrill, 1927.

Phillips, C. H. *The School of Oriental and African Studies University of London 1917–1967: An Introduction.* London: School of Oriental and African Studies, 1967.

Pierson, Donald. *The Negro in Brazil: A Study of Race Contact at Bahia.* Chicago: University of Chicago Press, 1942.

Pierson, George Wilson. *Yale: The University College—1921–1937.* New Haven, Conn.: Yale University Press, 1955.

Pike, Kenneth. *The Intonation of American English.* Ann Arbor: University of Michigan Press, 1946.

A Plan for the Study of Freshman English, 1923. Washington, D.C.: Howard University, 1923.

"Poet Wins Award." *Chicago Defender,* February 8, 1947.

Pollitzer, William. *The Gullah People and Their African Heritage.* Athens: University of Georgia Press, 1999.

Poplack, Shana, ed. *The English History of African American English.* Oxford: Basil Blackwell, 1999.

Powell, William S. *North Carolina through Four Centuries.* Chapel Hill: University of North Carolina Press, 1989.

"The Presidents of The University of Chicago: A Centennial View." *The University of Chicago Centennial Catalogues.* Special Collections of the University of Chicago Library, 1990.

Priddy, Gladys. "Roosevelt College Professor Collects Native Art on Study Trip to Africa: Latin American Music Traced to Origin—Africa." *Chicago Daily Tribune,* May 1, 1952, part 5, W10.

"Professor Studies Dialect: Lorenzo D. Turner." *Nashville Journal and Guide,* April 2, 1932.

"Profile of a Scholar: Lorenzo Dow Turner." *Negro History Bulletin* 21, no. 2 (November 1957): 26, 47.

Puckett, Nubell Niles. *Folk Beliefs of the Southern Negro.* Chapel Hill: University of North Carolina Press, 1926.

Quarles, Benjamin. *The Negro in the Civil War.* Boston: Little, Brown and Co., 1953.

Quick, W. H. *Negro Stars in All Ages of the World.* Richmond: S. B. Adkins and Company, 1898.

Rabinowitz, Howard N. "A Comparative Perspective on Race Relations in Southern and Northern Cities, 1860–1900, with Special Emphasis on Raleigh." In *Black Americans in North Carolina and the South,* ed. Jeffrey J. Crow and Flora J. Hatley, 137–59. Chapel Hill: University of North Carolina Press, 1984.

Ralston, Richard M. "An Independence Gift for Sierra Leone: A Krio Dictionary." *FREE: A Roosevelt University Magazine* 1, no. 1 (Spring 1962): 2–8.

Ramos, Arthur. *O negro brasileiro: Ethnographia, religiosa e psychanalyse.* Rio de Janeiro: Civilização brasileira, 1934. Translated by Richard Pattee as *The Negro in Brazil.* Washington, D.C.: Associated Publishers, 1939.

Rawley, James A. *The Trans-Atlantic Slave Trade: A History.* New York: W. W. Norton, 1981.

Raymundo, J. *O Elemento Afro-Negro na lingua Portuguesa.* Rio de Janeiro: Renascença Editora, 1933.

———. *O Negro Brasileiro.* Rio de Janeiro: Record, 1936.

"Records in Gullah Heard by Linguists: Dialect of Coastal Negroes of South Carolina Is Presented at Yale Session (Unique Study Described)." *New York Times,* January 1, 1933, 16, col. 3.

"Records of Strange Gullah Dialect Made for Scientists." *Pittsburgh Courier,* January 14, 1933.

Reinecke, John. E., Stanley M. Tsuzaki, David DeCamp, Ian F. Hancock, and Richard E. Wood, eds. *A Bibliography of Pidgin and Creole Languages.* Honolulu: University of Hawaii Press, 1975.

Reinhold, Meyer. *Classica Americana: The Greek and Roman Heritage in the United States.* Detroit: Wayne State University Press, 1984.

Report of the Governing Body and Statement of Accounts of the School of Oriental Studies, London Institution (University of London). Hertford: Stephen Austin and Sons, Ltd., 1917–37.

Report of the Governing Body and Statement of Accounts for the Year Ending July 31, 1932, School of Oriental Studies, London Institution. London: Waterlow and Sons, 1932.

Report of the Governing Body and Statement of Accounts for the Year Ending 31st July, 1936, School of Oriental Studies, London Institution. Hertford: Stephen Austin and Sons, Ltd., 1936.

Ribeiro, J. O Elemento Negro: História-Folclore-Linguistica. Rio de Janeiro: Record, 1939.

Richardson, Joe. *A History of Fisk University, 1865–1946.* Tuscaloosa: University of Alabama Press, 1980.

Rickford, John R. *African American Vernacular English: Features, Evolution, Educational Implications.* Oxford: Basil Blackwell, 1999.

———. "The Creole Origins of African-American Vernacular English: Evidence from Copula Absence." In *African American English: Structure, History and Use,* ed. Salikoko S. Mufwene, John R. Rickford, Guy Bailey, and John Baugh, 154–200. London: Routledge, 1998.

———. *Dimensions of a Creole Continuum: History, Texts and Linguistic Analysis of Guyanese Creole.* Stanford, Calif.: Stanford University Press, 1987.

———. Foreword to *African American English: A Linguistic Introduction,* by Lisa J. Green, ix–x. Cambridge: Cambridge University Press, 2002.

———. "Pidgins and Creoles." In *International Encyclopedia of Linguistics,* ed. William Bright, 3:224–32. Oxford: Oxford University Press, 1992.

———. "The Question of Prior Creolization in Black English." In *Pidgin and Creole Linguistics,* ed. Albert Valdman, 190–221. Bloomington: Indiana University Press, 1977.

———. "Some Principles for the Study of Black and White Speech in the South." In *Language Variety in the South: Perspectives in Black and White,* ed. Michael Montgomery and Guy Bailey, 38–62. Tuscaloosa: University of Alabama Press, 1986.

Rickford, John R., and John McWhorter. "Language Contact and Language Generation: Pidgins and Creoles." In *Handbook of Sociolinguistics,* ed. Florian Coulmas, 238–56. Oxford: Basil Blackwell, 1997.

Rickford, John R., and Russell John Rickford. *Spoken Soul: The Story of Black English.* New York: John Wiley and Sons, 2000.

Robbins, Richard. *Sidelines Activist: Charles S. Johnson and the Struggle for Civil Rights.* Jackson: University Press of Mississippi, 1996.

Robeson, Paul. "The Culture of the Negro." *Spectator* (London), June 15, 1934, 916–17.

Romaine, Suzanne. *Pidgin and Creole Languages.* London: Longmans, 1988.

Ronnick, Michele Valerie, ed. *The Autobiography of William Sanders Scarborough: An American Journey from Slavery to Scholarship.* Detroit: Wayne State University Press, 2005.

———. "Wiley Lane (1852–1855): The First Professor of Greek at Howard University." *Classical Outlook* 79, no. 3 (Spring 2002): 108–9.

———. "William Sanders Scarborough: The First African American Member of the Modern Language Association." *PMLA Journal* 115, no. 7 (December 2000): 1787–93.

Roy, Jessie Hailstalk, and Geneva Calcier Turner. *Pioneers of Long Ago.* Washington, D.C.: Associated Publishers, 1951.

Sakodas, Kent, and Jeff Siegel. *Pidgin Grammar: An Introduction to the Creole Language of Hawai'i.* Honolulu: Bess Press, 2003.

Sampson, Geoffrey. *Schools of Linguistics.* Stanford, Calif.: Stanford University Press, 1980.

Sandburg, Carl. "Chicago." In *Chicago Poems,* 3. New York: Henry Holt and Company, 1916.

Sankoff, Gillian. "The Genesis of Language." In *The Genesis of Language,* ed. Kenneth C. Hill, 23–47. Ann Arbor, Mich.: Karoma, 1979.

Sapir, Edward. *Language.* New York: Harcourt, Brace, 1921.

Schneider, Edgar W. *American Early Black English: Morphological and Syntactic Variables.* Tuscaloosa: University of Alabama Press, 1989.

Schneider, John T. *Dictionary of African Borrowings in Brazilian Portuguese.* Hamburg: Helmut Buske, 1991.

Schuchardt, Hugo. *Pidgin and Creole Languages: Selected Essays.* Edited and translated by Glenn G. Gilbert. Cambridge: Cambridge University Press, 1980.

Sea Island Translation and Literacy Team . . . with the Summer Institute of Linguistics and Wycliffe Bible Translators. *De Good Nyews Bout Jedus Christ Wa Luke Write: The Gospel according to Luke in Gullah Sea Island Creole.* New York: American Bible Society, 1995.

Sebeok, Thomas A., ed. *Portraits of Linguists: A Biographical Source Book for the History of Western Linguistics, 1746–1963.* 2 vols. Bloomington: Indiana University Press, 1966.

"Secretary's Report: The Detroit Meeting." *Publications of the American Dialect Society* 9 (November 1947): 85.

Sengova, Joko, "'My Mother Dem Nyus to Plan' Reis': Reflections on Gullah/Geechee Creole Communication, Connections, and the Construction of Cultural Identity." In *Afro-Alantic Dialogues: Anthropology in the Diaspora,* ed. Kevin A. Yelvington, 211–48. Sante Fe, N.Mex.: School of American Research Press, 2006.

———. "Recollections of African Language Patterns in an American Speech Variety: An Assessment of Mende Influence in Lorenzo Dow Turner's Gullah Data." In *The Crucible of Carolina: Essays on the Development of Gullah Language and Culture,* ed. Michael Montgomery, 175–200. Athens: University of Georgia Press, 1994.

Simms, William Gilmore. *The Wigwam and the Cabin.* London: Wiley, 1846.

Simpson, George Eaton. *Melville J. Herskovits.* New York: Columbia University Press, 1973.

Singler, John Victor, ed. *Pidgin and Creole Tense-Mood-Aspects Systems.* Amsterdam: John Benjamins, 1990.

Sklarewitz, Norman. "Dr. Turner's African Odyssey." *Chicago Tribune,* August 16, 1952, "Courier Magazine Section," 3.

"Slave Narratives: A Folk History of Slavery in the United States from Interviews with Former Slaves." Library of Congress Project, Works Progress Administration, 1936–38.

Smith, Bruce. "The Word Is Spread in Gullah Book of Luke Translated into Slave Language." *Chicago Tribune,* November 11, 1994, 9.

Smith, Reed. *Gullah.* Bulletin of the University of South Carolina Press. No. 190. Columbia: Bureau of Publications, University of South Carolina, 1926.

Smitherman, Geneva. *Black Talk: Words and Phrases from the Hood to the Amen Corner.* Boston: Houghton Mifflin, 1994; revised, 2000.

———. *Talkin' and Testifyin': The Language of Black America.* Boston: Houghton Mifflin, 1977.

———. *Talkin' That Talk: Language, Culture and Education in African America.* London: Routledge, 1999.

———, ed. *Black English and the Education of Black Children and Youth: Proceedings of the National Invitational Symposium on the King Decision.* Detroit: Center for Black Studies, Wayne State University, 1981.

SOAS [School of Oriental and African Studies] *Alumni Newsletter,* 17 (Winter 1998): 15.

"Society." *Louisville Defender,* July 8, 1944, 12ff.

Sollors, Werner, Caldwell Titcomb, and Thomas A. Underwood, eds. *Blacks at Harvard: A*

Documentary History of African American Experience at Harvard and Radcliffe. New York: New York University Press, 1993.

Spears, Arthur K., ed. *Race and Ideology: Language, Symbolism, and Popular Culture*. Detroit: Wayne State University Press, 1999.

Spears, Arthur K., and Donald Winford, eds. *The Structure and Status of Pidgins and Creoles: Including Selected Papers from the Meetings of the Society for Pidgin and Creole Linguistics*. Amsterdam: John Benjamins, 1997.

Stanfield, John H. *Philanthropy and Jim Crow in American Social Science*. Westport, Conn.: Greenwood Press, 1985.

Staples, Robert. "Race and Marital Status: An Overview." In *Black Families*, ed. Harriette Pipes McAdoo, 173–75. Beverly Hills, Calif.: Sage Publications, 1981.

Stewart, William A. "Creole Languages of the Caribbean." In *Study of the Role of Second Languages in Asia, Africa and Latin America*, ed. F. A. Rice, 34–53. Washington, D.C.: Center for Applied Linguistics, 1962.

———. "Toward a History of American Negro Dialect." In *Language and Poverty: Perspectives on a Theme*, ed. Frederick Williams, 351–79. Chicago: Markham, 1970.

———. "Urban Negro Speech: Sociolinguistic Factors Affecting English Teaching." In *Social Dialects and Language Learning*, ed. Roger W. Shuy, 10–18. Champaign, Ill.: National Council of Teachers of English, 1965.

Stoney, Samuel G., and Gertrude M. Shelby. *Black Genesis*. New York: Macmillan, 1930.

Storr, Richard J. *Harper's University: The Beginning—History of the University of Chicago*. Chicago: University of Chicago Press, 1966.

Strong, Mary Louise. "*Readings from Negro Authors for Schools and Colleges*, by Otelia Cromwell, Lorenzo Dow Turner, and Eva B. Dykes." *Journal of Negro History* 17, no. 3 (July 1932): 383–87.

Swadesh, Morris. Review of *Africanisms in the Gullah Dialect*, by Lorenzo Dow Turner. *Word* 7, no. 1 (April 1951): 82–84.

Sylvain, Suzanne Comhaire. *Le Créole haitïen: Morphologie et syntaxe*. Wetteren, Belgium: Imprimerie de Meester; Port-Au-Prince, Haiti: Chez L'Auteur, 1936.

"Teacher to Study Dialect of Gullahs." *Washington Times*, March 22, 1932.

Terry, Clifford. "Gold 'Dust': Julie Dash Evokes Gullah Culture." *Chicago Tribune*, January 3, 1992, section 7, 23.

Thomas, John P. "The Barbadians in Early South Carolina." *South Carolina Historical and Genealogical Magazine* 31, no. 2 (April 1930): 75–92.

Thomason, Sarah G., and Thomas Kaufman. *Language Contact, Creolization, and Genetic Linguistics*. Berkeley: University of California Press, 1988.

Thompson, Robert Farris. *Flash of the Spirit*. New York: Random House, 1982.

Thompson, Robert W. "A Note on Some Possible Affinities between the Creole Dialects of the Old World and Those of the New." In *Creole Language Studies II: Proceedings of the Conference on Creole Language Studies Held at the University College of the West Indies, March 28–April 4, 1959*, ed. Robert Le Page, 107–13. London: Macmillan, 1961.

"Topics of the Times: Gullah." *New York Times*, January 2, 1933, 22, col. 5.

Trager, George. *Outline of Linguistic Analysis*. Linguistic Society of America. Baltimore: Waverly Press, 1942.

"Tribute Paid to the Late Lorenzo Dow Turner." *Journal of the Chicago City Council*, February 24, 1972, 2636.

Tuttle, Kate. "*Plessy v. Ferguson*." In *Africana: The Encyclopedia of the African and African American Experience*, ed. Kwame Anthony Appiah and Henry Louis Gates Jr., 1531–32. New York: Perseus Books, 1999.

———. "William Edward Du Bois." In *Africana: The Encyclopedia of the African and African American Experience,* ed. Kwame Anthony Appiah and Henry Louis Gates Jr., 635–36. New York: Perseus Books, 1999.

Twining, Mary A., and Keith E. Baird, eds. *Sea Island Roots: African Presence in the Carolinas and Georgia.* Trenton, N.J.: Africa World Press, 1991.

"U.S. Profs Instilled Dream; Missionaries the Knowledge: Baptists Have Educated More than 50,000 Nigerians." *Jet* 28, no. 26 (October 20, 1960): 16–19.

Valdman, Albert, ed. *Dictionary of Louisiana Creole.* Bloomington: Indiana University Press, 1998.

———. *Pidgin and Creole Linguistics.* Bloomington: Indiana University Press, 1977.

Van Name, Addison. "1869–1870: Contributions to Creole Grammar." *Transactions of the American Philological Association* 1 (1869–70): 123–67.

Vass, Winifred K. *The Bantu Speaking Heritage of the United States.* Los Angeles: UCLA Center for Afro-American Studies, 1979.

Vaughn-Cooke, Faye. "Lexical Diffusion: Evidence from a Decreolizing Variety of Black English." In *Language Variety in the South: Perspectives in Black and White,* ed. Michael Montgomery and Guy Bailey, 101–30. Tuscaloosa: University of Alabama Press, 1986.

Voegelin, Carl F. "Edward Sapir." In *Portraits of Linguists: A Biographical Source Book for the History of Western Linguistics, 1746–1963,* 2:489–92. Bloomington: Indiana University Press, 1966.

Voget, Fred W. *A History of Ethnology.* New York: Holt, Rinehart and Winston, 1975.

Wade-Lewis, Margaret. "Beryl Loftman Bailey: Africanist Woman Linguist in New York State." *Afro-Americans in New York Life and History* 17, no. 1 (Spring 1993): 7–15.

———. "A Bridge over Many Waters: Mark Hanna Watkins, Linguistic Anthropologist." *Dialectical Anthropology* 28, no. 2 (June 2004): 147–202.

———. "The Contribution of Lorenzo Dow Turner to African Linguistics." *Studies in Linguistic Sciences* 20, no. 1 (Spring 1990): 189–204.

———. "The Impact of the Turner/Herskovits Connection on Anthropology and Linguistics." *Dialectical Anthropology* 17, no. 4 (November 1992): 391–412.

———. "Joseph Applegate," "Beryl Loftman Bailey," "Raleigh Morgan," "Mark Hanna Watkins," "Lorenzo Dow Turner." In *African American National Biography,* ed. Henry Louis Gates Jr. and Evelyn Higginbotham. New York: Oxford University Press (forthcoming 2008).

———. "Lorenzo Dow Turner: Beyond Gullah Studies." *Dialectical Anthropology* 26, no. 3/4 (November 2001): 235–66.

———. "Lorenzo Dow Turner: Pioneer African American Linguist." *Black Scholar* 21, no. 4 (Fall 1991): 10–24.

———. "Mark Hanna Watkins: African American Linguistic Anthropologist." In *Histories of Anthropology Annual,* ed. Regna Darnell and Frederic W. Gleach, 1:181–218. Lincoln: University of Nebraska Press, 2005.

———. "The Status of Semantic Items from African Roots in English." *Black Scholar* 23, no. 2 (Winter/Spring 1993): 26–36.

Ward, Ida C. *An Introduction to the Ibo Language.* Cambridge: W. Heffer and Sons, 1936.

———. *The Phonetic and Tonal Structure of Efik.* Cambridge: W. Heffer and Sons, 1933.

———. *The Pronunciation of Twi.* Cambridge: W. Heffer and Sons, 1939.

Watkins, Mark Hanna. "*Africanisms in the Gullah Dialect.*" *American Anthropologist* 52, no. 2 (April–June 1950): 259.

———. "Africanisms in New World Speech." *Journal of Negro Education* 19, no. 4 (Autumn 1950): 485–86.

———. *A Grammar of Chichewa: A Language of Central Africa.* Washington, D.C.: Linguistic Society of America, 1937.

———. "Race, Class and Caste in Haiti." *Midwest Journal* 1, no. 1 (Winter 1948): 6–15.

———. "The Social Role of Color in Haiti: Some Facts and Impressions." *A Monthly Summary of Events and Trends in Race Relations* 3, no. 8 (March 1946): 250–51.

W. D. W. "Gullah Use of African Names Is Cited in Mencken's Volume." *Charleston Post and Courier,* August 20, 1948.

Welmers, William E. *African Language Structures.* Berkeley: University of California Press, 1973.

Welmers, William E., and Ida C. Ward. *Practical Phonetics for Students of African Languages.* London: Kegan Paul International, 1933.

Wesley, Charles. *The History of Alpha Phi Alpha: A Development in College Life.* 14th ed. Washington, D.C.: Foundation Publishers, 1981.

Westermann, Deidrich, and M. Bryan. *Languages of West Africa.* Handbook of African Languages 2. Oxford: Oxford University Press, 1952.

Westermann, Deidrich, and Ida C. Ward. *Practical Phonetics for Students of African Languages.* London: Kegan Paul International, 1933.

Wilkinson, Frederick D. *Howard University Directory of Graduates 1870–1980.* White Plains, N.Y.: Bernard Harris Publishing Company, 1982.

Williams, Robert, ed. *Ebonics: The True Language of Black Folks.* St. Louis, Mo.: Institute of Black Studies, 1975.

Willis, Deborah. "African American Photography." In *Africana: The Encyclopedia of the African and African American Experience,* ed. Kwame Anthony Appiah and Henry Louis Gates Jr., 1518–23. New York: Perseus Books, 1999.

Wilson, George. Review of *Africanisms in the Gullah Dialect,* by Lorenzo Dow Turner. *Quarterly Journal of Speech* 36, no. 2 (April 1950): 261–62.

———. "Secretary's Report: The Detroit Meeting." *Publications of the American Dialect Society* 9 (November 1947): 85.

Winford, Donald. "Back to the Past: The BEV/Creole Connection Revisited." *Language Variation and Change* 4, no. 3 (1992): 311–57.

Winslow, Mrs. Watson (Ellen Goode). *History of Perquimans County: As Compiled from Records Found There and Elsewhere.* Baltimore: Genealogical Publishing Company, 1990.

Winston, Michael R. *The Howard University Department of History, 1913–1973.* Washington, D.C.: Department of History, Howard University, 1973.

Winton, North Carolina History. Winton, N.C.: Hertford County Tourist Bureau, 2004.

Wolfram, Walter. "The Relationship of White Southern Speech to Vernacular Black English." *Language* 50, no. 3 (September 1974): 498–527.

Wolfram, Walter, and Donna Christianson. *Sociolinguistics in Appalachian Dialects.* Washington, D.C.: Center for Applied Linguistics, 1976.

Wolfram, Walter, and Erik R. Thomas. *The Development of African American English.* Oxford: Basil Blackwell, 2002.

Wolfram, Walter, Carolyn Temple Adger, and Donna Christian, eds. *Dialects in Schools and Communities.* Mahwah, N.J.: Erlbaum, 1999.

Wolfram, Walter, and Nona Clarke, eds. *Black-White Speech Relationships.* Washington, D.C.: Center for Applied Linguistics, 1971.

Wood, Peter. *Black Majority: Negroes in South Carolina from 1670 through the Stono Rebellion.* New York: Alfred A. Knopf, 1974.

———. "'More Like a Negro Country': Demographic Patterns in Colonial South Carolina, 1700–1740." In *Race and Slavery in the Western Hemisphere: Quantitative Studies,* ed. Stanley

L. Engerman and Eugene D. Genovese, 131–71. Princeton, N.J.: Princeton University Press, 1975.

Wood, Phillip J. *Southern Capitalism: The Political Economy of North Carolina, 1880–1980.* Durham, N.C.: Duke University Press, 1986.

Woodson, Carter G. Review of *Africanisms in the Gullah Dialect,* by Lorenzo Dow Turner. *Journal of Negro History* 34, no. 4 (October 1949): 477–79.

Woofter, T. J. *Black Yeomanry: Life on St. Helena Island.* New York: Henry Holt, 1930.

Yale University. *Yale University Graduate School Bulletin for the Academic Year 1938–1939.* New Haven, Conn.: Yale University, 1938.

———. *Yale University School of Fine Arts Bulletin.* 1938–1939. New Haven, Conn.: Yale University, 1938.

Yelvington, Kevin. "The Anthropology of Afro-Latin America and the Caribbean: Diasporic Dimensions." *Annual Review of Anthropology* 30, no. 1 (2001): 227–60.

———. "The Invention of Africa and Latin America in the Caribbean: Political Discourse and Anthropological Praxis, 1920–1940." In *Afro-Atlantic Dialogues: Anthropology in the Diaspora,* ed. Yelvington, 35–82. Santa Fe, N.Mex.: School of American Research Press, 2006.

———. "Melville J. Herskovits and the Institutionalization of Afro-American Studies." Presentation for the International Colloquium on Brazil, UNESCO, January 12–14, 2004.

Zaluda, Scott. "Lost Voices of the Harlem Renaissance: Writing Assigned at Howard University, 1919–31." *CCC* 50, no. 2 (December 1998): 232–57.

Zumwalt, Rosemary Levy. *Wealth and Rebellion: Elsie Clews Parsons, Anthropologist and Folklorist.* Urbana: University of Illinois Press, 1992.

Dissertations and Unpublished Documents

Allsopp, Richard. "Pronominal Forms in the Dialect of English Used in Georgetown (British Guiana) and Its Environs by Persons Engaged in Nonclerical Occupations." Master's thesis, University of London, 1958.

Bucholtz, Mary. "Borrowed Blackness: Language, Racialization, and White Identity in an Urban High School." Ph.D. diss., University of California, Berkeley, 1997.

Cunningham, Irma Aloyce Ewing. "A Syntactic Analysis of Sea Island Creole (Gullah)." Ph.D. diss., University of Michigan, Ann Arbor, 1970.

Dorsey, Millard A. "Biographical Statement for Geneva Townes Turner's Retirement Dinner, June 17, 1954." Geneva Townes Turner Collection, Moorland-Spingarn Research Center, Howard University, Washington, D.C.

Green, John. Correspondence from Secretary, The Grand United Order of Odd Fellows. Philadelphia, September 3, 2002.

Hopkins, Tometro. "Issues in the Study of Afro-Creoles: Afro-Cuban and Gullah." Ph.D. diss., Indiana University, Bloomington, 1992.

Jones-Jackson, Patricia. "The Status of Gullah: An Investigation of Convergent Processes." Ph.D. diss., University of Michigan, Ann Arbor, 1978.

Loftman [Bailey], Beryl. "Creole Language of the Caribbean Area: A Comparison of the Grammar of Jamaican Creole with Those of the Creole Languages of Haiti, the Antilles, the Guianas, the Virgin Islands, and the Dutch West Indies." Master's thesis, Columbia University, 1953.

McDavid, Raven I., Jr., William A. Kretzschmar Jr., and Gail J. Hankins, eds. *Gullah: The Linguistic Atlas of the Middle and South Atlantic States and Affiliated Projects: Basic Materials.* Microfilm Manuscripts on Cultural Anthropology, 71.378. Joseph Regenstein Library, University of Chicago, 1982.

Mille, Katherine Wyly. "A Historical Analysis of Tense-Mood-Aspect in Gullah Creole: A Case of Stable Variation." Ph.D. diss., University of South Carolina, 1990.

Morton, David Lindsay, Jr. "The History of Magnetic Recording in the United States, 1888–1978." Ph.D. diss., Georgia Institute of Technology, 1995.

Morton, Lois Gwendolyn. "Illustrations in Recent Novels of Negro Life." Master's thesis, Fisk University, 1938.

Murrill, Harold Harvey. "A History of the Roanoke Missionary Baptist Association 1866–1886." Master's thesis, Shaw University Divinity School, 1979.

Nichols, Patricia Causey. "Linguistic Change in Gullah: Sex, Age, and Mobility." Ph.D. diss., Stanford University, 1976.

Osumare, Halifu. "African Aesthetics, American Culture: Dancing towards a Global Culture." Ph.D. diss., University of Hawaii, Manoa, 1999.

Reinecke, John. "Marginal Language: A Sociological Survey of the Creole Languages." 2 vols. Ph.D. diss., Yale University, 1937.

Rickford, John R. "Variation in a Creole Continuum: Quantitative and Implicational Approaches." Ph.D. diss., University of Pennsylvania, 1979.

Townes, Geneva Calcier. Diploma, 1916. Mathilda Minor Normal School in Washington, D.C. Geneva Townes Turner Collection. Moorland-Spingarn Research Center, Howard University, Washington, D.C.

———. Howard University Transcript, 1910–14. Geneva Townes Turner Collection. Moorland-Spingarn Research Center, Howard University, Washington, D.C.

Townes Maloney, Olivia. "Olivia Townes Maloney Biography." Circa 1964. Personal Collection of Eugene Townes, Bryans Road, Md.

Turner, Geneva Calcier Townes. European Scrapbook, Summer 1937. Geneva Townes Turner Collection. Moorland-Spingarn Research Center, Howard University, Washington, D.C.

———. "Geneva Townes Turner Biography." Circa 1964. Personal Collection of Eugene Townes, Bryans Road, Md.

Turner, Lorenzo Dow. "Obituary of Elizabeth R. Freeman Turner." 1931. Personal Collection of Lois Turner Williams, Chicago, Ill.

———. "Rooks Turner Biography." 1926. Personal Collection of Lois Turner Williams, Chicago, Ill.

———. "A Study of the Negro Family" Questionnaire. Survey No. 2588, completed for E. Franklin Frazier. E. Franklin Frazier Papers. Collection 131. Folder 8. Manuscript Division. Moorland-Spingarn Research Center, Howard University, Washington, D.C., circa 1933.

———. Transcript, Harvard University, 1915–17. UAV 161.272.5. File 1. Box 14. Harvard University Archives. Harvard University, Cambridge, Mass.

———. Transcript, Howard University Academy, 1906–10. Office of the General Counsel, Howard University, Washington, D.C.

———. Transcript, Howard University, 1910–14. Office of the General Counsel, Howard University, Washington, D.C.

———. Transcript, University of Chicago, 1919–26. University of Chicago Office of Registrar, Chicago, Ill.

Twining, Mary A. "An Examination of African Retentions in the Folk Culture of the South Carolina and Georgia Sea Islands." 2 vols. Ph.D. diss., Indiana University, Bloomington, 1977.

Wade-Lewis, Margaret. "The African Substratum in American English." Ph.D. diss., New York University, 1988.

Weldon, Tracy L. "Exploring the AAVE-Gullah Connection: A Comparative Study of Copula Variability (African American Vernacular English, South Carolina, Georgia Gullah)." Ph.D. diss., Ohio State University, 1998.

Wellens, I. H. W. "An Arabic Creole in Africa: The Nubi Language of Uganda." Ph.D. diss. University of Nijmegen, 2003.

Videos

Carrier, Tom. *Family across the Sea.* VHS. Columbia: South Carolina ETV, 1991.

Dash, Julie. *Daughters of the Dust.* VHS. New York: Kino Videos, 1991.

Opala, Joseph. *The Language You Cry In.* VHS. Los Angeles: California Newsreel, 1998.

Voices of the Gullah Culture: The Hallelujah Singers. Columbia: South Carolina ETV, 1993.

Government Documents

Clark, Walter, ed. *State Records of North Carolina.* Vol. 23. Winston, N.C.: Published for the General Assembly, 1905.

North Carolina Board of Health. *Fifth Biennial Report of the Board of Health, 1893–1894.* Raleigh: State of North Carolina.

Pasquotank County Records from the Office of Register of Deeds. Book 2. Elizabeth City, N.C., 1879, 78.

Pasquotank County Records from the Office of Register of Deeds. Book 6. Elizabeth City, N.C., 1885, 572.

Pasquotank County Records from the Office of Register of Deeds. Book 8. Elizabeth City, N.C., 1886, 43.

Pasquotank County Records from the Office of Register of Deeds. Book 13. Elizabeth City, N.C., 1892, 369–70.

Pasquotank County Records from the Office of Register of Deeds. Book 16. Elizabeth City, N.C., 1895, 116.

Pasquotank County Records from the Office of Register of Deeds. Book 20. Elizabeth City, N.C., 1899, 588–89.

Porter, Dorothy, comp. *The Negro in the United States: A Selected Bibliography.* Washington, D.C.: U.S. Government Printing Office, 1970.

U.S. Bureau of the Census. Data for Montgomery County, Maryland, for 1900 and 1920.

U.S. Bureau of the Census. Data for North Carolina for 1860, 1870, 1880, and 1890.

U.S. Bureau of the Census. Data for Washington, D.C., 1910, 1920, and 1930.

U.S. Bureau of the Census, Department of Commerce and Labor. *Heads of Families at the First Census of the United States Taken in the Year 1790: North Carolina.* Washington, D.C.: U.S. Government Printing Office, 1908.

INDEX

Please note that LDT stands for Lorenzo Dow Turner.

ABOUT THE AUTHOR

MARGARET WADE-LEWIS is an associate professor at the State University of New York at New Paltz, where she has served as chair of the Department of Black Studies and director of the linguistics program for the past fourteen years. The first African American woman to receive a Ph.D. in linguistics from New York University, she has taught at the University of California, Santa Barbara; the University of Nebraska, Omaha; and the University of Texas, Austin. Her writings on the contributions of black linguists have appeared in *Dialectical Anthropology, Black Scholar, The Encyclopedia of Southern Culture, African American National Biography,* and *lexicon Grammaticorum.*